An Anthropology of Things

An Anthropology of Things

Edited by

Ikuya Tokoro & Kaori Kawai

Translated by

Minako Sato

Kyoto University Press
Kyoto

Trans Pacific Press
Melbourne

First published in Japanese by Kyoto University Press in 2011 as *Mono no jinruigaku*.

This English edition published in 2018 jointly by:

Kyoto University Press
69 Yoshida Konoe-cho
Sakyo-ku, Kyoto 606-8315, Japan
Telephone: +81-75-761-6182
Fax: +81-75-761-6190
Email: sales@kyoto-up.or.jp
Web: http://www.kyoto-up.or.jp

Trans Pacific Press
PO Box 164, Balwyn North
Victoria 3104, Australia
Telephone: +61-(0)3-9859-1112
Fax: +61-(0)3-8611-7989
Email: tpp.mail@gmail.com
Web: http://www.transpacificpress.com

© Kyoto University Press and Trans Pacific Press 2018.

Copyedited by Karl Smith, Melbourne, Australia.

Designed and set by Sarah Tuke, Melbourne, Australia.

Printed by Focus Print Group, Melbourne, Victoria, Australia.

Distributors

Australia and New Zealand
James Bennett Pty Ltd
Locked Bag 537
Frenchs Forest NSW 2086
Australia
Telephone: +61-(0)2-8988-5000
Fax: +61-(0)2-8988-5031
Email: info@bennett.com.au
Web: www.bennett.com.au

USA and Canada
International Specialized Book Services (ISBS)
920 NE 58th Avenue, Suite 300
Portland, Oregon 97213-3786
USA
Telephone: 1-800-944-6190
Fax: 1-503-280-8832
Email: orders@isbs.com
Web: http://www.isbs.com

Asia and the Pacific (except Japan)
Kinokuniya Company Ltd.
Head office:
3-7-10 Shimomeguro
Meguro-ku
Tokyo 153-8504
Japan
Telephone: +81-(0)3-6910-0531
Fax: +81-(0)3-6420-1312
Email: bkimp@kinokuniya.co.jp
Web: www.kinokuniya.co.jp
Asia-Pacific office:
Kinokuniya Book Stores of Singapore Pte., Ltd.
391B Orchard Road #13-06/07/08
Ngee Ann City Tower B
Singapore 238874
Telephone: +65-6276-5558
Fax: +65-6276-5570
Email: SSO@kinokuniya.co.jp

All rights reserved. No reproduction of any part of this book may take place without the written permission of Trans Pacific Press.

ISBN   978–1–925608–98–4 (hardcover)

The translation and publication of this book was supported by a Grant-in-Aid for Publication of Scientific Research Results (#16HP6005) provided by the Japan Society for the Promotion of Science, to which we express our sincere appreciation.

Cover illustration: Paper-cuts from China's Shanbei region, a craft that adds color to the people's traditional cave-houses.

Contents

Figures   viii
Tables   ix
Photographs   x
Contributors   xiii

Prologue: Let Things Tell Us   1
Introduction: Why the Anthropology of *Mono* (Things)?
   Ikuya Tokoro & Kaori Kawai   18

Part I: The Genesis, Extinction and Continuation of *Mono*

1. Between Form, Word and Materiality: Shanbei Paper-Cuts
   Tomoko Niwa   37
2. *Mono* that lurk, retreat, or manifest: *Mono* and the body
   Kazuyoshi Sugawara   58

Part II: The Nexus Between *Mono* and the Environment

3. *Mono* beyond control: A New Perspective on Cultured Pearls
   Ikuya Tokoro   81
4. An Ecological Analysis of Pottery Culture: From Clay to "*Mono*" *Michiko Intoh*   96

Part III: The Dynamic Between *Mono* and the Body

5. Learning Pottery Making: Transmission of Body Techniques *Morie Kaneko*   115
6. Nature and the Body in Male Sex Stimulants *Masakazu Tanaka*   136

Part IV: The Agency of *Mono*

7. Masks as Performers: *Topeng*, a Balinese Masked Dance Drama
   Yukako Yoshida   155

8 "Living" Musical Instruments: On Changing Sounds of *Suling* *Kaori Fushiki*	171
9 *Mono* that Show and Tempt: Contingency by Fortune-Tellers *Ayako Iwatani*	189

Part V: Toward a New *Mono* Theory

10 The Origin of Tool-using Behavior and Human Evolution *Gen Yamakoshi*	207
11 "Things" and Their Emergent Sociality in the Primates' World *Suehisa Kuroda*	222
12 Livestock as Interface: The Case of the Samburu in Kenya *Shinya Konaka*	241
13 The Cicadas Drizzle of the Chamus *Kaori Kawai*	258

Epilogue: Stonehood: Agency as Inagency *Motomitsu Uchibori*	273

Essay I: The Appearance of "*Mono*"

I-1	Where a Name Acquires a Form: Motifs of Javanese Batik *Junko Sato*	281
I-2	Kashta Drives People: The "*Mono*" Power of Uzbek Embroidery *Emi Imahori*	287
I-3	"Play" Between Mono and Humans: Interdependence with bananas? *Kaori Komatsu*	293

Essay II: Mysterious "*Mono*"

II-1	Fetishism on Pagodas and Buddha Images *Keiko Tosa*	303
II-2	"*Mono*" Sucked Out of the Body: Shamanic Rituals of Ladakh *Kiyoshi Miyasaka*	308

Essay III: Fluctuating "*Mono*"

III-1 Globalization of Aboriginal Paintings, Localization of "Art"
       Sachiko Kubota — 315
III-2 The Bodies and Art Forms of Pacific Islander Artists
       Matori Yamamoto — 321
III-3 Staying Authentic: Between *bingata* and Ryukyu Bingata
       Akiko Muramatsu — 327

Notes — 336
Bibliography — 366
Index — 396

Figures

2.1 Manifestation of a ring	62
2.2 Negotiation for Kirin Orange	66
2.3 Manifestation of "Poppy"	72
2.4 Fantasy heist game	75
3.1 Stages of Akoya pearl culture operation	83
4.1 Map of Oceania	102
5.1 Study field	119
5.2 Four main types of pots used by the Aari people	120
5.3 Work and seating arrangements of a mother and two daughters	125
6.1 The male body and sex	141
8.1 Fingerings for *tekap lebang* (*lebang* key)	174
8.2 Pitung ilah	176
10.1 Substrate use in capuchin monkeys	217
I-2.1 *Qars do'z* (Stitch A)	288

Tables

5.1 The progression of pottery forming by three daughters in S Village (11/1999–03/2002)	127
5.2.1 The progression of pottery forming by six daughters in S Village (06–07/2001)	129
5.2.2 The progression of pottery forming by six daughters in G Village (05–06/2001)	129
5.3 Potters in S Village who can form pots other than the four main types (02/2002)	130
9.1 Images in cuvați	202
12.1 Correspondence between human and livestock body recognition (male)	250
12.2 Correspondence between human and livestock body recognition (female)	250
12.3 The classification of wild animals by the Samburu	253
I-1.1 The process of making batik in white, blue and brown	285
I-2.1 Comparison of *kashta* producers	289

Photographs

1.1	Cave-houses during the Spring Festival season	38
1.2	Female members of a farming family arrange various patterns on the kang bed-stove to choose window-flowers for the coming year	38
1.3	Gao Fenglian's paper cut (completed)	45
1.4	She watches TV and chats with her granddaughter during production	45
1.5–1.7	Impromptu "*maojiao*" for the work in Photo 1.3 (photographed from the reverse side)	47
1.8	"Wugefangyang" cut by Liu Xiaojuan several months earlier	49
1.9	A new paper-cut of the same motif based on the previous cut in Photo 1.8 as a "yangyang"	49
1.10	Ma Ruilan executing "maojiao" while humming a folk song	54
3.1	Pearl culture technician performing "nucleation (surgical grafting)" on a host pearl oyster	85
3.2	Memorial tower for pearl oysters	93
3.3	The 57th memorial service for pearls held on 23 October 2007	93
4.1	Small sand grains and grass root fragments are removed from a clay body	105
4.2	The pottery wall is built from the bottom, adding clay a little bit at a time	105
4.3	Once the top part is dry, the base is trimmed with the edge of a split bamboo	107
4.4	The surface of the dried vessel is moistened with water immediately before firing	108
5.1(1)	A potter breastfeeds her baby at her pottery making workplace	122
5.1(2)	Infants can help with forming pottery under their mother's instructions by the age of two or three	122
5.2(1)	The mother makes some adjustments to a pot-shaped plaything formed by her daughter	123
5.2(2)	The first pot (*bun til*) formed by the daughter	124

6.1	Tokay: Distribution & habitat – Southern China, Southeast Asia, India in the 18–32°C temperature zone	143
6.2	An advertisement for "Daikakumanseitan" (Shūkan hōseki, 20/27 December 1985, p. 229)	147
7.1	Masks laid out before a performance (Sidakarya at top left)	159
7.2	Bondres (left) and Penasar (right)	159
7.3	The Wijil mask missing half of its moustache	165
7.4	The mask reportedly given by Dewa Agung	167
8.1	Suling gambuh	172
9.1	Nāyakaṉ men	195
9.2	Cuvaṭi	198
9.3	Palmyra palm	199
10.1	A chimpanzee eating figs in Bossou	209
10.2	A chimpanzee inserting a stick into a tree hollow to catch carpenter ants in Bossou	220
11.1	A bonobo mother swinging infants playing with a sugari	229
12.1	An old man extracting a tooth from an infant	249
12.2	Boys after circumcision	251
12.3	Black crowned cranes (*Balearica pavonina*; local name: *nkaitoole*) with a characteristic crest on the head	251
12.4	Somali fiscal (*Lanius somalicus*)	254
13.1	A herd of cattle moving through an open acacia woodland and a lone Chamus herder following it	259
I-1.1	Wax resist filling using the canting (*nembok*)	283
I-2.1	*Qars do'z* (Stitch A)	290
I-2.2	*Qarso do'z* (Stitch B)	290
I-3.1	Intensive banana cultivation in western Tanzania, the Great Lakes region of East Africa (source: S. Maruo)	295
I-3.2	Extensive banana cultivation in southeastern Cameroon, Central Africa	296
I-3.3	Standardized banana planting at a plantation in Ghana	297

I-3.4	Different cultivars of bananas found in one day at a market in Tinambung, West Sulawesi, Indonesia	298
III-2.1	*Samoan Couple* by Yuki Kihara (2005)	323
III-3.1	The bark of *fukugi* (*Garcinia subelliptica*) is the source of a yellow dye, one of the base colors of bingata	328
III-3.2	Fabric for a Ryukyu dance costume	328
III-3.3	A paste bag used in a technique called *tsutsubiki* involving dyeing hand-drawn patterns used in making products such as *furoshiki* (wrapping cloth)	330
III-3.4	Nozzles from the postwar era	331
III-3.5	The underlay called rukujyū is made by drying *Okinawan shima-dōfu* in winter	334
III-3.6	Final checking of pattern carving. (*Futenma Bingata Kōbō*)	334

Contributors

FUSHIKI, Kaori
Associate Professor, Faculty of Literature, Taisho University

IMAHORI, Emi
Lecturer, Tokai University

INTOH, Michiko
Professor, Department of Modern Society and Civilization, National Museum of Ethnology

IWATANI, Ayako
Associate Professor, Graduate School of Human and Environmental Studies, Kyoto University

KANEKO, Morie
Associate Professor, Graduate School of Asian and African Area Studies, Kyoto University

KAWAI, Kaori
Professor, Research Institute for Languages and Cultures of Asia and Africa, Tokyo University of Foreign Studies

KOMATSU, Kaori
Professor, Faculty of Humanities, Hokkai-Gakuen University

KONAKA, Shinya
Professor, School of International Relations, University of Shizuoka

KUBOTA, Sachiko
Professor, Cultural Anthropology Graduate School of Intercultural Studies, Kobe University

KURODA, Suehisa
Emeritus Professor, The University of Shiga Prefecture

MIYASAKA, Kiyosi
Associate Professor, Faculty of Intercultural Studies, Nagoya Gakuin University

MURAMATSU, Akiko
Lecturer, Faculty of Human Society, Sagami Women's University

NIWA, Tomoko
Assistant Professor, National Institutes for the Humanities

SATO, Junko
Visiting Researcher, Centre for Asia Pacific Partnership, Osaka University of Economics and Law

SUGAWARA, Kazuyoshi
Professor Emeritus, Kyoto University

TANAKA, Masakazu
Professor, Institute for Research in the Humanities, Kyoto University

TOKORO, Ikuya
Professor, Research Institute for Languages and Cultures of Asia and Africa, Tokyo University of Foreign Studies

TOSA, Keiko
Professor, Graduate School of Global Studies, Tokyo University of Foreign Studies

UCHIBORI, Motomitsu
Professor, The Open University of Japan

YAMAMOTO, Matori
Professor, Faculty of Economics, Hosei University

YOSHIDA, Yukako
Assistant Professor, Research Institute for Languages and Cultures of Asia and Africa, Tokyo University of Foreign Studies

Prologue
Let Things Tell Us

Topeng – the masked dance-drama of Bali, Indonesia. This mask, which once danced with I Nyoman Kakul (1905–1982), now dances with his grandson I Ketut Wirtawan (photographed on 25 February 2007). One topeng performer says that a mask is like a wild animal and must be tamed. Another performer says that he is "married" to the masks he owns and never lends his "wives" to other performers. Thus, a topeng mask is more than "mere material thing". It often wields strong agency by connecting the performer to a symbolic meaning, personality or mysterious force. Yet, it exerts its powerful action on the performances and traditions of topeng precisely because it is a thing, i.e., having "materiality" that allows it to degrade, to be reprocessed, and to be transferred. (See Chapter 7)

The "paper-cutting" in China's Shanbei region is a craft that adds color to the people's traditional cave-houses called yaodong. The local women engage in this paper-cutting work for both pleasure and homemaking during the farming off-season. Paper-cuts pasted on lattice windows for the Spring Festival and other celebratory days (bottom photo) are transient; they are intended to be disposable decorations made of thin and fragile material that discolors and disintegrates over time (top photo: one year later). Nevertheless, papermakers commented that "I'm so engrossed in it that I forget sleeping" or "I like paper-cutting best because I can express what I want to". These paper "window-flowers" continue to exist as mono (things) through an expiration-renewal cycle in which they are replaced / replenished at the end of each year. To understand this elusive "humans-things" relationship, it is not enough to treat paper-cutting as a "mere" style of representation, a medium of meaning or value, or as an art system. Paper-cutting severely shakes up the foothold of anthropological material culture studies, which has emphasized the solid entity and inherent materiality of things and relied on their reality. (See Chapter 1)

Let Things Tell Us

The traditional Javanese batik involves drawing patterns on textiles using hot wax. The workers utilize "things at hand" and draw upon their experience to develop the motifs emerging in front of them. Traditional motifs finally appear on the fabric. The use of things and the use of human experience together constitute a single episode of motif drawing. (See Essay I-1)

One reason for the popularity of embroidery in so many societies is the simplicity with which one can produce an infinite number of decorative design patterns by combining three essential mono *(things) (needle, colored thread and textile), human hands, and techniques. Despite this simplicity, the relationships between embroidery and people are not homogeneous. A style of Uzbek embroidery called* kashta *involves different stitching techniques. Completely different business policies, production scales and employment relations are formed depending on which stitch the* kashta *producers use. (See Essay I-2)*

The nucleation operation in Akoya pearl culture. In simple terms, nucleation is a type of organ transplant operation in which a tiny sphere called a "nucleus" – made of the freshwater shell and a piece of the Akoya pearl oyster mantle (an organ that produces its shell) – are inserted into the vicinity of the gonad of the host oyster. In human activities involving living things such as aquaculture and farming, the context surrounding humans and things dramatically changes. Rapid fluctuations in the ecological environment demand technical innovations in response. One consequence of this is "the paradox of skill" in which "veterans have a harder time keeping up with changes". This is a phenomenon that cannot be fully explained by existing theories such as "communities of practice" based on a manufacturing and skills development model under relatively stable conditions. (See Chapter 3)

Banana varieties found at a market in West Sulawesi, Indonesia, in one day. Banana crops are cultivated under a wide range of regional conditions. There are very many cultivars. In East Africa, one village may grow over seventy varieties of bananas, a diversity which cannot be explained by functional reasons such as catering for different uses. The relationship between bananas and humans seems to have much room for "play" that produces diversity in their relationship. (See Essay I-3)

Let Things Tell Us

Tokay (Gekko gecko), an ingredient for sexual stimulant

* * *

Recipe for tokay liquor
Ingredients: 1 pair of tokays. Spirit (over 35%). No added sweeteners.
Steps: Scrub off dirt, dust and scales in running water. Remove skewers and dry separately. Chop into pieces of suitable size and macerate in spirit. The liquor becomes drinkable after two months. After six to twelve months, drain liquid and macerate for the second time. The finished product has pale yellow color. *Add 120 g of carrots and 1.2 l of spirit, and age for one to three years. It has beneficial action on the nervous, immune and endocrine systems and can be used as an everyday health tonic. (Source: Genki zake pawā ga minagiru yakuyōshu zukuri *by O. Watanabe)*

* * *

When the male body is considered as a sexual body, it is often regarded as an "active" body and the penis is regarded as an "instrument". Various discourses surrounding male sex stimulants strongly reflect this instrumentalist view of the body. Traditional male sex enhancement techniques relying on plant, animal and mineral sources – the power of "wild nature", so to speak – attempt to invoke the inner life force or wild nature of the body without completely alienating it. However, Viagra and other recent pharmaceuticals have the ability to induce erection with pinpoint accuracy. Both men and women are at the mercy of the penis prepared by Viagra because of this instrumental "reinforcement" approach. (See Chapter 6)

A cuvaṭi used for divination by the Nāyakaṉ, a nomadic people in Tamil Nadu, India. The Nāyakaṉ fortune-tellers associate the images on cuvaṭi with the client's properties, fortune and celestial bodies in an assertive and rhetoric-filled tone, drawing the client into their speech-act. Contingency, non-intentionality and indexicality embedded in things give the client a chance to retrospectively reinterpret events in their lives. The Nāyakaṉs' external appearances, their utterances and cuvaṭi cards are choreographed to maximize extraordinariness and forcefully inject foreign things into the regular and bland lives of people. They evoke the matters and situations, landscapes and experiences that have already been part of everyday life and activate reciprocally causal meanings. (See Chapter 9)

In Ladakh, professionals who perform healing rituals are called lha-mo *(female) and* lha-pa *(male). Their primary treatment method is* jip, *which means "sucking out". What is sucked out is usually a black slimy fluid or semisolid substance called* grib *(meaning "shadow", "dark" and "pollution"), which conjures up negative images such as illness and memories of actions that may have damaged a spirit. The thing constructs a system of explanations. It is not difficult to imagine that seeing this thing that invokes negative images removed can lead to healing. (See Essay II-2)*

Let Things Tell Us

Firewood is arranged in a conical shape around a dried vessel in the final stage of the traditional pottery making operation on Yap Island. Clay is transformed into pottery only through the firing process. Among all the things that have been produced by humankind, pottery is the oldest one requiring sophisticated techniques of the body. Potters need to use diverse materials and corresponding body techniques in order to prepare clay, form a vessel, dry it without cracking, and fire it intact. The firing process is a collision between the cultural factor (pottery making technology) and various environmental factors (clay, firewood, humidity etc.). In this sense, pottery is the perfect thing for attempting to decipher the dynamics between the body and the environment. (See Chapter 4)

A girl and her grandmother of the Aari in southwestern Ethiopia, forming clay pots in the workplace. The girl began forming pottery just three weeks earlier. She cannot see her grandmother's hands from where she is sitting and faces a partially formed pot in front of her. Woman potters say, "I came to know pottery making by myself". Just like them, their daughters establish their own pottery forming procedures through trial and error rather than exactly following their mothers' ways. Mothers do not correct pots formed by their daughters because "our hands are different". Finished pots are sold directly to users at the market. Users get to know the characteristics of individual potters through the use of the things called pots. (See Chapter 5)

Various shīgu (small knives) for carving stencil patterns and home-made rukujyū (underlays), which are made of dried tofu, used in Ryukyu Bingata, Okinawa's traditional textile dyeing craft. During the wartime shortages, craftsmen used umbrella ribs to make shīgu blades. The tale of postwar producers who made tools out of shell casings is still talked about among the craftsmen. During the Battle of Okinawa, which had a devastating impact on their society, they had no choice but to change raw materials and technology to suit the prevailing conditions. Yet, the craftsmen have maintained the authenticity of their craft as they talk about the "climate" to describe their relationships rooted in the fabric of life woven in Okinawa and their connection with their forefathers. (See Essay III-3)

For the coming-of-age ceremony in the Yolngu, an Australian Aboriginal people, the mythological story of the paternal clan is painted on the chest of each boy. The body paint disappears once the ceremony is over but similar patterns and motifs are painted on tree bark to teach their mythology to the young. These paintings gained commercial value during the 1970s. As they were incorporated into Australia's national identity, they came to be recognized as "high art." Some works have been sold for more than one million dollars. Nevertheless, the connection with the land and the world of spirits and myths at the core of their paintings has never been lost. Their "commercialization" and elevation to "high art" in fact serve to communicate and explain their local concepts to mainstream society. Aboriginal people continue to move between the local and the global through paintings of their mythology. (See Essay III-1)

A neon-decorated Buddha statue (Thanboddhay Pagoda in Monywa, Sagaing Region, Myanmar). This is a normal monastery that attracts local worshippers due to its reputation of being built by a high priest. Today its many kitschy statues and buildings also attract the interest of Japanese fans of bizarre temples. How does the neon decoration combine with the "sacred" in a religious context and "authenticity" as historical heritage? As well as questioning the legitimacy of this question itself, reconsidering the relationship between the objects of faith and people by temporarily treating the former as things offers a wealth of possibilities. (See Essay II-1)

Let Things Tell Us   11

Samoan Couple by Yuki (2005, by courtesy of Sean Coyle and Yuki Kihara). Kihara is what Samoans call faʻafafine *(one who prefers the feminine way although physically male). This photographic print is staged to look like a 19th century postcard but the faces of both the husband and wife are composites based on Kihara's own face. This work was produced as a challenge to dualist thinking about gender and the view of* faʻafafine *as "primitive peculiarity" and "exotic". Kihara's attempt to objectify her own body would not have been feasible without the body, but her works adapt and stage it in an ingenious fashion rather than a blunt exhibition of the object itself. What is interesting is the intense presence which she lets her body assert as a thing. (See Essay III-2)*

The player (front) and the maker (back) of suling gambuh, the main instrument of the gamelan ensemble which accompanies the Balinese dance drama of gambuh. The final stage of suling making, in which pitches are fine-tuned, used to be done jointly by the player and the instrument maker. While the sound of suling has been changing in recent years, the changing sound and music are left alone with no modification being made to the instrument. The "living" suling forces humans to accept the changing "sound," refusing to be modified. At the same time as being a material mono (thing), the suling exists as an aggregate of things, including physical vibration, manufacturing technology, playing techniques, memory and knowledge. It changes "sound," the sound structure and the human perception of it, shaking the existence of "music". (See Chapter 8)

Let Things Tell Us

Exchange of snuff between a man and a woman of the G|ui hunting-and-gathering people in the Kalahari Desert. (1) The man makes a verbal request as he extends his left hand. (2) The woman feels the back of her hip. (3) She opens a small bottle. (4) She takes snuff out on her palm. (5) She hands it over. (6) She adds more snuff. During the period of 106 seconds from the verbal request to the completion of the exchange, snuff is verbally expressed as a topic for a very short moment; the rest of the time is filled with gossip unrelated to the requested object. It seems as if the exchange of the thing is a "subordinate involvement" that flows through gaps in the "dominant involvement" of conversation. Conversation analysis reveals the place where things lurk, intervene and surface in the middle of a direct bodily interaction. (See Chapter 2)

A chimpanzee in Bossou inserting a stick into a tree hollow to catch ants. Tool behavior in chimpanzee and other great apes has the important ecological function of providing accessibility to otherwise unavailable food categories that cannot be accessed by the body alone. The most universal pattern of tool use behavior among great apes is to insert a string or stick into a hole or gap smaller than the hand. Surprisingly, this behavior is rarely seen in other primate species. Showing interest in holes and fissures and inserting a finger or stick into them is widely observed in both ape infants in captivity and human infants and interpreted as an expression of curiosity. Insightful intelligence, curiosity, and the existence of manipulable things unique to great apes – Is this where we find the origin of the evolutionary history of the relationship between things and humans? (See Chapter 10)

What is a thing for humans? Let us explore this fundamental question from an evolutionary point of view. Primates have created a rich world of things in which things manifest on multiple levels and mediate social interactions. Guessing from their behavior, any object of movable size and shape can be singled out as a "thing-like thing" in the first instance. On this basis, sugari *(support) and* sasae *(cling) are noteworthy. A sense of the reality of a thing is accumulated through the experience of grasping and moving it. For example, a branch growing out of a tree trunk provides the affordance of* sasae *(support) for climbing. Flexible small branches and vines are typical examples of* sugari *(clinger), which can be drawn closer, transformed into a manipulable thing when broken off, used to create movement for riding, and produce an elastic "counterforce". These senses are unique to primates, as in the case of bonobos who excite their infants by swinging the branch from which they are hanging in the manner of a cradle or a swing. At this time, the branch becomes a socialized thing as a piece of play equipment. Furthermore, bonobos and chimpanzees socialize their food by way of sharing. Food has a complex position in the sense that it serves as the object as well as the means of interaction at this time. (See Chapter 11)*

Young men belonging to the Samburu people of North Central Kenya, are castrating a male calf. The Samburu compare the castration of cattle to the circumcision of young men. Unlike Western thinking that draws a line between humans and animals, the Samburu see humans and animals on a continuum. The men confirm the position of the seminiferous tubules by hand and strike them with wooden clubs. The club can be regarded as an "extension" of the human hand. The affordance of "striking" provided by the club is transmitted to the hand every time the club strikes. Things, including livestock animals, are defined as continuous reciprocal interactions between the body and the environment. (See Chapter 12)

A herd of cattle resting and ruminating. In the life of the Chamus pastoralists in Kenya, each herder goes into the bushland alone to graze their livestock. With no company other than animals, the grazing area is filled with the loud chorus of cicada sounds. Here, "liiyo eats" the herder. The word liiyo means cicada in the Chamus language, as well as "ringing in the ear" and "loneliness (solitude)". The herder gets a strong sense of "solitude" in the midst of cicada drizzles that are felt via the auditory sense as well as the tactile sense of the entire body. This conceals the fundamental question of "What is (the materiality of) a thing?" Sound is intangible but people detect it through hearing as sound and/or the cutaneous sense in the entire body as physical pressure. The materiality of things is perhaps one aspect of things which is perceived only in the relationship with the human body, with the five senses that are always open to the environment. (See Chapter 13)

Let Things Tell Us

There is a plethora of discourses about things. Most of them seem to be fixated on man-made things and their production, and those which are not tend to find the significance of the existence of things in the arguments for the usefulness and symbolic value of things to humans. This relationship between humans and things assumes that "people" are the subject, the center of agency in the strongest sense. By contrast, the purpose of this book is to stop using utility and symbolism as guide for story-telling and let things tell stories. On this point, stones by the side of a road or on a river bank are typical of all the "meaningless things," situated in the farthest place from what we commonly call agency. However, this "meaninglessness" is an entirely human meaning, and meaninglessness exists only because meaningfulness exists. How can we escape from this cycle of self-contradiction? Stones are reluctant to tell us. Perhaps the fact that they vex us in this way is a proof of the "stones' agency without intention". (See Epilogue)

Introduction
Why the Anthropology of *Mono* (Things)?

Ikuya Tokoro & Kaori Kawai

1 Beyond material culture studies: An anthropology of *mono* (things)

"*Mono*" is a Japanese term that loosely corresponds to "things" or "objects" in English. This interpretation will suffice for reading this chapter, but there are some clear, albeit subtle, differences between *mono* and things/objects which are explained in Section 5 below.

The organization of the everyday lives of humans are inseparably linked to a great number of *mono* that surround us. Yet, we are often unaware of how significant *mono* are, because they are so commonplace that we take them for granted. Even when we are aware of them, we do not bother to assign meanings or values to the vast numbers of *mono* in our life-world. Sometimes we have assigned a meaning or value, but remain unconscious of having done so. Nevertheless, diverse *mono* assert themselves by their sheer presence, exerting some influence on us, or standing against us as entities beyond our control in various situations. Ultimately, we cannot ignore the possibility that our "life" is profoundly affected by all of the *mono* in our life-world; in some respects, at least, it seems that it is the *mono* which enable us humans to live our lives.

The aim of the authors of this book is to highlight the fact that *mono* play an important role in our life-world and to interpret the way in which *mono* and humans relate with each other, using the perspectives and methodology of anthropology. More specifically, we are attempting to establish "how *mono* and humans interact with each other" – a very simple question in itself – through an anthropological approach based on ethnographical data from Asia, Africa and Oceania.

What is referred to as "life-world" here is a field (time-space) in which people lead their everyday lives. It is a social environment (social world) in the sense that it is a field in which humans coexist with others. At the same time it is a natural (ecological) environment (natural world) in the sense that it is a physical space in which humans find themselves. In reality, however, humans live in a field where these two worlds are combined and overlap. The various *mono* that interact with humans also occupy this field.

This book departs from the so-called "material culture studies" framework in addressing the question of interaction between *mono* and humans. The subjects and methodologies adopted by the participants varied greatly. The data gathered and the ensuing discussions gradually highlighted a number of issues. It made us aware of questions that might lead to re-examining the fundamental theories and methodologies of anthropology itself. An ethnographical study of the relationships between *mono* and humans extends far beyond a simple re-evaluation of the relatively minor field of material culture studies. We became aware that focusing on *mono* might provide a foothold in forming a bridge over theoretical and institutional divisions in anthropology such as "nature/culture (ecological/symbolic)" and "cultural anthropology/biological (ecological) anthropology". More broadly, it provided an opening to an unfolding criticism and re-examination of the anthropocentrism that underpins the modern world view and which continues to plague anthropology). Redefining the relationship between *mono* and humans in anthropology might culminate in re-examining the ontological question of continuity and distinction between humans and non-human things, which might, in turn, lead to a redefinition of human being itself.

To date, anthropological interests in *mono* have been lumped together under the label "material culture studies." This has been generally regarded as a rather minor subspecialty in cultural anthropology, rather than a theme worthy of being the central focus of the field. Cultural anthropology ostensibly set out to explore all aspects of human activity from a holistic perspective, but the situation is changing dramatically. In contemporary anthropology, a wide variety of studies and conceptualizations are responding to emerging interests in the relationships between humans and material culture – the non-human beings surrounding humans – including various organic and non-organic things in the environment as well as man-made things.

This project is part of this trend. The (re-)invigoration of broad material culture studies in anthropology both within and outside of Japan is one of its background conditions. This book is not, however, a material culture study, despite the strong parallels. This work goes well beyond the pre-defined framework of material culture studies in its perspectives and contents. Our aim in compiling this study is to propose new perspectives and methodologies to portray various aspects of interactions between *mono* and humans by removing or crossing the boundaries of the sub-field called "material culture studies" in anthropology.

2 Where the problem is: Toward a new "human/mono" relationship

As mentioned, we humans are surrounded by vast numbers of *mono*. We interact with a wide variety of *mono* in our everyday lives. A cursory glance at our daily activities reveals that it is doubtful that we can even survive, much less live comfortably, without relying on various *things* from the time we get up until the time we go to sleep (and even during our sleep). For instance, we cannot survive without diverse relationships between a wide variety of *mono*, including food, clothing and shelter. Even the activities that seemingly belong to "non-materialistic" domains such as religion, where we relate to "meta-physical" entities such as "god", the "afterlife" and "spirit", are rife with physical objects such as gravestones, offerings or performing a ritual.

In the field of material culture studies, these relationships between humans and *mono* tend to be understood through the dichotomy between "subject and object". This schematic positions humans (and their society and culture) as subjects and *mono* as the subordinate and subservient objects under the control of human subjects. From this perspective, *mono* are seen as merely reflections of social relations and the cultural systems of their societies while their production, use and consumption by humans gets all the attention. Generally, our relationships with the various *things* in everyday life rarely enter our consciousness because they are extremely mundane and routine. Myriads of *mono* that are supposedly essential for living seldom come into focus. Instead, they are relegated to the background in our perception. In the terms of Gestalt psychology, they are part of the "ground" in the figure-ground grouping.

Long-term detailed studies of the interactions between *mono* and humans, however, have revealed that *mono* "quit" being the object in no small number of situations. These situations, which we either could not see or did not bother to see from within the theoretical frameworks and perspectives of material culture studies, expose the uncontrollability of *mono* that fill our life-world. We find that *mono* often resist and evade human manipulation, control or wishes. In this book, we shall attempt to deconstruct the traditional anthropocentric "human/*mono*" relationship in order to transcend the reductionism of material culture studies.

Our methodology is to pay attention to the activity, independence, compelling power and potential contained in *mono* in themselves as we attempt to discover how to properly recognize interactions between *mono* and humans. To do so, we must assess how they exist in our life-world, embedded in our life-world, rather than separating them from the social, cultural and natural environments in which they are found. This is a fundamentally different approach than that of the Western museums and private collectors who proliferated from the Age of Discovery through the colonial period, especially in the 19th century. They searched for various novelties (curio) in the non-Western world, removed them from their sources, and exhibited them out-of-context in their own countries. The material culture studies field in cultural anthropology followed a similar path in its earliest stages of development.

We have also sought to treat the social, cultural and natural environments in which *mono* exist as comprehensive space-times. A single *mono* presents differently depending upon time and context. So does its interaction with humans. We are trying to capture them in their entirety, holistically. Take a ceremonial mask, for example. In addition to trying to define and understand the mask solely in terms of its role in the ceremony, we seek to pay the same amount of attention to its life outside of ceremony, encompassing how it is crafted, prepared for the ceremony, stored afterwards, and repaired or modified. In short, we endeavor to comb through every space-time in which the mask exists and interacts with humans.

As a material entity, a *mono* continuously occupies a certain space-time and does not disappear very easily. In many cases, humans live in close relationships with such entities for long periods of time. These relationships can be either strong or weak. We often remain unaware of such relationships. Our aim in elucidating these fundamental interactions, of course, determines the ethnographical approaches that we can employ. Observational data obtained from tracking people's actions are combined with discursive data obtained through interviews to provide the evidence required for analyses in most of the chapters of this book. We observe concrete human actions rather than relying solely on linguistic (self-)representations in recognition of the fact that humans are inescapably physical beings. As we shall see, some of the theses presented in this book focus on the embodied interconnections between *mono* and humans. The critical importance of the body in human interactions with *mono* is a topic that our authors return to again and again.

Although the approach of this book differs from the material culture studies approach both epistemologically and methodologically, the *things* that we are concerned with here are neither special nor rare. A majority of them have been scrutinized by material culture studies for a rather long time. These include earthenware for daily use, traditional paintings and dyed goods, craft and folk art such as embroidery and paper-cutting (many of which are articles for daily use), jewelry, masks and musical instruments used in rituals and ceremonies, religious articles such as Buddha statues, mysterious objects used by fortune-tellers and shamans, and food items that are essential for survival. At the same time, it is the intention of this book to define *mono* as broadly as possible. Most of the things that have been dealt with in material culture studies are useful or meaningful for humans, be they substantive or symbolic, whereas this book also examines things that have no useful purposes, such as "stones". It recognizes that everything that can be perceived through our five senses belongs to the category *mono*. That is, it is not constrained by commonly accepted notions of materiality, such as visible and tangible (solid) objects. Consequently, it covers our own bodily interiority as well as intangible *things* which are not normally categorized as things, such as the "sounds" that are felt through auditory or skin sensation (as air vibration).

3 Genealogy of *mono* studies in and outside of anthropology

Space does not permit a comprehensive overview of the genealogy of material culture studies. There are numerous books and general reviews on the history of such studies, so we shall limit ourselves to some supplementary comments on the genealogy of *mono* studies to the extent that it is relevant to the contents of this book.[1]

The English term "material culture" was first coined by Prescott in *The History of the Conquest of Mexico* (1843) (Buchli 2002: 2–3). In these early days of anthropology, interest in material culture was interconnected with the Western-centric theories of social evolution. The emergence of museums from the 19th century formed an institutional backdrop for this. The museums were preceded by the collection and private exhibition of "curio" or unusual things from the non-Western world, which had been fashionable among the European aristocracy since the Renaissance. Thus, an interest in material culture and the proliferation of museums spread hand in hand in the West. The term "material culture" had become inseparable from anthropology by the latter half of the 19th century.

In the 20th century, however, material culture studies was gradually relegated to a relatively minor area within anthropology as the cultural anthropology of Malinowski and Radcliffe-Brown became an independent academic discipline within universities. To put it rather loosely, during the early to mid-20th century anthropology shifted its interest from concrete *things* discovered in the field to more abstract systems and relationships. In the development from structural functionalism to structuralism, to symbolic and interpretive anthropology, anthropologists shifted their interest from *things* to social relations, cultural codes, and representational systems abstracted from the objects they encountered in the field.[2]

We can say that anthropologists' interest in material culture receded into the "ground" in the aforementioned "figure-ground" analogy at the time. In the 1980s, amid rising interest in and attention to reflexive criticism of ethnographic writing and methodology following the publication of *Writing Culture* (Clifford and Marcus 1986), anthropological debate shifted towards reflexivity, epistemology and the politics of anthropological field work. An interest in material culture was not necessarily salient.[3]

Behind the exuberant debates surrounding reflexivity in ethnographic depiction, another movement, a quiet revolution, was inconspicuously yet steadily underway (Henare, Holbradd and Wastell 2007: 7–8). This movement can be seen as a *mono*-oriented anthropology trying to reposition material culture studies in a broad sense once again as one of the main themes of anthropology. While this movement can be found in the work of individual researchers, they are sometimes bundled into a number of loosely-connected schools or groups. Those which are worthy of special mention in relation to the present work include studies by Miller, Gell, Latour, Appadurai, and Kopitoff as well as current research being produced under their influence.[4]

Recent interest in *mono* is not limited to anthropology. In recent years, there has been a resurgence of academic interests in material culture studies across many disciplines, not to mention archaeology and museum studies for which *things* have always been the main subject. For instance, various approaches emphasizing *things* and the environment surrounding humans have been proposed in cognitive science, psychology and philosophy as they attempt to understand human cognition and intelligence, including situated cognition, distributed cognition and affordance theory. They are bringing about a new world view; one in which humans and the world form dynamic relationships by the agency of *mono* and the environment, replacing the dualistic Cartesian subject-object model. The theory of "embodied mind" proposed by Lakoff and Johnson (1999) in particular, argues that humans interact with the environment and things as concrete embodied beings rather than as "ghosts in the machine" (separated from the body and the world). It observes that many of our abstract concepts and arguments rely on metaphors based on concrete physicality.[5]

In other fields, such as history, studies in which the relationship between *mono* and the body is the central theme are gathering momentum, including historical studies of *mono* and material culture since Braudel's *Civilization and Capitalism* (1955–1979) and Hasegawa's history of birthing chairs (1997). The increasing interest in *mono* in anthropology appears to develop concurrently and to be inter-connected with the trend in related humanities and social science disciplines.[6]

4 Theoretical issues addressed in this book

The study of *mono* or material culture is extremely diverse, both in terms of the variety of *things* to be studied, the location and cultural background of their production and use, and the approaches and questions adopted in research. The following challenges exist for any anthropological studies on material culture. First, *mono* or material culture studies have a tendency to be preoccupied with paradigmatic case report of things from various locations. Second, they may contain well-researched catalog of ethnographical accounts regarding all sorts of things from all sorts of places, but it is difficult to assess how they could be anthropologically meaningful.

For these reasons, we have attempted to go beyond the existing material culture studies paradigm, deliberately positioning *mono* among matters of contemporary interest for anthropology and adjacent sciences. In the next section, we will outline our intentions for adopting the main theoretical issues in this book.

4.1 From meaning to agency: Against the linguistic turn

In this book, we posit that, through the study of *mono*, it is possible for anthropology to break away from its excessive reliance on linguistic models. In material culture studies in anthropology it is not uncommon to use linguistic modeling to understand a material culture, deciphering its meaning in the same way that one deciphers signs and discourses. In symbolic and interpretive anthropologies that have been influenced by structuralism or post-structuralism, *mono* are understood to be meaningful signs, symbols and discourses. Hence the anthropologist's job is understood as a kind of code breaking, to ascertain what a certain craftwork or decoration means (represents, signifies), or what the layout of a house or community symbolizes. In these endeavors, *mono* are treated as texts that reflect kinship or social relations, or in which some symbolic or cultural meaning is written (Miller 1998: 9; Tilley 2007: 23).

After the reflexive turn in late 1980s, material culture studies came under the influence of post-colonialism and cultural studies, criticizing the anthropological conventions for being static and indifferent to power relationships. This supposedly new, critical approach was not, however, as different from the model it set out to critique as its proponents would have us believe. It continued to treat *mono* as texts in which social and cultural meanings are inscribed, but with a new tendency to reduce the relevance of material culture to power relationships in particular social and political contexts. *Mono* continued to be regarded as merely illustrations or tokens of the social relationships or cultural systems in question. Hence, one of the challenges of this book is to find ways to approach *mono* without reducing them to mere signs, texts or representations.

As mentioned, Gell (1998) presents a useful perspective from which to approach *mono* in a non-reductive fashion. Gell proposed that we look at objects of art as agents of action, so to speak; agents that trigger reactions and actions – including awe, enchantment, fear and other emotions – in the viewer rather than as texts to be decoded by the anthropologist. This approach involves a shift in the questions that we ask of objects of art. Rather than "What do they represent?" or "What do they mean?" our question should be "What do they do (cause)?"

Gell further argued that an art object is a social agent which expands and transmits its producer's action. This provides a departure from linguistic modelling and interpretation. We can call this shift a change "from meaning to agency". It is a resistance to, or critical re-evaluation of, the logocentric tendency that originated in the so-called linguistic turn, which has been very influential in cultural anthropology as well as in the humanities and social sciences in general.

Let us be clear, though, that we are not suggesting that language and linguistic practice are unimportant in the study of humans and material culture. We are not suggesting that the use of *mono* is more important for humans than language or systems of meaning; they are complementary and often intertwined. Both practices are part of what Lakoff and Johnson call "embodied mind." In fact, much of our linguistic practice is essentially metaphorical, rooted in materiality (Tilley 2007). It is therefore of paramount importance when studying *mono* to pay attention to the materiality of linguistic practice, rather than either reducing *mono* to its linguistic dimension or neglecting the linguistic dimension completely.[7]

A similar change of direction can be found in the re-evaluation of non-discursive thought in the work of Bergson, Merleau-Ponty, and Deleuze, among others. For example, Bergson's focus on the material entity that is excluded when an understanding of the human is reduced to language and its biological generation is being reassessed by contemporary scholars (Higaki 2008: 60). This de-centering approach may help to develop a perspective that can understand life, the body, their autopoiesis and their interaction with the environment by capturing the materiality of production as it is (p. 62). The growing interest in *mono* in anthropology may also be attributable to an aspiration to distance oneself from debates about the linguistic turn or reflexivity in anthropology and to return to the tangible or textured reality, so to speak, which we encounter in the field. From this perspective, we suggest that the anthropology of *mono* has the potential to provide links to the anthropology of sentience or qualia in the future.[8]

4.2 Dynamics between the body and the environment with *mono* as agents

The body and its relationship to *mono* are important themes that are repeatedly referred to in this book. The embodied practical wisdom or tacit knowledge (Polanyi 1966) in the production and use of *mono* and techniques of the body (Mauss 1973) are important concepts in this work. Our interest in the body is also closely related to the departure from linguistic reductionism in the study of *mono*, as suggested earlier. This highlights the importance of paying attention to the embodied practical knowledge required for the production and use of *mono* as well as linguistic knowledge and its representations.

One example of practical knowledge in relation to *mono* which is frequently quoted is the knowledge (skill) of "how to ride a bicycle". It is possible, theoretically, to describe this type of knowledge (skill) in language (e.g., "Hold the handle with both hands, place one foot on a pedal..."). But it is not possible for a complete beginner to master bicycle riding by simply reading instructions. The knowledge of bicycle riding is the kind of knowledge that can only be learned physically, through repeated praxis, by actually using the body and the bicycle. Cases of embodied practical wisdom or tacit knowledge in the manufacture and production of *mono* are examined by Kaneko (Chapter 5: pottery-making) and Tokoro (Chapter 3: pearl cultivation).

Another important point is that the body actively interacts with the agency of *mono* in the surrounding environment. There is a dynamic relationship in which the boundary between the body and the external environment fluctuates and changes. This relationship has disappeared from view in the modern world, where the distinction between the subject and the object is understood in terms of a sharp boundary between human and environment. The predominant Western view sees the human body as a delimited and fixed entity.

With a slight change in perspective, however, we find that the boundary between the human body and the environment fluctuates considerably. For example, a tool is clearly an external object when it is not in use, but it can be seen as an extension of the human body when it is in use. In other words, the boundary between the human body and the environment can fluctuate and change dynamically by the agency of *mono*. As Konaka points out in Chapter 12, *mono* act as an interface between the body and the environment.

A walking stick for the visually impaired and a vehicle for a skilled driver are commonly quoted examples in relation to this fluctuation. The walking stick itself is part of the external environment outside of the biological body of the visually impaired but it functions as an extension of their body (hand) when it is being used. The "body" extends to the far end of the stick, where a new boundary is formed between the extended body and the ground surface. Similarly, skilled drivers experience the car as an extension of their own body. In fact, clothing, accessories, cosmetics and houses can all be experienced as an extension of the body or the skin in a broad sense when they are worn or inhabited, while simultaneously having the characteristic of a physical object outside of the body in a narrow sense (external environment) (Knapett 2005: 18).

In short, *mono* can be embodied according to the situation. The boundary between the "body" and the "environment" changes dynamically through the interface of *mono*. In this book, Sugawara (Chapter 2), Kaneko (Chapter 5), Tanaka (Chapter 6) and Konaka (Chapter 12) discuss questions about the interactions and the boundaries between *mono* and the body based on ethnographical data.

4.3 *Mono* and the environment

When we use the term "environment", we include not only the cognitive environment at the micro level as in cognitive scientific discussion but also the ecological (natural) environment and the social-cultural environment in a more ordinary sense. It is one of the aims of this book to elucidate how various types of *mono* are locally produced, traded, consumed, used, disposed and re-used in different environments (cultural, social and ecological) on the basis of ethnographical data.

Nevertheless, as discussed, we seek to highlight the real materiality inherent in *mono* themselves rather than reducing them to their social-cultural context. In other words, while we acknowledge the materiality constituted by the meaning system of the culture that creates it, we want to shed light on the particular materiality that constitutes a society or culture. Our objective is to demonstrate that *mono* and the human cultures that create them are mutually constitutive (Miller 1998: 3; Henare, Holbradd and Wastell 2007: 2).

We also recognize that studies in cultural anthropology tend to emphasize the cultural-social environments while overlooking the relationship between humans and the ecological (natural) environment – as well as *mono*/materiality. With this in mind, we have adopted an interdisciplinary approach in this book, including researchers from archaeology, ecological anthropology and (sociological) primatology (see Chapter 4 by Intoh, Chapter 10 by Yamakoshi, and Chapter 11 by Kuroda) as well as cultural anthropologists.

Archaeology, of course, has long grappled with *mono* and has established an almost dispassionately objective methodology with regard to its "materiality". As we aim for a comprehensive and empirical study of *mono*, we have much to learn from this aspect of archaeology.

Ecological anthropology is one field of anthropology that attempts to elucidate interaction and coexistence between humans and nature, principally through the detailed observation, description and analysis of subsistence activities. Long-term observation and measurement is its methodological mainstay, providing a perspective which can produce convincing empirical explanations as well as capturing human experiences that cannot be verbalized. In his essay on domestication (of animals and plants), Komatsu (I-3) argues that the process of domestication presents important information which demonstrates the end point (or pass point) of long-term interactions between humans and nature – in the form of concrete things such as livestock and cultivated crops – on an almost evolutionary time scale. Domestication also offers a chance to introduce temporal axes into the study of *mono* by examining the physical and physiological "changes" of plants and animals. Konaka (Chapter 12) also explores livestock as an interface between humans and the environment based on ethnographical data from East Africa.

The participation of primatologists is our bold attempt to incorporate an evolutionary perspective into the study of *mono*. While cases of the use and manufacture of tools found among non-human primates, especially the genus *Pan*, orangutans, and cebid monkeys in South America, and food-sharing found in the genus *Pan* are themselves intellectually stimulating, more importantly, the study of *mono* by primatologists poses fundamental questions about what *mono* are for humans in the first place. In the actions of primates we can identify something like a "primordial state" that may be indicative of the origins of the relationship between humans and *things*. "Tool-use" has become an important topic in the study of wild chimpanzees and the term "material culture" is used routinely in that field (e.g., *Chimpanzee Material Culture: Implications for Human Evolution* by McGrew, 1992). In subspecialties such as cultural primatology (McGrew 1996; de Waal 1999 among others) and cultural panthropology (Whiten et al. 2003), comparative research into the manners of tool-use and grooming in chimpanzees is conducted using an "ethnographic" method (Wrangham et al. 1994).

Of course, following these lines of inquiry raises the risk of producing yet another type of reductionism in the study of *mono*: reducing the condition of various *things* to natural or ecological factors. As Konaka (Chapter 12) points out, material culture studies to date have tended to fall into the dualistic trap of distinguishing between the cultural/social domain and the natural domain, and explaining material culture in terms of either "culture (society)" or "nature". In contrast, this book is an endeavor to capture the hybrid-like intertwining of the human body and the natural environment through *mono*.

4.4 De/re-commoditization of *mono*

It is impossible to avoid the question of commoditization in our discussion of the relationship between the social-cultural environment and *mono*. Addressing this issue, though, once again raises the challenge of how to avoid reducing material culture studies to cultural-social contexts. For instance, the Marxist concept "reification" was coined precisely to highlight the error of attributing value to things in themselves, suggesting that the perceived value of things (commodities) is in fact the value of social relations such as the relations of production. A similar perspective has dominated anthropological discussions of the exchange and consumption of things, maintaining that social relations are of primary importance whereas things are secondary media at best.

Appadurai and Kopytoff sparked a departure from this reductionist tendency in anthropology. They argued that the "social life of things" should be tracked in the same way that humans are and proposed that certain things de- and re-commoditize depending on context (Appadurai 1986). As we expand this perspective, we find that things can have different values or meanings in different social contexts, that things are circulated and utilized trans-locally across certain time periods or places, and that certain things are utilized and appropriated in very diverse ways. In short, it becomes quite clear that we cannot merely reduce things to the cultural contexts of the localities in which they are produced.

From a rather different perspective, Munn's study of the Kula exchange provides another important point of departure from the reductionist perspective. She points out that although humans have certainly ascribed value to the shells that they exchange, they have no way of representing value without shells. This suggests that shells and humans are reciprocal agents in defining the value of one another (Munn 1983: 283). This is an important point for the argument about the possibility of *mono*-centric description in the next section.

4.5 De-anthropocentrism and the possibility of *mono*-centric description

In common parlance, the distinctions between "humans" and "things", whether natural things or human-made objects, and between humans and non-human lifeforms, are generally understood as self-evident and beyond question. The dominant perspective in the modern world is that humans alone have the privilege of being subjects with agency (freedom to act) while non-human things are dead objects to be controlled and manipulated by humans (the so-called "instrumentalist world view": see Tanaka, Chapter 6). In this world view, even living creatures are implicitly regarded as if they were some kind of sophisticated but mindless automatons. The boundaries between humans and non-human things are considered absolute; border-fluctuations, border-crossing, or hybridization between them, rarely enter our awareness. In this paradigm, human superiority over non-human things is unshakable. This perspective, including a heavily anthropocentric view of *mono*, has been common sense in modern society.

This modernist view of *mono*, however, is not common to all humankind. Nor is it a universally appropriate paradigm for discussing the relationship between humans and various non-human things. This book attempts to realign our depictions and understandings of the relationships between humans, non-human things, and the environment. We aim to demonstrate the inadequacy of the anthropocentric framework for understanding things and humans while beginning to lay the foundations for a new model for understanding the humans/*mono* relationship.

Many of the discussions in this book build on the question of how to overcome the paradigm which sees humans as dominant subjects and *mono* as subordinate objects. This de-anthropocentric concept of agency has gained some traction in the humanities and social sciences over the past two decades thanks largely to the Actor Network Theory (ANT) proposed by Latour and others (Latour 1993; Knapett 2005; Knapett and Malafouris 2008 among others). ANT adopts a symmetrical approach toward humans and non-human *things* and proposes that we should understand agency to be distributed through the relational network of humans and things rather than as an exclusively human privilege. It considers humans and things to have the same level of importance as long as they participate in the network. In other words, actors and agency are seen as products of the complex and hybridized networks woven by humans and things. In these terms, another way of describing the aim of this book is to say that we want to examine the complex entanglement between humans and things through close analysis of ethnographic fields free from the dichotomizing prejudices of the anthropocentric paradigm.

5 The term *mono* in this book

We have mostly been using the Japanese term *mono* to describe matters for which a conventional material culture study would use the English term *things*. This is a conscious decision rather than a simple word choice preference. We have deliberately chosen *mono* as a keyword in this book because it contains highly complex and rich nuances that cannot be translated into English.

In the classical Japanese language, *mono* can mean "everything that can be perceived and discerned by humans, from anything that has a form and is palpable to any event in a broad and general sense" (Iwanami kogo jiten). In contemporary Japanese the term *mono* can be written in two different kanji (Chinese) characters – "物" and "者" – usually the former refers to (non-human) objects and the latter refers to humans. Thus, *mono* in Japanese contains both "human" and "non-human" meanings, depending on the context.

Moreover, when we look at the usage of *mono* in classical Japanese, we find colorful expanses of meaning containing not only external and objective matters but also human emotions, psyches and sometimes even invisible and spiritual beings interwoven with such matters. Some examples include, *mono no aware* ("pathos of things"; deep emotions triggered by external things, events or phenomena), *mono no ke* ("mysterious things"; live or dead spirits), and *tsuki mono* ("things that possess"; animal, human or dead spirits that possess people). Thus, *mono* in Japanese can be understood to be a term that covers a broader and richer semantic domain which cannot always be reduced to English terms such as thing or object. For this reason, we have chosen to define and use *mono* as a term in which its broad connotations and ambiguity in the classical Japanese context are deliberately embedded along with the implied narrower meanings, such as visible and tangible entities (solids), materials or objects.

It is fair to say that "material culture studies" in the narrow sense mainly deals with visible and tangible things. In contrast, the focus on *mono* in this book moves across the narrower boundaries of material culture studies while keeping material culture at its core. Our discussions of *mono* include not only man-made and craft products, but also material objects which have rarely been examined by "material culture studies" scholars, including natural objects such as "stone" (Uchibori, Epilogue), lifeforms such as livestock (Konaka, Chapter 12), biological products such as pearls (Tokoro, Chapter 3) and bananas (Komatsu, Essay I-3), and "sound" (Fushiki, Chapter 8 and Kawai, Chapter 13). In other words, not only those solid and liquid *mono* that are visually perceptible and tangible, but all phenomena that can be perceived and cognized through any or all of the "five senses" (visual, auditory, olfactory, taste and tactile senses) are potential topics for discussion in this book.

6 Contents

The chapters and essays in this book cover extensive regions in various parts of the world, including Asia, Africa and Oceania, as well as diverse types of *mono*. For the sake of convenience, we have grouped the chapters into five parts (and the essays into three groups plus one extra) according to their broad theoretical themes, keywords or questions.

Part I is entitled "The genesis, extinction and continuation of *mono*". It contains two theses concerning questions about the most fundamental aspects of the relationship between *mono* and humans, that is, how *mono* come to appear before humans (genesis), then get noticed, form relationships and fade from sight. In terms of the figure-ground relationship, the question is how *mono* shift from the "ground" to the "figure" and from the "figure" to the "ground" in their interactions with "humans". Both of these theses also present interesting discussions on the relationship between language and *mono*.

Part II is titled "The nexus between *mono* and the environment". It contains two theses examining the "environment", which cannot be ignored in anthropological discussions on *mono*. Tokoro (Chapter 3) reconsiders the commonly accepted view of the humans-*mono* relationship by analyzing the uncontrolled nature of the environment and *mono*. Intoh (Chapter 4) argues for recognition of the importance of the ecological (natural) environment, which tends to be overlooked in cultural anthropology in a narrow sense, through an archaeological analysis of pottery making.

Part III, titled "The dynamic between *mono* and the body", presents two theses that squarely address questions of physicality. These questions are crucial to any discussion of the production and use of *mono*. The body is a keyword whose importance has once again been recognized in philosophy and the cognitive sciences in recent years. Kaneko (Chapter 5) and Tanaka (Chapter 6) use ethnographical analyses of specific items of *mono* – earthenware and male sexual stimulants respectively – to highlight the importance of the body in the production and use of *mono*.

Part IV, "The agency of *mono*", includes three theses offering ethnographical materials that might severely shake up the dominant view of *mono*. These theses deal with masks, musical instruments and fortune teller's tools and demonstrate the validity of investigation from the perspective that *mono* are capable of exerting agency, rather than being merely inert objects or reflections of a particular culture.

Part V, entitled "Toward a new *mono* theory", presents four theses that contribute to expanding the horizon of the anthropological theory of *mono*. Yamakoshi (Chapter 10) and Kuroda (Chapter 11) offer some hints to re-position and re-capture the humans-*mono* relationship on a much longer evolutionary historical scale than the anthropocentric tunnel vision that traps cultural anthropology into narrow discussions of *mono* from a primatological perspective.

Konaka (Chapter 12) uses the techniques of both ecological anthropology and cultural anthropology to propose a new theoretical framework to overcome the two types of reductionism – "nature (or ecology)" and "society (or culture)". Kawai (Chapter 13) searches for the possibility of a new *mono* study that addresses the "*mono*-like property" of "sound" itself, which is not an easy topic to discuss in conventional material culture studies. It signals the impending birth of a new area of anthropological study concerning feelings (or perceptions) about *mono*.

In addition to the above theses, this book contains several shorter essays, which are divided into three groups: Group I "Emerging *mono*", Group II "Mysterious *mono*" and Group III "Fuzzy *mono*". In broad terms, Group I essays discuss interactions between *mono* and humans, Group II essays address the "mysteriousness (strangeness)" of *mono*, including fetishism and kitsch, mainly through studies of religions and ceremonies, and Group III essays deal with *mono* that fluctuate in the changing cultural and social contexts (primarily art). The final essay by Uchibori serves as the Epilogue of the book.

It is worth noting, however, that these theses and essays have been arranged in this way merely for the sake of convenience. The order of arrangement is in no way absolute. The themes of these groupings are certainly not mutually exclusive. For instance, the contents of Konaka's thesis (Chapter 12) in Part V are also relevant to the environment in Part II as well as the question of physicality in Part III. The reader, of course, should choose to read the theses and essays according to their interest, as independent pieces, rather than following the sequence in which they are presented.

Indeed, if we view these theses and essays as themselves *mono*, then clearly the editors' attempts to situate each thesis in a single context or to control its meaning is a futile effort. So we will stop talking and let these *mono* speak for themselves.

Part I
The Genesis, Extinction and Continuation of *Mono*

1 Between Form, Word and Materiality: Shanbei Paper-Cuts

Tomoko Niwa

Keywords: Shanbei paper-cut, appearance of things, sensory experience, materiality of symbolic things, repetition and creation

1.1 Shanbei paper-cutting: *Things* in sensory experience

There is a vast expanse of dry yellow earth along the upper reaches of the Huang River in inland China. Shanbei (the northern portion of Shaanxi Province) centers around Yan'an on the Huangtu Plateau. A majority of inhabitants make their living in agriculture and live in small villages consisting of a few dozen homes scattered across rolling hills and valleys. The typical dwelling in this area is a kind of traditional cave-house called "*yaodong*", an arched structure carved horizontally out of a hillside (Photo 1.1).

The subject of this chapter, "*jianzhi*" (paper-cutting) or – as the local people call it – "*jiaohua*" (flower-cutting), is carried out by farming women during the off season, partly for pleasure and partly as a housekeeping task. These women make paper-cuts to decorate the lattice windows on the façade of their cave-houses. When paper-cuts and spring festival couplets[1] are pasted on houses around the time of the Lunar New Year, the desolate wintry villages turn red, instantly restoring their liveliness. In Shanbei, paper-cuts are primarily decorations for the stark-looking cave-houses, which add color at the time of the Spring Festival as well as other special occasions. The brilliant red color of paper-cuts are said to carry auspicious omens or charms against evil (Photo 1.2).

In Shanbei, it is said that "paper-cuts are the songs of the hearts of women". Until the mid-20th century, skills such as paper-cutting and embroidering were regarded as indicative of a woman's capability. Still today, many men are of the view that "paper-cutting is an innate ability of women who bear and raise children". The norm of "Men work outside, women work inside" persists in these rural areas.

Photo 1.1   Cave-houses during the Spring Festival season. The inside and outside of the homes are decorated with deep red New Year couplets and paper cut-outs after the year-end cleanup.

Photo 1.2   Female members of a farming family arrange various patterns on the kang bed-stove to choose window-flowers for the coming year.

Accordingly, the locals say that men pour out their emotions by singing loudly in the mountains while women express their feelings through the needlecraft and paper-cutting that they do inside their cave-houses.

1.1.1 Another thing that is represented and mediated by a *thing*

Traditional paper-cutting was banned as a superstitious custom during the Cultural Revolution (1960s and '70s). Since the late 1970s, however, it has been experiencing a resurgence as a "folk art" (*minjian-yishu*). Theoretical support for the revival was provided by various iconic studies, which considered paper-cutting to be a repository of China's ethnic world view, symbolized by yin-yang philosophy and aiming to interpret the meaning inherent in diverse shapes (e.g., Jin 1994). At the same time, treating paper-cutting as a mode of women's self-expression facilitated its protection and promotion and provided an incentive for bringing its product to market as a kind of artwork from the 1990s.[2] More particularly, recent recognition of the art of paper-cutting as intangible cultural heritage has led to individual makers being applauded for their artistic creativity. In this vein, a number of books have been published that interpret the "work" of paper-cutting masters through the lens of the producers' personal histories (e.g., Qiao 2004).

Despite the difference in perspective between the realization of symbolism and self-expression, both views share a regard for paper-cutting as a medium – they are both interested in something else that is represented by paper-cuts rather than paper-cuts themselves.[3] According to the dualistic Cartesian subject-object model mentioned by Tokoro and Kawai in the Introduction, the commonsense view of *things* (*mono*) states that things are made, defined and mobilized as objects in opposition to terms such as "human", "language (sign)" and "mind" within the framework typified by the mind-body problem. This type of thinking is also found in explanations of how "objects" called artifacts or artworks come into being. Seeing "making things", for example, as the "act of giving a form to a material substance based on a content preconceived by the person who makes it" is rife with dichotomies such as "form/substance" and "meaning-content/form".

From the 1980s, anthropological material culture studies argued against this anthropocentric view of *things*, proposing instead to adopt a methodology focusing on things themselves. Appadurai (1986) and others argued that we must pay attention to things themselves as they move across different spaces and times. When applied to the study of so-called indigenous art, a new perspective was achieved which captured the processes through which artefacts and artworks traversed different value systems such as "West–Non-West" and "market commodity–personal property–museum". In this process, the things both generated and changed their meanings (e.g., Myers 2001). From this perspective, the process through which paper-cuts transformed from practical items in farming households to "folk art" seems to be a suitable subject for research. At the same time, however, Miller's (1987) argument for recognizing the agency of objects may also be applicable for those who focus on paper-cuts used as gifts between members of village communities or to subsequent generations. In these cases the paper-cuts can be seen as vehicles for personal memories or social relationships. From either perspective, though, the thing continues to function merely as a medium for the human objectification of things. In the end, things are absorbed by human meanings or values.

1.1.2 Appearance of *things* in the form of ephemeral paper-cuts

Yet, paper-cuts are at least as much things as they are meanings and values. In comparison with patchwork pictures (*budui-hua*) and peasant paintings (*nongming-hua*) that are produced to sell – both of which employ the art of paper-cutting – the actual paper cut-outs themselves are generally of little value. Their price tends to be discounted for sale to friends and family, either within or outside of the local area; or they are given away as "bonus extras" in the sale of "works" of other styles. Paper-cuts were originally disposable decorations that are repeatedly reproduced using thin and fragile materials. Pasted paper-cuts are normally discarded when they become old and worn. Hence, in contrast to the high value that researchers and artists in cities accord to "folk art", paper-cuts tend to be ephemeral in the places where they are produced and used.

But of course, financial value – or price – is not the only measure of value. Many of the women who create paper-cuts admit that "Once I start paper-cutting, I get so engrossed that I forget to sleep" or "I like paper-cutting because I can express what I want to express quickly." At the same time, some makers of handicrafts dislike it because of its high production and storage costs relative to its low commercial value.

Hence, if we are to examine this somewhat elusive "human-thing" relationship between the people of Shanbei and paper-cutting, it is not enough for us to treat paper-cutting as a style of representation, a medium for meaning or value, or to simply describe is as an art system. We need to examine the individual physical experiences of "holding a pair of scissors, cutting paper shapes, and pasting them on certain places" as the women lead their everyday lives in cave-houses.

One key can be found in answers to the question of "Why paper-cutting is loved by Shanbei women". The locals often explain "For many women who cannot read, paper-cutting is the best way to express themselves". In the long history of paper-cutting, the fact that many makers were illiterate women meant something more than the simple fact that they could neither read nor write.[4] For people in this area, especially the middle-aged and elderly women who are the main makers of paper-cuts, words definitely exist as sounds. The intimate relationship between the generation, extinction and continuation of words as voices and the generation, extinction and continuation of paper-cuts will be one of the central points of the discussion that follows.

This chapter, therefore, describes the way the things called Shanbei paper-cuts, which are transient and fragile in terms of their materiality and value, continue to exist as things not only as physical emergence but also as perceived and recognized images. To state our conclusion first, paper-cuts as *things* appear recurrently, so to speak, in concatenations of discrete yet contingent sensory experiences. In this appearance of things, we argue, the "word" which is typically contrasted to things, and "form" which is seen as a product of the mind, also have certain kinds of materiality. Words and forms relate with things in a mutually reciprocating manner. Our aim is to propose a fresh perspective to advance the anthropological study of things by refuting the conventional view of things as fixed and inflexible and focusing on the "human-thing" relationship.

1.2 "Flower-cutting" (*jiaohua*): "Flower" (*hua*) as a beautiful image

Firstly, we shall examine how "paper-cuts" (*jianzhi*) are perceived in Shanbei based on its appellation. In standard Chinese, "剪紙" (*jianzhi*) refers both to the things called "paper cut-outs" and to the act of "cutting out paper with scissors". In reality, however, this term is rarely used in rural Shanbei. The locals understand *jianzhi* to be a term used by urban intellectuals with the connotation of "artworks" made by professional "paper-cutting artists". The term ordinarily used in rural villages is "flower-cutting" (铰花 *jiaohua*), which can also refer to work using fabric material. Like "剪" (*jian*), "铰" (*jiao*) is a verb for cutting with scissors. The locals, especially the paper-cut makers, stress that their paper-cutting is different than a paper-cutting technique called "刻紙" (*kezhi*), for which a knife is used.[5]

Paper cut-outs acquire various names according to their uses. "Window-flowers" (*chuanghua*), for which the twelve animals of the Chinese Zodiac, other creatures and flowers are popular motifs, are also pasted on lanterns as "lantern-flowers" (*denghua*) and on walls as "wall-flowers" (*qianghua*). "Happiness-flowers" (*xihua*) – which are called "wedding-flowers" (*jiehunhua*) and "double happiness-flowers" (*shuangxihua*) locally – are decorations pasted on the bedroom walls of a newly married couple, on the bride's marriage furniture, on dough models (*mianhua*) of the food to be eaten at the ceremony, and so on around the time of a wedding. The inside and outside of the cave-house are covered in red paper-cuts on the wedding day. While these paper-cuts for decoration pasted on visible places are made of red paper, templates for embroidery for insoles, pillows and clothing are called "flower models" (*huayangzi*) or "patterns" (*yangyang*) (meaning samples) and are generally made of waste paper such as old magazines. These names categorize paper cut-outs as practical items according to their uses. The same paper cut-outs are called by different names depending on the situation.[6]

What do "flowers" (花*hua*) in flower-cutting and window-flowers represent? The women who make paper-cuts commented, "Flowers in the field, designs, everything that looks nice is a 'flower'". Some literate men commented, "Old women delight in new year pictures, saying '*huahua*', and praise beautiful dresses and well-made window-flowers as '*huabulanglang*'", and "For those women who don't know written Chinese, "flower" (*hua*) and "picture" (畫 *hua*: something picturesque) are similar things and not differentiated". Rural villages in Shanbei continue a so-called "oral culture" today (Ong 1991) – a culture in which "writing" is not internalized by people. Hence, for the illiterate women in this area, the word "flower" (*hua*) not only echoes the concrete image of a plant in flower but also refers to a wider range of objects.[7]

We shall therefore interpret the "*hua*" here as a "beautiful form". This is of course not simply a material form or a pattern decorating useful objects. The "form" (flower = *hua*) of a paper-cut is in a sense a thing such as a beautiful decoration or design. It demonstrates the condition of things, including amorphous images, before they are given meanings according to use. However, it acquires specific names such as "flower-cuts" and "window-flowers" when they are recognized in relation to their specific placement, the action used to make them, the tool used, or the places or situations for their use. At the same time, when these names (words) are uttered, Shanbei paper-cuts appear in front of people as "tangible images" (Iwaki 2001) with certain materiality.[8]

Similarly, it also demands a new concept of *things*. In the meantime, we shall define *things* as an overarching concept which includes both the physical dimensions of the materiality in which they occupy specific times and places (*things*) and another conceptual or imaginary dimension in which they emerge as tangible or intangible images as exemplified by the "flowers".[9] In a later section, we shall demonstrate that things are rather fluid and indeterminable; their materiality appears to people in a context-specific fashion.

1.3 Use of paper cut-outs: Disposal, storage and renewal

Let us step into a space in which paper cut-outs are used. The "red paper" used for paper-cutting and spring couplets (*chunlian*) is commonly purchased at New Year markets. The red paper is thin and light. The red dye fades when it gets wet, or is exposed to sunlight. It is difficult to store sensitive paper-cuts in a cave-house and their delicately cut details are particularly fragile. "Window-flowers" and "happiness-flowers" are left unattended after they have been pasted up and therefore destined to wither due to exposure to the weather and sunlight. Some may retain their original shapes but after a while the residents become so accustomed to their presence that they pay little attention to the symbolic meanings of the individual forms. This transience and fragility, however, signify something more than just the passing seasons.

When do paper-cuts surface to people's consciousness? It appears that, on the one hand, the moment of critical visual importance must be when sunlight hits the screen windows to bring out the color of the window-flowers and illuminate their forms like silhouettes. The only daylight windows in the cave-house construction are the lattice screen windows set in its façade. In the rural villages of Shanbei, window-flowers are considered essential, especially in households with children. Their importance can be seen in the saying that "children go blind if window-flowers are not pasted". This draws an analogy between the windows, which are regarded as the eyes of the cave-house and the children within the household. The window-flowers are things that are seen by the eyes. We can also find metaphorical uses of visual and auditory images in a legend that "window-flowers take away '天花' (*tianhua*) [smallpox]." The materiality of a paper-cut is recognized as a "form" (flower) in the process of its interaction with *things* around it as well as the environment (climate, outside light, cave-house etc.). We must nevertheless acknowledge that the appearance of this thing is always contingent and situation-dependent, rather than fixed or definitive.

On the other hand, the motifs of window-flowers include the Chinese astrological animal symbol for the coming year or one's wishes for the new year.[10] Once they are pasted on screen windows or mounting paper, they cannot be removed. They discolor and tear after a while. They are therefore renewed each year, when the screen windows are replaced before the end of the year. At the same time, it seems that the fragility of paper cut-outs continually generates the incentive for reproduction. One paper-cutting artist stressed to me, "An artwork can be framed and enjoyed for a long time but the window-flower is for a single-use." It is disposable. The window-flower is supposed to be reproduced seasonally and cyclically; it is a thing meant for renewal. Its fragility is itself an important factor for the continuation of a thing called paper-cutting.

Surplus paper cut-outs are inserted between the pages of old magazines or between the kang bed-stove and the mattress for storage as stock or samples (*yangyang*). They are taken out for use as required – for pasting at the end of the year or at the time of a wedding. Women in the neighborhood may ask for them as a gift or for exchange. These occasions are a time for stocktaking and sorting. In this way, good "forms" are passed on from one generation to another or spread and shared within and outside of the village.

1.4 Making process (1) – Improvisation of "*maojiao*"

Let us look at the process of "flower-cutting" next. In Shanbei villages, paper-cut makers often say "I can't do flower-cutting" or "I can't cut without a '*yangyang*' (template)". Using a template (pattern or sample) is called "*ti-yangzi*" (template replacement). Paper-cut makers distinguish this method from the "*maojiao*" method of cutting out a form directly with scissors without a sample or sketch. One's "flower-cutting" ability is judged on the basis of how well one can do the latter. This is because "*maojiao*" – literally meaning "impromptu cutting" – is regarded as the skill to create a design.

"*Maojiao*", which is a technical goal for flower-cutting, is described as "*xiang-zhe-jian*" (cutting using one's imagination) and "*yong-xin-lai-jian*" (cutting from one's heart). It is interpreted as "using imagination to conceive an image and converting it directly into a form as one chooses". As it seems to be an act of freely creating a form out of a blank sheet of paper, it is regarded as an improvisational practice of design "creation". The skilled makers are acknowledged as masters with "*chuanyi*" (creativity), akin to the singers who can "*bianci*" (create or modify lyrics on the spot). Like many artists, paper-cut makers often confess when they look at their own "*maojiao*" cut-outs of complex designs that "I don't know how I did that" or "I'm surprised how well I've cut it".

Photo 1.3 is an example of the process of "*maojiao*" practiced by Gao Fenglian, a female paper-cut artist in her seventies, who is well known in Shanbei.[11] The production of the work shown in Photo 1.3 was carried out intermittently over three to four days in mid-January of the Chinese calendar during the farming off-season in her own cave-house. The following description centers around the first half (one and a half days) of the making process for this work, together with her commentaries.

Between Form, Word and Materiality 45

Photo 1.3 Gao Fenglian's paper cut (completed).

Photo 1.4 She watches TV and chats with her granddaughter during production. She places a rough cut-out of an ox's head (made from a newspaper) on the red paper to work out the design.

On the first day, after feeding her family's livestock and having a late breakfast, Gao Fenglian began production by cutting a sheet of red paper into eight pieces, putting one on top of the other and clipping the edges to fix them together. According to Gao, the only thing in her mind before picking up her scissors was the central motifs of an ox and a tiger from the Chinese zodiac and "no idea of what else to cut". She cut out a template for the faces of the ox and the tiger from a sheet of newspaper, placed it on the red paper, and cut along the outlines with her scissors. She then cut the rough outlines of their bodies by way of "impromptu cutting" (Photo 1.5).

As she gazed at the picture, she said that she could "see a tree appearing" out of the shape of the background behind the two animal shapes and began cutting a tree trunk from the ground up between the ox and the tiger. She rested her hand a while later, then began cutting the outlines of a woman on the top right corner of the space by saying, "It would be nice to have a girl under the tree". After that, she returned to the cutting of the tree (Photo 1.6). She rested her hand frequently to stare blankly into space while humming a tune, to watch TV, or to converse with her family as she continued to work. Gao said, "If I don't know what to cut, I just leave it".

Work on the first day was finished before dinner preparation started and resumed in the afternoon of the second day. (Meanwhile she was busy preparing offerings for a temple fair (*miaohui*) in the evening, attending the temple fair the next morning, watching a play, and receiving visitors.) As if in response to a curve appearing as she was cutting tree branches at the center, she added two more women figures. She cut the tree and the women alternately to tidy up their shapes gradually. "The three women are standing around to chat. Perhaps an elderly woman and two daughters-in-law". After having an early dinner and sweeping the front yard, she came back to paper-cutting. She cut out the outlines of a cave-house using a newspaper template, then began adding windows and other details. "There is a cave-house behind the tree and the women in the front yard. Mobile things are at the front, immobile things are at the back" (Photo 1.7). The work continued until late at night.

From the third day, she moved on to the "decoration" (*zhuanxi*) within the outlines of each motif which she gradually determined as its form and balance emerged in the production process. What was striking was the considerable "waiting time" during which she rested her hand and appeared to daydream until she could see "the next form" (the image of a motif or decoration is evoked from the form of the blank space in the background). Other things that caught my eyes were: the way she tried, corrected and decided on which line to cut by applying a separate paper template to the outlines of the shape she wanted to stabilize; tracing a cutting line by moving her scissors in the air in the manner of a practice swing before actually beginning to cut, and; marking an approximate

Between Form, Word and Materiality

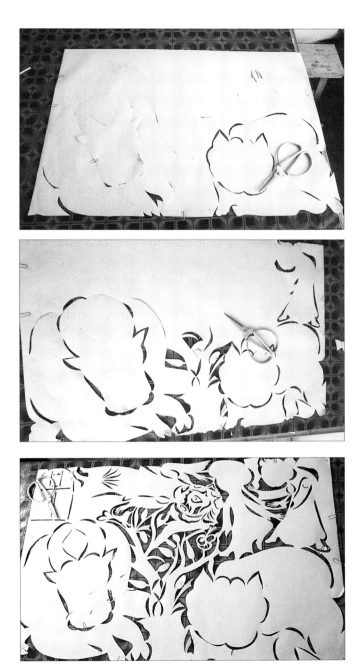

Photos 1.5–1.7 Impromptu "maojiao" *for the work in Photo 1.3 (photographed from the reverse side).*

line on the paper with the tip of her scissors. While avoiding the risk of failure ("Once it is cut, it's over") as much as possible in this way, she created a finely balanced composition with naturally blended motifs. On the other hand, once her scissors began cutting, the work was left to the interaction between the paper, the scissors and her hand movement. The fast and decisive use of the scissors produced clean lines and clean-cut "forms". For "decoration", the scissors were used in a more decisive and rhythmic manner because a repertoire of certain designs (to be discussed in the next section) were utilized. They are expressed through several different techniques, including "*wan*" to punch holes with sharp scissor tips and "*da-yaya*" to cut paper to hair-like fineness, depending on the condition and texture of each motif.

As we can see, in the "*maojiao*" process, the form of a paper cut-out is created by the skill of a highly trained hand while being subjected to certain kinds of resistance (constraints) from layered paper material and scissors, not from a pre-determined design or template. This supports Henri Focillon's argument that technique is a recognition method, that the form's life "develops in a space that is not the abstract frame of geometry; under the tools and at the hands of men it assumes substance in a given material" (Focillon 1992: 62). Yet, the work process of "flower-cutting" must go beyond the interactions between materials, tools and the body as Focillon conceived it, and find its place in a broader context incorporating production practices.

"Flower-cutting" is part of Gao Fenglian's everyday life. It happens in between farming work, animal husbandry and household chores, and is sometimes interrupted by seasonal events. Moreover, production itself is a kind of "multitasking operation" – she worked while humming a folk song, watching a period drama on TV, or chatting with people around her. In that process she was seen talking cheerfully with her granddaughter and visitors about paper-cutting, even asking them for advice. Her attitude of "I just leave it when I don't know what to cut" points to the contingency associated with the use of scissors and of the in-situ experience contained in the improvisational nature of the "*maojiao*" work. Paper-cutting production advances incrementally through the coordination of hands, scissors, paper, the work space environment, and the juxtaposition of everyday activities while drawing on a well-developed understanding of symbolic meanings as well as an insight for the object of depiction. The impromptu performance of "*maojiao*" becomes feasible when the practitioner embodies these skills and understandings.

Photo 1.8 "Wugefangyang" cut by Liu Xiaojuan several months earlier

Photo 1.9 A new paper-cut of the same motif based on the previous cut in Photo 1.8 as a "yangyang".

1.5 Making process (2): *Studies* and *"ti-yangzi"*

Paper-cut makers skilled in the "*maojiao*" method stress that they "cannot cut the same thing twice." They say that "it is rather cumbersome to reproduce old cut-outs; after all, they change while cutting". For those who have gotten to know the impromptu "*maojiao*" process, this assertion sounds convincing. But what if this assertion was made by the maker of the two paper-cuts shown in Photos 1.8 and 1.9?

This paper-cut maker says, "It's the same 'My Love the Shepherd' (*Wugefangyang*: the title of a folk song) but I changed what I didn't like about the previous cut (Photo 1.8) when I made the next version (Photo 1.9); it's completely different from the previous version". Although this person is a paper-cutting artist, this feeling is more or less shared by all women who love paper-cutting. This is attributable to the fact that Shanbei paper-cutting uses sources that are shared among local communities, which means that a relatively limited, albeit diverse, variety of stylized motifs (particular plants, animals, gods in folk beliefs, historical events, rural customs etc.) are used. It may look as if the same motifs are reproduced over and over but the "improvisational" *maojiao* practice necessarily involves some re-arrangement. Based on the image of a form which one has seen or cut before, one can "create" an infinite number of variations. In this sense, it is no exaggeration to say that each individual paper cut-out forms part of a series of *studies*.

Moreover, something similar can be said about the "*ti-yangzi*" practice (using samples or templates), which the locals see as a reproduction technique that can be used by anyone, unlike "*maojiao*". Broadly speaking, there are two types to "*ti-yangzi*". One is a "copying" technique that places a template on a stack of sheets of red paper and fastens them together. The other is an "imitating" technique; free-cutting following someone else's pattern. When using the copying technique, the maker does not have to think too much about the complicated cutting sequence or techniques required to complete a full, unbroken design. In the imitating technique, though, the maker has to introduce some degree of improvisation, because it is impossible to perfectly copy the original model. How the maker introduces her own innovations is a measure of her dexterity and "creativity" in both practices.

In the copying technique, despite using an overlaid template, children and unskilled people invariably end up with distorted forms. They nevertheless tend to mix their templates with their own paper cut-outs, pasting them all up. This frequently results in their own poorly made cut-outs being kept and used as templates next year. They seem to lack any notion of keeping the original templates for future use. In effect, then, the "*ti-yangzi*" process is quite similar to that of "*maojiao*", producing a series of motif *studies*.

The literal meaning of "*ti-yangzi*" is "replacing the sample/template". In the process of cutting a form using the hand, scissors and paper as well as one's own and someone else's products as a temporary template, paper-cutting – as a physical being as well as a tangible image – entails various arrangements and continually replaces the source for subsequent productions. Thus, paper-cutting is renewed and continued as a kind of fluid thing that is "the same but different". The boundary between copying, imitating ("*ti-yangzi*") and creating ("*maojiao*") in Shanbei paper-cutting production is thus considerably fuzzier than the makers think.

1.6 Resonance between word and form

As mentioned, the Shanbei paper-cut makers are predominantly illiterate women. "Spoken words" that are destined to vanish as soon as they are uttered resemble the transient and fragile paper-cuts which are repeatedly generated and extinguished. This similarity is not merely at a phenomenal level. When we consider the improvisational and repetitive experience of paper-cutting – creating new images through physical action from a diverse but limited shared repertoire – the parallels with an "oral tradition" are striking. We will tease out these similarities in this section, highlighting the scenes of interaction between spoken words, speech and paper-cutting.

1.6.1 Paper-cutting as a rebus (picture puzzle)

Paper-cutting images are sometimes evoked by the sounds of words. Common motifs in paper-cutting include auspicious patterns, myths and historical events, but the names of individual forms repeatedly appear as voiced sounds or spoken words, especially formulaic phrases that are traditionally uttered in narrative acts and ceremonial chants. Iconographic images that express desires for prosperity, happiness, fortunes and protection against evil, frequently use metaphors that combine animal or plant motifs with symbolic meanings.

For example, some of the favored images for *xihua* (wedding flowers) include "*yu-xi-lian*" (a fish playing on top of a lotus flower) and "*shiliu-zuo-mudan*" (a pomegranate on top of a peony flower), both of which represent yin-yang, which in turn symbolizes the union between man and woman. These are typical designs for wishing matrimonial harmony and fertility.[12] The main wedding ceremony in Shanbei is called "*shangtou*" (hair combing), during which an assistant alternately combs the bride's and the groom's hair while they are sitting back to back. While he is combing their hair, the assistant chants: "If you give birth to a daughter, raise her into a dexterous woman/ who can make pomegranates, peony flowers and impromptu paper-cutting… a pair of walnuts and a pair of red dates/ a pair of male and female children race one another." At the end of the ceremony, twelve pairs of walnuts and red dates are dropped over the heads of the bride and groom, who hurriedly pick them up. The shapes and colors of the walnut, red date, pomegranate and peony are metaphors for man and woman.

An elderly woman who I spoke to while attending a wedding told me, "We were married in our mid-teens in the old days. The fish is man and the lotus is woman. Even children would know what to do without being told (when they look at "wedding-flowers")". This narrative suggests that the form has a rebus-like structure. The Chinese language has many homonyms, and is also rich in "homophony" (*xieyin*: characters having the same or similar pronunciation), both of which are heavily used in overlapping the forms to produce multiple meanings.[13] Moreover, the Chinese characters themselves are pictograms, and younger paper-cut makers like to incorporate certain characters such as "囍" (*xi*: double happiness) and "寿" (*shou*: longevity) into their designs. Thus, Shanbei paper-cutting has in-built mechanisms for invoking images through the multilayered resonances between the forms and the sounds of words triggered by ceremonial chant phrases or various narrative acts, all of which enables individuals to share and interpret them in their own ways.

Spoken words naturally influence the paper-cutting process. One typical example can be seen in Jin Zhilin's, a painter and folk art scholar, "discovery" of the paper-cutting iconography called "*Zhua-ji-wawa*" when he visited Shanbei.

> Surprised by the form of holding up chickens with extended arms... standing with legs wide open which he had never seen before, he [Jin Zhilin] asked, "What did you cut?" "It's *Zhua-ji-wawa*." "What does it mean?" "'Her plaited hair is swinging, her matrimonial home is right there,' we used to say." As soon as Chen Shenglan [paper-cut maker] said so, elderly women around her all... started chanting [this set phrase] loudly. (Zhang 2009: 93)

According to Jin, these women suddenly became animated after that and began to cut various forms of "*Zhua-ji-wawa*" with their own decorations.

Interestingly, with its many homonyms, when Chinese words are memorized simply as sounds, the combination of word and form can lead to confusion, sometimes changing the meaning of the form itself. For instance, the Kitchen or Stove God "灶君" (*Zaojun*) is normally depicted as an old male figure riding a flying horse, but in some paper cut-outs it has been replaced with a valiant female deity riding a rooster. This is because "馬" (*ma*: horse) in the word "灶馬" (*zaoma*:

kitchen-stove horse) is confused with the similar sounding word "媽" (*ma*: mother or mature woman).

It is clear that not only symbolic meanings but also spoken words are embedded in the forms used for paper-cutting. Paper-cutting as a rebus associated with set phrases and word play exhibits clever interactions in which the forms appear out of the sounds of words and the words resonate with the forms.

1.6.2 Invocation of voiced words and songs

In Shanbei, an "oral culture" is still very much alive. Performances such as *"mingge"* (folk songs), *"yangge"* (song & dance), *"shuoshu"* (story telling) and *"daoqing"* (classic opera) remain very popular and elderly people enjoy impromptu reciprocal singing over drinks. Stories memorized as sounds are favorite sources for paper-cutting. As we saw above with Gao Fenglian, during paper-cutting we come across makers who are humming folk songs or mumbling verses from a play or a story while working on their paper-cutting. As these lines are murmured in the making process, they often evoke a form or design. The case of paper-cutting by Ma Ruilan, a woman in her sixties, is another example of this.

When Ma was a child, she enjoyed singing and dancing. Whenever *"shuoshu"* story-tellers or *"daoqing"* folk theater troupes came to her village, she visited them often enough to learn to recite lines and songs from their performances. Her favorite paper-cutting motifs are the characters and gods of oral folk stories. She says she never gets bored with cutting out her favorite scenes from folk songs and myths. Every time she cuts her specialty scenes, she mumbles songs or short lines – phrases that are melodic and pleasing to her ear such as "thousand-year-old ancient trees become spirits and ten-thousand-year-old stone mountains start talking" – repeatedly, as if to remind herself. She nods a little to the rhythm of her murmur as if to confirm something and cuts even the minute details of the scene by *maojiao* as she expands her concrete image of the story (Photo 1.10). According to Ma, "The same scene comes out differently each time. Human figures, and which animals or plants to cut, also change each time".

Sometimes "verse editing" (changing the lyrics) happens while she is chanting them, and the changes are reflected in the paper-cutting. One day Ma Ruiran visited the home of Mrs. Feng, where I was lodging. When Ma began to hum a counting folk song, which started with "When I entered the first door…", she made impromptu changes to the lyrics while maintaining the original tune and rhythm, suddenly uttering new verses. "When I entered the first door, the dog barked/ when I entered the second door, Mrs. Feng appeared/ When I entered the third door,

Photo 1.10 Ma Ruilan executing "maojiao" while humming a folk song.

there was an unfamiliar girl". She incorporated what was happening on the spot. The "unfamiliar girl", of course, was me. Ma continued repeating the new verses even when she got home and ended up making a new paper-cut incorporating Mrs. Feng, her pet dog and me in her garden based on these verses.

Ma makes paper-cuts based on a folk song called "*Xiaobaicai*" (Little cabbage) while singing the song. When she comes to the part of the song about the feelings of the main character, a girl who is abused by her stepmother, her voice quavers and her eyes fill with tears as she remembers her own childhood and continues cutting. This kind of synchronization between songs and feelings was frequently observed.

It seems that the act of vocalizing a series of words from memory has the effect of reverberating the content. When it is repeated almost mechanically in combination with the tune or rhythm of a song, it more actively evokes images that synchronize with memorized stories, recollections and emotions.[14] Moreover, the movement of the hands and tools generally follows the brisk rhythm of the words or songs, an interaction of the body and the sound that happens with work songs. This is a unique "sound guidance system" to transform the form of a paper-cut into "a song of the hearts of woman".

1.7 In closing: Generation, extinction and continuation of things

1.7.1 The perspective of the "appearance of things"

Shanbei paper-cuts are ephemeral due to their physical characteristics. It is difficult to find a strong emotional involvement of the maker or the user or any inherent meaning or value in a particular paper cut-out. They are physically fragile *things* whose existence is transient. This chapter has rejected the conventional research perspective of seeing paper-cutting as a representational medium and seeking to reveal the meaning or value of its "form". Instead I have focused on the presentation of paper-cutting as thing through people's sensory experiences in individual practices during the stages of use and making. What we have found through this approach was the generative and fluid mode of being of this thing, which appears and disappears to each person each time in various ways rather than being seen as a stable or fixed object.

We generally consider things as objects external to our self. However, our examination of paper-cutting in this chapter raises the distinct possibility that what people perceive in their experiences may be an "appearance of things" (phenomenon). This perspective severely shakes the foundation of anthropological material culture studies.[15]

Kenichi Iwaki, an aesthetics scholar, states that when we are at the scene of experience as physical beings, *things* "appear to us as images ("tangible phenomena")" (Iwaki 2001: 2–4).[16] This argument is quite suggestive with regard to how we are to understand the various practices surrounding paper-cutting. For example, the perception of window-flowers by people inside the cave-house when they are illuminated by sunlight and the renewal of things as "forms" promoted by the fragile materiality of paper-cutting are clear examples of things' appearance as images. In the making phase, when we redefined the "*ti-yangzi*" approach as an individual physical practice instead of a replication or imitative technique as it was normally regarded, we found that it was a "creation" that continues to produce new "forms" from existing "forms". The condition of being created by individual makers in a context of creation by the local community as a whole resonates strongly with Iwaki's view of things.

1.7.2 Between form, word and materiality

I have already mentioned that "form", which is the subject of this chapter, and words (language) have generally been understood as "representations" or symbolism. The unique contribution of Iwaki's argument lies in the notion that this "language-symbol" is also a type of "tangible phenomenon" (image) that is sensorily perceived in such a way that not only a "transparent concept" but also "opaque materiality" is recognized (Iwaki 2001: 270–271). For example, the description of the process of "*maojiao*" in this chapter has demonstrated that the "form", which tends to be the subject of semiotic analysis when viewed through a dichotomous framework such as material/mental, form/content and so on, appears as a tangible-material image which forms reciprocal relationships not only with materials, tools and the body, but also with the environment and the activities of living embedded in it.

How are we to view language, then, which is a product of symbolism? Let us recall "flower" (*hua*) in "flower-cutting" (*jiaohua*). In the cave-house space decorated with paper-cuts, the multiple elements of things which are present appear as fluid images in front of us. Both the "beautiful form" and the "flower" can be regarded as words that indicate the generation process of things, which accompany tangible and intangible images in various situations. When we think of the actual language use, however, we cannot help but elicit words such as "window-flower" and "flower-cutting" from the "appearance of things". Nevertheless, Iwaki's argument suggests that each word acquires a tangible image and the materiality of thing appears to be even more solid because of these words. The process of this "word-symbol" with "opaque materiality", so to speak, appearing as an image in one's sensory experience is also found in paper-cutting as a rebus prompting resonance between "form" and "word".

This chapter has also proposed that the things called paper-cuts are evoked by the words and songs that are voices in the process of their generation and renewal; and that the words and songs are themselves "forms" accompanying tangible images. It is also clear in our analysis of word play, poetry and concrete poetry featuring rhyming and repetitions that spoken words possess their own notes, colors and rhythms. Shanbei folk songs and formulaic chants evoke the shared stories and knowledge of the community as well as the memories and emotions of the individual paper-cut makers. They sometimes deviate from the song's original meanings, leading to new verses or motifs. It is clear that "words" surrounding the practices of paper-cutting possess a certain type of materiality and play a role in the appearance of the thing called paper-cutting as they resonate with "forms".

1.7.3 Generation and continuation of things through repeated practices

Finally, I would like to point out the importance of the repetitive nature of paper-cutting practices in the use and production phases. In its appearance as both an image and a physical object, a paper-cut is remade and its "form" is renewed, both repeatedly and cyclically. The continuation of paper-cutting as thing is perceived through these repetitive experiences, which encompass variations that are "the same but different". Repetition is also crucial to the resonance between word and form.

Ingold (2007) objects to the stereotypical view that creation is a "sequence of one-off events or novelties" whereas daily routine is constant and static. A routine or repetitive practice – which often accompanies rhythmic gesture – produces a certain phenomenon out of many latent possibilities in a situation-specific manner each time while incorporating the involvement of some contingent things or the environment. Creativity, according to Ingold, lays in a continual movement of *becoming* that is inherent in the ceaseless flow of life. A practitioner sometimes ends up creating something (often to her unexpected amazement) in the process of engaging in a routine practice, while building on existing knowledge or imagery. Thus, he also rejects the idea of "A unique and finished 'work'" linked to the agency interacting between subject and object or mind and material (Ingold 2007: 45–51).

Ingold therefore questions the view that creative agency is an internal property that resides in persons or in things, or even in persons *and* things. He suggests, instead, that "This agency could be none other than the generative flux of the world itself in its continual concrescence, from which persons and things emerge and take the forms they do for the duration of their existence" (ibid.: 52).

Consequently, a research perspective focusing on the appearance of things needs to describe individual specific interactions between humans and things and needs to position those interactions in relations to the continuation of things – for example, the generation and extinction of individual things, collective things, and so on. In the case of paper-cutting, we begin to see potential changes lurking in this continuity through ongoing participant observations of repetitive and periodic practices, including the annual cycle, the family life cycle, production embedded in everyday living, varying studies of the same motif, and paying attention to people's sensory experiences. The anthropological study of the appearance of things in individual practices that does not reduce things to meanings or values will only be achieved through such an undertaking.

2 *Mono* that lurk, retreat, or manifest: *Mono* and the body

Kazuyoshi Sugawara

Keywords: face-to-face interaction, intervention by *mono*, affordance, resource, deictic/deixis

Now I see: I recall better what I felt the other day at the seashore when I held the pebble. It was a sort of sweetish sickness. How unpleasant it was! It came from the stone, I'm sure of it, it passed from the stone to my hand. Yes that's it, that's just it – a sort of nausea in the hands. (Sartre, 1964: 10–11)

2.1 Introduction: Intervention by mono in human interactions

The aim of this chapter is to describe one aspect of the interactions between the body and *mono* in conversations based on microscopic analysis of video-recorded face-to-face interactions. Conversations were analyzed in three different situations: 1) triadic conversations between university students (recorded in Sapporo in 1986); 2) ordinary conversations and interviews with the G|ui hunter-gatherers[1] (the former was recorded at the Xade settlement, Botswana, in 1989, and the latter was recorded at the Qx'oensakene resettlement in 2005); and 3) an interview with a dancer of the traditional Japanese *dengaku* (*noh* troupe) of Nishiure district, Misakubo (presently part of Hamamatsu), Shizuoka Prefecture (recorded in 2002). Let us begin with a casual conversation between university students.

Case 1 "Something must have happened."[2]
[There are tea cups on a table from which they have just finished drinking tea. H-m has just finished talking about "sleep paralysis" he experienced at the dawn. An utterance in { } and one in the line immediately after that are simultaneous utterances in the original Japanese text.]

1. K-m: You were dreaming, {weren't you?}
2. H-m: {No, it wasn't a dream.} Too realistic
3. K-m: Is that so?
4. H-m: Yes, and then, a dream before it was set in the Warring States period or the Edo period →
5. And in that dream I double crossed my father.
6. K-m: You always do that {anyway}. ((M-m: Laughs))
7. H-m: {No,} it wasn't like that. ((M-m: Laughs)) In a castle or somewhere →
8. imprisoned him or that kind of story.
9. K-m: Oh, is that so?
10. H-m: Mm, something must have happened, · ↓ definitely. ((Slapping on the table with his right hand))

H-m experienced sleep paralysis immediately after having a dream about incarcerating his father. That is why he jokingly expresses his concern that "Something unusual might have happened to my father back home". During a short pause before "definitely" in Line 10, H-m slapped on the table with his right hand in a theatrical manner. The impact caused a spoon left in his tea cup to make a sharp clanking sound. The participants, though, did not pay any attention to the sound. Hence, it had no bearing on their interaction as a significant resource. Yet, it was surprisingly loud in the analyst's earphones.

This trivial yet typical event demonstrates the potential for *mono* to intervene in human interactions. The *mono*'s "action" is highly contingent, and independent of the intentions of participants in most cases. The potential for interactions to be disrupted by a chance intervention of *mono* remains ever-present. "Accidentally" dropping things or knocking them over are but two of the possibilities.

At least after World War II, the wildest ambition of anthropology has been to provide a corrective to the humanist view of the individual subject, who is self-constituted through their clear consciousness and who controls their action by their autonomous will. For example, a village man embedded in the cycle of "generalized exchange" might not know why he got his wife from the neighboring 'Village West' and married off his daughter into the 'Village East' (Lévi-Strauss 1969). Foucault claims that anthropology, as well as psychoanalysis, is the science of unconsciousness, because it aims to attain, by means of positivistic intellect, what exists outside the human and keeps escaping from the consciousness (Foucault 1966). Phenomenology, despite its ridicule by structuralists and post-structuralists, shared this ambition, positing the body as the central reference point for thinking.[3]

I wonder, however, if it is possible to rewrite the world with *mono* as the central character instead of "humans" or "the body"? At first glance, it seems to be fundamentally impossible. The substratum of the social world is constituted by interactions between bodies, especially communicative interactions. But there is no communication between the human body and *mono*. Putting it simply, *mono* is not the other. This is not my original view, but the outcome of a discussion in a study group. I had commented: "If I put money into a vending machine and my coffee didn't come out, I would kick the vending machine. At this moment, the vending machine would have manifested as the other, wouldn't it?" An attending ethicist disagreed promptly. "That would not be the case. Double contingency does not arise between you and the vending machine."[4]

Accordingly, it is not possible to set *mono* as a reference point for thinking in the same capacity as the body. However, it is also nonsense to assume that the body is separate from *mono*. A viable body is "carefully absorbed" (Heidegger 1962) by clothes, shoes, houses, tools, streetscapes and myriads of other things. The most essential characteristic of *mono* that are contiguous to the body is not being explicit. This is why Sartre's character Antoine Roquentin felt "nausea" when he encountered a naked being stripped of this self-evidence.

Where, then, is this chapter headed? I cannot promise to "conduct an analysis with *mono* as the central character" for the reasons just stated. The central player – the one who appears, moves of its own accord and vocalizes on the stage – is the human body, after all. Yet, *mono* do not resign themselves to being "stage props" manipulated by or subordinate to the human body. Although *mono* do not take voluntary action, they do intervene in face-to-face interactions in critical ways.

Let us clarify the meaning of the modifier "critical" by using a dramatic metaphor. A play whose every detail becomes obvious simply through the reading of its script is not worthy of being called a drama. To make it a drama, the bodies and voices of the actors must have a critical role in creating the world that the play is trying to express. Similarly, the transcripts (which are equivalent to play scripts) of the cases being analyzed in this chapter do not fully tell us what is happening at the scene no matter how carefully we read them. This is not only because we cannot grasp the meanings conveyed by gestures[5] but also because *mono* and bodies relate with each other in ways that create a critical momentum for the generation of meaning in an event.

Let me explain the term "intervention". My choice of this term does not carry an anthropomorphic intention to give *mono* agency. I would rather stress that things manifest in response to certain "resistance rates" according to various projects (*projet*) of the body (Sartre 1956). "Iron bars" or "glass windows" separating two lovers intervene in their interactions only when highlighted by their attempt to embrace. The involvement between the body and *mono* begins when the former refers to, orients to, or invokes the latter. However, the contingency of intervention by *mono* would fall outside of a field of vision narrowly focusing on the actor. Heidegger (1962) suggests that *mono* exist in the dimension of "instrumentality" when Present Being (*Dasein*) is involved in relationships with the constituents of the environment. However, the main thread of this chapter is to analyze the intervention of *mono* in interactions from a perspective that is tangential to "instrumentality".

2.2 Involvement between the body and the environment

The conversation between university students above takes place in a "modern" environment. The characteristics of such an environment, which is enclosed by solid walls and filled with numerous human-made things, define the context in which the body involves *mono*. This contrasts with the environment of the G|ui. Let me draw your attention to a specific relationship between *mono* and gestures which was observed in G|ui conversations.

Case 2 "That is precisely death"
(Two elderly women Qg and Go are talking about the epidemic of smallpox that happened more than half a century ago in response to questions from research assistant KA.[6] From left to right, Go, Qg and KA are sitting side by side in a cross-legged position.)

1. Go: Those are in this way, and they themselves, they become this way →
2. join together all over, {then collapse already}. ((Pressing down the sand eleven times with her right palm))
3. Qg: {Like that - like that} then it happens and dies.
3'. ((Running her right hand over the sand in front of her and flattening it))
4. Go: That is {that is precisely dying}.
5. Qg: {That is precisely, death}. Those do this way. ((Pressing the sand with her right hand nine times))
6. and, {do this, do this, and}
7. Go: {And --- and --- and --- and --- and ---} they join together
8. Qg: Do this way [[Go: eheh]], and, this happens [[Go: eheh]], look, this happens →

9. [[Go: eheh]] and, this {happens (-) this happens} ((Stabbing her right index finger in the sand seven times))
10. Go: {That, doing that}
11. Qg: People pricked and picked them.
12. Go: Ehay then it gets better =
13. KA: = The man survives.

The gestures of swiping and pressing the sand made by Go and Qg are not deictics, which is the topic of Section 2.5 below. They are using the sand as a canvas on which they depict the way smallpox rashes become blisters, which join up to cover the entire body. And Qg pricked the sand to represent the way scattered wounds are pricked with a twig and pus is removed once the blisters become separated. What is indicated here is the condition of the skin of smallpox sufferers. The sand is a material which is used to help to describe the condition. Sand is the most ubiquitous substance in the Kalahari Desert and forms the substrate of the inhabitants' environment. When the narrators tried to re-enact the disaster, they reached out to this material "function-specifically" and extracted an unexpected affordance from it (Reed 2000). They made impromptu use of the sand's plastic property to retain markings.

"Wait, suddenly but"

"I have an urge"

Figure 2.1 Manifestation of a ring

This highlights the limitations of lab-based gesture studies, such as having test subjects re-enact an animated cartoon (McNeill 1992). Conversations always take place in a specific environment. Gestures are generated through the direct involvement of the *mono* of a specific world and the body.

2.3 Thematization involving intervention by *mono*

Let us examine another conversation between university students. The body extracts affordances from *mono* along a gradient from implicitness to explicitness in the gesture and body motion channels. At the same time, the degree of thematization by utterance follows a gradually increasing curve in the linguistic channels. In this section, we analyze the thematization of *mono* that occurs at the linguistic level in conjunction with the extraction of latent affordances from *mono* by the body.

Case 3 "It's a diamond" (Figure 2.1)

1. M-f: What is it (1.2) nice – ↓① like Giselle or something.
1'. ((① N-f: Turning her face to M-f and touching her head with her left hand))
2. A-m: (Let me see) head (……) what is set in it?
3. N-f: Ah (set in) it's set in well.
4. M-f: What?
5. A-m: Like a gemstone.
6. N-f: Ah {ah}
7. M-f: {Aaah} diamond {it is}
8. A-m: {(……)} =
9. N-f: = It's a diamond ↑End of ① ((N-f: Removing her left hand from her head))
10. A-m: Wow.
11. N-f: It's about one carat {maybe, (I think)} ((Smiling at M-f))
12. A-m: {Real (thing) is it?}
13. M-f: Hang on, one carat is {(……)}
14. N-f: {(……)} It is one carat, darling.
15. M-f: It'll be nice when a fiancé buys it for me. Two and a half carat or (some unbelievable →
16. size) very big, tens of millions of yen is common now, because normally →
17. a diamond is – ((N-f's left hand touches her right ring finger)) →
18. zero point something carat or something =

18'. ((N-f looks down at her half-raised hands. She removes the ring from her right ring finger and holds it in her left hand))
19. N-f: = Wait, suddenly but ↓② I have an urge ↓③ Can I do it?
19'. ((② N-f switches hands to hold the ring in her right hand. ③ She puts the ring on the left ring finger.))
20. I've wanted to do this once ((Continuing the ring putting action until the beginning of Line 21))
21. M-f: (……) ↑End of ③ ↓④ That's quite big. [[N-f: Laughing]]
21'. ((④ N-f: Holding her left hand straight up with straight fingers, turning the back of the hand to M-f while smiling))
22. M-f: You look like Seiko.

From right to left, A-m, N-f and M-f are sitting side by side at a table. As N-f turned to A-m on her left to ask something, the back of her head came into M-f's field of vision. M-f twisted her face to see more closely. Her comment "What is it, nice" and so on was in reference to N-f's hair accessory. Comments about "diamond" and "one carat" from Line 7 onward are clearly jokes. M-f's utterance in Line 14 "It is one carat, darling" seems to be a theatrical mimicking of the way of speaking of a wealthy woman wearing expensive jewelry.

The second "gemstone" suddenly appears from Line 18 onward. There was a ring on N-f's right ring finger. When she heard M-f's fantasy about a future ideal fiancé buying her "an incredibly large diamond", she moved her cheap ring from her right ring finger to her left ring finger and acted as if she were showing it off. She was mimicking a scene in which a celebrity showed off her engagement ring in front of a battery of cameras.

Interactions can leap in unexpected directions, springing out of *mono* themselves, breaking loose from the constraints of linguistic relevance. Incidentally noticing something that is attached to another's body or casually involving something one is wearing can suddenly change the course of a conversation.

2.4 Negotiations over *mono* as resources

While the body continues to fuse with familiar things, it faces other things from a different direction. That is, it tries to "acquire" something. According to Sartre, the essence of desire is "appropriation". For instance, smoking can be seen as a destructive appropriation and a cigarette as the symbol of "appropriated being" (Sartre 1956: 761). For example, I have a hobby of collecting animal figures

Mono That Lurk, Retreat, or Manifest

(including dinosaurs) and a propensity to be attracted to transparent things. From Sartre's perspective, both the hobby and the propensity are oriented to some fundamental project or original choice about myself, which is expressed through a fondness for a certain type of "being-in-itself (*l'être-en-soi*)".

> We conclude that flavor [...] has a complex architecture and differentiated matter; it is this structured matter—which represents for us a particular type of being—that we can assimilate or reject with nausea, according to our original project. It is not a matter of indifference whether we like oysters or clams, snails or shrimp, if only we know how to unravel the existential significance of these foods. / Generally speaking there is no irreducible taste or inclination. They all represent a certain appropriative choice of being. (Sartre 1956: 784)

This section follows the way *mono* retreat from linguistic thematization in parallel with a body-level negotiation driven by a desire for *mono*.

Case 4 "Pass me the Kirin Orange" (Figure 2.2)
(From right to left, S-m, K-m and R-m are sitting around a low table. There is a large bottle to the right of R-m.)

1. K-m: Hey, pass me the Kirin Orange. ((K-m extends his right arm in the direction of the bottle))
2. R-m: Mm, uh, yes. ((R-m grabs the bottle with both hands and offers it to K-m, whose right hand moves toward the bottle))
3. K-m: Oh, I may finish {this} ((K-m's right hand holds the bottle and his left hand touches the cap))
4. S-m: {Finish} it, please.
5. K-m: Ah, you want it, too?
6. S-m: Oh, can you give me a little, ↓°please. Mr. Saitō <K-m's surname>, how about you?↓°
6'. ((① K-m removes the cap. ② The mouth of the bottle reaches S-m's glass.))
7. Oh, is it alright? Sorry, (it's from this morning). ↑°Sorry, uh. ((K-m finishes pouring))

The bottle of Kirin Orange was passed from R-m's hands to K-m's hands in the course of the first two lines. K-m (whose surname is Saitō) was about to drink the Kirin Orange. S-m was asking K-m to give him some of the juice. In this situation, "Mr. Saitō, how about you?" is a peculiar utterance. This is the sort of offer that

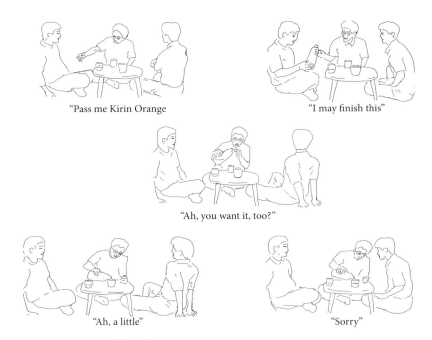

Figure 2.2 Negotiation for Kirin Orange

is made by the person in possession of the resource. To resolve this peculiarity, the following analysis assumes the presence of a desire to "drink Kirin Orange" inside S-m and tracks its behavior.

S-m had been sitting with his right knee tucked to his chest and his arms wrapped around it, facing the far wall until K-m's utterance in Line 1 at which point S-m began thinking. In Line 2, S-m turned his upper body to face forward and began to lean forward while keeping his eyes on the bottle. Psychological description: "I want to drink, too." In Line 3, S-m placed his left hand on the floor. He was still staring at the bottle. However, as K-m's left hand touches the cap at the same time as the utterance of "I may finish this", S-m leaned on his left hand. While Km was turning the cap, S-m made the utterance in Line 4 as he leaned backward on both hands and averted his face in the direction of the far wall. Psychological description: "Damn, no drink for me".

However, the situation changed quickly. His declaration of renunciation, "Finish it, please", was received by K-m as S-m's expression of desire. S-m began to think immediately after Line 5 but his upper body remained leaning backward.

S-m's upper body finally began to move forward as he said "Is it alright?" and his hands came off the floor by the time K-m finished pouring the juice. S-m's left hand was about to hold his glass as he uttered "Sorry, uh", but the hand ended up sitting by the side of the glass. After that, K-m poured the juice in his own glass, put the cap on, and placed the bottle on his right side.

As S-m gave up on his desire, his body took the posture of "placing both hands on the floor behind him and leaning backward", meaning "a retreat from a resource". It must have been difficult to switch to another posture, which meant "Thank you for giving me some", in such a short period of time. The body has an inherent inertia and breaking free from it requires intentional muscular action. A situation that is inconsistent with a logical textual structure is realized as a natural situation by the body in the course of interaction.

At the start of the conversation, a very simple form of deixis takes place with the bottle of Kirin Orange being on the scene as a referent. However, the true significance of this case is not found there. When attention is turned to a thing as a useful resource, it often becomes thematized by verbal expression. However, explicit gestures do not necessarily coordinate with such thematization. In fact, the body reveals one's interest in the thing in an implicit form, involving a secret negotiation for it.

In the next case of the G|ui, the object of desire is tobacco. For a majority of the G|ui people, leaf tobacco is a scarce discretionary item that stirs up intense desire. In one recorded story, someone travelled to a faraway place to get tobacco in the midst of a raging smallpox epidemic. The following case was recorded inside the home of Ga, a middle-aged woman. Her mother is the second wife of KK, an elderly man.[7] AR is an elderly man of KK's age who has been staying in Xade Settlement for a long time after leaving Mothomelo in the southwest. Ga and AR love taking snuff, finely ground leaf tobacco that is taken in the nose.

Case 5a "Let me hold marijuana"
(TR, a middle-aged man, who has just left the hut, was also a visitor from Mothomelo. He was (probably in joke) asking Ga to enter an extramarital sexual relationship (*zaaku*) with him. After giving evidence at the town court in relation to an assault case, TR arrived in Xade in the middle of the previous night. Half a day later (yesterday), several women, including Ga's daughter Qx'om, visited the camp of people from Mothomelo. TR came up and told her, "Tell your mother about my offer of *zaaku*". He visited Ga last night and talked about *zaaku* again.)

1. Ga: TR came last night and talked.
2. AR: He came last night and talked here.
3. KK: He has {walked past just now}
4. Ga: {He, yesterday, midnight, so} yesterday ↓① Qx'om [g's eldest daughter] and others there →
4'. ((① AR: Claps and rubs his hands [a gesture for admiration]))
5. {arrived during the day at their place,} they came.
6. AR: {Let me -- ↓② hold (marijuana)} ↓③
6'. ((② AR: Extends his left hand to Ga)) ((③ AR: Picks his nose with the right little finger/Ga: Feels the back of her left hip with her left hand))
7. KK: They said. You [two women] pass my [message] on.

In Line 6, AR begged quietly in the manner of stage whisper. Marijuana in this context was a tumid expression for snuff. Even though Ga's utterance in Line 5 overlapped with AR's request, Ga understood AR's intention accurately and began searching the inside of a small bag hanging near the left hip with her left hand immediately. However, the search was halted as she became engrossed in the conversation. The conversation eventually moved away from the topic and Ga spoke of a situation, which is summarized in brackets below.

Case 5b "Shake the plastic"
[A rumor about an incident in Mothomelo. TR and another man were using a dog owned by a third man to hunt a gemsbok (*Oryx gazelle*) when they were caught and punched by some wildlife protection officers.]

1. Ga: They [two men] sneaked up to a gemsbok ↓① and went into their place ↑②.
1'. ((① A: Extends his hand to Ga))
2. KK: Two Kua [a collective term for Bushmen] men ((Laughs)) Two Kua {men cried}.
3. Ga: {They said}
4. You are ↓③ *bolosh* [meaning unknown], without even asking us [two men]
4'. ((③ Ga: Holds a bottle in her right hand, takes snuff out on her left palm))
5. we {suffer whipping} ↑③ cont. ((③ [cont.] Ga: Places snuff on AR's left palm))
6. KK: {Without} they hadn't even killed it [female] [yet].
7. AR: Shake the plastic [loanword] and [give me what's] inside.
8. Ga: Where is it? ||Awasiexo's mother [Ga's classificatory elder sister] yesterday↓④
      gave me (+)

8'. ((④ AR: Takes his own bottle from a pocket))
9. We [female plural] begged for ↑④cont. (-) senior's ration ((④[cont.] AR: Begins to open the bottle))

After this conversation, they moved on to another topic, which was about the *zaaku* relationship involving a female relative of KK's and Ga's, told mostly by Ga. If we focus only on the exchange of snuff, it went as follows. A time lapse after AR's first request is indicated in angle brackets < > by seconds. (1) Ga took out the plastic bottle containing snuff and held it in her hands <44 seconds>. (2) Ga shook some snuff out on her own palm and passed it on to AR's palm <60 seconds>. (3) Ga placed some more snuff on AR's palm <76 seconds>. (4) AR put snuff into his own plastic bottle, sniffed a small amount left on his palm, closed the bottle, and returned it to the right pocket of his jacket <106 seconds>. During the period of one minute and forty six seconds from A's utterance of his first request to the completion of the exchange, tobacco was linguistically thematized only in Lines 7 and 8 in Case 5b. Most of that time period was filled with gossip unrelated to the object of the request. It even appears that the exchange of the thing is "a subordinate involvement" that flows through gaps in a conversation, which is "a dominant involvement" (Goffman 1963).

I have never witnessed a vociferous argument about the exchange of *mono* (except obviously in jest) throughout many years of field research.[8] If the act of "giving on request" is practiced as a natural event unworthy of particular attention, it may be regarded as a G|ui habitus which fundamentally characterizes the way *mono* are introduced into interactions.

2.5 Invocation of *mono* by deixis

A gesture that clearly expresses the body's orientation to *mono* is pointing, that is, "deictic". Deixis might be seen as the polar opposite of making *mono* explicit. In this section, we focus on deictics toward *mono*, one's own body, and the other. The following conversation between university students involves M-m, who is getting teased by two junior students for his fondness for Alinamin (anti-fatigue tablets).

Case 6 "You probably have it now"
.1. M-m: Only when I go skiing I {take the medicine}.
2. K-m: {Well, I} that · Mount Rishiri or →

3. { (……) }
4. H-m: {Ah} I had.
5. M-m: Ah, that, because {that was} →
6. K-m: {Ah, that was} [mimicking M-m's speech]
7. M-m: {That was}
8. H-m: {All the time} you carry it around =
9. K-m: = Yes yes yes yes =
10. M-m: = I don't carry it around.
11. K-m: Is that {so?}
12. M-m: {h'm}
13. H-m: You probably↓① have it now ((① Pointing at a case on M-m's right side with his left hand))
14. M-m: What ?↑End of①
15. K-m: ↓② Take the stuff out { (……) } ↑End of② ((②Pointing his right hand in the same direction while smiling))
16. M-m: {I don't} have it because · on travel (or -) →
17. going away or [the rest of the transcript omitted]

M-m insisted that "I am not a regular user of Alinamin". H-m and K-m responded with speculation that "You probably have it now", pointing at his belongings. We cannot say that the referent is M-m's case itself. Rather, the referent here is the invisible contents of the case, or a jar of Alinamin (allegedly) hiding there, and moreover, the personal "taste" of M-m who may carry a jar of Alinamin with him today (or in Sartrean parlance, his unique way of relating with the world). In this example, the thematization of *mono* by utterance and the explicitness of deixis show a clear correspondence.

In the following interview with Mr. S, a *noh* dancer of Nishiura *dengaku*, deictics with more complex meanings can be observed. Although the role of *jino* [entertainment for gods] in *dengaku* is traditionally passed on from the father to the eldest son under a strict hereditary system, occasionally the dancer was substituted. The verbal interchange between one of the researchers and Mr. S prior to what is transcribed below is summarized at the start.

Case 7 "Let me dance this year"
[According to Mr. S, it was customary for the *jino* dancer who was looking for someone to stand in for him to offer a gift of *sake*. Conversely, "If I ask him to let me perform the role this year, I must give him a gift, I hear". O-m (researcher)

asked, "Which dance do you like best?" Mr. S replied, "The monkey dance is nice." Mr. S revealed that because the hereditary performer of this dance had become unable to dance (for the reason described later), Mr. X, who was a brother of the previous *betto* [who plays the role of a priest], replaced him even though he was not a *noh* dancer. In one year, Mr. S thought "This is a nice dance".]

1. S: Well, uh, and, at that time asking to dance and that sort of things →
2. I didn't know that sort of things, so, to the younger brother of *betto*, excuse me →
3. "Please let me dance it this year" I said, and "Sure" he said, "Well" I said, →
4. and danced, then the next day Mr. X visited my home with *sake*, →
5. "Thank you very much" he said, I didn't know why he was doing it
5'. ((Cocking his head to the side))
6. O-m: Because the person who ask (+) normally (pays a visit) to bring it, so =
7. S: = Ah.
8. O-m: The one who has been asked haven't to bring =
9. S: = No, his family dance, he (can't) perform ↓① that's why · →
10. ↓② Thank you for dancing it, he said ↑$^{End\ of②}$ ((Gesturing to present a large bottle of *sake* with both hands))
11. O-m: Ah, I see what you mean.

At Line 9①, Mr. S used his right hand to point at his left upper arm. According to a previous interview, the original dancer of the monkey dance was no longer able to dance because he had lost his arm in forestry work. Accordingly, this deictic indicated "S's arm" as a "species", "human arm" as a genus, and "the loss of an arm" as a possible state of being for an arm. The referent of a deictic is not necessarily something that is present at the scene. The line of deictic force can reach an object (or situation) that is not present nor clearly thematized by utterance.

In the next example, a face-to-face deictic is used in an impressive form first, and the gesture itself is thematized by utterance. Then, something mysterious manifests at the scene through an iconic gesture (McNeill 1992).

Case 8 "What is this hand?" (Figure 2.3)
[K-m's narrative. An assistant lecturer in psychology showed some slides during class and said that their laboratory monkey's name was Michael. However, when K-m visited the lab later, he saw three monkeys. He asked postgraduate students there, "Which one is Michael?" and they replied, "They have never been named".]

"Yes, yes, yes, at night"

"What is this hand?"

"Um, unconsciously"

"Explain"

"Naming!"

"Peepoppee"

Figure 2.3 Manifestation of "Poppy"

Mono That Lurk, Retreat, or Manifest

1. K-m: He named it himself =
2. M-m: = Named.
3. K-m: He calls it at night, John, John.
4. H-m: Yeah?
5. K-m: He talks to it (-) well, I don't know about that, but, yes.
6. H-m: So, as if to a toy animal =
7. K-m: = Yes, yes, yes, yes, at night, to a toy animal
8. M-m: What is this hand, {what is this hand?} This hand =
9. K-m: {No, no, no, no}   = Um, unconscious {of}
10. H-m: {Naming!} Explain!=
11. M-m: = For what {(......)}
12. H-m: {Naming! } Peepoppee
13. M-m: Oh, come on [the rest of the transcript is omitted]

In Line 7, K-m extended his right arm toward M-m and pointed his index finger at a distance of thirty centimeters or so from M-m's face. M-m looked at the finger sharply, bent his right elbow into a V-shape and pointed back at K-m's hand itself while shouting "What is this hand?" and so on in Line 8. At that moment, K-m's arm was withdrawn as if it was pushed back by an invisible repulsive force. After that, however, K-m extended his arm again with an open hand as if to cover M-m's finger. In Line 9, K-m pointed his finger again while saying "unconscious". Then, K-m and H-m began to act jointly. In Line 10, H-m pointed his left and right index fingers at M-m while saying "Explain!" in a facetious manner. During transition from Line 10 to Line 11, K-m performed an odd action. He turned his right palm toward himself, extended his right arm toward M-m for show, and then bent his closed fingers toward himself twice. In Line 12, H-m also made a similar hand shape with curled fingers with his left hand placed in a lower position and uttered "Peepoppee" as if to call on his own hand.

Anyone who did not know what "Poppy" was would not understand the meaning of this interaction. I happened to discover a narrative about Poppy that K-m told in another conversation. It was M-m's soft toy rabbit, a glove puppet whose facial expression was easily manipulated by the fingers inside it. K-m described it as "strangely realistic and creepy". That strange hand shape formed by K-m and H-m represented this entity called Poppy.

K-m's first deictic referred to M-m as a variant of the "creepy man who talks to a monkey at night". The gesture was thematized by M-m himself, who was the target of that pointing gesture. Moreover, this deictic passed through the "immediate" world in which the participants were presently together and created a pathway to a different referent that could not be seen from here.

One common feature of all of the university students' conversations that I analyzed is that participants frequently referred to the fact that they were being videotaped or behaved in ways which indicated that they were conscious of that fact. This is called "frame reference". H-m's utterance of "Explain!" accompanying a facetious gesture in Line 10 is a typical case of frame reference.

Videotaping is also the backdrop of the next case in my analysis. S-f, a female student, asked her friends to have a conversation in her room for her graduation thesis and left the scene after setting up a video camera. When the flow of their conversation stopped, T-m came up with a unique way of "frame referencing". The participants would "state their wishes" to S-f "in exchange for their cooperation".

Case 9 "A rope over there" (Figure 2.4)
[T-m says, "I want a wrist watch" because "I lost one recently". K-m says, "I don't have a TV", "A TV would be nice". T-m asks Y-f (whose surname is Urabe) what she wanted.]

1. T-m: How about Miss Urabe?
2. Y-f: Oh, me.
3. T-m: Yes.
4. K-m: That chest of drawers looks nice.
5. Y-f: Mm, I want this. ((Pointing at a couch on which K-m is leaning))
6. K-m: This one, nice. ((Turning his head around to look at the couch))
7. T-m: Ah {(......) isn't it?}
8. K-m: {Transporting this} would be a bit hard →
9. K-m: Later we carry it together {shall we?}
10. Y-f: {But} My place is close ((Swinging her left index finger overhead to the right))
11. K-m: Ah, s{o}
12. T-m: {Ah} what =
13. Km: = Mm =
14. Tm:= a rope over there ((Swinging his left hand overhead backward))
15. Y-f: {Yes} yes, yes,   {yes} →
16. K-m: {(Do like) this} {creak}
16'. ((K-m: Bringing his right arm upright and extending it from in front of his face diagonally to the left))

Mono That Lurk, Retreat, or Manifest 75

"A rope over there"

"Creak"

"Swoosh"

Figure 2.4 Fantasy heist game

17. Y-f: {Swoosh} ((Gesturing to hold a rope with both hands with her right hand in front))
18. T-m: {Someone else's house}, that direction ↓① Should be over there ↓②
18'. ((T-m: ① Raising his left hand toward the left side of his head. ② Pointing his thumb directly behind him))
19. Y-f: Over there ↓③ ↓④ Please excuse me ↑$^{\text{End of }④}$ I say.
19'. ((Y-f: ③ Pointing her left hand overhead diagonally to the right.
④Making fists in front of her and making two small thrusting motions))

From Line 6 onward, the three became engrossed in refining the details of their fantasy heist. In Line 10, Y-f appeared to point in the direction of her own flat, which was close by. Then from Line 12 to Line 18, the three performed the imaginary act of "bringing the couch down through a window using a rope" together.

The room and the outside environment filled in the meaning of the deictics that were employed in this conversation. There was a sunny window behind T-m. In Line 14, T-m pointed in the direction of this window. The extension of K-m's arm in Line 16 was also in the direction of the window. "Creak" would be an onomatopoeic word imitating a sound from the rope squeaking under the weight of the couch. In Line 17, Y-f thrust her "hands gripping the rope" toward the window and performed an act of feeding the rope out. In Line 18, T-m used two kinds of deixis in different directions in quick succession. They corresponded to directional differences between "someone else's house" (that direction) and Y-f's flat (over there). At the end, in Line 19, Y-f pointed in the same direction as she did in Line 10, and then made a peculiar gesture. She seemed to act out the way she would push her way through "someone else's house" or the way she would feed out the rope tied to the couch.

Heidegger refers to a car's indicator, a mobile arrow in that era, to point out the inadequacy of seeing a "sign" as "a Thing which stands to another Thing in the relationship of indicating." He further argues that a sign *"explicitly raises a totality of equipment into our circumspection"* (Heidegger 1962: 110; emphasis original). The deictics in the case above overlap with the function which Heidegger finds in a "sign". They explicitly raise a complete set of equipment into our circumspection – in this case, the furniture in the room and Y-f's flat nearby. The hands gesture to create an imagined world in which the couch was being transported, highlighting the structure of the world to which the participants belonged, rather than signifying individual objects. Although the common definition of deixis is "to denote the present object", it is clear from this case that this denotation is only one very limited and specific way in which a wide variety of kinetic bodily forms point towards *mono*.

2.6 In closing: Between *mono* and the body

Non-explicit things always lurk on the stage of interaction, with the body in the lead role. The starting point for our analysis in this chapter was the possibility of *mono* intervening in human interaction following some largely contingent cues. As we have seen, though, even gestures, which supposedly service communication, act on *mono* in function-specific ways according to the environment and draw latent affordances from them. Similarly, speakers utilize *mono* in largely contingent (or arbitrary) ways and thematize them. Such interventions by *mono* deflect the relevance linking one utterance to another, causing deviations in unexpected directions. By contrast, when a *mono* is targeted by desire, it emerges and becomes explicit. Even then, it often retreats from vocal thematization, deferring instead to a directly embodied negotiation. However, when a specific *mono* is invoked by deixis, it is made explicit with unparalleled clarity at the scene. Of course, deixis is often coupled with vocal thematization. However, the *mono* is not always a "referent" that is present at the scene. Another important function of deictic gesture is to structure the environment itself.

Let us summarize this convergence on deixis in our analysis from another perspective. A majority of words in the so-called "deixic" category in linguistics are demonstratives. The intuitive distinction of "here" and "there" is embedded in a specific context always delimited by the field of vision of a speaker and fundamentally constrained by the way she or he perceives their social world (Hanks 2005). This is why the study of linguistic deixis has privileged importance in pragmatics and offers a potential breakthrough in demolishing the myth that the "proposition statement (representing function) is the essence of language". Either way, this privileged nature does not apply to physical deixis. All physical actions are embedded in the field of interaction to begin with.

To put it simply, the primary specificity of physical deixis is to make something explicit in the "now-and-here" field. What has been demonstrated by the case analyses in this chapter is the more interesting function of deixis. In a sense, it punches a hole in the "now-and-here" and creates a channel to invoke other entities that are not present (Poppy is a typical example).

From a strictly functionalist perspective, it is imperative that humans choose something that serves a particular purpose from among all the other things lurking in the "here-and-now" by deixis or a similarly demonstrative action if they are to meaningfully involve *mono*. As long as we are confined to pragmatic functionalism, extending a hand while saying "Pass me the Kirin Orange" is merely instrumental to "acquiring" the resource. But the act of pointing at something is not only a step for acquisition; it is just as often about creating a distance (space) between the body and the thing. The potential that could invoke contingent intervention by *mono* dwells in this distance (space) most abundantly.

The microscopic analysis of everyday conversations is a relatively new methodology in anthropology. It aims to understand the condition of a social world that is lived in the "here-and-now" field from within, beyond the distinction between "modernity" and "traditional society". The focus of this approach, including my research to date, has been "actions specialized for communication" (Kendon 1970)[9] such as "utterances" and "gestures". However, the human body is not simply supported in the interpersonal sphere; it develops in an environment in which interpersonal relationships and human-*mono* relationships seamlessly intertwine and overlap.[10] In all facets of our casual social intercourse, upon contingent cues, a *mono* intervenes in an interaction, sometimes explicitly and other times implicitly. In the process it becomes a material that constitutes a social reality at a level different from communication in a narrow sense. This chapter is an early attempt at systematic description of this process.

Part II
The Nexus Between *Mono* and the Environment

3 *Mono* beyond control: A New Perspective on Cultured Pearls

Ikuya Tokoro

Keywords: Pearl, the paradox of skill, uncontrolled nature (environment), dialogue with *mono*

3.1 *Mono* and uncontrolled nature

This chapter attempts to describe and re-interpret the relationships between humans, non-human entities and the environment. We will focus on the context of events that these relationships generate, mainly drawing on an ethnographic study of pearl culture in Japan.[1] Our intention is to critique the conventional anthropocentric understanding and develop a new model for understanding the *human/mono* relationship. To anticipate our conclusion, a problem that arises in describing the relationship between *mono* and *humans* in pearl cultivation is that *mono* inevitably eludes human control. Contrary to common understanding in modern society, *mono* refuse to be obedient objects controlled by human subjects, frequently resisting manipulation by, and/or deviating from, the expectations of humans.

The general background for this is precisely the instability of the environment itself. The natural environment surrounding and generating *mono* oscillates constantly and sometimes fluctuates greatly. This chapter attempts to capture pearl cultivation as a dialogical process in which humans negotiate with the uncontrollable natural environment and pearl oysters to produce *mono* called pearls.

3.2 Pearl cultivation: An overview

So what is a pearl? One succinct definition of a pearl says that it is "a spherical shell that has formed in the wrong place" (Matsuzuki 2002: 14). This is the broadest definition of pearls, which theoretically can be produced by all of approximately 100,000 species of shellfish in the world. However, pearls in the narrow sense commonly used for jewelry include only those which have a so-called "nacre" structure. These pearls are produced by a few dozen species of pearl oysters. Well-known among them are Akoya pearl oyster (*Pinctada fucata martensii*) found in Japan and other areas, Gold- and White-lip oysters (*Pinctada maxima*), Black-lip oyster (*Pinctada margaritifera*) and Penguin's wing oyster (*Pteria penguin*) that produce South Sea Pearls, and mussels such as *Cristaria plicata*, *Hyriopsis schlegelii* and *Hyriopsis cumingii* that produce freshwater pearls.[2]

Humankind began breeding pearls a surprisingly long time ago. Buddha-shaped blister pearls of sorts were grown in freshwater shells in China as early as the 5th century. However, systematic and large-scale pearl cultivation was made possible largely due to the development and expansion of pearl culture technology in Japan after the Meiji period. Japan's cultured pearl industry continued to grow in both production and the number of businesses even after the end of WWII through the expansion of the US market, reaching an annual production volume of around 150 tons by 1966. Although pearl culture was practiced in twenty-four prefectures across Japan at the height of the industry, now over 90% of the total production volume is produced in five prefectures – Mie, Ehime, Nagasaki, Kumamoto and Oita.[3]

3.3 The process of Akoya pearl cultivation

In this section, the specific process of Akoya pearl cultivation is introduced and discussed on the basis of a field study. The following information was obtained mostly from observations and interviews that I conducted at Akoya pearl cultivation farms in Mie, Ehime and Nagasaki Prefectures.

There are some important differences in details of the Akoya pearl cultivation process, depending on the location and farm operator, which we will discuss shortly. However, the basic operation is quite similar across all regions. Similarly, the general process and technology apply to pearl cultivation using White-, Gold- and Black-lip oysters, even though they differ in details. The common stages of the operation process are summarized in Figure 3.1 (although details and the timing of the process vary from one farm to another. as explained later).

Let us explain each stage of operation in the diagram briefly.

Purchasing spats and rearing pearl oysters
Pearl cultivation requires large quantities of pearl oysters that are used as the host and the donor for grafting (see below). Except for large-scale integrated producers, cultured pearl operations today tend to purchase spats from wholesalers or fishery

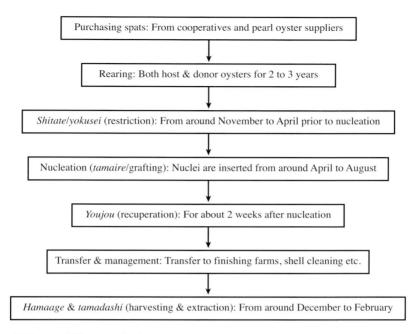

Figure 3.1 Stages of Akoya pearl culture operation

cooperatives. These spats are reared for two to three years before being used as either the host or donor for nucleation or grafting (see below).

Conditioning and restricting (*yokusei/shitate*)

The next stage is called *yokusei* (or *shitate*). This is a very important operation in Akoya pearl cultivation. It involves conditioning the oysters to prepare the base and materials for nucleation. In simple terms, *yokusei* "restricts" the physiological condition of the oysters. More specifically, it includes procedures such as increasing the density of pearl oysters in each net, changing the depth of the nets suspended in the sea, and changing the mesh size of the wire net, or a combination of some of them. In the case of Akoya pearl cultivation in Japan, *yokusei* is commonly implemented from the autumn of the year before nucleation until the spring of the year of nucleation. The success of *yokusei* significantly impacts factors such as the post-nucleation mortality, the percentage yield of pearls, and the luster of the harvested pearls. For this reason, the *yokusei* operation requires the same high levels of experience, knowledge and skills as the nucleation operation that follows.

Nucleation *(tamaire)*

After a successful *yokusei* operation, a nucleus is surgically implanted into the oyster in the nucleation or *tamaire* (grafting) stage. This operation is commonly carried out sometime between April and August depending on the location and the operator.

In simple terms, nucleation is a type of organ transplant operation. A tiny sphere, called the "nucleus", made of the freshwater shell and a piece of tissue from the Akoya oyster mantle (an organ that produces its shell) are inserted in the vicinity of the gonad of the host oyster. The oyster from which this piece of tissue is collected is called the donor oyster. When everything goes according to plan, the tissue piece that is inserted attaches to the nucleus, forming a membrane called a pearl sac, which completely encases the nucleus. As the oyster grows, layers of nacre are deposited around the nucleus to eventually form a pearl.

The nucleation stage is very delicate and cannot be mechanized. Multiple instruments are used in this operation, including a "*hikkake*" (hook), scalpel, graft-lifting needle and nucleus-lifting needle. In addition to manual dexterity and sharp eyes, detailed knowledge of the pearl oyster's life history and the ability to evaluate its physiological condition are essential. Hence, grafters are the core personnel for the process of pearl cultivation. Grafting skills require a lot of practice. It is said that "at least three years of experience" is needed for a person to become a full-fledged grafter (Photo 3.1).

Caring and management (*youjou, okidashi*)

The stage after surgical nucleation is called *youjou* (caring of grafted pearl oysters). During this stage the host oysters are kept in calm waters to recuperate from the surgery and recover their health. After *youjou*, the oysters are transferred to farms providing good growing conditions. This is called the *okidashi* (heading out to sea) operation. Once there, they are typically left alone to grow until they reach the harvesting stage, although they may be periodically taken out of the sea for cleaning.

Harvesting and extraction (*hamaage* and *tamadashi*)

The final stage of pearl cultivation is the *hamaage* (harvesting) operation, which is generally carried out in the winter months of December and January. After harvesting, the adductor muscle of the pearl oyster is cut, the shell is opened, and the pearl is extracted. The pearl extraction is called *tamadashi*. These are the main stages of the pearl cultivation process. Harvested pearls are then shipped to auctions and the market by the processors via distributors.

Photo 3.1 Pearl culture technician performing "nucleation (surgical grafting)" on a host pearl oyster

Now, having outlined the main stages of the Akoya pearl cultivation process that is most commonly used in Japan, it is necessary to discuss a high degree of variability in the details of these processes. Once one sets foot onto a site of pearl cultivation, variations in the stages of operation as well as the types of tools, technology and pearl oyster are as noteworthy as variations in farm scale and configuration.

In part, at least, this appears to be because pearl cultivation is not amenable to control techniques used in industrial production such as formalization and standardization. It is highly influenced by the natural environment in the place of production and heavily reliant on the embodied and individualized skills of the producers.

This contrasts sharply with the tendency found in factory production of industrial goods, where mass-production is achieved by negating the specific locality and workers' physicality through standardized procedures and mechanization.

3.4 Pearl cultivation skills as embodied practical knowledge

While observing the different stages of pearl cultivation at farms in Mie, Ehime and Nagasaki, we noticed subtle differences in the techniques and tools used by different workers at any particular work site. These individual differences cannot be explained by variations in the natural environment since they are all occurring on the same site.

One specific example can be found on a cultured pearl farm operated by Mr. F in Nagasaki. A special tool (a combination of a graft-lifting needle and a scalpel) is used, but only by one of the many grafters working at the farm (Mr. F's wife). She developed this combination tool herself, based on the idea that "if one tool could handle both graft-lifting and cutting, we wouldn't have to switch tools and therefore we could omit a step from the work process". By using this special tool, she was able to perform nucleation faster than the other grafters.

When I asked why the other grafters at the farm did not use the combination scalpel, I was told that they had tried it for a while but had reverted to the normal scalpel because "after all (the combination scalpel) did not fit their hands and they felt more familiar with the previous (normal) scalpel and made fewer errors". As this example demonstrates, a tool that is efficient and easy to use for a particular grafter is not necessarily suitable or convenient for others. This is due to the fact, as I've mentioned, that grafting is manual work that is highly dependent on the subtle embodied senses and skills of the worker.

Pearl cultivators recognize that micro-differences in the grafters' skills sometimes have a great impact on the cultured pearls as final products. It is therefore not uncommon for a pearl farm employing multiple grafters to introduce a tracking system to identify which grafter seeded which pearls. This system tracks oysters from the recuperation stage through to the transfer, harvesting and extraction stages by grouping and tagging the nucleated pearl oysters with the grafter's name. When pearl cultivation skills are considered a type of knowledge, it is clear that they are as individual as the workers who engage in the practice.

These skills are derived from accumulated experience, keen senses and manual dexterity, all of which vary greatly from one worker to the next. Although manuals and textbooks have been compiled for pearl cultivators, it is generally understood that these skills cannot be learned from book knowledge alone. Even on-the-job coaching by senior workers is not enough. One can only master the skills through personal experience. We were frequently informed that "listening to the words of senior workers is not enough; you cannot master it unless you experience it with your own body". In other words, the skills and knowledge that are considered to be necessary for pearl cultivation exhibit the characteristic of embodied knowledge – what Polanyi calls "tacit knowledge" – which can only be learned through practical experience, in contrast to propositional knowledge which can be learned orally or textually.[4]

Theoretical reflection on pearl cultivation process from this perspective may suggest affinities with anthropological concepts such as "artisanal" manufacturing in traditional craft making as well as the "communities of practice" described by Lave and Wenger (1991). It is certainly not possible to understand pearl cultivation without coming to terms with the necessity for technicians to master the embodied practical knowledge required at the crucial stages of the process, especially "nucleation" and "restriction".

However, another extremely important factor must also be taken into account: the "environment". Fluctuations in environmental conditions have a major impact on pearl cultivation. This dependence on the labile environment separates pearl cultivation from the production of other mass-produced goods as well as some traditional craft products. In the next section, we shall discuss the environmental factor and its effects on pearl cultivation.

3.5 The environmental factor

We cannot stress enough the importance of the natural environment in pearl cultivation. Be it Akoya, White-lip or Black-lip, cultured pearl oysters are delicate creatures whose survival is entirely dependent upon the sea. Any changes in their environment, even those which seem minute from a human viewpoint, have significant influences, including death. The conditions at each cultured pearl farm vary greatly from one another. It is not uncommon that a technology or technique that is successful in one place is ineffective in another because of differences in conditions such as water temperature, currents, planktons and tides. In fact, "the performance (of pearls) changes from one beach or inlet to the next" even in the same village or district, let alone between prefectures. Micro-variations between farms and their oceanic conditions have a great impact on the cultivation of pearls.

Furthermore, each particular environment is affected by constant temporal fluctuation. Particularly in recent years, deteriorating oceanic and climate conditions have been seen as a serious problem by pearl cultivators, who often complain that their cultivation environment is becoming unstable. Incidents such as the mass-mortality of Akoya pearl oysters (detailed below) are attributed to these changes in the environment. Pearl cultivators are responding by modifying and fine-tuning their technology, including introducing hybrid oysters.

Thus, pearl cultivators have been compelled to subtly change their technical know-how in response to the spatial diversity of cultivation environments as well as temporal changes at each environment. These are further reasons that, as previously mentioned, pearl cultivation is not suitable for standardization or mechanized processes; in each instance (site / season) it must be done in harmony with the local climatic and oceanic conditions, and must respond to their fluctuations.

Mass-mortality has become a major problem at Japan's Akoya pearl cultivation sites, especially since around 1997. It has had a devastating impact on Akoya pearl oysters (and their pearls) in Ehime, Mie and elsewhere. The exact cause of the problem is yet to be determined although various possibilities have been raised, including virus, aquaculture and overpopulation, and water contamination.[5]

3.6 "The paradox of skill" and meta-skills

In response to changes in the fisheries' environment, an increasing number of pearl cultivators are trying out different techniques and oysters. For example, Japan's Akoya pearl cultivators are introducing so-called "hybrid" species, crossbreeding Japan's native species with a Chinese species that is believed to be more resistant to warmer water. Even among hybrids developed from the same species, characteristics differ depending on the supplier, and pearl cultivators have to ascertain the subtleties of these variations if they are to successfully produce. Space does not permit us to go into similar details of the many new technologies being trialed by pearl cultivators.

One very interesting development in this context, though, is the suggestion that "the more experienced one is, the more difficulty one has in keeping up" with changes in pearl cultivation technology. Cultured pearl farms in diverse locations have observed this paradoxical situation in which the skilled veteran technicians have more difficulty dealing with changes in cultivation technology because they are more tied to their embodied experience.

We can see this in the following (abridged) narrative by Mr. A, who is widely acknowledged as a master pearl cultivation technician. Mr. A has been involved in the pearl cultivation industry in Ehime Prefecture for many decades.

> These days there are many more things to learn (about pearl cultivation) than before. For example, there were as many as eighty varieties of pearl oysters at the peak time and there are still many varieties today. There were too many to choose from. It was because increasingly more pearl oysters were crossed between different countries and different Japanese localities and so many phyletic lines were created. In the end, we had to choose based on the performance of the pearls alone. There are about twenty varieties of (graft) tissue donor oysters, too. So, at the peak time, there were about 1,600 patterns

of combination between pearl oysters and donor oysters (…) When we create a hybrid, the outcome is different depending on whether we cross a Chinese male and a Japanese female or vice versa. This kind of phyletic know-how varies from one operator to another and it is still a business secret. We never let outsiders enter our workshop in those days. Now some of the young people allow outsiders to look at their operation. Times must be changing. Young technicians come here to look because they are eager. They don't necessarily learn straight away by looking, though. We exchange knowledge at study meetings through our cooperative but subtle variations can be found in what we do not say. That part is sometimes the important part (…) We wouldn't need to make any effort if we could do it by just listening. After fifty years of experience, I'm still like a first-year worker. Yes, (the environment is) different every year. Like, water temperature, living things change amazingly. For instance, the water temperature now is 13 or 14°C, which is much lower than the usual temperature of 16°C or over. 13°C is almost the annual lowest temperature. Certainly, it goes below 13°C on several days a year but it is unusually low for January. It would be scary if this continues into February (…)

Up until now, we have been developing pearl oysters that are more resistant to higher water temperatures to deal with ocean warming. That's why the pearl oysters are susceptible to these low water temperatures. The water temperature was relatively low during the fall and now it dropped further suddenly. We are seeing adverse effects on nacre thickness in this year's harvesting…

Mr. A recognizes that the introduction of "hybrids" in response to the changing environment has increased the amount of knowledge required at an exponentially accelerating rate compared with the days when Japanese Akoya pearl oysters were used as well as how environmental changes are making the established technologies less effective. To put this in theoretical terms, learning through (routine) repetitions of embodied practices in a relatively stable environment, as described in the "communities of practice" theory, does not readily translate to the production of things such as pearls, which are dependent on environmental fluctuations and other external factors. We need to consider, instead, the so-called "meta-skills" (or higher order learning, in Bateson's terms [2000: 399–418]) involved in the continuous correction and re-optimization of skills based on the premise that the quantum of information and data to be considered is increasing exponentially (what cognitive science calls a "combinatorial explosion") and changing the context. (The explosion includes, for example, factors at each stage of pearl cultivation and associated information such as the best combination of pearl oyster and donor oyster out of many possibilities; the timing and degree of *yokusei*; the timing and method of nucleation; the amount of shell cleaning, and so on, in order to achieve the best possible luster, color and nacre thickness as well as survival rate at the harvesting time in view of the considerable fluctuations in water temperature and other environmental factors.)

Let us recap our observations so far. First, when we look at the pearl cultivation process as a type of "manufacturing", it shares distinctive characteristics with artisanal production of, for example, traditional craftworks, in that it is set up to suit the local conditions at individual sites (farms), that the practical knowledge and skills personalized and embodied at each site are important, and that the process of "embodiment" through collaborative work at each site is crucial for learning. At the same time, pearl cultivation processes contrast sharply to Fordist production systems in modern factories.

As we have seen, however, pearl oysters are marine creatures living in the ocean. The environment in which pearls are produced is changing dramatically. The introduction of crossbred pearl oysters and other technical innovations in response to those environmental changes are further changing the production context. On top of all of that, the industry is experiencing "the paradox of skill" in which "veterans have a harder time keeping up with changes". In summary, what is emerging with pearl cultivation in recent years is a phenomenon that cannot be fully explained by the model of "manufacturing" and skills development under a relatively stable context assumed by the existing theory of "communities of practice".[6]

3.7 *Mono* and uncontrolled nature

The importance of practical and embodied knowledge in pearl cultivation is not limited to the technicians. Interestingly, when the technicians try to understand the condition of their oysters, they treat the pearl oysters as living creatures that have the same physical senses as humans. For example, Mr. A, the previously quoted pearl culture technician, explains administering "*yokusei*" to Akoya pearl oysters in the following manner.

Until now, I know this doesn't sound nice but we've inflicted suffering on the body (of the pearl oyster) very slowly so as not to be noticed. The body gradually weakens as it doesn't get food. Then it starts to absorb energy within itself. It starts absorbing energy from the ovary first. It cleans out the inside of the ovary. If we insert a nucleus into it, we can get an excellent pearl. Those pearl oysters that are worked on softly and slowly do not have resilience. This robustness (posing by dropping his pelvis and putting his feet down firmly with his fists clenched) um... weak. Stronger oysters are firmer. So (the nucleus) is buried deeper (...) Akoya instinctively tries to push the nucleus out because it hurts. What I have been thinking for a long time is that when the nucleus is inserted closer to a vulnerable place (critical for its survival), the oyster tries harder to remove it by attacking it. In other words, the oyster tries to push it out by using its foot to stroke the nucleated part of the body.

Here, Mr. A captures the Akoya pearl oyster through a kind of embodied understanding. It is a perspective that sees the oyster as an embodied actor with agency, so to speak. It perceives "pain" and other sensations. It "tries to spit out the nucleus." He does not use abstract or mechanical terms to describe it. Mr. A also laments the fact that Akoya pearl oysters respond to fluctuations in the environment and sometimes behave in unpredictable ways that betray the expectations or intentions of their human operators when he says, "We are rearing living creatures after all and I've been desperately trying to catch them out every year but I haven't been able to".

Thus, even to a highly experienced technician such as Mr. A whose involvement in pearl cultivation spans many decades, the pearl oyster manifests as an autonomous agent who is not easily controlled by the technician. It sometimes demonstrates a certain kind of "resistance" or an unexpected reaction to human interference.

Among those involved in pearl cultivation, Mr. A is not alone in describing the pearl oyster as having capacity for action and acting according to its own senses or intentions. This narrative of the pearl oyster as an "embodied" entity like a human being rather than merely a tool to produce a pearl for economic profit is more prevalent among the more skilled technicians. For instance, senior technicians at some pearl cultivation sites in Nagasaki Prefecture have been heard instructing junior technicians to "Think how the pearl oyster is feeling!" and "Treat them kindly because the pearl oyster is hurting after nucleation surgery!" It is often reported that sites that train their staff this way generally exhibit greater care and sensitivity in their work, which results in relatively better oyster mortality rates and higher quality pearls.

3.8 Memorial service for pearl oysters

As discussed in the Introduction of this book, the dominant paradigm of the modern world, following Descartes, distinguishes between humans and non-human things (including life forms). It treats humans as active and sentient subjects and things as passive and mindless (lifeless) objects which are subordinate, subject to the control of human subjects. In this framework, even living beings such as animals and plants are seen as if they were mindless (soulless) machine-like beings. As we have seen, however, in the practices of pearl cultivation, pearl oysters are seen as sensitive and sentient subjects like humans, rather than merely subservient objects.

This attitude is not exclusive to the narratives and behaviors of pearl cultivation technicians. The entire pearl-related industry, including distributors, sellers and cooperative workers, gather together each year at various places to conduct memorial services for the pearl oysters that die in serving the industry. While details vary, the ceremony generally involves offering rice wine, flowers or some harvested pearls to the local pearl memorial tower and expressing gratitude for the year's harvest. Reverence for and consolation to the sacrificed pearl oysters are also expressed. Monks from a local Buddhist temple recite sutras in front of the memorial tower to comfort the spirits of pearl oysters while attendees burn incense in thanks and consolation. Prayers are offered for future successful harvests. In some areas, the pearl cultivators throw some harvested pearls into the sea after the memorial service at the tower (Photos 3.2 and 3.3).

These memorial services are simply one part of Japan's extensive tradition of memorial services for *mono*. Memorial services are held for whales and eels in various locations across the country. Tokyo's blowfish wholesalers conduct an annual ceremony in which fish are released into the Sumida River following a prayer service on the river bank. Other living and non-living things which are commemorated in Japan range from tortoise and chickens to sewing needles, dole, kitchen knives, eye glasses, computers and bras. This reverence suggests a perspective that treats *mono* as a subject with its own soul, rather than merely a passive object (non-living matter).[7]

The belief or philosophy underpinning these practices is hardly peculiar to Japan. In fact, the modern perspective that treats humans and non-human beings as if they are two ontologically distinct dimensions is not universally shared. Many cultures assume interaction, interpenetration and border-crossing between the human and non-human domains. The prevalence of totemism in a broad sense is one example of these beliefs. Beliefs about transformation between humans and animals as well as narratives and mythologies about personified animals are other examples.

The cognitive archaeologist Mithen (1996) hypothesized that the early human mind had a domain-specific (or moduled) structure consisting of natural history

Photo 3.2 Memorial tower for pearl oysters

Photo 3.3 The 57th memorial service for pearls held on 23 October 2007 commemorated the centenary of the development of pearl cultivation technology. A large gathering of industry personnel and Miss Ise-Shima contestants participated in the ceremonial release of about 200,000 pearls and 100 Akoya pearl oysters to the sea. Photographed by author in Kashiko Island, Shima City, Mie Prefecture.

intelligence, technical intelligence and social intelligence. In contrast, he suggests, the mind of anatomically modern humans functions unbound, interlocking these domains through "cognitive fluidity". This enables humans to think across boundaries and interpenetrate the human and non-human domains, for example (ibid: 218). Similarly, according to Ingold, there is no ontologically clear division in hunter-gatherer society between the social domain and the world of things (natural domain) (Ingold 1992: 42; Mithen 1996: 66).

In other words, as *Homo sapiens* emerged from the "moduled (domain-specific) mind" phase it was inclined to think primarily in terms of "personifying the non-human world". It was normal to think of nature using idioms of human society and to represent humans using idioms of nature (animals) (Mithen 1996: 217–218). The personification of animals and totemism are examples of these two tendencies. Thus, we might consider the treatment of the pearl as an autonomous subject to be a thought pattern that is potentially ubiquitous among *Homo sapiens* with "cognitive fluidity" rather than a uniquely Japanese perspective.[8]

3.9 From a control model to a dialogical model of *mono*

Finally, we would like to discuss the form of *human/mono* relationship that our discussion of pearl cultivation brings into view. We have examined the process of pearl cultivation as a "manufacturing" process in a broad sense, pointing out the "embodied knowledge" required of the pearl cultivation technician. This suggested a certain affinity with Polanyi's idea of tacit knowledge as well as Lave and Wenger's "communities of practice" argument. However, we also noted that our field study of cultured pearl farms highlighted a "paradox of skills" because pearls are environment-dependent products and some situations cannot be adequately explained by the communities of practice framework. What emerges here is the significance of the constantly changing environmental factor. We cannot talk about the production of *mono* called pearls if we ignore the fact that the natural environment remains beyond human control.

Our second (related) point, is that the narratives of technicians at cultured pearl farms portray pearl oysters as autonomous subjects with senses and agency. The scenes of annual memorial services for pearl oysters reveal a human attitude of gratitude, consolation and supplicating *mono* rather than one of ruling, dominating and controlling them.[9]

As mentioned in the Introduction, the common-sense distinction between *humans* and *mono* (both non-human life forms and human-made objects) is generally accepted as a self-evident division. Particularly in the dominant post-Cartesian modernist understanding, only humans are seen as subjects with agency; non-human *mono* are treated as passive objects subject to human control and manipulation. In this world view, even living creatures are tacitly regarded as mindless objects. Here, the distinction between humans and *mono* is seen as absolute; crossing the boundary and hybridization between the two domains rarely enters consciousness. In this paradigm, belief in human dominance over *mono* is unshakable. It has been a commonsense view in modern society, but it is a highly anthropocentric view of *mono*.[10]

In reality, as demonstrated by ethnographical case studies from various regions discussed in several chapters of this book, this modernist view of *mono* is neither a universal paradigm nor is it always an appropriate one. What emerges from the descriptions of pearl cultivation is a model that captures the *human/mono* relationship in terms of broader dialogues and interactions rather than a "control model" which explains it in terms of an active subject and a subordinate object. We shall conclude this chapter by pointing out that the unstable and uncontrollable natural environment underlies the need for this dialogical-interactive model, as the account of pearl cultivation in this chapter has shown.

4 An Ecological Analysis of Pottery Culture: From Clay to "*Mono*"

Michiko Intoh

Keywords: pottery technology, technological change, ecological environment, technological adaptation, embodiment of knowledge

4.1 Pottery technology and culture

It was once assumed that tool use was what differentiated human beings from other animals. However, it is now well known that tools are used by some animals, including certain insects (see Yamagoshi, Chapter 10, on tool use among primates). Nevertheless, the tools used by non-human animals tend to be very simple resources found in the natural environment and largely unaltered. In contrast, tools made by humans with a purpose in mind may mark the beginning of the history of making *mono* (things).

Early humans of the Paleolithic period made a wide variety of *mono*, including axe, knife, hammer, grinding stone, arrowhead, fishhook, etc. Most of these were made of stones and shells (marine or freshwater) that were readily available in the surrounding environment. It is highly probable that plant materials such as wood and leaves were also processed and used as tools, but they rarely survive archaeologically.

When humans transitioned into the Neolithic period, one of the major differences from the previous era was the use of pottery.[1] The earliest pottery in the world has been found in East Asia (about 16,000~18,000 years old). The clay from which pottery is made is natural, but pottery is not found in nature. It is clearly human-made *mono*. There is a considerable difference in manufacturing technology between stone tools and pottery. Stone tools are shaped by chipping and polishing while pottery requires more than shaping. Heat must be applied to affect a chemical change that transforms clay into ceramics. Pottery appears to be the earliest *mono* that humans made through intentional chemical action.

Making pottery is not easy. There is a lot more to it than working, shaping, and firing the clay. A variety of materials and appropriate bodily techniques must be used in order to form clay into a vessel, dry it without cracking, and heat it without inflicting damage. Hence, pottery is a suitable *mono* for deciphering the dynamics between the environment and the human body.

Pottery making requires combining available raw materials and developing technologies that cater for the particularities of each situation. A tradition of pottery making is a technology that has been embodied and stably operated through a prolonged process of trial and error peculiar to each specific locale. Potters are generally conservative about "change" (Rice 1984a). When local conditions change, however, the finished products and embodied techniques likely change as well. For example, if the traditionally used source of clay dries up, potters may find their technology unsuitable for the substituted new type of clay; they must then alter their techniques accordingly (Intoh 2006: 146).

A *mono* must be considered from two perspectives: production and consumption (Uchibori 1997). Although production and consumption appear to be quite separate, they are in fact closely interrelated. It is expected to consider how the products are to be used in the process of the production activity. The production of practical pottery reflects the shapes, sizes and physical properties appropriate for their functions. The spiritual images of the society are often expressed in the form of decorative patterns. The physical properties (thermal conduction, thermal shock, porosity etc.) of the pot need to be adjusted according to whether they are used for cooking or for storage (Rye 1981). Conversely, the production situation can influence consumption patterns in some cases. For example, if a certain *mono* cannot be mass-produced, shortages may lead to higher consumer prices or the development and use of substitutes. Moreover, the types of value that are added to *mono* are complicated through the act of exchange between producers and consumers. By interpreting these various factors comprehensively, we might decipher a system of meaning, that is, a culture (Hodder 1982; Stark & Longacre 1993; Gosselain 1998 among others).

Each pottery making tradition around the world can be interpreted as a relatively stable technology particular to its environment. A stable pottery technology becomes a cultural program for the society concerned, regulating the behavior of its potters. We must, however, consider the relationship between potters and their environment if we are to comprehensively interpret this cultural program. It is often difficult to accurately interpret a *mono* from an anthropocentric framework, especially where it is created through an intimate relationship between the environment and bodily techniques, as in the case of pottery making. Once a technology is established in a particular society, it can be difficult to ascertain why various elements of the tradition (e.g., raw materials, particular techniques, etc.) were selected initially.

For example, when damage to pottery at the firing stage due to inadequate drying is attributed to non-observance of conventions (e.g., sleeping with her husband the previous night), how are we to deduce these cultural meanings? To discover changes in pottery technology, it is necessary to reconstruct the real causes and technological responses which have been obscured behind various discourses.

In this chapter, the background for the change of pottery technology is explored using archaeological materials as well as ethnographic resources. When we study pottery technology using archaeological materials, we examine the finished product: pottery (either the whole or pieces). But this approach is not always conductive to a detailed reconstruction of the bodily techniques used in production. We deduce their characteristics from various factors, including the environment and the culture (Matson 1965).

In the next section, an overview of the making of the *mono* called pottery will be provided. Making pottery requires a wide range of knowledge and experience on the part of the potter. The general technological process in terms of its relationship with the environment will be described first. Then, the depth of the relationship between the technology and the environment will be discussed focusing on pottery making in Oceania.[2]

4.2 Pottery production: From earth to earthenware

Clay is an indispensable raw material for making pottery. Clay refers to a fine-grained material (up to 2 µm) of weathered or denaturalized rocks and minerals which becomes plastic when mixed with a limited amount of water, and hardens when heated. Geologic clay deposits are widely distributed as weathering turns most rocks into clays. However, not all clays are suitable for pottery making.

Basically, it is possible to make "earthen products" by kneading clay and firing at around 500 to 600°C (900 to 1100° F) or above. However, some improvements and modifications are required to produce earthenware that serves specific purposes, such as cooking pots. Above all, preparation of the clay body bearing appropriate plasticity and reasonable shrinkage is important. The success of pottery making essentially depends on adjusting these factors. Naturally deposited clay is modified by adding non-plastic additives or other clay with different qualities to control the workability of the clay. The forming and firing techniques applied must be altered accordingly to suit the particular material being used.

In addition to the clay, water and fuel, a variety of tools are used at various stages of pottery making, including temper materials (sand, plant material etc.), screens, forming tools (potter's wheel, paddle and anvil etc.), surface finishing tools (stone, bamboo, seashell etc.), and pattern engraving tools (wood, bamboo, rope, seashell etc.). The combination of these elements varies depending on many factors, including the ecological and social environments, bodily techniques, and the pottery's social function as *mono*.

When these combinations have been stabilized, the established pottery making technology is handed on from one generation to the next. Below is a brief outline of the basic stages and operations of pottery making followed by a discussion of the points at which the ecological environment tends to influence pottery making (Shepard 1956; Rice 1984b, 1987; Rye 1981; Intoh 2003; Kani 2005 among others).

4.2.1 Basic stages of pottery making

Clay, the main raw material of pottery, is characterized by its plasticity, which allows both free forming and retention of the final shape. Naturally found clays vary greatly in plasticity. This is largely determined by the type of base rock and the type and particle size of minerals contained in clay.

In order to make something for a specific purpose, potters need to improve the workability of the clay. The right plasticity contributes to good pottery making. Where more than one type of clay is available, those with extremely high or low plasticity are often avoided and those with moderate plasticity are preferred. Highly plastic clay (such as montmorillonite in the smectite group) is subject to a high level of shrinkage at the drying and firing stages, resulting in cracking. Thus, plasticity is modified either by adding a tempering agent such as sand, or mixing in other kinds of clays to reduce the shrinkage. The properties of the clay used impacts on the methods of forming, drying and firing pottery. Similarly, certain types of sand used for tempering adversely affect firing and require some technical solution (see Section 4.4).

Once potters are satisfied with the texture of the prepared clay, they proceed to the kneading and forming stages. The main forming methods include hand twisting, spiral coiling, ring building, paddle and anvil, slab building, molding and throwing (potter's wheel). Sometimes multiple techniques are combined. For example, potters of Yap Island in Micronesia use different forming techniques for the base, middle and top parts of a vessel (see Section 4.3). These techniques are influenced by the plasticity, shrinkage and other factors of the clay body used.

Once the overall shape is formed, it is further refined during the surface finishing stage. While the surface is finished by simple rubbing with hands, secondary surface finishing is often carried out using tools such as a stone or a seashell. The paddle and anvil technique of striking the walls of a vessel is another example.

Surface finishing is followed by the drying stage, which is divided into two parts. The first part is called leather hard, where further patterning and surface polishing can still be done. In the second part, a vessel is dried to the same level as ambient moisture. After this drying, the vessel is ready for firing. During drying, the clay shrinks and reduces in volume. Hence, when it is made from clay with a high shrinkage rate, a vessel is dried slowly over a prolonged period.

The firing stage effects a thermal transformation of the clay into pottery through a chemical reaction. Until this reaction is completed, the shaped vessel will revert to clay if soaked in water. The simplest firing technique is open firing, not using a kiln, in which a vessel is fired in an open fire on the ground. The firing temperature is between 700 and 900°C. The duration is often less than one hour. Firing causes three stages of change in the clay, the timing of which varies depending on the nature of clay and the firing temperature (Shepard 1956: 83).

During the first stage, at around 100°C, the moisture present between the clay mineral particles evaporates. At around 500–700°C,[3] chemically combined water in clay mineral molecules breaks down and escapes in the form of steam and the clay's crystalline structure vanishes. This marks the transformation of the material from clay to ceramics; after this the object will not resume its plasticity when mixed with water. If firing is too rapid, more steam is generated than can be released from the walls of the vessel, causing it to burst. Also, if heat distribution is uneven, cracking may result.

The second stage involves oxidation. This change begins while dehydration is taking place in the first stage as organic materials contained in the clay are carbonated and burned and iron compounds are oxidized to form ferric oxide.

The third stage involves vitrification. This change begins at around 1,000°C and glassifies silica. Vitrification can be achieved in kiln firing but is rarely achieved in open firing.

In some cases, the pots after firing are surface treated for water proofing. Resin or other substances are applied to the inside and outside of the still warm pottery to form a thin layer that repels water. Decoration with paint or other materials can be done after this.

4.2.2 Embodied knowledge

While pottery making typically involves the basic stages described above, there was considerable variation in technologies of traditional pottery making around the world. As mentioned, this is because varying combinations of techniques were adapted in each tradition for utilizing available clays and other raw materials. A series of actions based on accumulated knowledge about environmental conditions, techniques and their combinations (a technological system) has been passed down through the generations as techniques of the body. These techniques are tacit knowledge and built up further through interactions between production, consumption and the ecological conditions on top of individual variation of potters (see Kaneko, Chapter 5).

Issues, for example, of where to dig to obtain clay or how much of which temper materials to mix with the clay, are part of the inherited techniques. Across the world, diverse materials have been used for tempering, including beach sand, river sand, grain husks, grass, finely crushed pottery fragments, etc. Potters use their own bodies, touching and experiencing the texture of various clay bodies (plasticity, size and amount of temper etc.) to determine how much of which materials should be mixed into the clay. A prepared clay body with "correct feeling" tends to have good workability (optimum plasticity) and moderate shrinkage.

At the same time, potters must choose materials appropriate for the function of the product. For instance, a clay body to make a large vessel needs more non-plastic additives for increased strength, to prevent it from collapsing under its own weight (Braun 1983). For water vessels used in a hot climate, more porous vessel bodies are preferred as the walls absorb water and promote evaporation, keeping the water cool (Rye 1981). Details of potter's bodily techniques include both technological adaptation to the local environment and actions determined by the particular cultural and social background.

At the drying stage, the method and speed of drying depend on the weather and the clay's properties. In hot and dry weather, pottery needs to be dried in the shade to prevent it from drying too rapidly. In cold and humid weather, the drying room must be heated. In areas with wet and dry seasons, pottery needs to be made during the dry season with relatively short periods of drying and firing (Arnold 1993).

Firing is the final and most difficult stage of making pottery. Potters proceed very carefully in order to avoid failure at this stage. Some potters offer prayers to their deity before they begin firing. In order to prevent breakage, they need the right balance between moisture in the clay, the heating rate and the maximum temperature. The amount of firewood, the method of stacking firewood, the quantity of pottery to be fired and other such details are all passed on as part of the embodied knowledge and techniques of individual pottery cultures.

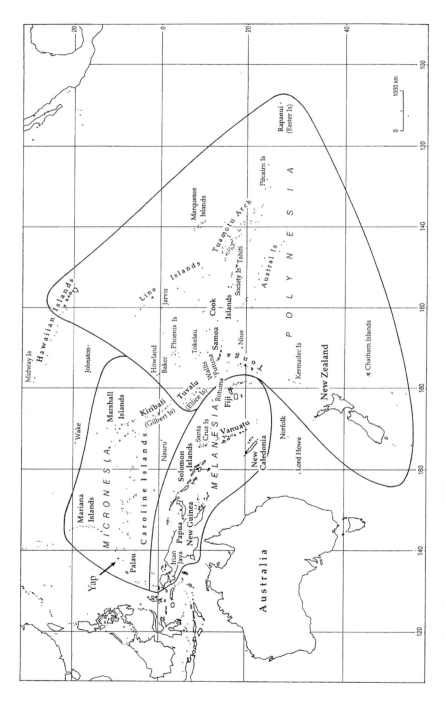

Figure 4.1 Map of Oceania (after Denoon 1997)

Traditional pottery making is thus a system of knowledge accumulated via repeated trials of technological options in response to particular ecological and/or cultural environments.

4.3 Environment and pottery technology

On an island with a relatively isolated environment, elements of pottery making are constrained in many ways. It is thus an ideal site for studying the relationship between pottery making and the environment. In Oceania, Austronesian-speaking people spread from the Southeast Asian islands about 3,300 years ago, expanding their settled areas from island to island (Figure 4.1). As the people settled on different islands and continued to make pottery, settlers on each island developed their own pottery culture over time. By considering this process of change and the diversity of the environment of each island together, we are able to demonstrate how the ecological environment has influenced both the pottery as *mono* and the techniques of the body to make them.[4]

Traditional pottery making on the Yap Islands in Micronesia, is described below. Pottery making was practiced on Yap continually for about 2,000 years. The oldest type of pottery is called 'CST (Calcareous Sand Tempered)' with calcareous beach sand being used as a temper material. Tempering with this fine sand was one of the characteristics of the pottery technology used by the early Austronesian people who migrated from Island South-East Asia. The characteristics of Yapese pottery continued to change over the subsequent 1,400 years or so (Intoh 1990a, b). At the end, 'Laminated pottery' with hard layered walls and no temper was developed, which persisted into the historic period (Müller 1917; Gifford & Gifford 1959). This pottery making technology exhibits some distinctive techniques of the body which highlight the impact that the local environment has on the production of *mono*.

I had the opportunity to observe the entire process of traditional pottery making by Ruetennigin, a sixty-two-year-old woman in Gitam Village on Yap, from 1982 to 1983 (Intoh and Leach 1985; Intoh 1990a; Intoh 2003). Ruetennigin was the last custodian of Gitam's pottery making tradition. She had grown up watching and learning traditional pottery making from her mother.

Yap is geologically unique in having exposures of pre-Tertiary metamorphic basement (greenschist) unknown elsewhere in Micronesia. Deposits of clay formed from weathered greenschist are found across a wide area. The ratios of montmorillonite (silicate) exceed 50% in most of these clays, which have very high shrinkage rates (Claridge 1984). Montmorillonite rich clay tends to expand and becomes very plastic when it absorbs water and to shrink severely when dried. Generally, clay with such a high shrinkage rate is seldom used alone for making pottery. If it has to be used, it is generally mixed with other lower shrinkage clays or tempered with non-plastic additives in an attempt to reduce plasticity and shrinkage (Rice 1984b; Arnold 1985: 21).[5] All clays in Yap have high montmorillonite content, so local potters had no other choice. Consequently, Yapese potters were obliged to make various technological adaptations and developed a unique pottery making method and process at the end involving a long production time.

The characteristics of traditional pottery making on the Yap Islands are summarized below. We shall look at the relationship between environmental conditions and body techniques developed for making pottery with montmorillonite rich clay (see Intoh 1990 for technological details).

1. **Not tempering clay**

    The clay body is made by removing impurities such as sand and organic matter from the dug up clay against the expected action such as adding tempering materials (Photo 4.1). Naturally its shrinkage rate remains high. This clay body is therefore highly susceptible to cracking during drying and to breaking during firing. It is known that montmorillonite loses more than ten percent of its moisture rapidly when heated to 100°C or so, increasing the risk of cracking (Tite 1972: 297).

    The earliest Yapese CST pottery, about 2,000 years old, demonstrates that the potters added beach sand as a temper. This is typical solution to make use of a highly plastic clay. However, Yap is surrounded by coral reef, and all of the beach sand contains a high proportion of calcium carbonate derived from corals and seashells.[6] Hence, tempering with beach sand causes other problems during firing (see Section 4.4). With calcareous sand mixed in the clay body, the success rate of firing pots could have been low. Although some evidence of using different temper materials were noted, Yapese potters chose to make pottery without mixing temper to the clay in the end, resulting in high plasticity and high shrinkage.

2. **A very long forming stage**

    Ruetennigin spent more than a month in forming a vessel. The clay was formed into a cylindrical shape and the top part was pushed to form a hollow. Some clay is taken from the lower part of the cylinder to make sausage-shaped rolls of clay to put on around the edge of the hollowed

An Ecological Analysis of Pottery Culture

Photo 4.1 Small sand grains and grass root fragments are removed from a clay body. This type of modification is rare in pottery making using highly plastic clays with high shrinkage. (Photos 4.1–4.4 were taken by author on Yap in 1983)

Photo 4.2 The pottery wall is built from the bottom, adding clay a little bit at a time. The inward curvature is formed with a conus shell.

cylinder. After building up to the half-height of the vessel, smaller pieces of clay are then added to form the incurved rim (Photo 4.2). She work on it a little bit each day, building it up slowly because the walls will collapse if too much clay is added on top before the lower part dries. This is a technological adaptation to the un-tempered plastic clay with low

Photo 4.3 Once the top part is dry, the base is trimmed with the edge of a split bamboo

strength. Once the vessel is fully formed, it is dried over eight days. She then places it upside down on her lap to trim surplus clay off the base using the edge of a split bamboo stick (Photo 4.3). The final surface of the inner side of the inverted rim was made with the curved surface of a cowrie shell tool.

3. **Drying slowly over 3–4 months**

    The surface finished vessel is placed in a purpose-built hut away from the village and slowly dried under the cover of large taro leaves for three to four months. This is a much longer drying period than is typical of other pottery making traditions in the world. Normally, the drying time is kept to a minimum because longer drying time increases the susceptibility of the pottery to breakage from unexpected mishaps. In the case of the Yapese pottery made with montmorillonite-rich clay, however, rapid drying would cause cracking, so a longer and slower drying period has been adopted.

4. **Wetting the surface of the vessel immediately before firing**

Photo 4.4 The surface of the dried vessel is moistened with water immediately before firing. Although it seems to contradict the effort to dry it over several months, it makes practical sense.

As soon as firewood starts to burn on the ground, the surface of the dried vessel is moistened with water. Once firewood is burned down to coals, the wet vessel is placed on it upside down. More firewood is placed around it in a vertical cone arrangement to create a strong upward draught.

Moistening the surface immediately before firing (Photo 4.4) seems contradictory to a long drying process, but this technique has scientific merit. It may have been intended to prevent cracks which could be caused by heating the un-tempered, high-shrinkage Yapese clay. An explanation for the wetting of the surface can be found in the practice of putting the pot directly on hot coals (about 600–700° C) rather than heating it gradually. When a pot is placed on a hot fire, the surface layer will be dehydrated rapidly by the heat, while the core is heated slowly and dehydration takes longer. Different rates of dehydration in different parts of a pot will cause cracks. An increase in the moisture content of the surface layers can equalize the dehydration period. While the temperature of the core rises high enough to drive the moisture out, the surface layer can retain enough moisture to prevent cracking. (Intoh 1990b). This is a very logical solution. The laminated vessel wall structure characteristic of the Yapese ethnographic pottery is likely created at this stage by strong steam pressure. Hence, it takes four to five months to make one piece of pottery, making this a very inefficient practice compared to other traditional pottery making around the world. There must have been a reason to have retained this tradition.

Pottery on the Yap Islands was traditionally made by women of the lowest ranked villages (*milingay*) in the social hierarchy.[7] The pottery size varied greatly (12–70 cm in diameter) but there was little variation in shape. They were all simple bowl-shaped vessels with sharply inverted rims used exclusively for cooking.

The completed vessels were delivered to the highest ranked village once or twice a year. The landless *milingay* villages supplied pottery to the highest ranked villages as tribute in exchange for permission to live on the latter's landholdings. Potters were therefore not free to give or trade their products to others. The chiefs of the highest ranked villages redistributed the collected pottery to other villages. They also traded the pottery with the inhabitants of coral islands to the east of Yap (through the *sawei* exchange system) (Intoh 2000). Pottery could not be made on these coral islands due to the absence of clay, so they obtained pots in exchange for craft products such as shell beads, coconut rope and turtle shells.

This is a significant point: pottery in Yapese society served not only for cooking but also for the social function of exchange between Yapese villages and other societies. It is most likely that the social value was one of the reasons that pottery making was not abandoned in Yap despite the extreme inefficiency of the technology. The fact that specialization of pottery making involved social obligation must have prevented *milingay* villagers from abandoning the practice.

4.4 Extinction of pottery and the environment

Another cultural change in Oceania involved abandoning pottery making. In some cases the discontinuation of pottery making led to the discontinuation of pottery use while in other cases the use of imported pottery continued. Where the use of pottery was discontinued, the functions that had been performed by pottery began to be performed by a new cooking method without using pots. Such examples are found on the islands of Polynesia and eastern Micronesia (Intoh 1995).

Lapita pottery making people migrated from the Southeast Asian islands to southern Oceania about 3,300 years ago, settling across an area that extends to

Tonga and Samoa. While early Lapita pottery featured fine dentate decoration, within a few hundred years the design patterns had become much simpler on most of the islands. Pottery making completely ceased in Tonga and Samoa. The cessation of pottery making in a finely developed pottery making culture such as Lapita is a very rare occurrence in world history. We shall examine the possibility that environmental factors were the principal cause for this change.

Besides design changes, there were other technological changes on many islands prior to the extinction of Lapita pottery. The most marked change of all was in the choice of temper materials. As discussed in section 4.3 above, the beach sands of Oceania often have a high content of calcium carbonate derived from shells and corals surrounding the islands, which makes it difficult to control firings. Studies on temper sand mixed in the Lapita potsherds have found that the use of calcium carbonate derived sand decreased while the use of volcanic sand increased on some islands. Pottery made in Fiji (Best 1989), Tonga (Poulsen 1988) and Samoa (Green 1974) are typical examples. Nevertheless, pottery making ceased completely in Tonga and Samoa within a few hundred years but continued in Fiji.[8] Archaeologists offer various hypotheses to explain these difference.

1. Pots were necessary for cooking rice, but when root crops became the staple food, cooking was done in earth ovens and pots were no longer required (Leach 1982).
2. Clays available on Tonga, Samoa and other Central Polynesian islands were not suitable for pottery making (Claridge 1984).
3. Lapita pottery was made for trade between islands. Pottery making ceased as the trade activity diminished (Irwin 1981; Marshall 1985).
4. Due to all of the reasons above, the need for pottery making decreased and the practice was eventually stopped (Le Moine 1987).

As Lapita pottery was used not only for trade, but also for daily cooking, Hypothesis 3 is unlikely to have been the primary factor. Also, it is hard to believe that people chose to cook without pots, as earth oven cooking coexisted with pottery cooking in Fiji and other places. Moreover, archaeological evidence indicates that some islands where there was no tradition of pottery making had imported pottery from Fiji. Hypothesis 1 is thus ruled out. While it is possible that it was caused by a confluence of all these factors as suggested by Hypothesis 4, I am assured that the factor proposed by Hypothesis 2 had the greatest impact. According to Claridge (1984), the difference lies in geological structure. Andesite-based islands from Fiji to the west have highly weathered clays suitable for pottery making. By contrast, many of the islands from Samoa to the east (except New

Zealand) are built on young basalt basement and their clays are unsuitable for pottery making. These islands are divided by the andesite line that runs between Fiji and Tonga; no andesite is found to the east of this line.

A similar phenomenon can be found in Micronesia, north of the equator. Western islands such as Marianas, Yap and Palau continued making pottery more than 2000 years. In contrast, on Chuuk, Pohnpei and Kosrae in the eastern part of the region, pottery making was practiced by people who settled there about 2,000 years ago but was soon abandoned. These islands are also younger basalt-based islands east of the andesite line. The poor quality and high shrinkage of the available clays are likely to have been the primary cause of the extinction of their pottery culture.[9]

Of course, good clays are not necessarily available on all islands to the west of the andesite line. Such is the case in the Yap Islands. As mentioned earlier, the rocks in Yap are mostly metamorphic. There is no andesite and the clays are very poor quality. The fact that pottery making had continued in Yap for 2,000 years contrasts sharply with the abandonment of pottery making on Polynesian and eastern Micronesian islands despite the similarly poor clay. This difference may provide the key to understanding the cessation of pottery making and will be discussed in the next section.

4.5 *"Mono"*, culture, and the environment

Among all the *mono* that have been produced by humans, pottery is one of the oldest and demands advanced physical techniques. Technologies in pre-industrial society were adaptations to the physical and human environment (Nomura 1999). Those which are stable under particular environmental conditions are thought to satisfy the following three conditions.
  1. Practical satisfaction with the completed *mono* (function, hardness etc.)
  2. Social and cultural satisfaction with the completed *mono* (form, decoration, commodity value etc.)
  3. Social and cultural satisfaction with production time and energy consumption (short production time, high success rate etc.)

The first two conditions are perceived by the user and the trader while the third condition is perceived by the producer. When the user and the producer are the same person (no division of labor), all three conditions are evaluated together. If the level of satisfaction is low for any of these three conditions, attempts are made to improve the production technology. However, as so many factors influence each other in making pottery, a change to any single factor is highly likely to affect other factors. These complex inter-influences can be reflected in the final pottery product as a *mono* itself (Intoh 1990b).

In this chapter, we have examined how pottery culture built upon stable techniques alters in response to changes in the environment (resource depletion, migration etc.). The island environment of Oceania has been used as a laboratory to examine how changes in the environment cause changes in the final products. When skilled potters migrate to a new environment, they begin to make pottery by adapting their existing techniques to new materials. When they encounter a problem, they either change materials or modify production techniques. Such adaptations are influenced by various social and cultural choices and, hence, different groups may choose different solutions to the same problem (Intoh 2006: 146).

Evaluations of the time and energy invested into making a single pot vary according to diverse social and cultural factors. If the success rate at the firing stage is, for example, 30%, the decision to either try to improve the success rate, accept the 30% success rate, or to abandon pottery making altogether is determined by social and cultural factors, rather than simply material or technological determinants. Where there is a relation of social domination between the consumer and the producer, it is more likely that pottery making will continue despite the awkward process or the poor success rate, as we saw in this study of pottery making on Yap.

In Polynesia where pottery making was abandoned, some evidence that pots were imported from other islands strongly indicates that pots as cooking utensils still retained value in the culture. It is possible that the potters' inability to improve their success rate curtailed their motivation to make pottery, leading to the culture abandoning pottery making. Although pottery making ceased on Tonga and Samoa, nearby Fiji had good quality clays and continued to make pottery till now.[10] The fact that pottery has coexisted with earth oven cooking in Fiji, undermines the suggestion that pottery disappeared due to the introduction of alternative cooking methods. Ultimately, there is a strong association between the continuation of pottery making and the availability of good clays.

Although pottery making survived in Fiji, it was specialized in some areas and abandoned in others. Along the Rewa River and the Sigatoka Valley on Viti Leve Island, where there are deposits of clays and volcanic rock-derived sands suitable for pottery making, there are long-standing traditions of pottery making (Claridge 1984). It is obvious that the specialization occurred in a suitable environment in terms of resources available.

This chapter has mainly discussed the relationship between the technological features of pottery making and the characteristics of pottery products is, emphasizing the relationship between pottery making and the environment. In the process, we encountered social factors that cannot be determined by the ecological environment alone, but which significantly influence the materiality of pottery as cultural and social *mono*.

Part III
The Dynamic Between *Mono* and the Body

5 Learning Pottery Making: Transmission of Body Techniques[1]

Morie Kaneko

Keywords: Ethiopia, pottery, female potter, bodily techniques, technique learning process

5.1 Daughters say: "I came to know pottery making by myself"

I have been practicing pottery making as an apprentice for the female potters of an ethnic group called Aari in southwestern Ethiopia in order to study the diversity of techniques involved in forming and firing pottery as well as the background for their generation. While there was already an influx of aluminum and plastic products in this area when I began my field research in 1998, the people have continued using clay pots as well as the introduced cooking utensils.

Local pottery making technology initially brought me endless surprises, including how they formed round-bottomed vessels and how they could produce pottery that is durable enough for practical use after only a couple of hours of firing. After visiting the field-site many times, however, I gradually came to see their various techniques as "normal". Yet, one of the things that did not seem "normal" to me, no matter how many times I witnessed it, was the fact that girls as young as six years old were able to form clay pots without their mothers' help from their first attempt, and these products were sold at the markets.

When a daughter attempts to form pottery for the first time, her mother, who is a pottery maker, takes a lump of clay, forms it roughly, and hands it to her daughter. The daughter receives it and continues forming until it is completed. The mother seldom makes adjustments to her daughter's work. Once the daughter has completed her first pot, the mother begins to tell people that "(She) forms pots by herself". One of the potters even moved to another village to remarry, leaving her daughter with the grandmother. The girl had been making pottery for only three weeks, when the mother said, "My daughter's *aani* (hands) know. She can do the forming by herself from now on".

In my observations, though, I almost never witnessed a daughter gazing intently at her mother forming a pot. What I saw most of the time was the daughter facing a lump of clay and forming it into a pot by using her own small fingers. I asked, "Did you learn how to form pots from your mother?" and many of the girls replied, "I know how to form pottery"[2] or "I've come to know it by myself".

Using the pottery makers' daughters' statements as cues, this chapter shall describe and examine the transmission of pottery forming techniques from mother to daughter in order to elucidate how these techniques are learned. It will focus on the sequence in which a young girl "comes to know" different types of pottery, how to move her body in forming pottery, and the interactions between mother and daughter in their workplace. In this article, the term "pottery making process" refers to the entire process (including clay excavation and transportation, forming, firing, and selling at a market) while "forming" refers to the task of manually shaping a clay body into greenware.

5.2 Overview: Learning techniques and the field-site

5.2.1 From observation and mimicry to participation in a community of practice

It would be possible for a researcher to assume that, even though the daughters of Aari potters declare that "I have come to know pottery forming by myself", they in fact "observe" their mothers' body movements in daily living and acquire pottery forming techniques by "mimicking" their mothers.[3] This approach would lead to further analysis of the transmission of particular techniques from one generation to the next through the medium of the body.

Marcel Mauss conceptualized the techniques of the body, pointing out that human action is a series of movements which individuals borrow from the actions executed in front of him or with him by others (Mauss 1950). His insights into bodily techniques shed light on the social generation, transmission and preservation of the bodily actions of individuals (Tanabe 2002: 543). Arguably, though, there has been insufficient research into the processes of learning basic constituents of production style (e.g., design concepts in material culture, techniques of the body) (Herbich and Dietler 2008: 223).

The concept of legitimate peripheral participation (LPP), however, was a major turnaround in the notion that "techniques are passed on from one generation to the next". According to LPP, the idea that techniques are learned through observation and imitation is largely incorrect (Lave and Wenger 1991: 95). It suggests, instead, that technique acquisition (learning) happens through interactions with others, not on one's own. This same process leads to the establishment of an individual's identity. Learning occurs through participation in a community (Lave and Wenger 1991). This perspective led Lave and Wenger to focus on groups in which techniques are transmitted under an apprenticeship-like system. They named these groups "communities of practice".[4] According to Lave and Wenger (1991: 95), the apprentices' "legitimate peripheral participation" provides them with more than an "observational" lookout post. This helps to explain how tacit knowledge can be transferred through community participation (practice) (Wenger 2002).[5]

While LPP highlights new participants in communities of practice, some researchers argue that focusing on this process alone is not sufficient. Gosselain, for example, studied the transmission of pottery making techniques among female potters in Niger. He acknowledges the importance of Lave and Wenger's argument, but also points out that cultural transmission should be distinguished from cultural dynamics or cultural change. He argues that transmission occurs through the ceaseless contribution of people constructing the repertoires of their local culture (Gosselain 2008: 175–176). At the same time, he argues that transmission is merely part of the overall repertoire structure and not singularly important (ibid.: 175). In the context of our discussion in this chapter, this means that there is not much point in examining the transmission of techniques to daughters if we fail to look at the entire pottery making process.

This chapter embraces Lave and Wenger's approach in considering that people learn techniques through interactions with others. However, we aim to describe the processes through which the daughters come to know pottery making while considering interactions between the environment (e.g., material) and people in acquiring techniques. These interactions, in our view, were not addressed sufficiently by Lave and Wenger. The subjects of this study range from infants to unmarried girls. In my understanding, the acquisition, change and creation of pottery making techniques constitute a history of the life of a potter (a "techno life history" (Kaneko 2007a)). The chapter focuses on the period from when the daughters initially establish their basic pottery making techniques until the time that they become recognized as fully-fledged potters within a professional group. Studying the manner of technique acquisition during this period will help us to understand the technical changes of the individual potters in the context of their life practice.

In Chapter 4, Intoh examines changes in pottery making in Oceania over a period of a few thousand years, mainly from the perspective of interrelationships with the natural environment. She explains the influences of pottery as cultural and social *mono* on changes in technological practices that cannot be fully explained by the natural environment alone. This chapter's main purpose is to describe the processes through which young girls learn bodily techniques over a period of three to four years, but it also examines the ways in which techniques develop through the interplay of various elements of pottery making over that short time span.

The girls' claims that "I came to know pottery making by myself" is analogous to my experience of learning as a potter's apprentice. I was given very few verbal instructions while learning to form pottery. I repeatedly had the experience of not understanding how to form pots, no matter how much I observed a potter's technique, until I felt the clay with my own fingers. This chapter uses the testimony that "I came to know pottery making by myself" as a clue that the girls had experiences similar to my own: learning how to form pottery first and foremost through embodied interactions with the material.

This perspective has the potential to confirm the conclusion that "many of our abstract concepts and arguments rely on metaphors based on concrete physicality" proposed by Tokoro and Kawai in the Introduction. This chapter attempts to describe the process of learning pottery making techniques using important non-verbal elements of the process, including *mono* (i.e., an order in which different types of pots are made), "the body" (i.e., body movement patterns, including finger movement patterns (Kaneko 2007b)), and "field and space" (i.e., the spatial configuration of the mothers and daughters in a workplace)[6] as indicators. I aim to elucidate the characteristics of technique acquisition by Aari pottery makers on the basis of such descriptions.

This study was conducted intermittently over a total period of about nine months between November 1998 and March 2002. The main subjects included twelve mother and daughter pairs in S and G Villages in the South Aari District of South Omo Zone, southwestern Ethiopia. The descriptions of the daughters before they take up pottery making are based on observations of five to six children in S Village. Twelve daughters were observed for a tracking study of their learning processes during five periods: November 1998 to January 1999 (Period I), December 1999 to March 2000 (Period II), November 2000 to February 2001 (Period III), June to July 2001 (Period IV), and January to March 2002 (Period V).

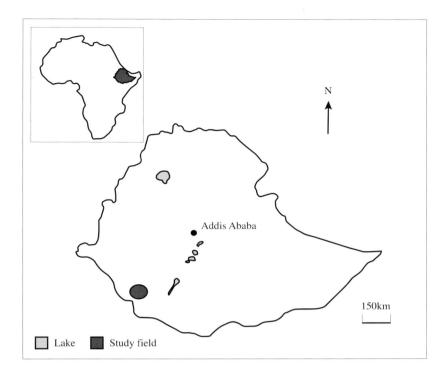

Figure 5.1 Study field

5.2.2 Research Site: The natural environment, pottery, and the potters' community

The Aari people engage in sedentary agriculture activity in the highlands of southwestern Ethiopia, approximately 1,500–2,500 meters above sea level (Figure 5.1). They are subsistence farmers, growing root vegetables such as *Ensete ventricosum*, taro and yam, as well as cereal crops such as corn, sorghum and barley. They also cultivate cash crops such as coffee and cardamom to participate in the cash economy (Shigeta 1988).

The Aari people use different food and cooking methods for each meal. Their rich dietary habit is supported by a wide variety of crops and pottery for cooking. They use over sixty types of clay vessels, about two-thirds of which are used in cooking. There are four major categories of cooking pots (Figure 5.2) based on their shapes. Pots in the same shape category are distinguished by the size of a certain part and are used for different purposes under different names. For example, the type of pot for brewing coffee leaves is called *bun-til* (*bun*: coffee, *tila*: a collective

Name (notation in the text)	Shape	Variations	Word origin Pot usage
Tila (A)		20 approx.	Aari. Cooking root crops, brewing alcohol, carrying water.
Disti (B)		10 approx.	Amharic. Cooking side dishes.
Jabana (C)		1	Amharic. Brewing coffee.
Aksha (D)		10 approx.	Aari. Baking bread, roasting coffee beans.

Figure 5.2 Four main types of pots used by the Aari people

term for pottery (broad definition) or a collective term for pots in Category A (Figure 5.2) (narrow definition); pronounced as *til* in compound words). This pot is about twenty centimeters high and its mouth is a few centimeters smaller in diameter than the type of *tila* used for cooking cabbage. The Aari people use different types of pots not only for different ingredients but also for different dishes using the same ingredient, as well as when cooking for different people and different occasions (e.g., communal work gatherings, having visitors).

These pots are made by women who belong to a vocational community called *tila mana*. The population of the Aari people was estimated to be between 120,000 and 180,000. There were about 350 female potters of *tila mana* at the time of this research (in 2002). There were about twenty *tila mana* settlements in the Aari area (in 2002). The people of *tila mana* have settled near clay sources. Each village was formed by a patrilineal kinship group. Among the Aari potters, the clan was the unit for exogamy and children belonged to their father's clan. The women of *tila mana* engaged in pottery making full time throughout the year while men farmed small plots while helping their mothers, wives and daughters. The potters formed one to fifteen pots in a day at their workplace in a hut adjacent to their home. The pots were sold directly from the potters to the end users without middlemen at periodic markets of their own and neighboring villages. The proceeds from the sale of pots paid for household living expenses, including daily food purchases and medical expenses.

5.2.3 The daughters play at the mother's workplace

The children of *tila mana*, both girls and boys, grow up practically in the hut where their mothers make pottery. It is common for a potter to take her infant to her workplace and carry on forming pottery as she breastfeeds (Photo 5.1(1)). The mother sometimes forms a clay object to soothe a crying child. While I was observing a workplace for a period of thirty minutes or so, children engaged in all sorts of activities by the side of their mothers who were concentrating on forming pottery. An infant who could sit on her own was playing at her mother's side, hitting a stone with pottery fragments. By the time a child could walk on her own, she would be playing with clay. Some of the objects made by the child looked like the pots her mother was making. I saw an infant take a broken pot and make forming actions similar to the ones employed by her mother.

When children reach the age of two or three, they provide assistance with tasks related to pottery making under their mother's instructions just as they help with household chores. They perform tasks such as carrying partially formed pots and covering pots with a cloth or taro leaves to prevent over drying (Photo 5.1(2)). As partially formed pots break if they become too dry, the potter instructs the children to cover the pots according to the sun's intensity at the time. Children might also transport water to be used in forming or fetch a stone for surface polishing from the main house.

Young girls begin to form shapes with clay as they spend time with their mothers at their workplaces. At this stage, however, the daughters are rarely seen to form pots using particular finger movement patterns under the mother's instructions. While playing at their mother's workplace, children sometimes make objects that look similar to the mother's pots. However, the mother calls this act "play" (*reeGa*) and distinguishes it from "pottery forming" (*tila mishikan*; the term *mishikan* is used only in the context of pottery making). I once observed a potter correcting her playing daughter in pot forming in response to my persistent questioning about how to acquire pottery forming techniques (Photo 5.2(1)). On that occasion, the potter showed the infant her finger movement pattern to tidy up the rim of the pot, saying "This way".

Photo 5.1 (1) A potter breastfeeds her baby at her pottery making workplace.

Photo 5.1 (2) Infants can help with forming pottery under their mother's instructions by the age of two or three. The children in this photo are covering partially formed pots with taro leaves to prevent over drying.

Learning Pottery Making

Photo 5.2 (1) The mother makes some adjustments to a pot-shaped plaything formed by her daughter. She demonstrates her finger movements with very little verbal information.

5.3 Pottery forming

5.3.1 The type of pot for the first-time forming

The potters said that the first pot their daughters would form would be *bun til* (for brewing coffee leaves, Photo 5.2(2)). In fact, all of the girls I surveyed started forming pottery with *bun til*. Some of the potters I interviewed claimed that "If you start learning with another type of pot, you won't be able to make *tila*".[7] The forming procedures for *tila*-shaped pots in Category A included finger movement patterns and drying techniques used in forming all of the other types of pots (Figure 5.2). For example, forming pots in Categories A and C was carried out in four stages punctuated by drying steps. Forming was divided into three stages for B and two stages for D (Kaneko 2005: 113). Twenty "finger movement patterns" were used for forming type A whereas B used three additional patterns not observed in forming A. C and D used two additional patterns not observed in forming A (Kaneko 2005: 114).

Aari potters work individually on their own home grounds in most cases. They do not form or fire pottery with their neighbors. It is not taboo to watch each other work, though, and potters do visit one another's workplaces. Nevertheless, married women rarely visit other potters' homes. Mothers and their unmarried daughters form pottery on the same site, however. In the early days, they sit within a meter of

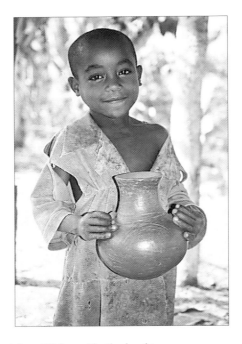

*Photo 5.2 (2) The first pot (*bun til*) formed by the daughter*

each other, often at an angle of forty-five degrees. When I watched a potter's finger movement and did not understand it, she only had to adjust her sitting position slightly so that I was able to see her finger movements.

Before the daughter forms her first pot, the mother roughly shapes a lump of clay and hands it to the daughter. The daughter receives it and continues forming it. By this time, the daughter can already mimic her mother's finger movement patterns. From then on, the mother begins to tell other people that her daughter has started forming pottery, using the term "pottery making" (*mishikan*). When I asked the potters why they would not correct the pots formed by their daughters, they replied that "(My and her) *aani* are different". The Aari word *aani* means "hand" and has many usages. Many Aari expressions associated with pottery making contain the word *aani* (Kaneko 2005: 164).

In the early days of the daughter's pottery forming, the mother and daughter tend to perform the same procedures at the same time. When the mother was forming a large-sized pot, however, they might work at a different pace. Once the daughter had formed pots for a year, she would sometimes work in a place from which she

Learning Pottery Making

	9/12/1999	10/12/1999	20/12/1999	22/12/1999	27/12/1999
S22 (mother)	●	●	●	X	●
S3 (4th year)	●	●*	X	O	●
S5 (7th year)	●	●*	●	O	X

● Different work   O Same work   X No work   * Sitting face to face

Figure 5.3 Work and seating arrangements of a mother and two daughters

could not see her mother's work, or work at a different time of the day from her mother. During my study, I never saw any mother-daughter pair engaged in the same procedures and they rarely sat face to face (Figure 5.3). Only once did I find two sisters performing the same procedures, but they were more than two meters apart and could not see one another's hand movements.

5.3.2 The process of forming large pots

According to the potters I interviewed, after mastering the *bun til* they next learn to form the *ekena til* (pots for cooking Ethiopian cabbages). When I asked the potters about the order in which they learn to form different types of pot, many explained that they learned "from small pots to large pots," using their hands to indicate the pot height or the size of the round base. Let us look at the cases of three daughters in S village (Itayata, Asa and Simiya) to examine this process.

Itayata was in her fourth year of pottery (as at 2001). Her parents were alive. She was the youngest of seven siblings. Two of her three older sisters had been married off to other villages. Itayata practiced forming pots with her mother and her unmarried older sister, Asa. Asa had been forming pots for over seven years.

Simiya had also been forming pots for more than seven years (as at 2001). Her parents were also alive. She was the oldest of five siblings (one son and four daughters).

Itayata, Asa and Simiya learned to form eight types of pots over the five study periods. Five of them were *tila*-shaped (A). Each of the other three had the shape of *disti* (B), *jebena* (C) and *aksha* (D) (Figure 5.2). An analysis of the forming of these pottery types, especially the *tila* types, revealed characteristic patterns at least with regard to the following four points (Table 5.1).

1. **There is an order of learning.**
   All three girls reported *bun til* (A^1) as their first pot. Itayata reported *ekena til* (A^2) as her second pot. I saw her forming B-type pots as well during Period I (Table 5.1). Asa reported that she had been forming pots in the same order as Itayata. I saw her progressing to *mosa til* (A^3) during Period I (Table 5.1). Simiya reported that she had been forming pots in the same way as Asa and progressed to A^3 during Period I (Table 5.1).
2. **Increased drying steps and repetition of the "finger movement patterns" for forming large tila pots.**
   The methods of forming small and large *tila*-shaped pots have different procedures and finger movement patterns. For example, the number of drying steps during forming is higher for large pot types than small ones. There are twenty finger movement patterns for both large and small pots, but two of the patterns are used more often in the forming of large pots than small pots.
3. **Forming more than one pot at a time.**
   The three girls reported that they had initially formed a single A^1 pot and subsequently learned to form multiple pots at once. They used the phrase "*aani* are soft" when they stated that they were able to form more than one pot at a time. When I accidentally made a hole in a pot I was forming, the potter told me, "Your *aani* are hard". Her daughter, who was forming a pot with us, explained to me that "If your *aani* are soft, they are like this (letting her hands dangle loosely) and you can form many fast, but if your *aani* are hard, you can't form many fast". In fact, both the mother and the daughter explained that when a girl was able to form a single pot fast, she could form multiple pots of the same type at the same time. That was when she could move on to form the next type of pot.
4. **They start forming large pots based on their own judgment.**
   Itayata progressed to forming B during Period I (Table 5.1). When I asked her, "Do you form *mosa til* (A^3)?" and "Do you know how to form *mosa til*?" she replied, "I can't form it" and "I don't know". Her mother listened by her side and said to me, "I tell her to form it but she doesn't". When I visited during Period II, Itayata reported, "I have formed *mosa til*".[8] While it was nearly two years before she was able to form A^3, Asa and Simiya learned to form three more types of pots in the same period. One of the reasons for this is that *gabija til* (A^4) and *sika til* (A^5) are almost the same size except for their mouth diameters. During these periods, they started forming the next type of pots based on their own rather than their mother's assessment.[9]

Table 5.1 The progression of pottery forming by three daughters in S Village (11/1999–03/2002)

	A¹	A²	B	A³	C	A⁴	A⁵	D
Itayata: In the 4th year of pottery forming								
I	●	●	●	X	X	X	X	X
II	●	●	●	O	X	X	X	X
III	●	●	●	●	X	X	X	X
IV	●	●	●	●	X	X	X	X
V	●	●	●	●	X	X	X	X
Asa: In the 7th year of pottery forming								
I	●	●	●	●	X	X	X	X
II	●	●	●	●	●	O	X	X
III	●	●	●	●	●	●	◎	X
IV	●	●	●	●	●	●	◎	X
V	●	●	●	●	●	●	◎	●
Simiya: In the 7th year of pottery forming								
I	◎	◎	◎	◎	X	X	X	X
II	◎	◎	◎	◎	◎	X	X	X
III	●	◎	●	●	●	◎	◎	X
IV	●	●	●	●	●	◎	◎	X
V	●	◎	●	●	●	●	◎	●

Note. A¹: *bun til*, A²: *ekena til*, B: *disti*, A³: *mosa til*, C: *jabana*, A⁴: *gabija til*, A⁵: *sika til*, D: *buna aksh*
▓ = Tila-shaped, ● = formed (confirmed by observations), O = formed multiple times (stated in interviews), ◎ = formed frequently (stated in interviews), X = never formed
Period I: 11/1998–01/1999, II: 12/1999–03/2000, III: 11/2000–02/2001, IV: 06–07/2001, V: 01–03/2002

5.3.3 The progression of forming pottery types other than *tila*

The narrative of progression "from forming small pots to large pots" is also applicable to pottery types with a globular base other than *tila*. For instance, the circumferences of B-shaped pots at the largest part of their body were either smaller than or about the same as those of A² pots. C-shaped pots, which Asa and Simiya formed during Period II, were slightly smaller the A³ pots in terms of the maximum circumference and the overall height (Table 5.1). A majority of the girls in my study went on to form B, C and D after forming *tila*-shaped pots. As mentioned in Section 5.3.1, forming B, C and D involved different techniques, at least in terms of finger movement patterns and the frequency of drying; they entailed additional finger movements that were different from those for A and fewer drying times in the forming process.

The same analysis was carried out on six mother-daughter pairs in S and G villages respectively (Tables 5.2.1 and 5.2.2). All six daughters in S village lived with their mothers and practiced forming pottery. Among the six daughters in G village, Aba and Suna lived with their grandmothers and practiced forming pottery. They had only been forming pots for six to twelve months. While none of the girls in S Village went to school, some potters' daughters in G Village were in school.[10] Among the girls listed in the tables, Taka and Masa were in lower grades of an elementary school at the time (Taka progressed to a junior high school while Masa was married with two children as at 2010). Table 5.2.2 shows that Suna, with one year of pottery experience, was able to form more pottery types than Taka. This was probably because Taka was attending school. By 2010, however, Taka was able to form all of the pottery types listed, just as Suna was.

The order in which the pottery types are arranged in the top row of Tables 5.2.1 and 5.2.2 represents the progression of pottery forming among the girls in S Village. When I compiled the progression of pottery forming among the girls in G village according to this order (Table 5.2.2), I found that they also progressed from small pots to large pots as far as *tila*-shaped pots were concerned. Some of the girls in G village progressed to the differently-shaped D pots earlier than the girls in S Village, though.

There were two daughters in G village who started forming D pots before they started forming A^4 and A^5 pots. It appears that Masa was influenced considerably by her mother, who was forming D-shaped pots almost daily although she had never instructed Masa to start forming D. Masa's elder sister Maga made D-shape pots less frequently and was more inclined to form A^4 and A^5 pots. This suggests that although the girls are influenced by the potters around them, they make their own judgment about which type of pottery they would like to form next.

According to the potters who were born and raised in G village and later married to men in S village, the clay found in G village is more suitable for forming large pots than the clay found in S village. Hence not only unmarried daughters but also married potters in S village do not make D-type pots very often.[11] According to Tables 5.2.1 and 5.2.2, however, the daughters in both S and G villages are able to form D-shaped pots after about six years of experience. It is therefore reasonable to say that the daughters in the Aari area learn to form various types of pots after certain periods regardless of the type of clay.

Among married potters, some may concentrate on making large pots such as *mosa til* and *gabija til*, which sell relatively well at the periodic markets. Others begin to specialize in different types of pottery in response to their aging or

Learning Pottery Making

Table 5.2.1 The progression of pottery forming by six daughters in S Village (06–07/2001)

	A^1	A^2	B	A^3	C	A^4	A^5	D
Kariya (6 months)	●	X	X	X	X	X	X	X
Masa (3rd year)	●	●	◎	X	X	X	X	X
Itayata (4th year)	●	●	●	●	X	X	X	X
Mariya (over 4 years)	●	●	●	◎	●	X	X	X
Asa (over 7 years)	●	●	●	●	●	●	◎	●
Simiya (over 7 years)	●	◎	●	●	●	●	◎	●

Note. A^1: *bun til*, A^2: *ekena til*, B: *disti*, A^3: *mosa til*, C: *jabana*, A^4: *gabija til*, A^5: *sika til*, D: *buna aksh*
▨ = Tila-shaped, ● = formed (confirmed by observations), ◎ = formed frequently (stated in interviews), X = never formed

Table 5.2.2 The progression of pottery forming by six daughters in G Village (05–06/2001)

	A^1	A^2	B	A^3	C	A^4	A^5	D
Aba (6 months)	●	●	●	○	●	X	X	X
Suna (1st year)	●	●	●	●	X	X	X	●
Taka (1st year)	●	●	X	X	X	X	X	X
Liya (2nd year)	●	●	●	○	●	X	X	X
Masa (over 6 years)	●	●	●	●	●	X	X	●
Maga (over 8 years)	●	●	●	●	○	●	●	○

Note. A^1: *bun til*, A^2: *ekena til*, B: *disti*, A^3: *mosa til*, C: *jabana*, A^4: *gabija til*, A^5: *sika til*, D: *buna aksh*
▨ = Tila-shaped, ● = formed (confirmed by observations), ○ = formed multiple times (stated in interviews), X = never formed

changes in their family's social and economic situations (Kaneko 2007a). Moreover, some potters start tailor-making pots[12] for their customers (Table 5.3). In this sense, we can surmise that potters continue to change their techniques and learn different techniques in response to changing social and cultural circumstances, not only when they are unmarried girls, but also after marriage and even when much older.

5.4 Pottery forming and *aani* (hands)

5.4.1 Aari pottery making permits the generation of diverse techniques

We have been examining the process of learning pottery forming techniques in twelve daughters in two villages using the young girls' comment "I came to know pottery making by myself" as a clue. The following characteristics have been found.

Table 5.3 Potters in S Village who can form pots other than the four main types (02/2002)

	A¹	A²	B	A³	C	A⁴	A⁵	D1	A⁶	D2
S2	●	X	X	X	X	X	X	X	X	X
S3	●	●	●	O	X	X	X	X	X	X
S4	O	O	O	O	X	X	X	X	X	X
S5	●	●	●	●	●	O	X	X	X	X
S6	●	O	O	●	O	X	X	X	X	X
S8	●	O	O	●	O	X	X	●	X	X
S9	O	O	O	●	O	●	●	O	O	X
S10	O	O	O	●	O	●	●	O	O	X
S11	O	O	O	O	O	O	O	O	O	O
S13	●	●	●	●	●	●	●	●	O	●
S15	O	O	O	●	O	●	●	O	●	O
S16	O	O	O	O	O	O	O	●	O	●
S17	●	●	●	●	●	●	●	●	O	O
S18	O	O	O	●	●	●	O	O	O	O
S21	O	O	●	●	O	●	●	O	●	O
S22	O	●	●	●	●	●	●	●	●	●
S23	O	O	O	O	O	O	O	O	O	O
S26	O	●	O	●	O	●	O	O	O	O

Note. A¹: *bun til*, A²: *ekena til*, B: *disti*, A³: *mosa til*, C: *jabana*, A⁴: *gabija til*, A⁵: *sika til*, D: *buna aksh* Potters in the list are arranged from the youngest to the oldest. ▨ = Tila-shaped, ● = formed (confirmed by observations), O = formed multiple times (stated in interviews), X = never formed

The potters' daughters grew up touching and feeling clay, spending time beside their pottery forming mothers from infancy. They appeared to have been exposed constantly to finger movement patterns and procedures for forming pottery as well as information about how to avoid breaking pots in the course of performing their daily tasks under instructions from their mothers. The daughters sat close to their mothers in the early days of forming pottery but the mothers never actively intervened with the daughters' pottery forming. They appeared to watch over the daughters' trials and errors with positive attitudes. This was suggested by expressions such as "(Mine and my daughter's) *aani* (hands) are different" and "(My daughter's) *aani* know".

The mothers understood the progression of their daughters' pottery making to different sizes and shapes in relation to the growth of their hands as they matured and became increasingly adept ("*Aani* become soft"). As far as learning to form *tila*

(A) is concerned, the daughters progressed from forming small pots to large pots. Forming larger pots, however, was not something that the daughters could learn to do by being instructed. The daughters got to that stage as they continued to interact with clay through their fingers and made their own judgement. Interviews of potters indicated that daughters start by making a certain type of pot and proceed to form other types of pots in a certain order. However, analysis of the progression of girls of two villages revealed that some girls proceeded to make pots in a different order from the one generally assumed by the potters.

The daughters of potters learn pottery forming techniques in consideration of a wide variety of conditions, including types of clay, fuels for firing, air temperature and humidity on a given day, and relationships with other tasks (e.g., household chores). It is likely that they learn the type of pot they are supposed to make by forming it and the order of progression for pottery forming as they live with their mothers, other potters, and relatives. At the same time, they sit face to face with their material as they work. In the process, some girls begin to employ procedures that differ from their mother's and others in their village (Kaneko 2007b; Kaneko 2007; Kaneko 2010) or progress through a different order than others.

The potters would not talk much about pottery making matters unless I asked them rather persistently. When they talked about matters pertaining to forming pottery, however, they used the expression *aani* (hands) very often. The condition under which the daughters are able to face the material on their own and continue to learn through trial and error seems to be supported by expressions such as "Our *aani* are different" and "Her *aani* know" and a way of thinking based on *aani*. This permits individuals, even those who engage in forming pottery for the first time, to continually change and create techniques through their interactions with the material and the environment. In this sense, the manner of learning techniques in Aari pottery making can be defined as a system of technical learning that allows the generation of diverse techniques. And because the system permits the daughters to learn pottery making through trial and error, these pottery making techniques can be transmitted in the context of changing environment and social situations.

5.4.2 Exploring *mono* using bodily experiences as clues

This chapter has described the process of learning pottery making techniques using important non-verbal elements as indicators: "*mono*" (an order of progression from one pottery type to the next), "the body" (patterns of movement of fingers and the rest of the body), and "field and space" (spatial configuration of the mother and the daughter at their workplace). As a result, it has found variations in the techniques of individual potters although the final products (*mono* as specific types of pots) appear to be identical. It is supposed that these variations are generated in the background of a system of learning pottery making techniques.

The Aari pottery makers' technique acquisition entails learning techniques through interactions between their body and the material and/or *mono*. This is similar to other types of handicraft practiced by the Aari people. The Aari produce a wide variety of *mono* through their handiwork. The *mono* are traded at local markets in most cases. Markets are held twice a week in at least ten locations in the area populated by the Aari people (Kaneko 2006). The *mono* sold and bought at these markets includes not only agricultural produce and foods but also handmade *mono* such as farming equipment and cooking utensils. Very few words are exchanged at the scenes of trading any type of *mono* at the markets (Kaneko 2013). For instance, it might take people more than ten minutes to complete a transaction for the exchange of a pottery product but they said little more than "How much is it?" and "It's XX birr" (birr is the Ethiopian currency unit). While exchanging *mono* involves little verbal information, such exchange contains many social and cultural meanings and much room for interpretation, it is at the same time an interesting point to consider in analyzing the acquisition of conventional techniques and knowledge.

One of the important *mono* traded at markets is the bamboo cylinder for bee keeping (hereinafter "bamboo cylinder"). Honey is a precious source of cash income. Bamboo cylinders are therefore owned by many households and traded frequently at the markets. They are produced in an area of wild bamboo growth more than 2,000 meters above sea level. At least three of several local cultivars of bamboo are used for bee keeping. According to the producers, honey productivity, bee aggression and honey quality are influenced by such factors as the bamboo cultivar, the bamboo weaving pattern, the set up location and the kind of wood used for smoking the bamboo cylinder. Yet, the bamboo cylinder producers almost never made a sales pitch to their customers about the bamboo cultivar, weaving method or set up method at the markets. When I asked them why they would not explain these matters, they replied as follows. "Those who know know. Those who don't know don't know. They have the set up location and the set up method in mind and assess the cultivar and the weaving pattern, then hear the seller's asking price. Those who understand buy and those who don't understand cannot buy". By extensions, we can assume that when the Aari people are trying to acquire some *mono*, they evaluate the *mono* in front of them on the basis of their own experience of interacting with that *mono* before they decide whether to acquire it or not.

This commentary about the bamboo cylinder is a reflection of the view that one acquires techniques and knowledge through experiences mediated by one's body. At the interchange of *mono* between the producers and the customers at markets, evaluations based on verbal expressions are rarely encountered. This parallels beliefs about how pottery making techniques are learned as well.

There are times, however, when evaluations are exchanged between the customers and/or pottery makers who have spent many years interacting with particular *mono*. They evaluate someone's pots and pottery making techniques using expressions such as "*Aani* is good" and "*Aani* is bad". For example, customers used the expression "*Aani* is good" about potters who made durable pots. Potters used the expression "Her *aani* is good" about a reputable potter when they emulate her techniques unsuccessfully. When a purchased pot did not last long, the purchaser might exclaim loudly at the market that "This potter's *aani* is bad". However, the assessment with the expressions "good" and "bad" was continually changing rather than permanent. Even a potter who was assessed as having "good *aani*" by the users of her pots sometimes made pots which were assessed as "bad *aani*" when she failed to adapt to variations in clay and other environmental conditions. In some situations, a potter with "good *aani*" to a certain user was considered as a potter with "bad *aani*" by another user.

Incidentally, I did not find Aari words corresponding to "adept" and "inept" and seldom heard users and potters use comparative adjectives to refer to someone's skill level. This seems to indicate that the users evaluate pottery making techniques according to various criteria of their own while the potters believe that good pottery making techniques vary depending on the individual potter and cannot be determined by simple comparison.

Some of the daughters with six or seven years of pottery making experience and the newly married potters visited the workplaces of other potters who were reputed to have "good *aani*". In most cases, the potters would graciously allow visitors to watch them work.[13] Several years ago, one young married potter of my acquaintance began to form and sell a type of pot that her mother couldn't form. She explains that she had visited and observed many potters in their workplaces before she began trying to form this type of pot. Her attempts to emulate their techniques resulted in a broken pot every time, though. Ultimately, she developed techniques that suited her own *aani* by trial and error.

Aari pottery is made primarily with fingers (the body) and few tools. There is an intimate connection between the diversity of evaluation criteria towards pottery as *mono* and the positive manner in which variations in pottery making techniques are evaluated. To the Aari potters and their daughters, pottery making techniques they have learned contain variations that developed through the accumulation of trials and errors made by an individual. The generation of techniques that allow such variation is the process that has been practiced by all potters, not only as girls, but in day to day pottery making over a long period of time.

The daughters of Aari potters do not learn to form pottery by borrowing their mothers' patterns and styles of certain body movements and procedures. Of course, being present where they can easily observe the way their mothers form pots is an important background condition for learning techniques. However, girls learn techniques through the practice of making pottery as they communicate with the environment in a broad sense, including clay, fuels, temperature and humidity, more than they are influenced by their social relationships with their mothers and female relatives. The communication between the daughter's body and the material is not the same as that between her mother's body and the material. Potters recognize that there are individual variations in the way each potter communicates with her material and these variations lead to the generation of diverse techniques.

As well as daily communication with the general environment represented by clay and other materials, potters must also juggle other chores and information (noise) not directly relevant to pottery forming. For the daughters who have been forming pots through daily communication with the material, dealing with noise is something they have already mastered in the process of learning their techniques. Users also rely on their experiences, mediated by their own body to evaluate the pottery thus produced as *mono*. Each user comes to know the potters who make the pots (*mono*) that suit her way of using the body in the process of repeated experiences. This can be seen as a process in which the user meets the potter whose body (*aani*) resonates with the user's way of using her body through the agency of the pottery (*mono*).

Potters sometimes form pots to cater for the personal requirements of users they have met in this manner, creating new forms in the process. This creativity is one of the abilities acquired by the potters in the process of learning to communicate with the material. Thus, diverse manners of communication between the potter's body and the broader environment and human relationships mediated by *mono* are believed to be the sources of the creation of new techniques and new shapes of pots (*mono*). We can surmise that the acquisition of these techniques and abilities by the potters has been realizable thanks to the system of learning techniques that prompts the daughters to say, "I came to know pottery making by myself". We have been able to arrive at this conclusion by analyzing and examining the technique learning process with a focus on pottery as *mono*, the body that makes pottery, the manner of evaluation, and the verbal representation of the evaluation of the formed pottery.

6 Nature and the Body in Male Sex Stimulants

Masakazu Tanaka

Keywords: traditional Chinese medicine, vitalism, advertisement, sex

Have an erection from the heart! (*Ai no mukidashi* or *Love exposed* 2008, directed by Shion Sono; words of a master stealth photographer)

Superstition and folk belief die harder (and far, far more slowly) than Viagra and other pharmaceutical concoctions make any penis firm (Hopkins 2006: 23).

6.1 What if you can't have an erection?

What can you do when you suddenly find yourself failing to attain an erection? The first time you might be able to dismiss it as a one-off incident. What if it continues to happen every time? They may tell you to have an erection *from the heart* but it is not that simple. Actually, you can give up if it happens all the time. If erectile dysfunction becomes permanent, you can simply stop having sex. You may eventually forget that you are suffering from erectile dysfunction. But what can you do when it happens "occasionally"?[1] It is much more troubling if it happens occasionally for no reason. You become worried when it will happen again.

This chapter considers the relationship between the body and *mono* (things) through an examination of erections and remedies for erectile dysfunction. More specifically, we investigate the magical nature of male sex stimulants (virility enhancers)[2] based on the names of the products, advertising copy, photographs and illustrations, recommendations from grateful users and other information found in magazine advertisements.

6.2 Thoughts on the male body

6.2.1 The instrumentalist view of the world
The Cartesian theory of the body is widely considered to be the archetypal modernist view of the body. It is understood to be the view that lies at the base of the development of modern medicine.[3] From this perspective, the human body is a large complex instrument comprised of various smaller instruments (parts). A human being (the mind) first uses the body as an instrument, and then extends the body endlessly by making more instruments and machines through the agency of the body. Many things have been made as an extension of the human body: the telescope (an extension of the eye), clothing and housing (extensions of the skin), bicycles, motor vehicles and trains (extensions of the leg), telephones and other communications devices (extensions of the ears and mouth), as well as robots and spaceships, for example. These artefacts – so-called modern conveniences – are extensions of the body. They are human instruments which ideally exist to obey humans and to contribute to the better life that humans seek.

Situated at the center of this "instrumentalist view of the world" is the subject or the mind that uses them – the master of the body. The instrumentalist view of the world and mind-body dualism are closely linked. Both see the body and the world (environment) surrounding it merely as "resources" waiting to be approached by the mind. In this view, the subject-object relationship is fixed.

6.2.2 The male body as an instrument
When the male body is studied as a hetero-sexual body, it is generally presented as an active body. This activity is closely linked to power relations between men and women, differences in physical strength, and the activity expected of men in sexual intercourse. The male sex organ plays an important role in sexual intercourse in which the man is expected to be the active participant. In sexual intercourse, the man inserts his protruding sex organ into and rubs against the female sex organ. This instrumentalist view of the penis gives rise to an alter ego of the penis, that is, an "extension". Men have produced numerous instruments that resemble, represent or emulate the penis.

From an instrumentalist perspective, sex for a man consists of finding his own sexual pleasure (by ejaculation) and giving sexual pleasure to his female partner (Tanaka 1999). Generally speaking, a woman also has these two goals in mind. As I shall explain later, however, the penis becomes an instrument in only two of the four situations – where he gives pleasure to a woman and where a woman seeks pleasure. The man is the subject who uses the penis in the former situation. The man uses his penis for the clear purpose of stimulating the woman's sex organ and giving pleasure. Any physical pleasure felt by the man is relatively small in this situation. His pleasure here is in leading the woman to an orgasm by using his own body. What matters here is "erectile ability, expandability, sustainability, recoverability" (Sotomori 1989: 24) and enlarging and penetrating power, and ejaculatory force (Leonard 1983). The man therefore worries if his gun (penis) will operate properly and if it has enough bullets (sperm) (Tamura 1996).

What happens when the man seeks his own physical pleasure, though? Although masturbation is an act of obtaining sexual pleasure (ejaculation) for himself, the means for achieving this is his own hand and not his penis. From this perspective, when a man has sex with a woman for his own pleasure, his instrument is the female sexual organ, which corresponds to the hand in masturbation, rather than the penis. So who is using that instrument? When the woman is voluntarily involved, the woman is using her body as an instrument to give pleasure to the man. Conversely, we can suppose a situation in which the man uses the female sexual organ and the attendant body. It is not so strange to see this situation as the man using the woman's body instead of his own hand. Considering that most manufactured aids to male masturbation come in the form of either a female body (sex doll) or a vagina, it is obvious that this supposition is correct. Men often pay money to temporarily "own" women's bodies, especially female genitals and mouths, to satisfy themselves. This is why the sex industry is accused of commercializing the female body.[4] A similar view underlies the criticism that a selfish man is merely using a woman's body to masturbate. When a man's pleasure is the only goal, the penis cannot be an instrument because it is the pleasure organ.[5]

When a woman seeks gratification by using a male body (penis), the situation is opposite to the male-female relation in the sex industry. Here it is the woman with power or financial resources who uses the penis.

In view of the above clarification, I would like to confine our discussion to the situation in which the penis is regarded as an instrument and used by the man.[6]

6.2.3 When the instrument is broken

How should you respond when the penis is "broken," when it cannot achieve an erection? To many men, a flaccid penis means that they cannot have sex. Just as when you are sick, you feel that your body does not listen to what you tell it to do, you experience a sense that this part of your body is no longer yours. This is the opposite of a situation in which, say, a master craftsman skillfully uses his tools as if they are part or extension of his own body. In the latter case, a tool that is separate from the body becomes integrated into the body whereas in the case of erectile dysfunction something that is part of the body feels as if it is not. Just as a broken down car is merely a bundle of metal scraps, a non-erectile penis is merely a piece of flesh.

We can think of two ways to repair the non-erectile penis. One is to repair the instrument using an instrument, or to reinforce it with another instrument. Let us call this the "reinforcing" approach. It involves the use of erection sustaining rings, hard condom-like devices, vibrators and the like. In this situation, the level of pleasure obtained by ejaculation is dramatically reduced even though that is probably quite natural because the penis is an instrument. The more instrumentalized it becomes, the more efficiently it can give pleasure to the partner, but these instruments do not produce pleasure for the male body. The male body is no longer present when a man makes contact with a woman via an instrument. The sense of unity that arises when a master craftsman uses his hammer or chisel does not arise here.

The other way may be called "untaming", which is a rather magical approach. Untaming is not quite anti-instrumentalist but it features a more holistic approach to the body. It can be called vitalism in a sexual context which attempts to invoke "the power of nature" which lies dormant in the body.[7] According to Suzuki, who reviewed studies of vitalism from the Taishō period (1912–1926), vitalism is defined as:

> A general philosophical theory that holds the concept of "life" as the fundamental principle of its world view and a trend of thought that opposes the conquest of nature by teleological and mechanistic world views based on 19th century positivism. (Suzuki 1995: 3)

Suzuki contrasts vitalism with an orientation towards taming nature. Note that this orientation towards the conquest of an object and what we call purposive rationality and instrumentalism in this chapter are two sides of the same coin. First, one must conquer (master) the instrument (i.e., the male body) itself. Next, one must conquer nature (the female body), the object of the instrument's action, using all sorts of information. The man must have an intimate knowledge of the female body and guide her to an orgasm using his own body. This is the ultimate goal of the conquest in sexual intercourse.

Nevertheless, we must remember that the untaming approach is still governed by the instrumentalist world view in the context of sexual intercourse although the underlying philosophy is different from the reinforcing approach. It is incorrect to say that the vitalism in untaming "opposes the conquest of nature by teleological and mechanistic world views based on positivism". As long as the untaming approach upholds the goal of giving women pleasure, the penis is merely an instrument whose sustained hardness and thickness are desirable. Unlike in the reinforcing approach, however, the penis is not externalized, replaced or alienated by another instrument. In untaming, the pursuit of male pleasure remains a possibility, albeit secondary.

Let us summarize the argument so far. Erectile dysfunction is a denial of (heterosexual) male sex, which is in effect a "death". One of the means to defy, overcome or recover from this death is to use the male sex stimulants we will discuss later in this chapter. Another means is the use of auxiliary instruments and penis substitutes. This latter, reinforcing, approach belongs to the technological (cultural) domain. It can also be called a metonymic (adjacent) approach to the body in that it involves at least a partial substitution of the male sex organ; to repair or reinforce an instrument (penis) using another instrument. By contrast, the use of male sex stimulants is an attempt to stimulate and "revive" the natural power (vitality) mystically lying somewhere inside the male body, at least before Viagra, when traditional Chinese medicine-type remedies were predominant. In this sense, these remedies belong to the natural domain.[8] Their use is an attempt to revive the wild nature hidden inside one's own body by taking in the essence of wild nature. It can be considered metaphorical in that it concerns a mystical whole called vitality rather than a part (component). This means that the male body with erectile dysfunction is placed at an intersection of nature and culture or wild nature and technology (instrument) and exposed to two gazes (Figure 6.1). Penis reinforcing rings and penis mimicking products such as vibrators exist under the technological gaze whereas male sex stimulants are ingested under the gaze of wild nature. Exceptions include topical stimulants such as "bull frog oil" (Ōkubo 1989: 96) and Viagra. Bull frog oil is more of a metonymic as it is applied directly to induce erection. Viagra is ingested but this pharmaceutical product does not reflect any vitalist idea of life and nature.

6.3 The world of male sex stimulants

6.3.1 Male sex stimulants, aphrodisiacs, tonics

Male sex stimulants are important in untaming the male body. Let us provide a brief definition for a male sex stimulant by comparison with similar products.

Nature and the Body in Male Sex Stimulants

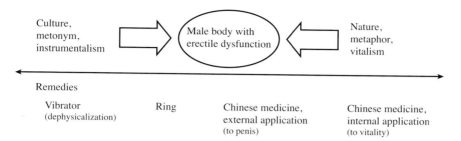

Figure 6.1 The male body and sex

First, an aphrodisiac is a fast-acting substance that arouses sexual desire. A general assumption is that it is used by men to arouse women. Typical products include yohimbine[9] and charred newt.[10]

Male sex stimulants deal with erectile dysfunction and include drugs containing male hormones, various animal body parts, yohimbine, *hachimigan*,[11] goji berries (from the *Lycium Chinese* tree of the Solanaceae family), and *ikarisō* (horny goat weed; *Epimedium violaceum* of the Berneridaceae family) which is said to make sheep and deer frisky. Some of these treatments put more emphasis on increasing the length or thickness of the penis than on the erection, but it is difficult to separate them.

Tonics or invigorants such as winter worm-summer grass are not only effective for erectile dysfunction. Tonics can improve general heath and restore the body's metabolic function. Although male sex stimulants are categorized as pharmacological products while tonics are categorized as health foods in some cases, this chapter treats those which are considered effective for erectile dysfunction as male sex stimulants. As some aphrodisiacs are said to work for erectile dysfunction as well, it is impossible to draw clear boundaries.

I shall describe male sex stimulants in a little more detailed manner, especially in relation to their ingredients.[12] A majority of products available in Japan are based on traditional Chinese medicine ingredients, which can be broadly classified as either plant- or animal-type.[13] Monnier's snowparsley (*Cnidium monnieri*), horny goat weed, seahorse (*Hippocampus coronatus*), and tokay (*Gekko gecko*; Photo 6.1) are four well-known ingredients. Also widely-known are Erabu sea krait, mantis, ant, cobra, soft shell turtle, *habu* (venomous snakes in the Ryukyu Islands), Japanese pit viper, and deer horn. Snakes are generally steeped in liquors with at least a 45% alcohol content and the infusion is ingested. The penis and testicle of deer, fur seal and dog are used to make medicinal products. Among larger animals, tiger, bear and ox (especially dried testis essence and gallstone) as well as rhinoceros horn are famous. There are plant-derived male sex stimulants such as maca (*Lepidium meyenii* root) from South America and guarana (*Paullinia cupana* seed, also a well-known aphrodisiac) from Brazil.

Male sex stimulants can be divided into four groups based on active constituents and efficacy (Tamura 1996).

1. containing male hormones and zinc which are important for sex drive and sperm production
2. deer horn, Asian ginseng, Japanese pit viper and the like that act on blood vessels and circulation
3. *hachimigan* and the like that improve organ functions
4. those which act on psychogenic erectile dysfunction by invigorating or relaxing.

6.3.2 Law and history

Do male sex stimulants really work? What evidence is there that they do? Male sex stimulants are supposed to be subject to laws and regulations concerning pharmaceuticals. People must be thinking that they are sold at pharmacies legally and therefore their effectiveness must have been recognized by the state authorities. Let us look at the relationship between male sex stimulants and the Japanese Pharmaceutical Affairs Act.[14]

The key principles concerning manufacturing approval and other matters were legislated in 1967. The legislation prohibited misleading advertising among other things. A re-evaluation of medical products began in 1971, at which time many male sex stimulants were allowed to continue on the basis of "vested rights". In other words, the manufacture and sale of many of these products was approved without re-examination of their efficacy on the basis that they had previously been sold as drugs.

There are of course many new products on the market. They are sold as health foods, which do not come under the Pharmaceutical Affairs Act. Words such as "effective for…" and "stress" cannot be used in advertisements for these products (Nakata 1996).

There are several possible reasons for a rapid increase in the sales of male sex stimulants from the 1980s. First, it is assumed that the number of men with erectile dysfunction has been increasing. Is this true? An increase in the number of erectile dysfunction cases does not necessarily mean that all the sufferers start buying

Nature and the Body in Male Sex Stimulants

Photo 6.1 Tokay: Distribution & habitat – Southern China, Southeast Asia, India in the 18–32°C temperature zone. Characteristics – Gekko gecko. 20–35 cm in length. Agile nocturnal geckos inhabit rocky mountains and tree hollows. The common name "tokay" comes from the sound of their loud calls. It was speculated that they were sexually vigorous animals because they copulated for a long time and a copulating pair of geckos could not be separated. In fact, they have male hormone-like substances with known aphrodisiac effects. In a natural medicine form (gōkai), the tokay is gutted, attached to a bamboo skewer with fully opened limbs in the shape of a double cross, and dried. In China, freshly killed and gutted tokays are pickled in liquor (Watanabe 2004: 130). A male-female pair of tokays were sold with their bellies together (in Singapore).

male sex stimulants. Another possible reason is that older men, who tended to step back from sexual activity in the old days, now want to continue to have sex. There is a possibility that the percentage of men who suffer from loss of virility is rising in our aging society (Hidaka 1996). It is also possible that sex life plays a more important role in contemporary society for both men and women. Sex life has joined the part of the world that is too good for premature retirement[15] because people's views have changed. Looking at the supply side, the improved availability of male sex stimulants must have been a significant factor.

The Nagoya-based Akahige Pharmacy chain, which opened its first store in 1988, introduced an innovative marketing approach for male sex stimulants by advertising nationwide and making ED issues more visible and less shameful. The company now has eleven stores with professional consultants (2017) and annual sales of 1.8 billion yen [~14.8 million USD] as at 2007. The male sex stimulant market reportedly reached 20 billion yen [~16.5 million USD] during the 1990s.[16] It is also notable that mainstream companies such as Suntory, famous as a whisky distillery, which once had nothing to do with this type of product, began manufacturing and selling "maca" products as health foods early in the 21st century.[17]

The appearance of large advertisements of male sex stimulants (mostly maca and other plant-derived products) in major national newspapers has become especially conspicuous in recent years. How should we interpret this change? It is worth mentioning that some advertisements about ED (erectile dysfunction) have appeared on the front page several times. It is possible to consider that people have become more permissive with words such as ED ("impotence" is no longer used) and virility enhancement. The government policy to try to counter the falling birthrate may also have something to do with this trend towards a more open discussion about male sex stimulants as well as ED.

While the sales of male sex stimulants looked destined to expand steadily, crises came from unexpected quarters. One was the ratification of the Washington Convention (The Convention on International Trade in Endangered Species of Wild Fauna and Flora, 1975) in 1980. Importation of certain animal ingredients for male sex stimulants was prohibited under the convention. For example, manufacturers were forced to discontinue the use of musk in their male sex stimulants.

Another was the launch of Viagra by Pfizer in 1998. The patent for this product was applied for in 1996. This was soon followed by Levitra and Cialis.[18] These pharmaceutical drugs promise results but also carry some risks. However, they are not as readily available, as they must be prescribed by a doctor. Their sales channel is a drawback even though they can be procured in a black market or on the Internet.[19]

6.4 Advertisement of male sex stimulants

6.4.1 Product names

Let us move on to analysis of advertising data. To begin with, we look at the status of advertisements for male sex stimulants among all advertisements in some recently published weekly magazines for adult men, including the May 2008 issues of *Shūkan jitsuwa*, *Asahi geinō*, and *Shūkan taishū*. Their share is not high. Even when advertisements for male sex stimulants and reinforcement devices, clinics (penis augmentation, hardening etc.), and sex toys for sexual enhancement are included, the highest share among the three magazines is only 21% in *Shūkan jitsuwa*. Advertisements for sex trade shops and dating services dominate all three magazines.

Next, we examine advertisements for male sex stimulants found in the end of December issue of the same three magazines in each year between the year of their first issue and 2005. I also use other magazines such as *Shūkan hōseki*, *Shūkan posuto* and *Shūkan gendai* just for reference. Sports and tabloid newspapers and pornographic magazines (including erotic comic magazines for adult men) are excluded from this analysis.

A chronological arrangement of advertisements for 292 kinds of male sex stimulants shows a gradual increase from the 1960s. Advertisements for ten or more new kinds of products begin to appear in the 1970s.

About 49% of them are orally administered. Products for topical application such as sprays and liniments account for 30%. Advertisements with unknown dose methods account for 21%.

The product names can be grouped into three broad types based on the meaning and style. The largest group consists of names containing some sexual metaphors. There are 124 of them (69%), excluding overlapping similar names, of which 61 are in kanji, 47 in katakana, eight in hiragana, five in English and three others. "Tengu jūōsei", "Ryūko", "Indoshinyu", "Seiryokugen", "Power Life", "Superman Gold", "God Lotion", "Missus Killer", "ACT", and "GREAT SEX" are some examples. They are broadly divided into two subgroups – the names associated with sexual acts such as ACT (18%), and the names associated with images such as *tengu* (long-nosed goblin) (51%). The second group of names features ingredient names. There are 36 of them (20%) which contain words such as *suppon* or soft shell turtle (*Pelodiscus sinensis*), guarana and garlic. "Yatsume no sei" or the essence of lamprey (*Petromyzontiformes*), "Otto pin" (from *ottosei* or fur seal, pin implies an erection), and "Guarana choc" are some examples. The third group contains nonsensical names in numbers and letters of the alphabet such as ESS which account for 20 (11%).

6.4.2 The representation of snakes and women

The large sales volume of male sex stimulants and their dubious effectiveness suggest the importance of images (Natsuhara 1996).[20] When we look at one- and two-page advertisements in magazines, we see the prominence of photographs and illustrations. They can be divided into four broad types – powerful looking animals (including mythical creatures such as dragons), young women, photos of the sellers, and photos of the merchandise. A small number of advertisements such as one for "Tengu jūōsei" carry photos of hard-bodied men such as professional wrestlers (*Shūkan jitsuwa*, 27 April 1970). Some of these types are used together in some cases.

The animal images include illustrations and photos of cobras, Japanese pit vipers, other snakes, tigers, ants and soft shell turtles. For example, an advertisement for "Iki-Iki Power" features a cobra with an ant on each side and the phrase "Make erection happen" in large letters (*Asahi geinō*, 26 December 2002, p. 165).

In a rare example, an advertisement for "Vigaretto Sara" explains the effectiveness of "horse penis essence" as follows: "Horses have remarkable sustaining power. (…) Their 'sustaining power' gives the male body strength" (*Shūkan jitsuwa*, 23 December 2004, page number unknown).

Images of animal ingredients are combined with women in some cases.

A combined advertisement for "Cobrapin" and a female stimulant for vaginal application called "Kiritsubo" spreads over two pages with the copy emphatically declaring "Women's pleasures are men's delights" (*Asahi geinō*, 26 December 1985, pp. 44–45). The head of a cobra is represented on the right page and a woman letting out a joyous cry is depicted in the Ukiyo-e style on the left page. The headline exclaims, "One spray makes a man's erection last for a very long time (…)!?" The main ingredient of "Cobra pin" is the "testis essence" of the cobra, whose mating behavior is said to last for hours. Spraying this stimulant immediately before intercourse supposedly sustains an erection for at least 60 minutes. Feedback from users are also included. Mr. Kubota, aged 32, suffered from mild premature ejaculation, but his erection lasted for one hour and gave him "a sense of triumph for the first time". Mr. Iwata, aged 48, enjoyed sexual intercourse twice for the first time in years and looked forward to continuing his sex life.

An advertisement of "Daikakumanseitan" stands out for its artwork combining the main ingredient of an eel with a semi-naked woman (*Shūkan hōseki*, 20/27 December 1985, p. 229) (Photo 6.2). Needless to say, the eel symbolizes an energetic penis. This male sex stimulant claims to have turned the vitality of the guts of natural giant eels into a tablet form. The woman and the eel are overlaid with the copy "The talk of the town! Amazing virility and power now!" In addition to information about ingredients, effects (painful morning erection etc.) and usage, it curiously carries a photo of Managing Director Suzuki, the developer of the product, and his official girlfriend.

Here are several examples of advertisements carrying images of women. An advertisement for "Seimonkei" shows a woman with an ecstatic expression on her face and the copy "This has resolved my discontent!!" (*Shūkan hōseki*, 20/27 December 1985, p. 234). The product was developed by a Chinese medicine doctor in Taiwan and has reportedly been used by more than 50,000 customers. The prominent headline emphasizes its fast-acting property by claiming "Only 3 tablets

Nature and the Body in Male Sex Stimulants

Photo 6.2 An advertisement for "Daikakumanseitan" (Shūkan hōseki, 20/27 December 1985, p. 229). "Managing Director Suzuki calls himself an international playboy and practices sex once a day at the age of 60. The secrets of his super stamina and adventurous spirit are 'love' and 'eels'. Because 'Daikakumanseitan' has been developed based on his own experience and practice, it is easy to guess its effectiveness" (from the advertisement). The copy makes it sound effective.

to get an erection!!" Accompanying information says that it contains a species of tokay that is found only in the Takla Makan Desert, soft shell turtle, red pit viper, and fur seal penis as the main ingredients. Its effects are immediate and sustaining. The advertisement includes a comment from a 45-year-old male user, who says, "I was somewhat doubtful but I began to get a hard-on within only five minutes of taking the tablet (…)".

The photo of a smiling woman with a bare breast jumps out of an advertisement for "Fuyumushi-natsukusa E" (*Shūkan hōseki*, 26 December 1996, p. 108). The headline says "Increase male virility! Fuyumushi-natsukusa E makes you strong, strong, strong!" As well as information about the main ingredient of winter worm-summer grass and feedback from users, it makes the unusual claim that winter worm-summer grass was behind the excellent performances of Chinese women athletes at the Olympics. Mr. Takahashi, aged 51, is "happy with my regained virility" as he can satisfy his wife who is 19 years younger. Mr. Narita, aged 49, says his self-confidence was boosted by "Fuyumushi-natsukusa E", which his wife bought for him.

Not all of the women in advertisements for male sex stimulants are sexy looking or smiling happily. An advertisement for "Zetsurinfuneki" carries a photo of an elderly man and a younger woman sitting back to back and looking troubled (*Shūkan hōseki*, 26 December 1991, p. 170). It probably represents the mood immediately after a failed sexual intercourse. There is a message at the top saying "Your trump card to restore confidence".

There are some other styles of advertisements. One for "Suppon daiogen" shows a photo of the energetic-looking company owner standing with *suppon* or a soft shell turtle in his hands (*Shūkan hōseki*, 25 December 1997, p. 50). One for "Tengu jūōsei" has a photo of a man, who is believed to be the developer of the product, surrounded by its ten ingredients (*Shūkan taishū*, 26 December 1968, p. 74). Some advertisements carry the photos of the products and/or the main ingredients, but they are omitted from our discussion here.

The textual content of the advertisements can be divided into efficacy, ingredients, and anecdotes or users' comments.

Sensory descriptions on the part of men are quite interesting. These include explicit phrases such as "a storm of swirling pleasures", "undulating groin", and "restoring manhood". There are references to youth such as "painfully young days" and "racing young blood" as well as numbers such as "three rounds a night". Perhaps for married couples who are bored with each other, "Dad, energetic everyday, Mom, cheerful everyday".

Just as the previously mentioned claim that "This has resolved my discontent!!", references to women from a man's point of view are notable. For example, "My wife admires my remarkable erection" and "She asked for it again and again".

The developers of soft shell turtle-based "Daiōgen" and the aforementioned "Daikakumanseitan" appear in advertisements as virile men themselves. The former is described as "Now he can go on for a couple of hours" (*Shūkan hōseki*, 24 December 1998, p. 75) while the latter is portrayed as an "international playboy" who "has sex once a day at the age of 60" (*Shūkan hōseki*, 20/27 December 1985, p. 229).

6.4.3 Wild nature in raw materials

From an anthropological point of view, references to the places of origin of raw materials are interesting. Here are some examples (scientific names are author's additions).

- Used in rituals by indigenous Africans, "*kota*" nut essence dynamite. ("SEX Gold", *Shūkan posuto*, 3 August 2007, p. 108)
- Yohimbine is, *Pausinystalia yohimbe* from West Africa (...). ("Akahige Yakkyoku", *Shūkan posuto*, 4 January 2002, p. 171)
- *Herba epimedii*, routinely eaten by northern tribes according to the "food is medicine" principle. This is said to be the source of their robust body and amazing stamina that enable them to survive in a frigid climate. ("ECSTARIN", *Shūkan hōseki*, 23 December 1983, page number unknown)
- *Li ke chong cao wang* (winter worm-summer grass drink) was instantly made famous as a favorite drink of the world's greatest Chinese women's track and field team. "Mushikusaō Royal" uses the highest quality winter worm-summer grass collected in the Tibetan Qinghai Plateau. ("Mushikusaō Royal", *Shūkan taishū*, 26 December 1994, p. 133)
- *Butea superba* is a legume plant found near the Mekong River in Thailand. (...) It has been eaten by men of ethnic minority groups for fertility through the ages. ("Bagas II", *Shūkan taishū zōkan paparachi*, 10 March 2005, p. 745)
- An assassin from the last frontier Tibet! ("Zōbinhō", *Shūkan jitsuwa*, 22 December 2005, page number unknown)
- Tonic medicine used by the indigenous American Indians, saw palmetto (*Serenoa repens*). ("Shōbenkozō", *Shūkan hōseki*, 25 December 1997, p. 182)

Besides male sex stimulants, similar references are also notable among aphrodisiacs such as "Bangarara", which an advertisement claims has been used by the Zulu people in South Africa (*Asahi geinō*, 26 December 1985, p. 85).

It transpires from these references that the power of male sex stimulants is found in the outlying or peripheral regions close to the wilderness (nature). Certain things support the lives of those who survive in the harsh natural environment. Unlike those of Chinese or Indian origin they are discovered by Westerners, processed into male sex stimulants and win popularity. They are finally brought to Japan and so the story goes.

6.5 The body responding to marginal power

Male sex stimulants reportedly invigorate the potency or vitality of the male body by incorporating the power of wild nature. This is why the sex organs of animals such as fur seals and deer are used; they are known to form harems or to reproduce profusely. The same analogical reasoning is at work when matters such as the duration of copulation are emphasized. Rhinoceros horns and camel humps evoke images of strength and endurance. Dried tokays were sold in male-female pairs in a belly-to-belly position (Photo 6.1) that suggests sexual intercourse or coupling. There is even a product containing copulating lizards pickled in liquor (Koizumi 2010: 30). For plant-derived products, one theory for the potency of horny goat weed (*yin yang huo*) says that sheep go into a sexual rut when they eat this plant while the other theory claims that a sheep-like deer called *yin yang* is famous for mating up to 100 times a day because the animal grazes on this plant (Koizumi 2010: 48). As typically seen in *Zetsurin shoku* by Koizumi, it is possible to corroborate the effects of male sex stimulants by highlighting individual ingredients. The psychological placebo effect cannot be ignored either.

Despite the difference between the scientific approach and the magical approach, these are all discrete explanations. From a structural viewpoint, three kinds of otherness are involved, namely, bizarreness, different cultures and illicitness.[21]

The facts that the ingredients for male sex stimulants are often bizarre things (insects, guts, penis etc.) which are not normally eaten by people,[22] their associations with people who are "close to wild nature", and their dubious legality even though they are not illegal, all point to a perception that the potency of male sex stimulants resides in things that are normally excluded or discarded. Snakes and geckos steeped in liquor appear more bizarre and hence more effective than tablets containing the same ingredients. However, I must state that popularity in developed countries is used as a selling point in many of the advertisements for male sex stimulants (e.g., "Powerup Zinc Plus Maca" exclaims, "All the rage in major SEX power the U.S.A.", *Shūkan taishū zōkan paparachi*, 10 March 2005, 198–199) and that wild nature has been imported via the West as mentioned in the previous section. Wild nature is emphasized only with regard to raw materials.

According to Douglas (1966), pollution is "out of place", marginal, situated on the periphery of society. It is marginalized and concealed by exclusionary forces that try to maintain order. However, pollution is not simply abhorred and excluded. It has dangerous latent powers. These powers may be destructive, but at the same time they are beneficial in limited situations. Douglas refers to the pangolin cult of the Lele people of Central Africa as an example.

Pangolin, the scaly anteater, does not fall within the Lele system of animal classification. It is covered with scales but it is not fish; it looks like a lizard but it suckles the young. It gives birth to only one offspring at a time. Such creatures are normally taboo; but pangolins are eaten by young Lele men during their initiation rites. This is believed to ensure both women's fertility and successful hunt.

According to Douglas, the pangolin cult is a circuit that unifies the contradictory attributes of this animal to generate strong and benevolent powers.

The "bizarre things" and other kinds of otherness contained in male sex stimulants possess the powers of wild nature and effect the human body. In other words, male sex stimulants can be regarded as pangolins in contemporary society. Contemporary versions of the pangolin are of course secularized and commercialized; their effects are suspicious. Yet, they seem to be analogous to the pangolin cult in terms of the seriousness of the men who seek them and the expectations of activated masculinity – which is not the question of the penis alone; it is the question of masculinity because of its association with the penis.

Since male sex stimulants are medicine or food, their ingredients are naturally absorbed into the body to produce effects. Furthermore, the process in which wild nature acts on the human body appears to coincide with interactions between nature, things and other bodies which have been described with terms such as "call and response" (Minato 2009), "synchronization" or "sympathy" (Sugawara 2000: 205), and "correspondence" (Imamura 2001: 121). Hence one's communication with wild nature begins at the very moment he spots the advertisement.

6.6 The launch of Viagra

Finally, let us return to the comparison between reinforcing and untaming, the two ways to restore male sex function suggested at the start.

On the one hand, the reinforcing approach increases the instrumentality of the penis, alienating the body and sexual pleasure as a result. It relates to a part, metonym and adjacency. On the other hand, the untaming approach invokes latent powers or the vitality of the male body. The vitality is supposed to be an aggregate of certain chemicals such as male hormones but the causal relationship to their reputed effects are not always clear. Masculine nature (wild nature) supposedly resonates with the wild nature of the sex stimulants and is revitalized. This is a kind of sympathetic magic effect, seeking a metaphorical relationship with the body.

Although the untaming approach fits within the framework of instrumentalist thinking in the sense that it is employed for the purpose of restoring the inherent function of a pleasure instrument called penis, it does not completely alienate the male body. It tries instead to invoke the inner life or wild nature of the body rather than seeking to replace it with another instrument. The reverberation between wild nature and the male body discussed in this chapter is analogous to a physical sensation in sex – reverberation between the two bodies. We surmise that this is where we find the possibility of Eros, which destabilizes, criticizes and overcomes an instrumentalist perspective to see the body as an instrument or a Logos viewpoint from within.[23]

This classification, however, is drastically changed by the appearance of Viagra. This product is a pharmaceutical drug that makes erection happen with pinpoint accuracy based on the instrumentalist view of the body. The launch of Viagra signified the relocation of the penis from the mysterious world of male sex stimulants to the realm of modern medicine. It is a consequence of the medicalization and demystification of the male body. The penis can attain an erection anytime as demanded, thanks to Viagra. However, it contributes to greater dependence on modern medicine. Both men and women are at the mercy of the penis erected by Viagra. The apparent popularity of male sex stimulants suggested by the never-ending cycle of advertisements despite the existence of Viagra may be a show of modest but firm resistance put up by men against Viagra's control of the body.

Part IV
The Agency of *Mono*

7 Masks as Performers: *Topeng*, a Balinese Masked Dance Drama

Yukako Yoshida

Keywords: mask, materiality, performing arts, thing-centered description, unthing-like thing

7.1 A mask: An un*thing*like *thing*

A mask is said to be both a thing and not a thing at the same time (Hashi and Moriya 1981: 158). According to one performer of *topeng*,[1] a masked dance drama of Bali, Indonesia, a mask is like a wild animal and one needs to tame it (by learning to use it well). Another performer says that he is "married" to his masks and would never lend his "wives" to others. We can see that a mask is more than a "mere material thing" in the context of Balinese society. A mask, which often exercises strong agency[2] by connecting with symbolic meanings, personalities or mysterious forces, can be defined as a *mono* (*thing*) at the opposite end of a spectrum from where we place a "stone", which according to Uchibori (Epilogue in this volume) is the farthest place from agency in the ordinary sense.

In this chapter I examine ways in which the mask is a "material thing" in the context of the study of *mono/things*. Of course the mask is a "material thing". Wooden masks used in *topeng* are tangible, transferrable and exchangeable. They can deteriorate, be reprocessed or reproduced. The aim of this chapter is to examine how the materiality of masks effects the performance and succession of *topeng*. What is the effect of a tangible mask when introduced as an agent to an intangible dance drama? How does this materiality intersect with the un*thing*like condition of the mask? This chapter attempts not only to analyze the activity of *topeng* through descriptions of things (masks), but also to treat *topeng* as a subject to examine the "mutually constitutive" (Tokoro and Kawai in Introduction) relationship between things, culture and society. Culture or society provides contexts and meanings to things, however at the same time, things at least partially constitute culture and society.

This chapter concentrates on the mask in post-performance scenes. It will not consider the mask production process or the behavior of the mask during performances due to space limitations. Some studies of dance and theatre have treated thick facial makeup as a temporal mask (e.g. Beeman 1993: 382). However, facial makeup is applied prior to a performance and wiped off post-performance whereas a mask continues to exist and be used in repeated performances. This allows a mask to work very differently from facial makeup. Regarding this material characteristic of occupying a certain space for a certain period of time as our first clue, we shall consider various events that are caused after performances by the masks, the performer, and other associated people.

During my study over a period of thirteen months from August 2006, I had the opportunity to learn part of the *topeng* dance and to take part in *topeng* performances with various actors. The advice and opinions that *topeng* performers gave me as a novice dancer, are analyzed in this chapter as well as their interviews.

Several different performances are categorized as *topeng* in Bali. Our discussion will focus on a form called *topeng wali*, which is performed as part of rituals.[3] *Topeng wali* is considered to be an essential part of temple anniversary festivals (*odalan*), cremation (*ngaben/pelebon*) and subsequent rituals (*nyekah/ngasti/maligia*), tooth filing (*matatah/masangih/mapandes*), weddings and other religious events of a certain scale. It serves to bring the ceremony to a successful conclusion as well as entertaining the humans, deities and evil spirits (*buta kala*) who gather at the ritual. In this chapter, any reference to *topeng* means *topeng wali* unless otherwise specified.

7.2 Preceding studies on *topeng* and masks

Preceding studies of *topeng* have focused on the connection between the performance narrative and prevailing social conditions. Consequently, the scope of discussions of the masks themselves was limited until the turn of the 21st century. These limited analyses and more recent works with masks can be divided into two groups, based on their approach.

One group describes and analyses the characters represented by individual masks and the divinities that reside in the masks (Young 1980; Dunn 1983). In particular, they commonly associate figurative features with symbolism. For example, Young associates three types of masks – refined, coarse, and strong – with the castes of the figures that they represent. She argues that the characters expressed by respective masks play a part in teaching etiquette and norms related to the caste (*kasta*) system in Balinese society (Young 1980: 155–195).[4] This type of study considers the meanings and characters that the masks represent and the invisible beings that reside within them by ignoring their materiality. In so doing, they overlook various events caused by the masks' materiality.

The other group of studies treats a mask as a source of otherness. These focus on the relationship it forms with the selfhood or personhood of the actor who wears it (Emigh 1996; Coldiron 2004). Emigh defines the relationship between a mask and a performer as "a paradigm for the relationships between self and other (and self and self) that lie at the heart of theatrical process" (Emigh 1996: xvii). As far as *topeng* was concerned, however, Emigh was more interested in masked performances than masks themselves. Coldiron treats a mask as a more central subject. She is concerned with the effects of a mask on its wearer. The mask facilitates the performer's transformation by covering her/his face. The face has a central place of importance in the performer's identity. Concealing the face with a mask can give her/him a new identity (Coldiron 2004: 43–44). Her study shares some of the interests of our discussion in this chapter in its multilateral consideration of the action of a mask during a performance without reducing the mask to the character that it represents or its spiritual force. For example, the mask gives the performer a sense of separation from her/his own body during a performance, not only hiding her/his own face but also constraining her/his field of vision and breathing (Coldiron 2004: 194, 200–201). This analysis reveals that the mask acts on the performer's body in multiple ways during a performance on a material level as well. Nevertheless, Coldiron's primary interest is in deciphering the transformation process and little attention is paid to the behavior of the masks in situations outside of the context of the performer's transformation. By examining the continuing interactions between masks and people after performances, this chapter reveals the diverse ways the masks work beyond their function as a transformational device.

7.3 An overview of *topeng* and *taksu*

Many of the masks used for *topeng* are made to order by craftspeople over a period of several days. The traditional method of coloring is called *warna Bali*, which entails the application of dozens of coats of natural coloring, but acrylic paints are predominantly used these days. Among several types of suitable wood, *pule* (*Alstonia scholaris*) is preferred. It is easy to process, sufficiently strong, and compatible with paints. The spiritual power of this tree is also important. This tree species has a special place in Balinese mythology and commonly grows in temple yards and cemeteries (*setra/sema*). It is said that the tree grew out of drops of semen from the god Siwa.

Topeng accompanies various rituals and is performed during them.[5] Some temples have masks, but a majority of *topeng* masks are owned by the performers, who bring their own masks to each performance. In most cases, one to three actors share five to ten roles, which they perform by switching masks. The performance is improvised within the bounds of some loose rules. Based on a dynastic genealogy of Java or Bali (*babad*), a drama unfolds with additional commentaries on mythology, traditions and teachings as well as contemporary jokes and social/political commentaries. Common characters include the king (*dalem*), the minister (*patih*), the servant and story teller (*penasar*), and various comical villagers (*bondres*). In the final scene, a character called Sidakarya appears and performs certain movements while chanting mantras. The supposed function of *topeng* to bring about a successful conclusion to a ritual is mainly performed by Sidakarya.

Prior to a performance, the actors offer prayers to the god of *taksu* in their family temples (*sanggah/marajan*) at home. It is not easy, even for the Balinese people, to explain *taksu*. In rather simple terms, it is the power to charm people. It is often translated into English as "charisma" and "aura" but strictly speaking, it has different nuances.[8] All actors agree, though, that *taksu* in *topeng* is, first, the state of vividness/liveliness (*idup*) of the mask. When the mask, a lifeless object, is animated – dancing, speaking and singing – it captivates people. Some say that the mask acquires a "character" (*karakter* [I]). Another manifestation of *taksu* is when the audience is so drawn into an actor's performance that they are enthralled by every word and movement.

The actors explore gestures, movements, voices and speeches befitting the characters of respective masks in order "to inject a spirit or a soul in the mask" (*menjiwai topeng* [I]) or "to bring the mask to life" (*menghidupkan topeng* [I]). A substantial part of improvisational acting in *topeng* performances is guided by the expressions on the masks. The actors pray to the god daily for *taksu* and invite deities to visit their masks and theater before each performance. Furthermore, they aim to make their *topeng* performance more appealing by deepening their bonds and giving spiritual power to the masks.

7.4 Daily lives of masks and actors: Nurturing the masks

Some actors spoke of "nurturing the masks" (*memelihara topeng* [I]) in their interviews, referring to both their ownership of the masks and the dedication of rituals and offerings to the masks. We shall consider the process by which actors nurture a mask and the various ways masks act on actors.

Photo 7.1 Masks laid out before a performance (Sidakarya at top left)

Photo 7.2 Bondres (left) and Penasar (right)

7.4.1 Storage of masks

Masks owned by a performer are stored in their homes. It is said that a new mask should be kept within view, gazed upon and handled from time to time, rather than being stored away. Some actors reportedly try to take on the mask's persona by sleeping with it and dreaming about it (Emigh 1996: 117; Coldiron 2004: 199). Older masks are normally stored in a basket. They are treated as sacred objects in the home. Masks are not placed directly on the ground or floor, for the lower world (anything below or underneath) is associated with uncleanliness in Balinese cosmology. Those who are in a state of uncleanness, including a recent death in the family, having visited a dead person's house, and menstruating, do not touch the masks.

In contrast to the masks' vivid and vibrant movement during performances, they appear to remain static in storage. As discussed later, however, the masks undergo subtle changes as they slowly deteriorate or become discolored. In some contexts, the stored masks can appear to be more dynamic, as in the following example.

The actor K kept his masks in a pavilion on the eastern side of his house compound (*bale danging*). One day they all went up in flames along with the storage basket. K had offered incense to the masks earlier in the day, but had forgotten about it by the evening. Apparently the masks caught fire from the incense. Oddly enough, the fire did not spread to the pavilion itself, although it destroyed all of the masks and head dresses (*gelungan*). K consulted a priest with whom he was on friendly terms about this incident. The priest told him that storing the masks in the eastern pavilion instead of inside of the family temple was what caused the incident. The eastern pavilion was adjacent to a walkway along which menstruating women, for example, might come and go. They concluded that the masks combusted because the deities residing in them objected to where they were stored.

In considering the actions of *mono* (*things*) in Bali, one must take Balinese cosmology into account. In Balinese cosmology, the world consists of *sekala* (a visible and perceptible realm) and *niskala* (an invisible and intangible realm). In general terms, the realm to which human bodies and materials belong is *sekala* while deities and evil spirits live in *niskala*. The two realms are inextricably linked and many of the events and phenomena we see and experience daily are understood to be consequences of what is happening in *niskala*.[9] In this context, each and every thing (even a mask in storage) is potentially a medium for messages from *niskala*. For example, a car broken down in the middle of the road or a large sum of money unexpectedly falling your way *can* be attributed to invisible forces at work. This *sekala-niskala* world view plays a significant part when people are captivated by the lively dances of the supposedly lifeless masks and see the deities acting in the form of *taksu*, or when people interpret the combustion of masks as an expression of the deities' anger. Following the priest's advice, K conducted a purification ritual for the eastern pavilion. He has subsequently had new masks and head dresses made and stores them in the family temple within the home compound.

7.4.2 Rituals and offerings: Relations between masks, humans and deities

Some rituals are conducted specifically for masks. *Melaspas* is a ritual to purify by removing pollution. *Pasupati* is a ritual to confer spiritual power. One performer explained these two rituals using a house as a metaphor: *melaspas* cleans the house and *pasupati* opens the door to invite in deities. The ritual *masakapan* is performed to "marry" masks and a performer. The mask (or the deity residing in it) and the performer form a strong bond through this ritual. Additionally, the actor who plays the Sidakarya generally must purify him- or herself through a ritual called *pewintenan*, performed with the actor wearing a sacred mask and chanting mantras.

I was able to observe the rituals of *pewintenan* for an actor, *melaspas* and *pasupati* for masks, and *masakapan* for masks and the actor in a village in Badung Regency, on 8 March 2008. The series of rituals was conducted beginning around nine o'clock in the evening. It was conducted by a priest at the actor's home, where a small pavilion was set up and large numbers of offerings were prepared, including a roasted pig. The Sidakarya mask was placed at the center, surrounded by a head dress, a sword (*keris*) and other *topeng* accessories. Other masks were placed on a separate table along with some offerings, suggesting that these rituals were primarily for the Sidakarya mask. After following various procedures over a three hour period, the actor put on the Sidakarya mask and its head dress, performed a short dance, and chanted his newly learned mantras. The rituals were attended by his family, relatives, and a dozen or so of his fellow *topeng* performers and friends. These acquaintances were there to witness the rituals. In Bali, "three witnesses" (*tri saksi*) – deities (*dewa saksi*), humans (*manusa saksi*) and evil spirits (*buta saksi*) – are considered necessary for the successful conclusion of a ritual, hence, those family and friends are important participants. Their participation functions as recognition by the community that the actor has been purified and the mask has been deified.

Besides these rituals, various offerings are given to masks. Small offerings are made daily. Larger offerings are made at full moon, new moon, and *kajeng kliwon* (a sacred day that comes around every fifteen days). Even larger offerings are made on the day of *tumpek* –every 210 days. Priests are sometimes invited to conduct rituals. While a majority of actors are men, most of the offerings are prepared by women. The masks do not 'belong to' the individual actors alone. The act of owning and nurturing the masks inevitably involves spouses and other family members.

The offerings serve to appease and strengthen the spiritual power of the mask. But they do more than that too. Some offerings are eaten by people after they are taken down from the shrine. In Bali, leftover food offerings are called *lungsuran*. They include fruit, sweets, meat and rice and are considered to be more than just food. The people say they are tastier and better.[10] I was often encouraged to eat the leftover food offered to masks, as it would make me "perform *topeng* dances better". *Lungsuran* is a gift from the deities residing in the masks to people. An offering is in fact a reciprocal interaction between deities and people, mediated by things such as masks and the things being offered.

A mask that has become "home" for an invisible being is said to be *tenget*. This word is often used interchangeably with the Indonesian word *keramat* (sacred), and refers to a force or condition associated with a certain kind of fear or danger. The Brahmana man A, who is also a mask maker and actor, explained to me: "We are not at liberty to place it indiscriminately or talk (about it) indiscriminately. We must have respect and value it highly. This is *tenget*" (A's interview, 25 August 2008).

The sacred powers of masks are inextricably linked to a number of taboos and dangers. They demand the ongoing dedication of offerings and special treatment. Basically, the degree of sanctification of masks varies depending on its owner's attitude or disposition. For example, A avoids sanctifying the masks he makes for his own use in performances. He says, "Masks are just tools". He has only one underage son. He is concerned with the future of his masks. "Once you sanctify them, you have to do a lot of things. Who's going to take care of them after my death?" And he is critical of other actors who are more concerned with conducting rituals for their masks than developing their skills. While *topeng* is an important part of rituals, its other function is to entertain people with songs, dances and jokes (Yoshida 2009). Whereas masks used in other masked drama genres such as *wayang wong* and *calonarang* are usually owned by temples, as discussed, many *topeng* masks are privately owned by actors. Their treatment varies greatly from one actor to another. The double function of *topeng* permits a wide spectrum of representations from a "deified vessel" to a "mere stage prop". Among a variety of masks owned by each actor, those of the characters with godhood or similar attributes such as Sidakarya, the king and the high priest (*pedanda*) tend to become the subject of rituals.

However, A does make an offering – albeit a small one – on the day of *tumpek* despite his objection to the sanctification of his masks mentioned above. In sum, *topeng* masks in Bali, especially those used in ritual performances, are more-or-less associated with sacred beings. I was likewise reluctant to conduct a ritual for my mask, considering that I would take it to Japan in the future. Nevertheless, my host family began to place a small daily offering on the basket in which my mask was stored as soon as I bought it. And a dancer in the same village recommended that I should conduct a ritual for the mask. For him, owning a mask that has not been sanctified in a ritual is "like having a bird cage and not opening its door". He told me, "Perform a ritual. Sang Hyang Taksu [the god of *taksu*] may come in".

Upon discovering that I had not performed a ritual for my mask, another actor, W, earnestly invited me to bring my mask to his *tumpek* ritual for his masks. W conducts a very large ritual for his Sidakarya mask. When he has troubles, he consults this mask. He receives messages from the mask in his dreams. W persuaded me by saying, "You don't have to be afraid of performing a ritual for your mask; having a sacred mask is just like having an amulet". In this way, my mask was gradually pulled into relationships with deities, monks and offerings even though I, its owner, did not actively seek them.[11]

7.4.3 Repeated performances and the changeability of masks

After the aforementioned fire, the actor K conducted a much larger ritual for the new masks he bought. He looked pleased as he said he had better masks now, but he also appeared to miss his old masks.

> What is sad for me is that the old masks were one with me. They performed *ngayah* in various places and already had aura… (K's interview 14 March 2008).

Ngayah means voluntary religious service and, in this context, refers to the experience of performing *topeng* at rituals.

The actors say that masks grow in appeal, gain more *taksu* and blend with their actors better when they are used repeatedly. Actors develop their skills to tap into the characters of their masks and deliver more lively performances as they gain experience and refine their performances based on feedback and advice from the audience. In addition to this technical improvement, it is important to note that many *topeng* performances are staged as *ngayah* of which part or all of the proceeds are donated. The *ngayah* is an act similar to prayer. Actors receive *taksu* from a god as they repeatedly perform it. Actors also point out that repeated use increases the appeal of the masks because they absorb the actors' sweat during every performance. In fact, some actors rub their sweat into their masks after a performance. The masks are also sprayed with holy water and receive offerings before and after each performance. Furthermore, it is said that the power of the "place" of performance also accumulates in the masks in some form.

The masks change physically, as well. Those painted with the natural colors of *warna Bali* in particular slowly discolor over time. The color of the king and Sidakarya masks gradually changes from white to cream. Masks are seen as more attractive as they age. The discolored *warna Bali* masks are treated with great care and affection.

Performance is an intangible thing. Each time it is born it disappears again. *Topeng* is performed in a small corner of a ritual space without any large stage props. When a performance is over, the audience surrounding it disperses and the space is dismantled, returned to the previous state as if nothing had happened. Furthermore, as *topeng* is unscripted and highly improvisational, dances, songs, narratives and jokes are all influenced by the circumstances of the performance and the preferences of the audience. The program content changes every time it is performed. The characteristics of masks to store the history of repeated performances and to accumulate appeal and spiritual power provide an interesting contrast with the once-only and transient nature of *topeng* performance.

In addition to slow and gradual changes such as those mentioned above, the masks can also change their expressions suddenly and drastically. A young actor named I Wayan Sunatra has a *wijil* mask that is missing one side of its supposedly symmetrical moustache.

Wijil is a somewhat comical character. He is the younger brother of *penasar* and a servant to the king. One day one side of *wijil* mask's moustache broke off accidentally, but Sunatra used it on stage and elicited more laughs from the audience than he expected. Since then, he has been using this mask without repairing it because he thinks it is funnier. When *wijil* is on the scene, the moustache is an object of laughter. The goofy appearance becomes a device to make *wijil*'s jokes sound funnier. Through an accidental partial detachment of its moustache in the course of repetitive use by the actor, the mask has acquired a new face which the mask maker and the actor never expected and brought a new expression out of the actor. Masks undergo subtle and sometimes drastic changes of expression after leaving the hands of their makers as they age, break, get repaired or modified. When we talk about a mask as a "persona", we tend to think of its pre-determined and fixed nature (e.g., Watsuji 1988). If we reduce a mask to a persona, we overlook the dynamic nature of the mask that changes its complexion with time or through accidents.

7.4.4 Inheritance and bestowal – Masks motivating people

Masks can be used for more than 100 years depending on how they are used. Longstanding families of *topeng* performers keep old masks that have been passed

Photo 7.3 The Wijil mask missing a half of its moustache

on from their grandfather's or even older generations. I Ketut Wirtawan (1969–) is the grandson of the former leading *topeng* actor I Nyoman Kakul (1905–1982) who has inherited a set of masks from the grandfather. Wirtawan learned dance basics and *topeng* skills from his grandfather Kakul and his father (I Ketut Kantor 1943–2008), who in turn had studied under Kakul. Wirtawan trained under other dancers in his village as well. He is also a graduate of the Institute of the Arts and incorporates various elements into his dance techniques. While the art of performing changes in various ways over generations, masks are passed on as they are from earlier generations. When actors perform *topeng* as they switch their masks one after another, the masks may seem to be "temporal faces".[12] Yet, when we remember that masks are passed on across generations from a parent to a child and a grandchild as in the case of Wirtawan, and that the masks owned by some temples have been worn by generations of local community members in performances, we can see another aspect of masks: the actors are "temporal bodies" for the masks.[13] In the photo at the beginning of the Prologue (p. i), Wirtawan is performing in an old man mask inherited from his grandfather Kakul. Kakul had participated in making this mask. In an earlier study, Emigh (1996: 124) presents a photograph of Kakul dancing as a "temporal body" for this mask in 1975. Among the masks Wirtawan has inherited, however, the *penasar* mask is too small for him to wear. As masks are material objects, their inheritance may be limited for physical reasons in some cases.

These family heirloom masks motivate the descendants to become *topeng* performers. The former president of the Institute of the Arts I Made Bandem mentions ownership of masks as one of the reasons for the prevalence of hereditary succession of the *topeng* art form in the past.

> In the old days, people usually received their masks from the royal court. If a person is a descendant [of an actor], he owns sacred masks from the royal court he has inherited. That's why he *must* perform. (Bandem's interview 28 July 2007; brackets and emphasis added)

Bandem inherited masks from his father I Made Kredek (1909–1979), who was a master *topeng* actor, and sometimes wears them in performances. Bandem's sister Ni Nyoman Candri is one of a small number of female *topeng* performers in Bali. She used to be a famous *arja* dance-drama performer. Her late father's masks are one of the reasons why she took up *topeng* (Yoshida 2008: 79). Her brother Bandem was extremely busy in his capacity as a scholar and educator and rarely used his father's masks. That was why she considered using those masks.

Masks are sometimes acquired by means other than inheritance, too. As Bandem mentioned, masks were traditionally given by the king to performers as rewards. Actors showed me seasoned masks that they said were royal gifts on many occasions during my research. While these royal masks are still valued highly, it is easy to imagine the intense appeal they had to an audience when the court was a powerful presence. An attractive mask given by the king is testament to the power of the king who could command a craftsman to produce such an excellent mask as well as testament to the patronage of the king which the actor was privileged to receive. It is possible to say that the king's capacity and favor were "objectified" in the form of a mask. During his interviews, Bandem showed me a minister mask, which was given to his father Kredek by the last Klungkung king I Dewa Agung Oka Geg (1896?–1965)[14] in around 1963 (16 July 2009, 21 August 2009). This mask was given to Kredek when he performed *topeng* at a ritual hosted by Dewa Agung. On the back of the mask, there were some words reportedly written by Dewa Agung.

The relationship between the two deceased people, the king and Kredek, is still visible today in the form of a mask. The mask is passed on to the next generation, forms part of the appeal of the art, and confers a kind of prestige to the family line that inherits it.

Photo 7.4 The mask reportedly given by Dewa Agung

Unlike self-contained and stationary art objects, masks are imperfect entities; they exist in a strange state of being, in a sense, as bodiless faces. Mask makers in turn exercise their ingenuity so that they present their characters and appeal in the strongest possible way when they are worn by humans and move with specific musical accompaniment. Furthermore, there are masks that only cover part of the human face which are made to complete a facial expression by blending with the human face. The inherent incompleteness of masks motivates their owners to wear them and perform. In addition, gifting or handing down masks may encourage the recipient to perform *topeng*. For example, Cokorda Raka Tisnu, a mask maker and faculty member at the Institute of the Arts, sometimes donates masks to actors and temples in order to promote the activity of *topeng* performers or to introduce *topeng* to communities that do not have a strong tradition of performing *topeng* at rituals (interview, 16 Sept 2010). When he receives orders for other types of masks such as *barong*, he sometimes uses wood offcuts to make Sidakarya and other *topeng* masks and give them to the clients for free.

People also factor their hopes and expectations for the future into their masks. Many of the actors I interviewed appeared to expect that their sons or young relatives would become actors and inherit their masks in the future (regardless of whether they were hereditary actors themselves). As a society-wide norm, such expectations lead to a sense of security, or a feeling of hope, that the art of *topeng* will continue into the future as long as the masks exist. In an article about the rise and fall of Balinese performing arts, through which he examines how a once predominant genre can lose popularity and decline, the journalist Putu Setia states:

> Among them, only *topeng* is unlikely to disappear completely, unlike *gambuh* and *arja*. This is because many of the masks used in *topeng* (*tapel* in Balinese) are in the custody of temples.[15] Those masks are regarded as sacred and stored safely. (Setia 1994: 173)

Both *gambuh* and *arja* are performed with facial makeup. Comparing *topeng* to these similar dance-drama genres, Setia observes that the continuous presence of the tangible things, masks, supports the transmission of the art form. In reality, some masks are stored and unused for a long time. But someone may come along in the future who becomes motivated to "inject life into those masks" as long as they are kept in storage. The continuing presence of the masks not only provides connections to the experience of past performances but also bring people hopes and possibilities for the future.

7.5 The actions and materiality of masks

The primary role of a mask is to attach to the face of an actor and help him/her to express the personality and attributes of the mask's character. Unlike facial makeup or an abstract "role" given in a script, however, a mask is a concrete object that is taken back to the actor's home after each performance and continues to interact with people off-stage. With the mask's materiality enduring for a considerable length of time as a starting point, this chapter has examined interactions between the mask and people that continue after performances. If having an influence on people or drawing some act or emotion out of people can be called an "action" of the mask, the mask certainly has been acting in many different ways outside of the context of the "transformation of the actor" (Coldiron 2004).

First, as we have seen, many *topeng* masks are vessels or "homes" for deities. It is important to note that sacred masks do more than conferring supernatural power onto the actors who wear them. The masks as things turned deities into a visible and tangible existence, influenced people to engage in the act of making offerings on an ongoing basis, gave leftover food offerings to people, and expressed their anger when they were stored in the wrong place.

And masks are more than mere vessels for deities. Once they leave the hands of their makers, they individually accumulate episodes of their involvement with actors and other people. The sort of response a mask evokes (or does not evoke) depends largely on these episodes. The episodes, including the rituals it has experienced as well as where it came from and how many performances it has experienced with whom, are physically engraved in the mask and sometimes accumulated in people's memories. The mask with a history of these episodes, sacred power and *taksu* does more than captivating the audience from the stage. It continues to attract people, bringing various acts and feelings out of them even after it leaves the stage. So how does the mask's materiality exert influence in the many different actions performed by the mask off stage?

First, the characteristic of a mask to "continue to exist for a long time" confers a certain continuity on repeated performances. As mentioned earlier, each *topeng* performance has a singular and transient nature. Through its repeated use in performances, the mask continues to exist in this world, accumulates attractiveness and spiritual power from past performances, and carries them into future performances. As a consequence, it has created a path of succession that is unique to masked dramas and not available to other facial makeup-based performing arts; the ongoing presence of masks has promoted the continuation of this art form.[16] The ability of the mask to be passed down from generation to generation is also important. We asked at the beginning of this chapter what effects the addition of tangible masks has on intangible performing arts. Strictly speaking, however, the actor's body is also tangible. Just as masks are vessels for deities, human bodies are temporal vessels for souls according to the Balinese-Hindu world view. In the light of these points, it is possible to say that *topeng* is a performing art form nurtured by two things – the human body and the mask – together. Yet, the mask and the body exist in different time streams. Masks made by deceased craftspeople and masks that have gathered experience together with deceased grandfathers have been carried down to the present time and continue to experience more performances.

Second, the mask facilitates the transmission of the original owner's intention, power and experience as it passes from hand to hand because of its material characteristic of transferability. When the mask is passed on, the intention and social prestige of the original giver of the mask – the king and the craftsman, for example – the cumulative experience of performances of its past owners (actors) whose sweat has permeated the mask, and many rituals performed by them for the mask exert influence on the new owner; it motivates him/her to become a performer, brings about new expressions, and arouses a sense of attachment. These effects augment the attractiveness and spiritual power that the mask radiates to an audience during performances. Combined with continuous presence, the material characteristic transferability turns a *topeng* performance into an intersection of the performer's intentions and actions with those of many other people who have been involved with the mask offstage even though they do not appear directly in the performance. Only a few actors and a set of masks appear on stage. However, the actions of the craftspeople, the actors' families, priests, and friends who witnessed rituals for the masks as well as the past owners and the original giver and those involved in making and "nurturing" the masks all support the masks to captivate and awe the audience in performance.

Third, the physical changes masks suffer through use such as deterioration and breakage can also be a source of "actions" for the masks. The materiality of masks which manifests in discoloration, deterioration or burning persists as a record of the "ages" of individual masks or, for example, an expression of the anger of deities who have deserted them. There is contingency in the masks' physical changes, as we saw in the example of a mask missing one side of its moustache. Under such circumstances, masks may acquire new expressions or bring out new *topeng* performances that people never expected. The "unthing-like" actions of the masks such as aging, venting anger and refreshing performances are generated by very "thing-like" phenomena such as deterioration and breakage.

Thus, masks nurture the activity of *topeng* in manners that are unique to things and different from the way the human body works. The masks accumulate a wealth of episodes and power in the course of their interactions with people over a long time. When they are inherited, they motivate the next generation to learn *topeng*. This is considered to be one of the most important actions that the masks undertake offstage.

8 "Living" Musical Instruments: On Changing Sounds of *Suling*

Kaori Fushiki

Keywords: Indonesia, Balinese gamelan, musical instruments, sound change, "materiality" of sound

8.1 Prelude – *Suling gambuh*

A Balinese dance drama form called *gambuh* is believed to be one of the original forms of Balinese dance. It tells the story of the Javanese hero Prince Panji and features lines of script in the ancient Javanese language of Kawi, delivered by the dancers themselves.[1] *Gambuh* is accompanied by music played by a gamelan ensemble called *gamelan gambuh*. The focus of this chapter is the changes in the sound of *suling gambuh*, the main instrument for this gamelan genre. There has been a subtle change in the sound of *suling gambuh* in recent years. Despite some people being concerned about it, they have not adjusted *suling gambuh*. My motivation for this study was the question of why the sound and music were allowed to undergo this gradual but major change.

Most of the previous studies that have been conducted on the musical instruments of gamelan have been in the fields of organology, acoustic engineering and psychoacoustics. Most of them assumed the perspective of human actions on *mono* (things), where the *mono* are musical instruments with material properties (e.g., orchestration), physical phenomena in the absence of human factors (acoustical engineering studies), and human interpretations of sound (ethnomusicological studies to decipher symbolism in gamelan sounds etc.) and their uses (psychoacoustical studies). Musical instruments as *mono* were not the subject of these studies.[2]

In contrast, this chapter shall discuss invisible sounds from alternative viewpoints, including the dynamics between humans and visible *mono* (musical instruments). We will also consider material elements besides musical scores,

Photo 8.1 Suling gambuh. Suling gambuh is the longest type of Balinese bamboo flute. Suling gambuh of this village is the longest among them with an overall length of approximately 1 meter. The player in the photo (who is normally a dancer) is the son of a man who passed on a suling sample and manufacturing knowledge to a suling maker. The suling gambuh being played in the photo is that sample, which is currently kept by the suling maker. (See Section 8.3 for the circumstances of the transmission of manufacturing technology.)

whether musical instruments as *mono* can be a philosophical subject, and what to think of the "force"[3] that musical instruments exert on sounds and humans.

The object of this study is the *suling gambuh* used in Batuan village (Gianyar province)[4] which I have been playing for many years. In general, *suling* refers to a down-blown type of bamboo ring flute.[5] *Suling gambuh* is the longest *suling* used in Balinese gamelan. It is about one meter long, has a range of two and a half octaves, and is played using a circular breathing technique.[6] The *suling gambuh* used for this acoustic analysis was made around 1999 by a *suling* maker named C of P village in G province (pseudonyms). Five others are used for comparison, including one made around 1994 by an unknown maker, and a set of four made around 1995 by the aforementioned *suling* maker C. Changes in sounds in recent years were analyzed based on DVD recordings of a few *gamelan* groups in B village.

8.2 Out of tune *suling*?

Badly tuned notes in Balinese gamelan are called *bero*. I shall begin by identifying the conditions that are perceived to produce incorrect notes based on an acoustic analysis of *suling gambuh* sounds.

There are no technical words referring to tuning in the vocabulary of Balinese gamelan manufacturing. Instead, a scale called *laras* and the terms that are generally interpreted as key or tonality – *pathetan, saih*[7] and *tekap/tetekap* – are used.[8] In these terms, *gambuh* in B village is a *laras pelog* (seven tones) gamelan with four keys (*selisir, baro, lebang* and *senaren*).[9] These four keys are defined by *tekap* (meaning "closing of holes" = fingering, in this case). A series of pitches made by such fingering is also called *tekap*. In order to identify these four keys, fingerings need to be determined. As the fingerings of B village which have been reported (Formaggia 2000; Rembang 1973 among others; Tantra 1992 and Suharta 1994 also report fingerings without specifying which village) varied from one study to another and were different from the fingerings actually used for playing in B village,[10] they could not be used for this analysis. Consequently, I have decided to adopt the fingerings actually used in playing by N group (pseudonym) of B village in this chapter.

First, I used spectrum analysis[11] to identify individual notes in each fingering in an attempt to determine the sounds that are perceived to be out of tune. The result showed that most problems were found in *tekap lebang*, especially with the most characteristic sounds of *tekap* which were used heavily in playing *tekap* compositions. Please excuse the use of the term *tekap* as I do here; it is difficult to find a translated word that is appropriate for every situation. The ongoing confusion surrounding the question of whether *tekap* should be interpreted as "key/tonality" or "fingering" is one of the reasons for the change in sound and shall be discussed in a later section.

In *tekap lebang*, different fingerings are used in the base range, the first octave range and the second octave range which produce different sounds, that is, the constituting notes for different octaves are in different keys. The notes in question include 5a and 6a in the base range and 4a and 5b in the first octave range in Figure 8.1.[12] The sound spectrum of each note varies from one *suling* to another

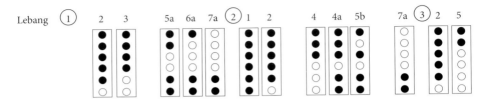

Figure 8.1 Fingerings for tekap lebang *(lebang key)*[12] ① *indicates the fingerings in the base range,* ② *in the first octave range, and* ③ *in the second octave range. This key is characterized by a small number of the same fingerings in each range but even the same fingerings produce different pitches in this key. A lack of precise sound periodicity is therefore its prominent feature.*

in my comparative analysis. The frequency ratio between each note and the notes above and below it are highly inconsistent. In addition, a characteristic note of *tekap lebang*, 5b, is part of these inconsistent frequency ratio relationships. Since differentials between individual *suling gambuhs* in other keys are not as great as for these notes, it is suspected that these frequency ratio differentials prompt people to decide whether the music is played out of tune and have a major impact on people's sound perception when they play or hear these notes.

As I will discuss later, however, *tekap lebang* is unfamiliar to those who do not play *gambuh* of B village as it is not a *tekap* (fingering/key) commonly used in gamelan music. In fact, the very root of the problem is found here. There is no sound problem in *tekap selisir*, which is widely used in other genres of gamelan. Even with *tekap lebang*, there would have been no sound problem when the instrument maker and the performer were the same person. These days, the instrument maker and the performer are different and the former may know the fingerings of *tekap lebang* but he may be unfamiliar with the actual sounds of *tekap lebang* when played. It is likely that this has caused the change in the sound of *tekap lebang*.

Before we consider the change of sound, let us clarify *suling* manufacturing technology and how *suling* makers transmit the technology to the next generation as well as the knowledge, problems and awareness of *suling* players below.

8.3 *Suling* making technology

Suling manufacturing in B village today is entirely contracted out. Only a few decades ago, performers made their own instruments. Today, only one *suling* maker-player remains in the village, but he is unable to make instruments due to old age and illness (as at August 2009). As few villagers have *suling* making skill, all orders are sent to C (pseudonym) of P village whose *sulings* were used for the above analysis. He is also the only person in G province who can make *suling gambuh*. Although he was a good player of other types of *suling*, he had no knowledge of *suling gambuh* playing techniques or compositions to begin with.

He became involved in *suling gambuh* manufacturing when approached by a performer (dancer) from B village. He was playing *suling* as a member of an ensemble for a performance of masked dance drama *topeng* at one ritual, at the time.[13] K (pseudonym), the former leader of N group of B village, actively invited C to make *suling gambuh* every time they saw each other at a performance as C already had *suling* making skills and excellent playing techniques. K gave C one of the *suling gambuhs* he was using at the time as a sample and taught him sizing (ascertaining ratios). Sizing is the most important task in *suling* making, and *suling gambuh* in particular.[14] As fine tuning in the production process requires knowledge about instrumental characteristics, playing techniques and compositions, K and C worked together over a long period of time.

Two previous studies on *suling* making technology are worth reviewing. It seems that the first report contained a brief account of *suling gambuh* sizing as it was presented by Rembang at a *gambuh* workshop in 1973 (Rembang 1973). The report mentions that the sizing method for *suling gambuh* is either *sikut kutus* or *sikut sanga* but does not provide any diagrams. More detailed data were released in Suharta's report in 1994. This report is based on a detailed study of *suling* used in various genres of gamelan on Bali. Suharta explains production techniques and sizing (ratios) using numerical data and diagrams (Suharta 1994). Once this study was released, instructions on *suling gambuh* manufacture technology were introduced to *gambuh* classes at the department of traditional music (Jurusan Karawitan) of Sekolah Tinggi Seni Indonesia Denpasar (STSI-Denpasar; now Institute Seni Indonesia Denpasar (ISI-Denpasar)) and the knowledge was made accessible to the public.[15] However, it was impossible to apply the theories of the two reports to *suling* of B village. Although a *suling* maker in B village was also interviewed,[16] both studies gathered data on *suling gambuh* mainly in P village of D city (pseudonyms) which formed the basis of their terminology and ratios.[17] In fact, I was given theoretically very different terminology and ratios when I interviewed a *suling* maker in P village of G province. For this reason, I shall use numerical data obtained from C of P village, G province, in this chapter while I use the aforementioned reports as references for theoretical frameworks only.

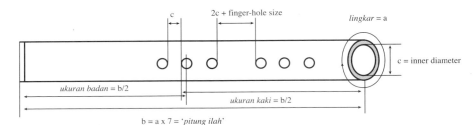

Figure 8.2 Pitung ilah. Pitung ilah *(seven circumferences) is the ratio principle (sikut ibane) applicable to suling gambuh in suling making. Where a is the circumference, b (overall length of the flute) is seven times a. However, as the length needs to be adjusted by half the length of the second finger-hole when its position is being determined, b is shortened by half the length of the second finger-hole, in theory. In practice, though, the multiple of seven is just a guide and the suling maker starts work by listening to the "sound of the bamboo" first. (The inner diameter of the bamboo c is used for spacing between finger-holes.)*

Sizing or the ascertaining of ratios, which is the most important piece of knowledge in *suling* making, is called *sikut ibane* in Balinese (or *ukuran tertentu* in Indonesian; hereinafter called ratio principle). Based on the base units of the diameter and the cross section circumference of the bamboo tube, the flute length and the distances between finger-holes are calculated using the inner diameter and the circumference respectively.[18] The ratio principle used in B village is called *pitung ilah* (seven circumferences) which derives the basic length as approximately seven times the circumference.[19]

It is an "approximate" value as the length is measured roughly using a palm leaf rather than by exact calculation and a cut is made with a large margin of error because bamboo has uneven thickness and warpage which can cause change of sound.

The process of *suling* making according to this ratio principle is described as follows.

1. **Bamboo selection**

    The type of bamboo used for *suling* making is *Tiying tali* (*Bambusa* sp.), which produces strong and sharp sounds. While *Tiying tali jajan batu* (perhaps a species of *Bambusa*, but that is unconfirmed) is a straight bamboo with glossy surface used for *suling*, the bamboo used to make *suling gambuh* is *Tiying gedanpal* (*Phyllostachys aurea* A & C), which is only found in a limited area of Bali.[20] An almost straight and thick *nguyung* (old bamboo; a dead standing one is desirable) is selected for use.

2. **Cutting**

   The bamboo is harvested on an auspicious day (*dewasa*) to ensure *taksu* (spiritual power that confers ability, power or certain charm on a person). The day is called *saniscara-paing-kajeng* (derived by combining the 7-day week, 5-day week and 3-day week cycles). The bamboo must be cut either before dawn or *jejeg* (*jegjeg*) *surya* (generally means "before noon").

3. **Drying**

   Once all leaves drop naturally, branches are trimmed off and the trunk (culm) is laid horizontally in the roof space of traditional kitchen until it is completely dry. In some cases, bamboos are stored for ten to twenty years in the roof space directly above the hearth to promote drying.

4. **Sizing and cutting**

   The process from here on is also carried out on an auspicious day so that the instruments will acquire *taksu*. The day is called *karna-sula*, the day "to open ears". The day is suitable for tasks such as making holes in a *suling* and beginning to study *suling*.

5. **Beck (*pemanis*) making**

   The windway and the labium should not be made too large. They are carved with a *mutik* (curved knife with its blade on the outside).[21] The *siwar* (a ring fitted around the beck) is made.

6. **Finger-hole (*lubang*) making**

   The second hole is opened first, followed by other holes. The position of the second hole is determined according to the ratio principle. The finger-holes are made initially to the size of the beck[22] and adjusted later on. Fine adjustment is made by a method called *ngirik* using sandpaper wrapped around a thin bamboo stick.

7. **Arasan**

   Arasan is the final stage in the process of *suling* making. Pitches are fine-tuned and finalized. This task is carried out jointly with the player. The final fine-tuning involves playing compositions. As they listen to the played notes, they may make fine adjustments to the beck by whittling with the *mutik* or apply oil inside the bamboo tube. This task demands the highest level of sensitivity and concentration; many days are devoted to this stage. The *suling* is complete when pitches are perceived to be invariable over three consecutive tests.

The noteworthy stage in the manufacturing process is the final stage of *arasan*. The perception that "pitches are invariable" is emphasized here but there is no numerical guideline for it. In the past, it was decided by K of B village who was a player; it was not a decision made by a manufacturer. Even today, a *suling* player participates in this process and determines the final sounds, not the *suling* maker. Now that K is deceased, the final *arasan* stage is carried out by C on his own. This is likely to be one of the causes of the change of sound.

8.4 What is *tekap*?

Let us look at the musical knowledge of a player and attendant problems.

The word *tekap* is problematic in itself. While it literally means "the manner of covering finger-holes (*penutup*)",[23] it also refers to a series of notes produced by a certain manner of covering finger-holes (fingering) as well as the key or tonality played with these notes, as mentioned above. The differing interpretation of this word is partially responsible for varying perceptions of acoustic change in the sounds that are made.

When *tekap* is understood as "the manner of covering finger-holes", or for those who believe so, the perception of being out of tune does not arise. "Wrong sounds, would that be possible?", said a former member of an ensemble affiliated with the national radio station (*Keluagra Kesenian Bali, Radio Republik Indonesia Stasiun Denpasar* (KKB RRI-Denpasar)), who originally learned the instrument and playing techniques of P village, D city, and subsequently learned compositions independently. "Because the ratio principle is correct, it is still *suling gambuh* even if (played) sounds are different", said a researcher and player from P village, D city, where the instruments and the produced sounds began to change dramatically from around 1999. They both say that they used *suling gambuh* of almost the same length with *suling gambuh* of B village and produced almost the same sounds until about 1999, but *suling gambuh* used in P village today are shorter by ten centimeters and smaller in diameter.[24] Also in B village, few questions are raised about the changes of sound and the pitches of *tekap lebang* played by T group, B village. They have changed remarkably from around 2001.

When *tekap* is understood as "key", on the other hand, people use different note names for the same sound partly because of a confusion surrounding note names in fingerings. This has caused major confusion. Individuals are compelled to learn compositions according to their own principle or system. In *tekap lebang* of B village, "the manner of covering finger-holes" reportedly has note names corresponding to a five-note scale and a seven-note scale. It doesn't help that this system assigns different note names to the same fingerings in the first place. Another factor exacerbating the confusion is the fact that one *suling gambuh* player of B village used a different system of note names to sing and teach compositions to young people in the past. He assigned names to the pitched notes and sang freely to teach compositions to others but those note names did not always correspond to his idiosyncratic system or the names used in the fingerings, creating confusion between "the manner of covering finger-holes" and "key/tonality" among his successors. On this point, they tried to avoid this confusion by calling the fingering "*nglubit*" (the manner of opening hands) in order to distinguish it clearly from the other meaning of *tekap* which is "key".

The dance drama *gambuh* once suffered a period of severe decline, which evoked a sense of crisis among the village's youth and spurred them to learn the art. The confusion about note names provided a major obstacle and added to their frustration with the slow pace of succession. Inheriting a dance drama entails learning many scripts and different compositions used in each script so that the construction (*susunan*) of compositions can be adapted in a flexible manner along scripts. Learning compositions alone does not make a dance drama, but the inability to learn the basic compositions is worse. As the confusion remained, players aged and some compositions were lost or partially missing due to incomplete succession. It reached the point that some programs could no longer be performed. In order to remedy this situation, the youth resorted to preparing musical scores. Although the scores were prepared by individuals as their own memoranda and not for sharing with others, they formed the basis for a collective attempt to restore incomplete compositions and vanishing programs. It eventually gave rise to a group of people who consciously addressed the musical aspect of the dance drama. They were the people who began to feel that "something is wrong with *suling gambuh*".

The problem here is that the players had no means of solving the question when it arose. Let us go back to the final *arasan* stage in *suling* making. It involves the task of finalizing sounds for which technology is supplied by the manufacturer and decisions are made by the player. As the people who had both the knowledge and technology of *suling* making and the knowledge and technology of *suling* playing passed away one after another, including K, who passed his *suling* making knowledge to C and acted as a tenuous link, there was no one who could integrate the two bodies of knowledge and technology in himself. *Suling* makers do not know "the (supposed) sounds of the notes" when played in "compositions" whereas the players with no knowledge of instrument making do not know "how to fix" a problem even if they notice that "something is wrong". The sounds continue to change but they have no choice but to keep using the instrument even if "something is wrong". As a result, the sounds of *suling gambuh* played by T group of B village and a group affiliated with the village temple have changed, and the sounds of *tekap lebang* performed by them in 2001 were different from those performed in 1992 when they sounded much the same as N group.

8.5 "Living" *suling*

8.5.1 The living *suling* phenomenon

Why has so little been done to modify the *suling* that are considered to be "wrong"? Although the manufacturing technology is challenging, some fine-tuning procedures such as adjusting finger-holes or length are relatively feasible. Why are people still using their *suling* without modification?

The answer to this question may be found in the statement of the *suling* maker C, "*Suling* is alive (*idup*)". His accounts of the process of *suling* making contain a number of phenomena hinting that *suling* is "alive" and inhibiting people from taking certain actions.

First, he says that "sounds change shortly after holes are made" during the manufacturing process. Not surprisingly sounds may naturally change depending on the manufacturer's physical and mental conditions; therefore he needs to be fit when he sets out to make an instrument. *Suling*, however, also changes its sounds on its own. There are times when he makes finger-holes, leaves the instrument alone for a while, and retests its sounds later. Sometimes he finds that the *suling* has changed its sounds on its own. He says that he must not engage in *suling* making in a state of *runtag* (feeling restless, hurried or unsettled) if he wants to judge the situation accurately. As things tend to go wrong when he feels unsettled, he must settle his mind before proceeding to work (especially with the hole making and *arasan* stages).

In the final stage of *arasan*, he says that an instrument sometimes "cowers" (*getap* = (a *suling* or instrument) is feeling scared). The term *getap* is used not only for *suling gambuh* but also all other gamelan instruments in the final stage of tuning. It refers to the phenomenon in which an instrument plays well with perfect sounds on its own but its sounds are overwhelmed by other sounds when played with other instruments.[25] The sounds of a seemingly well-tuned *suling* are drowned out when played with other *suling* or other instruments when the *suling* is *getap*.[26]

C also says that a decision to cut the lower end of *suling* should not be made lightly because it is equivalent to cutting a person's legs. Once I had a pair of *suling* which I could not use in performances because their sounds were different from those of my other pairs and I attempted to adjust the sounds of one of them by cutting a little bit off the end. The sounds did not change in the way I had expected and I ended up shelving the pair as I did not know what else to do with it. When I mentioned this episode to C during an interview, he and another player from B village who happened to be present were visibly alarmed and gave me the aforementioned warning. The taboo "not to cut a used *suling* indiscriminately" is apparently well known among not only *suling* makers but also the *suling* players of B village. They say that *maut* (having performed everywhere) *suling* in particular should not be cut and that "the more the player cuts, the stupider he becomes" in an attempt to modify his *suling*.

At the same time, he says that as *suling* grows older (*ungkur*), its sounds also age (*umur* (Indonesian)). He also says that old *suling* tend to suffer splitting but they can be repaired by gluing and strapping tightly. He showed me an amber colored old *suling* still in active use even though it had experienced splitting and repair once during its fifty years of service by saying that old *suling* produce nice sounds. In general, bamboo culms used for *suling* making have thin walls, which are prone to cracking or splitting. However, there is an established repair method for *suling*, which in most cases are repairable with much care and time. A *suling* becoming completely unusable is very rare. C is another professional *suling* player who says, "Very few *suling* have become unusable in my hands" among many he has inherited from his grandfather. The unusable *suling* are not thrown away; they are stored in the roof space until they reach a certain number and buried in the ground with a ritual although it is not as formal as a funeral.

The aliveness of *suling* is sometimes felt with immediacy at the scenes of performance. While a *suling* is a *mono* (things) with material characteristics, it is never spoken of in terms of "injecting a soul/animate" (*menjiwai*) or "bringing to life" (*menghidupkan*) unlike the Balinese masks discussed by Yoshida in Chapter 7. Expressions used about the *suling* include "getting *taksu* (from a *suling*)" and "(this *suling*) has *taksu*" but none refers to any action taken by a player to give life to his *suling*. An important requirement for the player is "to know *rasa*"[27] (*tahu rasa*) and "feel" (*merasa*) in the sounds of his *suling*, which means that "*rasa*" is already present in the melody produced by the *suling*. In fact, what I was constantly instructed to do while I was learning to play *suling* was to know the sounds of my *suling* and its *rasa* rather than handling procedures or playing techniques. *Suling* itself already has its sounds and does not need to be inspired by humans to make them.

8.5.2 Handling *suling*
In general, people who potentially handle *suling* on a routine basis do not have a clear knowledge of how to treat them or rituals for them. This includes the players

of *suling* other than *suling gambuh*, gamelan performers, and people associated with gamelan. *Suling* are commonly hung when stored but as people do not know why it is done, they sometimes pack them in plastic bags and keep in a cabinet or store them in a poor condition when they do not have suitable space for hanging. As a result, all too often they take out their *suling* to play only to find them moldy or missing its *siwar* (a ring around the beck). Some *suling* players may have inherited their instruments as well as knowledge about them and how to play them from family members such as the father. Normally, these players are the only people who know proper storage and management, keep their own *suling* in good condition and mention rituals for *suling*, albeit on very rare occasions.

The careless manner of handling *suling* may be attributable to their position in the usual set of gamelan instruments. Among the set of bronze instruments, *suling* are treated as complements (*pelengkapan*) that complete the set. For this reason, gamelan retailers do not bother questioning the quality of *suling* or paying attention to *suling* when they handle gamelan sets because *suling* are generally considered cheap. In storage, *suling* are often found together, hung in a simple drawstring pouch on the end of a gong rack. Many of the *suling* owned by village assembly halls are covered with grime and dust. But good *suling* players never use these low quality, poorly maintained *suling*. *Suling* players usually own various types of *suling* to use. Those who use poorly maintained low quality *suling* are insignificant players who are added to complete an ensemble for performances. As anyone can make at least some sounds by blowing air into it, the *suling* section is usually crowded with "complement players" at performances. These "complement players" have little or no knowledge of *suling* quality, proper handling, and the importance of knowing *rasa* in playing.

Respected *suling* players, however, know taboos about *suling* and proper handling. They routinely care for their *suling*. The aforementioned *suling* maker and master player C is conversant with taboos and proper handling with respect to *suling*. He is particularly knowledgeable about rituals for *suling*. He considers the *suling* itself to be *taksu*. It therefore should not be put down directly on the ground. He normally lays his *suling* out on his bed so that they do not lose their *taksu*. He recommends putting them in storage bags or carry bags and hanging them from the ceiling or on the wall for storage so that they do not have direct contact with the ground. He says that rituals for *suling* are conducted on the day of *tempak krulut* (the day for rituals concerning sound-related or performing art-related instruments and groups) and declares that "*suling* is the most important instrument for rituals on this day". The day of "*tempak*" is the birthday of the subject of the ritual and the offering made on this day is the same as the offering made on the human ceremonial birthday called *otonan*. Birthday rituals are conducted for *mono* (things) such as *suling* and other sound-related instruments, musical instruments and performing art-related instruments and groups (as a whole and not for members) just as for humans.

8.5.3 Characteristics of *suling* as *mono*

In Bali, the subject of these rituals are believed to have a soul, which can be removed temporarily at the time of repairs or transportation. The Balinese mask discussed by Yoshida in Chapter 7 is one of the *mono* treated in this way. A ritual called *pelarina* is conducted to remove its soul before the mask is modified in any way. Similarly, *pelarina* can be conducted to remove a soul from a shrine before rebuilding commences. However, no "soul removal" rituals exist for *suling*. Although *suling* does not require "consecration" by humans, it is natural for us to assume the existence of a life or a soul in it if *suling* is believed to be alive. However, the step for the removal of a soul or a life by humans does not exist for *suling*. Why is that?

As mentioned earlier, *suling* is treated as *mono* to complete a set of gamelan instruments. It is generally thought that as a material object it is easier to make than bronze musical instruments and both the raw material cost and the selling price are far cheaper than those of bronze instruments. Although it is conceivable that its low value is denying the conduct of the very costly *pelarina* ritual, I have never heard from anyone that they do not conduct the ritual for the low value *suling* because it costs too much. The careless treatment of *suling* by the public may suggest that this instrument is unappreciated but even the *suling* maker, who said that good *suling* should be repaired despite difficulty, never mentioned the conduct of a *pelarina* ritual in the repair process. It indicates that people may make an offering in exchange for *taksu* from *suling* but they have never envisaged a ritual to remove a soul from it. In other words, humans are submitted to the action of *suling* but human action on *suling* cannot provoke a change in the life of *suling*.

The low pricing of *suling* also tends to make people think, "I could repair the cracks but I would rather buy a new one" even if it plays beautifully or there is a way to repair it perfectly. The *mono* wasted here is *suling* and its sound but the latter drops out of their thinking process in which *suling* as a material object surfaces to the conscious mind as an item to be replaced. In fact, many people handle *suling* carelessly because they think that they will simply replace it when it spoils. Only very few *suling* makers undertake difficult and cumbersome repairs as they do not want to waste a *mono*, which is the lost sound.

The *suling* spoken of by their makers contain a wide variety of *mono*. When C talks about his own old repaired *suling*, it includes various *mono* such as its aged sound, a number of episodes that hint at the aliveness of *suling*, its treatment, the tunes it plays, and memories of the process of inheriting playing techniques and compositions, besides the aged material object. *Suling* appears before us as an aggregate of *mono* in the form of sound and invisible physical vibration, *mono* in the form of manufacturing technology and playing techniques that produce them, and *mono* in the form of memory[28] well beyond the mere material existence of *mono*.

However, when we are confronted by the undeniable fact that *suling* is *mono* called a musical instrument as well as its material characteristics, we often tend to fail to see *suling* as a holistic *mono*.

8.5.4 The action of *suling* on people

Let us recapitulate the findings and narratives so far to elucidate the action *suling* exerts on humans. First, an elderly manufacturer-player from B village commented on the question of *taksu* concerning harvesting bamboo: "a *suling* made of bamboo harvested at a particular time of a particular day imparts *taksu* (*metaksu*) to its player". It is the earnest desire of dancers and instrument players to acquire *taksu*. They try to secure it by restricting the cutting of raw material to specific days called *saniscara-paing-kajeng*. Making finger-holes and learning to play *suling* on the *karna-sula* day is also an attempt to secure *taksu*.

There are of course those who think these customs are "irrelevant" and do not practice them, even though they know about them. However, those who seek to acquire *taksu* by following the customs pay careful attention to these matters. This is because, to performers, *taksu* is neither something they can gain through skill development nor a sense of unity between the player and the instrument. *Taksu* is a thing that is given to an entity as a player by a living musical instrument or some other being. The entity that acquires *taksu* may be a material *mono* such as a musical instrument, head dress (*gulungan*), a tool, or the body of a player or dancer, or a *mono* such as the being of a player or dancer itself. This entity expresses the force of *taksu* and enthralls people. At the same time, taboos such as those about putting *suling* down on the ground and sayings such as "the more a player cuts, the stupider he becomes" indicate that the musical instrument will take away a person's abilities and appeal if he treats it inappropriately, affirming the agency of the musical instrument *suling*.

The kind of action that *suling* exerts on humans makes it difficult for people to carry out modifications to it. As the "living" *suling* has the power to influence humans, people regulate their own behavior so that *suling* will not take away their abilities. Once used, *suling* must not be cut; the most one can do is to make fine adjustments to finger-holes. When minor adjustments are made to a used *suling*, its friend (*teman*; the other *suling* in a pair) must be adjusted, too. This means that when people find that one *suling* is developing some subtle problem with its sounds, they are not at liberty to rework it so easily. In other words, *suling* as *mono* creates a situation in which the eventual sound changes have to be accepted.

8.6 Conclusion – From thoughts on sound to acoustic structure

8.6.1 Sounds heard but not listened

Taboos about the musical instrument *suling* have not been widely known in the past. However, as I investigated the changing sounds of *tekap lebang* from *suling gambuh*, I came to face the fact that there are certain taboos concerning *suling* just like other musical instruments (especially bronze ones) and that *suling* is a "living" instrument with the power to exert influence on humans.[29] So what should we make of this power to act?

Musical instruments are sometimes discussed from the perspective of a cult. Looking at the "living" *suling* from this angle is talking about the musical instrument *suling* from a human perspective, that is, describing the dynamic relationship between humans and *suling* in terms of the instrumentalist world view or the symbolist world view.[30] This perspective fails to capture the power of "living" *suling* accurately. Another option would be the anthropomorphization of musical instruments, but this approach suffers from similar limitations.

In contrast, the action force exerted by the "living" musical instrument on humans discussed in this chapter is a force humans cannot escape or break from no matter how hard they try. The musical instrument has the power to give *taksu* to people and to take their abilities away. This cannot be changed by human effort. The force of this action from the *mono* to humans led to the change of sound. While new *suling* can be reworked as needed, it is practically difficult to readjust *suling* that have already been used in performance. This cannot be explained adequately from the perspectives that see "musical instrument" and "sound" as controlled by humans. Here we find a clue to take us beyond the instrumentalist and symbolist world views in order to study the concatenation of sound, *mono* and humans.

Through the relationship between *tekap* and the sound of *suling gambuh*, the idea that *tekap* means fingerings can produce a sense that the sounds are the same as long as the fingerings are the same, even if the physically produced sounds are different. This is equivalent to the bodily sense or perception about the xylophone, another keyed gamelan instrument, for which people feel that the sounds made by keys in the same position must be identical. Strictly speaking, this does not mean that people stop listening to the sounds just because the key positions are fixed. The view among experienced xylophone players that they should be able to play the xylophone from the rear side of the keyboard where lower pitch keys come to the right side of the player's body instead of the usual left side, and their tendency to look down on those who cannot play it this way, indicates that not everyone has the sense that the key position equals the pitch position. Nevertheless, based on comments by the previously mentioned member of the national radio ensemble and the researcher from P village, D city, to the effect that the same fingerings means the same sounds, and the fact that changes in the *suling gambuh* played by T group of B village go unnoticed, this kind of sensory reception cannot be ruled out.

In this situation, the sounds of *suling gambuh* are absent even though they are present in front of people. Kawai states in Chapter 13 that human beings "are helplessly passive against the sound environment". Sound is an inescapable sensation for humans. Even the "act of covering the ears cannot overcome the passivity of 'hearing'." Kawai is not talking about man-made artificial sounds; she is talking about natural sounds, the unstoppable cacophony of cicadas, for example. In the case of the *mono* called *suling gambuh*, however, people deliberately "do not listen" to the sounds they artificially bring out of *suling*. Human ears do receive the sounds as physical vibrations, and the sounds create a melody. The *mono* appears as a musical accompaniment to a dance, and acquires *taksu* to captivate people. In spite of this, people consciously "do not listen" to *mono* called sounds.[31] Consequently, the sounds continue to change.

8.6.2 Changing sounds and sound perception

It is also true that there are some people who have come to feel that "something is wrong" about the change of sound or "it sounds out of tune". How is this change brought about?

I would like to return to Kawai's discussion, referring to her comment that the meaning of *liiyo* as "loneliness/solitude" is about the passive acceptance of the "*mono* nature" of sound. Borrowing an expression from Schafer's concept of soundscape, accepting the "*mono* nature" of sound refers to a situation in which "the ears are opened" to non-artificial sounds. This is contraposed with the act of focusing on controlling artificial sounds, that is, to "close the ears" and perceive the world of artificial sounds alone. This focusing on the world of artificial sounds by "closing the ears" and the rigorous theorization from the accuracy of pitch aspects of sound were promoted in the world of Western music. Weber described the creation of the equal temperament in Western music as the "rationalization" of music. However, the sound of *suling gambuh* has existed as sound which one hears but does not listen to even though it is artificial sound. There were differences in the size of *suling*, the fingering and the tune between villages in the past but *suling gambuh* as *mono* has continued to be *suling gambuh* and continues to be *suling gambuh* today.

If people are getting the sense that "something is wrong" with the sound as *mono*[32] in this situation, there must have been some change in the concept of sound as *mono* or their perception of sound. Young people who desperately tried to learn playing techniques and compositions for *suling gambuh* in order to inherit the traditional performing art had to identify and understand the sounds by reading musical scores and using recording devices as aids. It is likely that, through their effort to carefully listen to and reproduce the sounds that are normally heard and not listened to in this process of introducing the musical scores and recording devices, they acquired a sense to perceive sound as *mono*, which is to be fixed and controlled. Through the use of the very Western musical means of scoring and the ubiquitous presence of the sounds and songs of popular music, they probably accepted Western sounds and sound concepts.

However, any action that was supposed to arise from their sense that "something is wrong" was denied by the living *suling*. The living *suling* evokes a desire to rework it in the minds of the young people who feel "something is wrong" with it, but this desire is never fulfilled. When they face the living *suling*, they hope to acquire *taksu* from it. They fear that *suling* as *mono* may take something away from them. Thus, even though it is perceived as "wrong", the sound of *suling* continues to change once again in contexts and meanings that are different from those of the sound heard and not listened to. It becomes *mono* that exists as a context-dependent variable.

8.6.3 The condition of *mono*: a sound structure, a sound-related phenomenon, or an aggregate

Changes in the sound of *suling gambuh* is a problematique that points to the need to reconsider the dynamic concatenation of sound, *mono*, people, nature and the environment as well as the relationship between self and other *mono*. The *mono* called musical instrument with materiality exists as an aggregate of associated knowledge and technology (including scientific knowledge and technology as well as raw material-related natural and environmental changes)[33] and playing techniques. It creates a sound structure by constructing sounds or vibrations (movements) in a space called time.

While this sound structure has generally been called "music", the concept of "music" heading toward Western modernity has come to refer to a sound structure produced as a result of consciously disconnecting the concatenation of people, nature and the environment, philosophy and the cosmos. For this "music", human beings have been paying meticulous attention to specifying "sounds" and making strenuous efforts to control them as Weber and Adorno pointed out. At the same time as controlling "sounds", however, "music" as a sound structure has been treated as an autonomous ("spontaneous") entity in itself. Adorno criticized fetishization of voices and musical instruments, saying that voices and musical instruments are mere 'materials'.

Suling gambuh poses questions to us about the idea of controlling "sounds" and the existence of "music", voices and musical instruments. As *suling gambuh* changes in its sound by rejecting control, the human bodily senses and perception concerning sound and sound structures become undermined and shaky. As an aggregate of *mono* in the form of sound and physical vibration, *mono* in the form of manufacturing technology and playing techniques, and *mono* such as memories and knowledge beyond the place of *mono* as a simple material entity, *suling* changes an important element of the sound structure. The changed "sound" forces humans to accept it, changes the form of "music" as a sound structure, and undermines the characteristic of autonomy ("spontaneity") of "music". In this place, the sound structure is reduced to an aggregate thing that appears in a space between *suling* and humans, which is a phenomenon that only occurs in relation to sound (hereinafter called "sound-related phenomenon").

In the circumstances surrounding *suling gambuh*, the sound-related phenomenon is a *mono* that has what Adorno calls "fetish character" (*fetischcharakter*). But it is spun amid interactions between humans and the environment. Hence, it is only able to exist as a network connecting them. Human action on *mono* and *mono*'s action on humans are different forms of action mechanisms, each of which has multiple vectors and intensities. Perhaps *mono* as phenomena emerge temporarily among those vectors in a form of temporal materiality and an entity with agency. And perhaps a sound-related phenomenon is this kind of aggregate *mono*. *Suling gambuh* provided impetus to start thinking about these things.

9 *Mono* that Show and Tempt: Contingency by Fortune-Tellers

Ayako Iwatani

Keywords: divination, contingency, index, Nāyakan̠, cuvaṭi

9.1 No divine behind divination!?

Why are people tempted by divination? Are they seeking knowledge of future events that are supposed to be unknowable? Are they simply amazed by fortune-tellers who seem to know them better than they know themselves? Even self-professed non-believers of divination are sometimes tempted to try it. This chapter discusses the role of *mono* (*things*) in making divination tempting.

What are the *things* that are used in divination? Divination is defined as "a means to gain information about future events, concealed facts of the past and the present, and the appropriateness of an action one is about to take, using some forms of sign as clues" (Tomikura 1973: 40). The *things* that are used as signs include human beings (dreams, mediums' words and actions, birth dates, the lines of the palm etc.), nature (solar/lunar eclipses, celestial motion, animal calls, animal entrails etc.), and symbols artificially derived from instruments (lots, cards etc.). In this chapter, the *things* that are represented as the "signs" of events of the past, the present and the future through visual, auditory and other senses are treated as *things* involved in divination.

There is a tendency to think that people pay more attention to the meanings indicated by *things* used in divination rather than the *things* themselves. Past studies on divination have centered on analyses of its functions and interpretive acts. *Things* involved in divination have only been given the status of "signs" symbolically expressing something "behind" them – social values and world views, so to speak.

Recent anthropological studies of *things* and materiality, however, point to the actions that *things* themselves exert on divination. From this perspective, *things* can function as nodes or build networks between different communities and individuals through their use and exchange (Appadurai 1986; Miller 1987; Uchibori 1997; Boivin 2008). The important point here is that *things* are capable of becoming agents which act on people and compel them to restructure relationships. They are not merely objects of instrumental use by humans (Gell 1998; Knapett and Malafouris 2008). In recent years, the process by which *things* achieve agency has also been studied from the perspective of fetishism (Tanaka 2009).[1]

In this chapter, we apply recent theories and interests surrounding *things* to the *things* used for divination. We shall examine the cases of a group of people called Nāyakan̲ who practice divination in the South Indian state of Tamil Nadu with a special focus on the *things* they use in divination. *Things* that are "contingently" brought into the "here, now" of the client receiving divination are received in the process of divination as special *things* that are "already involved" in part of the "past", "present" or "future" life of that person. I would like to shed light on the process in which surprise or pleasure is expressed by people when material *things* are revealed as their "destiny" in front of their eyes in the context of the divinatory act.

9.2 How *things* manifest in divination

Let us begin with an overview of how *things* have been treated in functionalist and interpretationist analyses found in previous divination studies and elucidate our perspective in order to draw focus to *things* used in divination.

In functionalist analysis of divination, *things* are seen as the "means" to facilitate and justify diviners' interpretation or people's understanding. Discussions between diviner and client center on explanations of interpersonal relationships or psychological effects surrounding *things*.[2] For example, Nakata (2002), in her study of divination using coconut shells in South Laos, analyses divination as a scene of conflict where symbolic capital manifests as reputation and prestige within a community. The spontaneous spinning of the coconut, that is, contingency incorporated in divination, "results in the greatest justification of divination, and also functions as a strong fortress for misrecognition of the reality of struggle" (ibid.: 39). Here, contingency provided by the coconut is noticed but the coconut as a *thing* is only given a supporting role to confirm a symbolic struggle.

In contrast, interpretationist studies of divination focus on words and manners of speech chosen by diviners and clients to analyze how they appeal to people's emotional and perceptual frameworks or change such frameworks (Nuckolls 1993).

This means that uncertainty introduced to the result of divination by the *things* used in divination can always be controllable by way of interpretation or redoing of divination. Some questions such as why *things* are purposely used in divination are left unanswered.

The discussion below is based on the claim that it is precisely this contingency and paradox which *things* bring to the process of divination that gives "verisimilitude" to divination. Hamamoto points out that unlike everyday interpretive acts, divination is "a peculiar method for social and situational awareness that forces people to reflect on the way they look at the situation by revealing a paradox before their eyes" (1983: 43). The fact that the diviner, who is a stranger to the client, and cards, which cannot possibly have any causal link with the client's life, are encountered "here, now" by chance makes this encounter seem like destiny.[3] Sugishita also describes the characteristic of an interpretive act in augury as "being embedded in technical procedures that are unrelated to it" (Sugishita 1996: 361). She continues:

> An interpretive act in augury always converges on the presentation of a "judgment", which is given the value of an "objective finding" acquired through a specified procedure rather than "an interpretation". It is evaluated on the basis of the value of "verisimilitude" that provides a maximum denial of the relativity of "an interpretation". (ibid)

For Sugishita, who claims that "interpretive acts are concealed in augury" (ibid.: 362), the act of perceiving *things* is the interpretive act peculiar to divination.[4]

Perception of *things* in divination can be discussed on the basis of Gell's (1998) argument equating *things* and "persons" to "agents". Gell has applied Pierce's theory of signs to it. According to Gell's theory, when a person faces a thing (or a person), the thing becomes an agent to evoke a known relationship and generate some meaning. These arguments do not assume a transcendental being or culture behind things. An equal and interactive relationship between a thing and a person generates a concatenation of meanings and prompts known and future signification (Watts 2008; Uchiyamada 2008).

The agency of *things* is activated through the process of abduction by humans, who overlay their known experiences on *things* and perceive connections between various facets of the world by inference (Peirce 2001). This resembles the image of "déjà vu" generated by inferential imagination which was discussed by Yoshimoto (1984). The diviners present the image of "knowing from an unknowable place" or the image of "seeing a scene, including myself, from where it is supposed to be unseeable" (Yoshimoto 1984: 60) when they face their clients. Various *things* used in divination become indexes for scenes known to the clients. By sharing these indexes with the diviners, the clients retrospectively make sense of what has happened to them. According to Yoshimoto, "An understanding begins because there is the result of understanding; it's not that there is an experience of a certain matter because I encountered that matter; it's that I encounter a matter because there is an experience of the matter preceding it" (ibid.: 62). As he says, people deduce the cause of an ongoing event through their encounter with *things*. What is happening here is a "reversal of time experience" in which the cause and the effect are reversed. And at this point of time, the unknown self or event becomes something for the clients "to understand" rather than "to believe" (Hamamoto 2006).

Thus, *things* in divination do not function as mere tools for interpretation or reflections of some world view. In divination, contingency is deliberately introduced between persons and *things* for the purpose of artificially creating distance between the client and the diviner. Here, *things* acquire a position that is independent of someone's interpretation or intention. *Things* act as indexes for events that are already underway and events that will happen in future. They enable the subject perceiving them to retrospectively infer and signify the causal relationships of the events. Let us examine some specific examples below to see how *things* become agents that guide the destiny of people and how they turn a person from an object whose destiny is being read into a subject who reads its destiny in the divination procedures.

9.3 The Nāyakaṉ: Itinerant fortune-tellers

Divination has been practiced in India through the ages[5] and various types of it remain ingrained in the everyday lives of modern Indians. They can be divided into two broad categories – astrology and street fortune-telling.

Horoscopes of Western origin are used in Indian astrology. The astrologer compares personal information of the client, including her/his exact birth date, time and place, with the lunisolar calendar and prepares a horoscope of celestial positions at the time of birth. The client's fortune, personality etc. are read on the basis of this horoscope. In India, astrology is a very familiar practice. It is particularly common in matchmaking to refer to each party's horoscope; people who advertise for a marriage partner in newspapers request applicants to send their horoscopes.

Astrology traditionally was practiced mainly by members of the Brahman caste as it requires knowledge of astronomy and almanacs.[6] However, many Indian villages had no Brahman astrologer, so many people had no access to information required to make horoscope charts. These people relied instead on "people who practice divination by summoning gods" (according to a sixty-year-old woman). Most of these street fortune-tellers belong to some particular sub-castes in the business of fortune-telling. Others are individuals of other castes who have learned the practices of divination. They visit homes from door to door in villages and towns to engage in divination, or wait for clients on the street or in the vicinity of temples.

Varahamihira, who compiled a treatise of astrology in the 6th century, distinguished these street fortune-tellers from astrologers, saying, "Do not pose questions to people who fake divine possession and issue prophecies as if they were messages from gods" (Varahamihira 1995: 21). They are also maligned as beggars "under the disguise of Jogis (religious practitioners) or astrologers" (referring the Vaghri, nomadic people in West India (Enthoven 1990:405) and "through face reading" (referring to a Nāyakaṉ; Parthasarathy 2001). They certainly lack the knowledge of complex astronomy or astrology. Nevertheless, it has been said that they have achieved "rural cosmopolitanism" (Misra 1992), appropriating the knowledge and format of astrology systematized by the elite at the populace level and traversing between cities and villages in person.

Below are some examples of divination practiced by the Nāyakaṉ, a sub-caste of street fortune-tellers who are active in the South Indian state of Tamil Nadu.

9.3.1 Nāyakaṉ fortune-tellers as show *things*

The Nāyakaṉ (pronounced as Nāyakan, also called Kāṭṭunāyakaṉ, meaning "forest chiefs", among other names) is a group of Telugu-speaking people who migrated to Tamil Nadu from Andra Pradesh in South India during the 14th century. The "Kāṭṭunāyakaṉ" population in Tamil Nadu according to the 1981 national census is 26,383 but the actual number is unclear.

While Nāyakaṉs once led a nomadic lifestyle, making a living from hunting and gathering, divination and magic, since 1954 they have been increasingly subjected to the state government's permanent settlement program, the Backward Class House Scheme. According to Mr. K (aged 52 as at 2008, 3 years of schooling), who is the representative for Manapparai in Tiruchchirappalli district where 194 Nāyakaṉ families live, until ten years ago he regularly travelled to Delhi to practice divination.[7] His grandfather travelled as far as Kolkata, staying in each village for a year or so before moving to another village. Although only about one half of the Nāyakaṉ population are thought to earn their livelihood from divination these days, they believe that they "must practice divination for at least six months of the year; otherwise Jakkamma (a goddess they worship) will get angry" (a man aged 39, with 7 years of schooling). Hence, many Nāyakaṉs still travel in and out of the state to practice divination. Their children began to receive school education from the 1970s, but many go to work as street fortune-tellers from the age of ten or so, even today.

They practice divination in the following manner. Each group, comprised of a few families, stays in a camp site and does the rounds of nearby villages to offer divination services. When they have visited all the villages, they move on to another area. It is said that they choose places where they can expect payment for divination in agricultural crops during the harvesting season. Men and women, and adults and children, set out to work separately. In the traditional way of divination, men go to a cemetery at night, sacrifice a chicken for Jakkamma with offerings such as lemons and coconuts, and pray until divine possession takes place. When the goddess descends, they visit individual houses and announce divine revelations. In the morning, people go to see them and find out the meaning of the divine revelation from the previous night in exchange for goods. Nāyakaṉs need to be careful so that their divination is not regarded as "begging". Their visits are not always desired by people. And their divination is not supported by special knowledge such as astrology. They therefore ensure that the external appearances and words of the fortune-tellers who turn up unexpectedly are seen as special *things*, which reorganize the logic of everyday lifefor people.

For example, a sixty-year-old woman (of the Pallar caste) says that she did not know of the existence of astrology until she had divination by an astrologer for her first child in 1972. The only type of divination she had known was of the Nāyakaṉs who had visited her village. The Nāyakaṉs were tall and carried a cane and a drum. Men wore black clothes and turbans which were uncommon in South India. They sang songs and engaged in divination until they were given rice. Her grandfather called the Nāyakaṉs "people from North India" but he did not know exactly where they were from.

Nāyakaṉs shake up the things that anchor people's everyday lives by the way they clothe themselves for their village rounds. They paint their faces with holy ashes in a showy fashion, wear black shirts and turbans which local people rarely wear, carry an umbrella and a cane under their arms even on a fine day, sling large bags over their shoulders conspicuously, and walk around playing an instrument (kuṭukuṭupai)[8] (Photo 9.1). Although their external appearances are somewhat grotesque as if to evoke an association between them and cemeteries,

Photo 9.1 Nāyakan men

they open a crack in people's everyday relationality by putting themselves on show.

By suddenly showing up from nowhere, they disrupt people's everyday lives and promote the idea that there is a special meaning to encounters with the Nāyakans. For example, a thirty-eight-year-old man (of the Vellalar caste) believes in astrology but, because of the following event, he does not reject "intuitive divination" by Nāyakans, either. His younger sister was back at her parents' home after a miscarriage and one day she was visited by a Nāyakan girl around twelve years of age. The girl abruptly told his sister, "You will be pregnant again within several months and give birth to a child". The sister suspected that the girl was begging and asked her, "What do you want?" The girl replied, "I'll be back after you get pregnant; give me anything then", and went away. His sister became pregnant and gave birth to a child later on just as the girl had predicted, but the girl did not come back. "We don't have to give them money and they are quite accurate", said the man. Here, his sister's pregnancy as the result was retrospectively connected to the words of the Nāyakan girl and engendered the sense of "accuracy" in divination.

According to a Nāyakan woman (aged 34), the market rate for divination ranges from twenty five to one hundred rupees (USD 0.35–1.50) but the fee can be paid in rice rather than money and the amount varies depending on the client. She said that "the trick of divination" was "not to demand (payment)". She used to knock on doors to practice divination until ten years ago but now she walks down the streets and only goes to houses when she is called. Here we can see their strategy to not let their divination be perceived as mere "begging" or "a means of livelihood".

9.3.2 Words uttered in divination

The words that are uttered by Nāyakans in divination also act as *things* that are unexpectedly cast at the client rather than words as a medium of communication in the ordinary sense. Let us examine a case study.

Case 1: In a camp area

In September 2008, fifty two Nāyakans (from age 0 to 92) were living in six tents pitched in a part of the predominantly Muslim K village (pseudonym, a population of approximately 3,700) five to eight kilometers from their usual settlement of Manapparai. Forty eight of them had been staying there for about one month. According to villagers, the Nāyakans came to the village and stayed for three months or so every year. At around half past seven in the morning, they, including men, put on face paint and conspicuous clothes and went out to work. I accompanied a Nāyakan man (aged 24) who was visiting six homes near his camp.

When he arrived at the door of each house, he played his kuṭukuṭupai to gain people's attention and began to fire off words in one burst.

> **Nāyakan (N)**: I came all the way to be at your feet. You are blessed with livestock. You are blessed with tableware, too. But you have something that is stagnated.
> **Girl**: We don't want to know. You should leave.
> **N**: I came all the way to be at your feet. You are blessed with livestock. You are blessed with tableware, too. But your wishes are frustrated because of envy. Various people are envious of your family. Your wishes will be granted by the end of this year. You will build a house in the near future. That's for sure. This is a good time. Whatever you hope for will be fulfilled. There won't be any problem. (He hits the drum.) But something is frustrated by envy. Please give something because a Nāyakan is here.

The Nāyakaṉ held his ground in the face of repeated rejections, saying, "I came all the way to be at your feet". The householders paid no heed at the beginning, but soon began to nod and listen to the words of the Nāyakaṉ who spoke of various matters fluently and without hesitation. He asked at the end of it, "Please give something because a Nāyakaṉ is here". After visiting six houses, he was not given any money but he managed to receive some rice.

Once Nāyakaṉs get a chance to speak, they begin talking in full flow, no matter where. They need neither pleasantries nor situation setting which are normally made when people meet for the first time. By abruptly thrusting themselves into people's lives and speaking assertively, as if they already know the villagers' lives, they lead people to project their own lives on the uttered words. These words must not change in response to communication with the people. The more material and absolute the words are, the more they resonate as utterings free of the diviner's intentionality.[9]

The words the man delivered at the six houses in the case above had formulaic elements. The first element included blessings and harms from beings such as spirits and gods, and envy. The second element was a reference to "good" or "bad" fortunes in the people's future. The third element included references to tangible assets such as tableware, livestock and house, and children. The fourth was a reference to the client's work or education, and the fifth was a request for alms for the Nāyakaṉ. Except for the fifth element, which must be placed at the end, all of these elements were mentioned in random order. The properties and children that catch the Nāyakaṉ's eye on the spot are adopted as indexes that point to the "destiny" currently underway. While the first element is not mentioned as a persuasive message per se, it can evoke a causal link in the person's imagination when presented in association with the person's concerns (children, work). The Nāyakaṉs who appear out of the blue and the words that they utter are cast in front of people as *things* that connect "the present that is already underway albeit unseen" and "the future yet to be seen" in people's imagination.

9.3.3 Divination by cuvaṭi

Sometimes, what are more fascinating than the diviner's words to the client are the objects used in divination. The objects are used as cues to direct the clients' attention to the diviner's words. Let us look at the case of cuvaṭi (a sheaf of divining cards; Photo 9.2) used in divination by Nāyakaṉs. Just as kuṭukuṭupai, Nāyakaṉs make their own cuvaṭi and carry them around when they go door-knocking. They

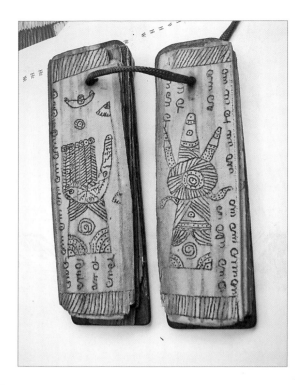

Photo 9.2 Cuvaṭi

make cuvaṭi by cutting the leaves of palmyra palm (*Borassus flabellifer*) (Photo 9.3), applying coconut oil, turmeric and coal to partially dried leaves, and drawing images on their surfaces before drying them completely. The whole process takes about two weeks. The cards remind people of ancient palm leaf books.[10] To do divination, the Nāyakaṉ presents a sheaf of cuvaṭi to the client, who inserts a metal stick between cards to open. The Nāyakaṉ looks at cards on both sides of the opening and tells the client his/her fortune. Diagnosis by cuvaṭi costs ten rupees or so and the client can try as many times as she/he wants. Here is one example.

Case 2: A Nāyakaṉ visit

On 31 July 2005, two Nāyakaṉ women arrived in the settlement of the Vaghri people (commercial nomads in Tamil Nadu). Two sisters (aged 40 and 35 respectively) were doing their rounds of nearby villages. At one house, a Vaghri woman in her forties was enticed to receive divination. She looked reluctant at the start when she

Photo 9.3 *Palmyra palm*

inserted a metal stick into a sheaf of cuvaṭi offered by one of the Nāyakan̠ women. The Nāyakan̠ began talking as she looked at the drawings on the cards.

> A tiger is on the watch. There are no stars (meaning that the planet alignment shows no bad signs). You don't have warm feelings toward others. There are ten fangs. Trust planetary positions and don't be afraid of envy. Bad signs seem to have passed. You are planning something now. Don't desire things like clothes and jewelry. Your wishes will be granted. And peace will come to you. Your wishes will be doubled. You must be patient. You must not rush if you want to accomplish something.

As the Vaghri woman listened to the Nāyakan̠'s words, she was gradually drawn into them and began to nod halfway through. When the flow of the Nāyakan̠'s speech paused, the Vaghri woman voluntarily inserted the stick into cuvaṭi again.

Look, you've got Bhadrakāli (the Hindu goddess Kali; a good omen)! You have never been bitten by a snake. Your horoscope indicates that all of the bad signs of the past have gone. You are an object of a little envy. Don't look for an astrologer or a sutra for him (her son). He will become an official in the future. He will have no problem in the future.

This divination was purely based on the images shown on cuvaṭi cards; the Nāyakaṉ did not ask the Vaghri woman's birth date. Therefore, "stars", "planetary positions" and "horoscope" she referred to had nothing to do with the actual positions of celestial bodies. Nevertheless, as in Case 1, the Nāyakaṉ associates the images on cuvaṭi with the client's properties, fortune and celestial bodies in an assertive and rhetoric-filled tone and draws the client into her speech. The act of inserting a metal stick into cuvaṭi is an important procedure in prompting the client to change from an "object" of divination to a "subject" who actively engages with *things* and deciphers their meanings.

So what are the characteristics of the images on cuvaṭi? Although each cuvaṭi consists of mysterious cards, contrary to expectations, the images are not loaded with significant meanings. Table 9.1 compares the cuvaṭi images of different Nāyakaṉs. Images are usually found on the front (odd numbers in the table) and back (even numbers) sides of each card, with signs resembling letters written in the blank spaces. The diviner interprets the images on both sides of the inserted metal stick, thus often relating the images on the back of one card and the front of the next.

Cuvaṭis 1 and 2 in the list belong to fifteen-year-old Aruputaṉ and Muhāi, cousins who began practicing divination at around the age of eleven. At the time of my study (August 2008), they were soliciting clients at Vīramma Kali temple in Thanjavur, a well-known gathering spot for fortune-tellers. Their party of four families moved to and stayed in nearby villages from an adjoining district. Cuvaṭi 1 was one month old and cuvaṭi 2 was four years old. Although they were made at different times, both were made by the same person (Muhāi's father). However, the two sets are completely different in terms of the number of cards, motifs, and the order of motifs.

Cuvaṭi 3 belongs to Cinnarāj (age 48, male), who was living in a tent outside of Chennai in August 2008. His home is in Vellore district but he was on the move for ten months of the year. The contents of his cuvaṭi were also totally different from those of 1 and 2.

The three sets of cuvaṭi have certain things in common, too. First, they all incorporate widely-known Hindu gods and themes from the mythological epics. Interpretations of cards are associated with respective mythologies. For example, if a card is drawn depicting Sītā, the wife of Prince Rāma in the Ramayana who reportedly lived in the woods for fourteen years after being abducted, it is interpreted as a sign of "separation from family". If a card is drawn showing Arjuna, a hero in the Mahābhārata who was forced to fight against his relatives, the interpretation for it is "a breakdown in family relationships". However, the diviners say that the interpretations are not standardized, but are adaptable to individual clients. Second, a majority of cuvaṭi motifs are Hindu-related but some are derived from Islam and Christianity. This is perhaps because of an assumption that some clients belong to different religious communities. Third, motifs that are incorporated that are appropriate for the area of travel. For example, cuvaṭi 1 and 2 contain many cards depicting Mahamāi or Murukaṉ,[11] which are not found in cuvaṭi 3. This is likely to be in recognition of the famous temples dedicated to these two gods within their owners' main area of travel. The fourth common feature is a card depicting "a snake and the moon". This motif represents "the waning moon", a symbolism which also represents declining energy in astrology. In all three of these cuvaṭi this card is interpreted to mean "being betrayed by others" and "suffering losses" or similar. Incidentally, cuvaṭi 3 had more cards with astrological motifs such as Saturn, lunar eclipse and Jupiter. The use of astrological motifs and letter-like signs adds authority to cuvaṭi, as we saw in Case 2 above.

9.4 The "truth" of divination

We have so far discussed the diviners themselves, the words of divination, and cuvaṭi cards as *things* used in divination. This chapter is critical of the perspective that *things* used in divination are mere reflections of the cultural contexts in which they are placed, or merely symbolic of the astrological knowledge behind them. Cuvaṭi is certainly reminiscent of ancient palm leaf books and the cards' motifs do suggest astrological and theological knowledge. However, when we examine the way they are made and used (arbitrary interpretation, non-standardization), we find that cuvaṭi does not merely function as vessels of authority or knowledge. More important were the contingency, non-intentionality and indexicality embedded in *things* which give the client a chance to reinterpret events retrospectively. The Nāyakaṉs' external appearances, their utterances and cuvaṭi cards are choreographed to maximize extraordinariness and forcefully inject foreign *things* into the regular and bland lives of people. They evoke matters and situations, landscapes and experiences that have already been part of people's everyday living and activate reciprocally causal meanings.

Table 9.1 Images in cuvaṭi

Owner (age, sex)	1: Aruputaṉ (15, female)	2: Muhāi (15, female)	3: Chinnarāj (48, male)
Made by	Maternal uncle (Muhāi's father)	Father	Self
Location	Vīramma Kāli temple in Thanjavur	Vīramma Kāli temple in Thanjavur	Avadi camp in Chennai
1	A vehicle and a wounded person	Mahamāi	Saturn moving away and a monster
2	A person climbing a tree	A man with an injured leg	Lunar eclipse
3	Hanuman climbing a mountain	Karuppucāmi	A snake and lunar eclipse
4	Murukaṉ, Śiva symbol	Nallataṅkal	Arjuna
5	Śiva, Hanuman a person	A snake following	Arjuna
6	Karuppucāmi	A snake (= Nagamma)	Śaiva and Vaiṣṇava
7	Kāli	Broken	Three gods in prayer
8	Maria	Mahamāi	Sītā sitting in the woods
9	Jesus on the cross	Maria (Samayapuram Muttumary)	Sītā sitting in the woods
10	Hanuman	A church and Maria	A Muslim
11	Mahamāi, Murukaṉ's weapon	Broken	Fish
12	Murukaṉ	Anjaneyar	Harishchandra's son
13	Vināyakar	Aiyanar and a dog	A house and a man
14	An elephant clothing a Śiva lingam	A snake eating the moon	A turtle with a human head
15	Ayyappaṉ	Vināyakar	A mermaid
16	Mahamāi and a trishūla	Vīramma Kāli	Hanuman
17	Mahamāi	Angara Kāli	Arjuna
18	Rāma with a bow and arrow	A mosque	Nagore Andavar
19	A snake following a person	A mosque	Nagore Andavar
20	A cobra (Sriranganagar)	A snake and Rāma	A giant and a ladder
21	A snake and the moon	Samayapuram	Bhadrakāli
22	Nagore Andavar (= Allah)	Murukaṉ and a peacock	A snake and the moon

23	A mosque	Mahamāi	A person
24	A woman near a hut (Nallataṅkal)	Rāma fighting Mahamāi (Krishna hunting)	Letters
25	A biting dog	Broken	A person praying and a plant (influences of Jupiter)
26	Murti	Broken	Kuṭukuṭupai
27		Hanuman is carrying a mountain	Kuṭukuṭupai
28		Vijayakanth (actor)	
29		A mongoose and a snake	
30		Broken	
31		Broken	

What is deliberately concealed from the client despite being a condition for divination is that the *things* used in divination are *replaceable*. Cuvaṭi cards can be chosen multiple times by the same procedure and some cards carry the same motifs.[12] There are formulaic sayings in the Nāyakaṉ's utterings, too. Nevertheless, what is emphasized more than anything at the scene of divination is that particular cards have appeared as special *things* before the client "here and now" out of the many cards in the set. This is applicable to the way the Nāyakaṉ shows up and repeatedly states, "I have come all the way to be at your feet". Here, *things* that were supposed to be replaceable with others are functioning as metonymy for matters that are already underway "here and now" although they have not been seen. At the same time, "I", as one of the clients of the Nāyakaṉ, becomes a subject who holds the key to my own life, by my own action "here and now".

The fact that divination is a business is concealed. The diviners deliberately avoid coercing people to do divination. They avoid setting a price for divination. And they happily do divination multiple times for one price. These practices are intended to demonstrate that the diviners' intentions are not reducible to the profit-motive, and that divination is performed free of the diviners' arbitrary interpretations and motivations. We surmise that these are attempts to prevent the "verisimilitude" of the diviners' words from being relativized. Nevertheless, clients "shop-around" in an attempt to avoid the result of one divination from becoming absolutized, seeking answers from more than one and sometimes different types of divination. Divination is realized at the intersection of people's desire to "know the future" and the diviner's desire to earn a livelihood by offering knowledge and words that might satisfy this desire.

Thus, when *things* work in divination, they deny the intention and meaning of divination, their replaceability as goods, and the fixed relationality and social circumstances of people who are involved in divination. Previous studies have focused on the social functions of divination or the process in which the "plausibility" of divination is created by interactions between the diviner and the client. The focus of this chapter, however, is not on the persuasive aspect of divination. Divination is not about persuasion; it entails the "showing" of unknown landscapes by enticing the client to encounter known matters and situations in a new space-time set up by *things*. People can stand in the entrance to the knowledge of their own destiny only when they are "tempted" by various *things* provided by the diviner.

This chapter has examined the mechanism by which the "verisimilitude" of divination arises with a focus on *things* that introduce contingency into divination. In our examples, the diviner's interpretation process was rarely explained and the client rarely spoke; only a categorical conclusion was provided. If this is a type of divination that is highly dependent on *things*, so to speak, there must be a type of divination which is less dependent on *things* and in which "problems" are explored through interactions between the diviner and the client. This point, including how divination types with different levels of dependence on *things* coexist, will require further study.

Divination gives people the pleasure of speculating and discovering the mystery of life by creating contingent encounters between people, and between *things* and people "here and now". Its major premise is that we are temporarily separated from our daily thoughts and expectations when we confront *things* or the diviner. In this place, we are given a chance to be released from the social meanings and relations of people and goods and to grapple with the world of new meanings again. The secret behind the popularity of divination among people may be found here.

Part V
Toward a New *Mono* Theory

10 The Origin of Tool-using Behavior and Human Evolution

Gen Yamakoshi

Keywords: chimpanzee, Africa, primate, bipedalism, feeding technique

10.1 The origins of human material culture and tools

An exploration of the relationship between *mono* (*things*) and chimpanzees, the extant species most closely related to humans, would provide us with suggestions about the evolutionary origin of the relationship between *things* and humans.

Things in the life-world of modern humans cover absolutely all domains that support our survival; an aggregate of material culture constituting our civilization. Although this material culture has grown so complex that it no longer seems possible to grasp a general overview, we should be able to arrive at some simple tool-using behavior of our ancestral species if we track the history of human evolution to its origin. What is the simple primordial tool that dramatically changed the relationship between humans and *things*? Was the primordial tool developed after early humans had diverged from the common ancestor of humans and chimpanzees as it has often been assumed? Or is it something with a much older origin; something which was developed before the last common ancestor and can still be found in the behaviors of wild chimpanzees today? In an attempt to find answers to these questions, we will trace the origin of the relationship between humans and *things* by examining the history of human evolution and comparing the tool-using behavior of early humans to today's wild chimpanzees.

10.2 The life-world of wild chimpanzees

Observing wild chimpanzees is hard work. As diurnal chimpanzees begin their activity at dawn, observers head for their sleeping nest, previously identified, in the faint light of the early morning. We follow them, ensuring that we do not let them out of our sight. On lucky days we can observe them until they make their beds in a tree at sunset and go to sleep. I chose the feeding ecology of wild chimpanzees for my academic dissertation, and led this kind of life in Bossou, Guinea, West Africa, for a total of twenty months between 1992 and 1996.

Generally speaking, feeding ecology is an approach to understanding the behavior and society of target animals by focusing on their diet. Wild chimpanzees are omnivores who feed mostly on fruits. They use a wide variety of foods, including leaves, tree bark, tree sap and insects, depending on availability, which varies greatly from day-to-day and month-to-month (Photo 10.1).[1] My daily tasks involved recording the place of feeding, the food species and which parts were eaten, the time and manner of feeding and so on for each food item eaten by the target chimpanzee. Observing these matters is not a simple task. When a chimpanzee is feeding on fruit at the top of a very tall tree, I must continue observing through binoculars while enduring pain in my neck. When it feeds on the pith or fruit of herbaceous plants of the ginger or arrowroot family in the dense undergrowth of the shadowy forest floor, I must crawl on the ground to get close enough to confirm the face of the feeding animal and which part of the plant it is eating.

A maxim often quoted as guidance to those studying the feeding ecology of chimpanzees. "You must try everything that the chimpanzee eats". There is a slight concern about poisoning and other risks, but it is relatively safe to assume that if it is edible for chimpanzees it is edible for humans, since we are very similar genetically and physiologically. Based on my experience, most of the fruit varieties that make up their staple diet are moderately sweet and palatable to humans, although some are strongly astringent or bitter. In order to try their food and identify plant species, I often need to collect some leaf or fruit sample from the high branches of tall trees. Doing so often requires ingenuity and considerable efforts, for example, using a very long stick or making a slingshot with a rubber band, for example.

Chimpanzees climb up the tree trunk, move on large horizontal branches on four limbs, and gather fruits and leaves while hanging from the thin end of the branch with their long arms. Their feeding behavior is founded on this ability to move freely in the spatial structure of the forest. All chimpanzees except for infants are able to gather necessary food using their own bodies alone. In contrast, humans are completely helpless in the forest environment without the aid of civilization, despite our biological proximity to chimpanzees. Be it in the forest or the savanna, humans require at least some simple tools, such as those used by hunting-and-

Photo 10.1 A chimpanzee eating figs in Bossou

gathering peoples, in order to acquire food to survive in the natural environment. Today, humans can only secure food within the massive civilization system based on agriculture and trade.

The ecology of wild chimpanzees, however, has shaken the classical dichotomy of humans-civilization and animals-nature from its foundation. Wild chimpanzees use tools. Field studies of wild primates, which gained momentum from the 1960s, revealed that chimpanzees in the wild routinely used natural objects such as twigs and stones to catch ants and termites and to crack nuts. Various types of tool-using behavior were observed during my fieldwork in Bossou, including using a pair of stones as hammer and anvil to crack oil-palm (*Elaeis guineensis*) nuts, hunting army ants with long sticks, and pestle pounding using the oil-palm petiole (frond). Tool-use in Bossou accounted for approximately ten percent of the total feeding time throughout the year, but there was a high level of seasonal variation, peaking at about 32% in June. The chimpanzees in Bossou spend 30–40% of their twelve-hour day on feeding activity, so if we track them in June, we can observe their tool-using behavior for one hour or so every day (Yamakoshi 1998, 2001).

The life-world of wild chimpanzees is very different from the modern human life-world surrounded by *things*. In terms of the total volume of *things* (or biomass), arboreal and other plants are the predominant component in the forest environment inhabited by wild chimpanzees. What we typically call *things* (i.e., discrete objects of manipulable size, according to Kuroda's definition in Chapter 11), though, are limited to such objects as plant waste products and stones. In particular, the arboreal environment to which primates are considered to have adapted is almost devoid of *things* that can be manipulated by hand. We can say that the life-world of wild chimpanzees is made up of "substrates," which support locomotion such as the ground and trees, "foods" (which are attached to plants in most cases and do not manifest as discrete *things*) used in feeding behavior, and social beings such as other conspecific individuals. *Things* in the narrow sense of being manipulable and usable are rare. It is likely that the relationship between chimpanzees and *things*, which shares common origins with human material culture, evolved in this kind of environment.

10.3 The grand narrative of the origin of tools

The question of when human kind developed tool culture and came to depend on tools for living was once an important part of the grand narrative (Lyotard 1984). Engels considered bipedalism to be "the decisive step in the transition from ape to man" (Engels 1968: 482). He considered bipedalism to be significant because "the hands had become free" (ibid.: 485) as a result. Relieved of the function of walking, the hands could specialize in carrying out other functions. "The specialization of the hand – this implies the tool, and the tool implies specific human activity, the transforming reaction of man on nature, production" (ibid.: 353).[2]

"Production" in this sense began with tools. Humans became animals who "labor". Humans began to transform nature in a planned manner through labor, enabled by tools. "Man by his changes makes it serve his ends, *masters* it" (ibid.: 491). Engels theorized that the most ancient tools were "hunting and fishing implements, the former at the same time serving as weapons" (ibid.: 487). The acquisition of tools, he argued, enabled the transition from an exclusively vegetable diet to the concomitant use of meat, and the improved nutritional condition resulting from meat in the diet prompted brain development. The development of labor necessitated joint activity, and language became necessary because "they had something to say to each other" (ibid.: 485). Improved nutrition and the development of language led to the development of the large and complex human brain. This grand narrative, incorporating the coherent causal relationship between bipedalism, tool use (labor), meat in the diet, language development, and encephalization provided a guiding framework that oriented empirical studies of human evolution following the Second World War.

10.4 Testing the grand narrative

While the "end of grand narratives" is talked about in the social sciences, studies of human evolution have nevertheless provided a paradigm for comprehensive empirical research centering on paleoanthropology and incorporating studies of the subsistence technologies of hunting-and-gathering peoples, the ecology and comparative cognitive science of extant primates, and the study of genetics, which has advanced dramatically in recent years. What is the empirical evidence provided by these studies for and against Engels' hypothesis of human evolution today?

The importance Engels accorded to the development of bipedalism has not diminished to this day.[2] The exclusive locomotion by upright walking is rare among vertebrates in general and mammals in particular. There is no conclusive theory about why this evolutionary adaptation occurred, but some of the competing hypotheses include: the efficient transportation of food (Lovejoy 1981); the thermoregulatory advantage – a claim that uprightness reduced the body's surface exposure to direct sunlight, thus aiding adaptation to a hot and humid environment (Wheeler 1991); and the energy efficiency hypothesis, based on a comparison of energy efficiency between quadrupedal and bipedal primates (Rodman and McHenry 1980).

Bipedalism developed specifically in the human lineage after separation from the last common ancestor of humans and chimpanzees. The oldest fossil hominine species indicating bipedalism is *Sahelanthropus*, dating back six to seven million years (Brunet at al. 2002). However, the subsequent "progress" outlined in Engels' grand narrative was not a consistent succession in the manner of the domino effect. Bipedalism in early humans such as *Australopithecus* is incomplete compared with that of modern humans. Modern human-like vertical bipedalism appeared during the early period of the genus *Homo* (so called *Homo erectus*) less than 2 million years ago.

Returning our focus to tool use, the aforementioned field studies of wild primates since the 1960s discovered that chimpanzees and other species do use tools in the wild. Among other things, this means that primates, especially apes, began to use tools although their hands were not freed by bipedalism, and their use of tools did not free them from dependence on dietary conditions imposed by nature (Yamakoshi 2001). The first major change in tool culture was observed in Oldowan stone tools excavated from geological layers up to 2.5 million years ago in East Africa (Semaw et al. 1997). It is unclear who manufactured and used these tools, but the time-frame overlaps with the emergence of the genus *Homo* from *australopithecines*. Since the use of stone tools bearing processing marks has not been observed in animals other than humans, we surmise that the behavior was unique to humans. While there is no conclusive theory about the function of these stone tools as yet, the prevailing view is that they were for cutting up animal carcasses. The causal relationship between the development of uniquely human tool use and the emergence of bipedalism is also unclear.

What about the function of tools to actively influence natural resources in order to acquire products as per Engels' "tool = labor" hypothesis? As mentioned earlier, wild chimpanzees in Bossou spend around 10% of their annual feeding time using tools. Food items such as nuts and ants, which become available through tool use, are physically protected by some form of defense such as hard shells and nests and cannot be readily accessed using their bodies alone. In other words, chimpanzees would lose significant sources of nutrition if not for their tool use. Chimpanzees in the Taï Forest of Côte d'Ivoire, for example, obtained 3,762 kcal of energy through a nut cracking behavior they carried out for just over two hours per day (Gunter and Boesch 1993). This provides a basis for comparing the value of tool use between chimpanzees and the San people – hunter-gatherers of the Kalahari Desert, Botswana – who reportedly outperform contemporary society in labor efficiency by obtaining 2,000 kcal from four hours and thirty nine minutes of labor per day (Tanaka 1971). In other words, becoming dependent on tools for survival while actively changing the availability of natural resources can be seen in the lives of wild chimpanzees.

It is well established that encephalization was achieved incrementally with the emergence of early *Homo* species. The brain consumes a lot of energy, and major changes in nutrition are believed to have been required to develop such a large brain (the "expensive tissue" hypothesis: Aiello and Wheeler 1995). Empirical evidence is scant, but the adoption in the diet of meat and /or cooked root vegetables have been suggested as the cause of encephalization (Yamakoshi 2001; Wrangham 2010).

As for language development, empirical evidence is extremely scant because it leaves very little archaeological evidence. The current best estimate for the time of language development based indirectly on morphological and genetic studies is between 100,000 and 300,000 years ago. This rather recent date appears to synchronize with qualitative changes that are different from those that herald the birth of the genus *Homo* (2–2.5 million years ago), and marks the emergence of so-called human species (*Homo sapiens*).

In summary, Engels' hypothesis seems to fit accounts of the emergence of the genus *Homo* (*Homo erectus*), with the almost simultaneous occurrences of important events, namely: the completion of bipedalism, uniquely human stone-tool making, the adaptation to highly nutritious foods (meat diet?), and the beginning of encephalization, although there still are many contentious issues outstanding. Two important components of the scenario missed the mark considerably: the origin of tool use traces back much earlier, to the common ancestors of humans and chimpanzees, and the use of language appear to have developed much later, at the birth of *Homo sapiens* (*Neanthropines*). Some predicated causal relationships are not supported by empirical evidence; especially the claim that the use of tools arises after bipedalism freed the hands, which is contradicted by the discovery that quadrupeds use tools. The fact that major transformation points in the hominization process center around 2–2.5 million years ago means that many Australopithecines had probably begun walking on two legs about seven million years ago, but were actually little more than "standing-only apes" for four to five million years, or three quarters of human history. We know almost nothing about the function of the hands freed by bipedalism during that period, especially the Australopithecine age. Empirical evidence suggests that transformation was stepped rather than gradual as some important changes happened simultaneously and very few changes took place for the rest of the time.

It appears that we need to look back at least to the common ancestors of humans and chimpanzees in our search for the origin of tools in human evolution. How far back shall we go to find the origins of tool-using behavior shared by humans and chimpanzees? And what was the very first tool-using behavior that spawned other tool uses? In the following sections we will look for the origin of human tool use in the evolutionary history of primates.

10.5 The definition of tool

We are surrounded by many different tools and live our lives by using them daily. The presence of tools has become so ubiquitous that we rarely wonder what is or is not a tool. However, ethologists, who study the behaviors of non-human animal species living in different *umwelten* than humans, need a strict definition of what tool use is. Beck offers the following practical definition:

> the external employment of an unattached environmental object to alter more efficiently the form, position, or condition of another object, another organism, or the user itself, when the user holds or carries the tool during or just prior to use and is responsible for the proper and effective orientation of the tool. (Beck 1980: 10)

It may not be a refined or elegant composition but this definition was formulated with careful consideration for a diverse range of examples and has been used widely as the de facto standard since its publication.

> Tool use is the exertion of control over a freely manipulable external object (the tool) with the goal of (1) altering the physical properties of another object, substance, surface or medium (the target, which may be the tool user or another organism) via a dynamic mechanical interaction, or (2) mediating the flow of information between the tool user and the environment or other organisms in the environment. (St Amant and Horton 2008: 1203)

For example, Beck's definition of a tool as an "unattached object" results in some inconsistencies. For example, catching ants with a broken-off branch is regarded as tool use but bending a stem from a nearby shrub to dip into an ants' nest is not. The revised definition avoids this problem by describing a tool as "a freely manipulable external object". And it successfully excludes tricky marginal cases such as "ceremonial gifts" that are assumed to change "the interior" of the target by limiting the effect of tool use to "altering the physical properties".

This refinement of the definition is very important in a practical sense. Nonetheless, I cannot help but find something tautological in such an activity; it is in a sense mere semantic refinement for the purpose of sorting without contradictions what we intuitively regard as typical cases of tool use out of a continuum where various marginal cases exist side by side with "instrumental behaviors". The harder we try to increase its objective precision as a practical definition, the more anthropocentric we have to make it. Such a dilemma may be another major characteristic of the behavior of tool use.

10.6 Distribution of tool-using behavior

Only a small number of animal species fulfill the above definition. However, they are not limited to primates closely related to humans; they include insects, fish and birds. For instance, ants belonging to the genus *Aphaenogaster* transport hard-to-carry liquid food such as honey and ripe fruit sap by soaking things such as snipped leaves and wood debris in them, then carrying it to their nest. Using tools, ants can transport this type of food ten times more efficiently (Fellers and Fellers 1976). And various bird species, including finch, crow and great tit, have been observed using a stick, held in their beak, to dig out insects hiding behind or inside something (Gifford 1919; Orenstein 1972; Boswall 1977).

The fact that these observations have been made in genealogically distant taxa suggests that tool use has evolved independently in different clades. What is the reason for the evolution of tool use in each of these taxa? Many of the tool-using behaviors that have been reported so far function to obtaining less accessible food items more efficiently. In other words, feeding advantages seem to have promoted the evolution of tool use in many cases.

10.7 Tool use in primates

It has been long known that primates reared by humans use tools with dexterity (Köhler 1962). And many accounts by local inhabitants of tool use by primates are also found in travel journals left by explorers who had visited various parts of the world during the Age of Discovery (Sept and Brooks 1994, and others). The first report of a directly observed case of tool use by wild primates with the location and target species specified was about nut cracking by chimpanzees in Côte d'Ivoire made by Savage and Wyman (1843–44). It was followed by, for example, a report by Carpenter (1887) of macaques (*Macaca fascicularis*) on the Andaman Sea islands using stones to open oysters on the beach. The number of credible observations reported increased from the 1960s when field studies on primates began in earnest.

Observed cases of tool use by primates are no more common than for all animals, and are mainly distributed across only three taxa, namely, the subfamily *Cebinae*, the subfamily *Cercopithecinae*, and the family *Hominidae* (humans and great apes). Tool use has been observed, including anecdotal and marginal cases, in only twenty or so of over 200 primate species, including humans (Yamakoshi 2004). These three taxa are independent of each other in the evolutionary tree and each taxon exhibits unique behavioral characteristics, as discussed below. It is highly likely that the tool behaviors found in extant primate species have also evolved independently. In other words, it seems reasonable for us to look to the common ancestors of great apes in our search for the origin of human tool-using behavior. We will compare the characteristics of tool use in these three taxa in order to understand what great ape-type tool usage entails.

10.7.1 The Cebinae

Capuchin monkeys, belonging to the subfamily *Cebinae*, are omnivorous primates occupying the forests in Central and South Americas. They feed on a wide range of food, including fruits, insects, and small animals. They are known for their "destructive feeding" pattern because they eat every food they find as they travel. While they were found to use various tools deftly in captivity, only a handful of cases of tool use in wild forest species have been reported, including using an oyster shell to break open another oyster on the beach (Fernandes 1991) and using a leaf to drink water (Phillips 1998). In terms of frequency, these behaviors were sporadic rather than habitual. In recent years, however, the use of a stone as a hammer to crack open hard palm nuts has been observed in several savanna-dwelling populations (Moura and Lee 2004; Fragaszy et al. 2004; Waga et al. 2005; Canale et al. 2009). It has been confirmed that they engage in this behavior very frequently and routinely.

It was observed some time ago that capuchin monkeys held a hard nut such as a palm nut in their hands and smashed it against a sturdy substrate such as the ground and the tree trunk in order to open it (Izawa and Mizuno 1977). It appears that this behavior had become a basic feeding pattern for the species as it has been observed frequently in almost all capuchin monkey populations (Figure 10.1). Holding the target object directly in the hands and altering it by using the substrate cannot be considered a tool use according to the definition above. Functionally, however, it is no different from using a stone to crack nuts, and this use of the substrate is structurally more complex than their ordinary feeding behavior. In this chapter, we follow Boinski et al. (2000) and apply the term "substrate use" to this behavior. Because capuchin monkeys rely on palm nuts and other hard-shell nuts during the period of low food availability (Terborgh 1983), feeding on palm nuts using the substrate seems to play a very important role in their survival. It is conceivable that the recently found tool-using behavior in the savanna-dwelling populations has been

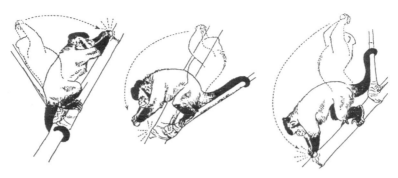

Figure 10.1 Substrate use in capuchin monkeys: Opening a palm nut by smashing it against a bamboo node. (Source: Izawa & Mizuno 1977)

developed from the basic feeding pattern of palm nut cracking behavior (substrate use), which is universal to the species. Perhaps for the forest-dwelling capuchin monkeys, it is more efficient to smash nuts directly against the tree trunk rather than fetching a stone from the ground and using it to crack nuts on a tree branch. In the case of capuchin monkeys who have moved into the savanna and live on the ground where stones are readily available, however, it appears that cracking palm nuts with a tool has developed as an extension of their substrate use.

10.7.2 The subfamily *Cercopithecinae*

Cercopithecine species such as baboons and macaques are highly omnivorous with a wide range of diets. Green monkeys in Kenyan savannas have been found to eat the viscous sap of Acacia trees gathering in unreachable tree hollows by dipping hard seed pods in it (Hauser 1988). This behavior was observed during the dry season in an extreme drought year but not in years of average rainfall before and after it. Other observed cases of tool use include the use of leaves to remove ants crawling all over small fruits in crab-eating macaques (Chiang 1967) and to remove poisonous stings from chrysalis in lion-tailed macaques (Hohmann 1988). These are anecdotal observations and cannot be regarded as routine behaviors. More recently, as mentioned above, two different types of oyster opening behavior in crab-eating macaques were observed in detail (Malaivijitnond et al. 2007; Gumert et al. 2009) in the Andaman Sea region where they had been observed to use stones to open oysters in the nineteenth century. The frequency of these observations indicates that this behavior is well established in their everyday life.

It is interesting to note that tool use has been observed in the more terrestrial species among *Cercopithecines*. Terrestrial baboons and macaques eat less accessible foods that are protected by hard shells or poisonous stings by pressing, smashing or rubbing them against a substrate such as the ground surface. This type of substrate use has become a basic feeding pattern of the species, which is observed regularly. The macaques are often seen washing dirty food with water; this is considered to be a type of substrate use to prevent excessive dental abrasion from chewing soiled food. As in the case of palm nut cracking by capuchin monkeys, oyster opening behavior found in crab-eating macaques is thought to have developed as an extension of the previously established substrate use, especially their tendency on the ground and near water.

10.7.3 The *Hominidae*

The family *Hominidae* is the taxon most closely related to humans. It includes orangutans, gorillas, chimpanzees and bonobos. The origins of human tool use are highly likely to have derived from these great apes' tool use.

Chimpanzees are the species most closely related to humans. They occupy a wide range of habitats from African tropical forests to open woodlands and have fruit-based omnivorous diets. They are the only primate species other than humans who engage in species-wide tool use. Habitual tool use has been observed in all long-term observational research sites. Tool use patterns vary greatly from one study field to another. As many of these variations cannot be explained by environmental differences alone, they are considered to be "culture" transmitted via social learning (McGrew 1996; Whiten et al. 1999). Tool use patterns observed in relatively large numbers of sites include termite fishing with flexible grass stems and twigs, which are inserted into termite nests and pulled out together with biting termites, ant dipping also with twigs inserted into army ant nests, and nut cracking using stones to smash hard nuts. Some patterns are specific to small numbers of communities, such as carpenter ant fishing in Mahale, Tanzania, (Nishida 1973) and pestle pounding in Bossou (Yamakoshi and Sugiyama 1995).

Orangutans in Sumatra, Indonesia, routinely use a twig held in the hand or the mouth to extract ants, termites and honey and to remove protective spikes from fruits (van Schaik et al. 1996). Among non-human primates, holding and manipulating a tool in the mouth is peculiar to orangutans. Curiously, major observations, including anecdotal reports, are limited to the subspecies on Sumatra Island and very few are found in the subspecies on Borneo Island which has been thoroughly studied in the wild. Van Schaik et al. (1999) suggest that this due to differences in social tolerance between the two subspecies. They conclude that tool use is more developed in the Sumatran subspecies, which has higher social tolerance, because there are more opportunities to observe the behavior of others in the community.

10.7.4 Tools and feeding niches

In comparison with the capuchin monkeys and *cercopithecines*, great apes exhibit a broader variety of tool use but their substrate use appears to be less significant. While there have been a relatively large number of cases reporting smashing hard food items against the ground, many of the other patterns reported are only anecdotal. Hence, it seems unlikely that tool use developed from great apes' substrate use as suggested by observations of capuchin monkeys and *cercopithecines*.

Another characteristic of the feeding technique of great apes is that its relationship with morphological adaptation is different from that of capuchin monkeys and *cercopithecines*. Capuchin monkeys possess hard enamel teeth and a powerful jaw adapted to eating hard food. Their feeding technique basically supplements these morphological adaptations and is applied to the foods typical of the species. Similarly, *cercopithecines* use their feeding technique to protect their teeth against excessive abrasion from eating hard foods, unripe fruits, and soiled terrestrial foods. In contrast, no such coordination between morphology and feeding technique has been found in great apes. The enamel layer of hominid teeth is relatively thin. And while the proportion of ripe fruits in their diet is higher in comparison with capuchin monkeys and *cercopithecines*, the social insects and hard nuts that they obtain via tool use are not the typical foods to which their bodies have adapted and are not usable without tools.

In other words, tool use allows great apes to acquire new feeding niches that are normally inaccessible through morphological adaptation alone, whereas capuchin monkeys and *cercopithecines* use feeding technique as a supplementary means to access foods to which they are morphologically adapted within their normal feeding niches. This tool behavioral tendency in great apes is highly suggestive, considering the fact that early humans subsequently shifted their feeding niches from fruit-based diet to meats and root vegetables.

10.8 The original type of human tool-using behavior?

The above overview of tool behaviors in primates indicates the possibility of finding the origins of human tool behavior in the tool usage found among extant

Photo 10.2 A chimpanzee inserting a stick into a tree hollow to catch carpenter ants in Bossou

great apes. This hominid-type tool behavior has some interesting characteristics, as previously mentioned.

Which hominid-type tool behavior became the archetype for human tool use? The most commonly observed pattern in great apes has been "inserting" a cord-like or stick-like object into holes and gaps that are smaller than their hands (Photo 10.2). Surprisingly, this is a uniquely hominid pattern that is seldom found in capuchin monkeys and *cercopithecines* (but see Souto et al. 2011). If we estimate the origin of tool behavior in hominids, including humans, by comparing extant species, the most likely scenario is probably the emergence of the primordial form of the behavior to extract social insects and their products (honey etc.) by inserting sticks in some species of Miocene hominids prior to the last common ancestor of humans and orangutans about 13 million years ago.

"Insertion feeding" (Yamakoshi 2004) has some indicative characteristics, including the need for precision gripping, the invisible site of action, which makes mimicking others difficult, and the absence of alternative substrate use in contrast to cracking open hard shells. As we have seen, the function of tools such as a stone to crack nuts can be performed by, for example, holding the target nut in the hand and smashing it against the ground or a tree trunk. Hence, we can conceive of the gradual development of tool use from the more primordial substrate use. In insertion feeding, however, the target of tool application is an unmanipulable substrate such as the ground and the termite nest and it is structurally impossible to achieve the same function with substrate use. The evolution of this type of hominid tool behavior may have required more insightful intelligence. It is perhaps too early to draw conclusions about the evolution of this unique behavior at this point in time.

Interest in holes and crevices and inserting fingers and sticks into them is observed widely in both non-human hominids in captivity and human infants. It is often interpreted as an expression of curiosity. Sartre gained insight into the relationship between holes and human nature from psychiatric literature on this behavior in human infants. "A good part of our life is passed in plugging up holes, in filling empty places, in realizing and symbolically establishing a plenitude" (Sartre 1956: 458). I wonder if we can see the evolutionary history of hominids over 15 million years behind this insight.

11 "Things" and Their Emergent Sociality in the Primates' World

Suehisa Kuroda

Keywords: primates/non-human primates, hand, *sugari*, socialization of *things*, equality principle

11.1 The socialization of things

This chapter focuses on non-human primates and discusses their direct physical involvement with *things* (which, for the purpose of this chapter, are manipulable physical objects; see 11.3 for a more detailed definition). Our discussion will demonstrate that the complexity of the way things appear was conditioned prior to the emergence of language, that things cannot be separated from the bodies that operate them, and that the participation by things in social intercourse can only develop in societies with a prevailing coexistence principle, which Itani (1987) named the equality principle. The equality principle is a constitutive principle of human society, containing the seeds of freedom and equality (Kuroda 2010, 2013). Things in the non-human primates' world overlap considerably with things in a human sense in terms of both the bodies that operate them and their relationship with society, although they are also different in important respects. Our discussion addresses a history that precedes the birth of things in the human sense.

In the history of human evolution, major events in the development of primates' relationship with things include the beginning of manipulating things by hand, rather than by mouth (the birth of true primates), the beginning of tool use by hand (see Chapter 10 by Yamakoshi), and the beginning of the "socialization" of things in the form of "food sharing" (Kuroda 1999). These developments each added layers of complexity to the meaning of things. The first two events are self-explanatory, but the third requires further explanation before we proceed.

The 'socialization of things' refers to the role of things as either the objective or the medium in peaceful interactions between individuals. According to Itani

(1987), who defined food sharing as an objectification of the equality principle, a necessary precondition for the ability to conduct social interactions via things is that society is constituted by the equality principle. The 'socialization of things' is a form of short-hand for incorporating things into a network of social relations, or assigning sociality to things. Of course, this is characteristic of things in the human world. In most primate species, in contrast, the handling of things is restricted to the individual level; things are rarely used as a means or a goal of social interaction. However, chimpanzees and bonobos[1] (the genus *Pan*), which are phylogenetically the closest species to humans, routinely share food between independent individuals (Itani 1987).[2] Additionally, for example, dominant male chimpanzees prioritize their supporters in sharing food (Nishida and Hosaka 2001) and female bonobos invite males in possession of food to mate in exchange for a share of the food (Kuroda 1982, 1984).[3] In terms of social intercourse, this means that food becomes a goal as well a means for achieving and maintaining affiliative relationships. As primates do not routinely share or transfer things other than food, we surmise that food sharing was the first form of the socialization of things in human evolutionary history as well (Kuroda 1999).

Food sharing appears to be the origin of economic behavior, creating both the producer and the consumer, and allowing valuable things to circulate between individuals (Itani 1987). However, interactions concerning food are not yet to lead to exchanges of things in the genus *Pan*. There is no evidence of reciprocity involving exchanges of food for either food or other things (Kuroda 1999). In this sense, primate things have not developed the complexity of things in the human world. Hobbes (1992 [1651]) considered the true meaning of things to lie in their exchangeability, and Levi-Strauss (1969) sought to understand human cultures in terms of their specific exchange behaviors. We can conclude that the essence of things in the human world lies in their exchangeability.

So, what is the significance of searching the primates' world for things prior to their transformation into the complex form of things (with exchangeability)? In the absence of the veil of language or institutions, relationships between things and society are more visible, enabling us to review the evolution of these relationships. For example, concepts of ownership, value and freedom are assumed in human exchanges of things, but their generation is difficult to discern from human exchange behavior. In contrast, observations of food sharing in the genus *Pan* find correspondence between behaviors and relationships. For example, adults never take food that lies within reach of another party without permission, regardless of their relative social status. With this observation, we can verify the emergence of a relationship between the thing and the subject that can be called "ownership" upon acceptance by others.[4] Food sharing relies on the autonomy of an owner who is free to decline. Food in an individual's possession becomes a valuable thing for another and the object of the other's desire precisely because of the possibility of sharing. Consequently, it becomes clear that food in the *Pan* world does have some circulatability (semi-exchangeability). In sum, food sharing is a form of socialization, which is generated along with primordial forms of ownership, value and freedom.

Moreover, although the socialization of things assigns social relationships to things, it also adds degrees of complexity that make identifying whether the thing is a means or a goal rather confusing (see 11.4.6). This is generated by the characteristics of social intercourse, rather than by language.

In the next section, we shall describe and examine developments in the world of primates' things in the first and third epochs. The second epoch – tool use – is discussed by Yamakoshi in Chapter 10.

11.2 Methodology

We shall touch on the perception of the environment, awareness and senses in non-human primates in this chapter. Conjectures are derived from both my observations and my experiences of eating primates' feeds and climbing trees to pick fruits ("ecological participant observations": Kuroda 2002). Recent findings in neuroscience, especially about the mirror neuron system (Rizzolatti and Sinigaglia 2009; Iacoboni 2009), seem to offer support for the appropriateness of humans drawing inferences about the awareness and senses of apes.

Mirror neurons become excited when an individual observes an action or emotion expressed by another, as if the observing individual is performing the same act or feeling the same emotion. They are understood as a mechanism that simulates the other's action in the observer's brain (Rizzolatti and Sinigaglia 2009; Iacoboni 2009). Mirror neurons in macaque monkeys appear to respond to human actions as well. Let me explain step by step. For example, when a macaque monkey with prior experience of drinking juice from a glass sees a glass, his neurons for grasping an object of a particular shape as well as neurons for drinking are already excited. In effect, a glass "appears" in the monkey's brain accompanying not only visual recognition of the form but also excitation of the neurons for grasping and drinking – the glass is "represented", so to speak, including its affordances. When the monkey sees a researcher reaching for the glass, these neurons fire more strongly. In the same way that we see the monkey's action and understand its goal, the monkey sees our action and knows our goals. It is reasonable to assume that the same thing is happening in mutual action recognition between individual macaque monkeys (and therefore other apes).

While some may criticize me for oversimplification if I infer various senses in primates on these grounds, I do not believe that I am too far off the mark as we are dealing with simple senses, desires and emotions. Furthermore, this neuroscientific finding of a cognitive structure which provides an empathetic understanding of the actions of others is consistent with, and provides support for, the theory of spatial awareness through motion (H. Poincaré), the concept of affordances, and Merleau-Ponty's phenomenology of the body (Rizzolatti and Sinigaglia 2009; Iacoboni 2009).

11.3 Things for primate individuals

11.3.1 A rich world of things created by hands

The archetypal primate species is estimated to have come into existence about 70 million years ago, while the extant primate species are characterized by hands and feet that are capable of grasping objects, which appear to have developed some 55 million years ago, according to fossil evidence. For hands and feet to have an ability to grasp, they principally need (apart from the nervous system) long fingers/toes with nails and the thumb located opposite the other digits of the hand/foot (the 'opposable thumb').[5] Moreover, long arms that can extend beyond the proboscis forward and upward as well as some degrees of freedom at the hand, elbow and shoulder joints are necessary for an ability to manipulate things by hand. Thanks to their flexible limbs and grasping ability, primates have followed a unique course of evolution in the arboreal world. These characteristics have been preserved even in the clades that subsequently spread their habitats on the ground. Needless to say, there would be differences between past and extant primates in their capacities for precision grasping, and there are undeniable differences in the inter-digit proportions and the muscular/nervous systems between extant ape species and humans.[6] Nevertheless, we shall set aside such differences and discuss their almost common features below. As for *things*, let's just say for the moment that they are objects that can be handled by the hand until we discuss their characteristics in more detail in the next section. Attributes of things such as color and taste are beyond the scope of this chapter.

In primates, the main organ for grasping, holding and manipulating things is the hand (forepaw). Animals other than primates touch things with their whiskers, snout or tongue and grip things between the teeth. Consequently, they can only manipulate things by pushing, biting and gripping when things are very close to their proboscis. Bears and cats which use their forelegs to attack prey have no ability to grasp, while squirrels and mice with short forelegs and weak grasp have very limited ability to manipulate things. By contrast, primates who use their hands have a wide manipulable space within their reach and are able to manipulate various objects in many ways. In other words, they have more objects that might be handled as things, and each thing has more affordances. Their long-reaching hands led to the emergence of diverse things with multilayered meanings.

The ability to grasp and manipulate is used for moving around on a tree, pulling fruit-bearing branches closer, and catching insects and small animals for food. In order to perform these actions quickly, they need short-range stereovision and linkage between optic nerves and motor nerves. One of the consequences of these requirements is the formation of a face with a relatively anterior eye position and shortened proboscis. For primates, things are connected to the face through the hands.

In primates, it appears that the hand provides an important benchmark for the visual structuring of space. According to neuroscientific findings, spatial recognition of the close range within hand-reach and that which is out of reach are performed in different parts of the brain. Visual contact with things at close range is linked to tactile perception in the parts of the body close to them in both humans and macaque monkeys (and perhaps apes).[7] By comparison, when humans touch things using a tool, we get a sense of directly touching it at a short distance from ourselves. In such cases, the domain for visual contact in close-range space also operates in our sight faculty. This has been confirmed for humans in brain damaged patients with hemispatial neglect of proximal space and that of distal space,[8] and for macaque monkeys in a tool use experiment by Iriki (2004). In short, the medium (things, especially tools) that transmit a tactile sense of contact with things causes both humans and macaque monkeys to recognize the objects as things within their hand-reach as well. Tools are an extension of both the hand and the eye.

According to Rizzolatti and Sinigaglia, neurons for goal execution by hand become excited when a macaque monkey sees a glass (Rizzolatti and Sinigaglia 2009). This means that the glass which appears for the perceiving macaque monkey is the simulation of a series of motions to perform some action based on his experience, i.e., explaining the representation using affordances. Rizzolatti and Sinigaglia (2009) say, this is consistent with Merleau-Ponty's (1945) observation: "In the action of the hand which is raised towards an object is contained a reference to the object, not as an object represented, but as that highly specific thing towards which we project ourselves, near which we are, in anticipation, and which we haunt".[9] This representation / anticipation is the same for macaque monkeys and humans (and apes) in the domain of affordances. The representation of a thing is constructed from the subject's experience of reaching for and manipulating the thing or similar things and comprised of the readiness to anticipate and make the interaction possible once again while predicting the outcome.

11.3.2 A sense of movable things

So what constitutes things for primates? We shall attempt to answer this by finding commonalities between human senses and primate behaviors. In the case of humans, we seem to intuitively perceive objects of movable size as things ("thing-like things"). Humans consider large trees and mountains to be "obstructive things" for certain purposes and rightly describe them as such, because they can imagine a space or an action in the absence of such things. In other words, movability is a condition for our sense of things, even if it is only imaginary movability. In contrast, non-solid objects such as water, air and fire should perhaps be categorized differently because we have a different sense of their manipulability. Thus, we shall begin by separating the objects of movable size and shape in terms of bodily senses as "thing-like things".

An example of non-human primates that manipulate things are Japanese macaques. They climb trees, pull branches toward themselves, and sometimes break them to eat fruit or leaves. On the ground, they use their hands to sweep aside and overturn fallen leaves, stones and dead wood to collect acorns, insects and mushrooms. When grooming, they part their partner's hair, pinching and removing lice eggs from the base of the hair (Tanaka 1999). Infants sometimes pick and chew fallen twigs or hit or press sand and pebbles. All these manipulations are performed by their hands. They normally avoid, climb over, or go around large, immovable objects. An alpha male might, however, use his full body to shake a large tree branch while barking loudly at an intruding male from another troop. In chimpanzees, males may try to move large rocks during displays of aggression, but they give up quickly. This seems to be a simple misjudgment about its movability. Manipulation of things by primates in general is the same as that by Japanese macaques. The differences between things they can move by themselves and things they cannot move is crucial for all of them.

Accordingly, we shall extract solid objects (including plants and excluding animals) from the physical world of primates, treating movable objects as things and the rest as "substrates". Under this classification, tree leaves and branches are things, but the tree trunk and the entire tree are substrates as far as primates are concerned.

11.3.3 A sense of self, *sasae* and *sugari*

In terms of the physical ability and locomotion of primates, an immovable part fixed to a substrate which can be grasped like a handle (*sasae*: support) and a part attached to a substrate like a small branch which is movable within a limited range (*sugari*: clinger) have special meanings as things because they are graspable. Both *sugari* and *sasae* are functionalized by the primates' unique physical ability to grasp and use them as media for moving their own bodies on and around substrates.[10] Of course, all land animals are movable bodies on the ground surface, but primates can extend their mobility three-dimensionally, moving up and down through the medium of *sasae* or *sugari* they grasp. These two categories, which appear to be unique to primates with grasping ability, are positioned between immovable substrates and movable and manipulable things, but we add these to the ranks of things because animals seem to have tangible senses of them as discussed below.

While a sense of things ("representation" and affordances in 11.3.2) is accumulated in the brain through grasping and moving, a sense of *sasae* is acquired by grasping it, giving one's weight to it, and a sense of extending one's body and muscular flexion/extension even though it is part of the immovable substrate. This also applies to *sugari* but we suppose that *sugari* offers a more dynamic sense, incorporating ever-changing senses of self due to its elasticity and the inertia of body weight. Of course, substrates and things are both the reflection of the animals' sense of itself in space. However, the *sasae* and especially the *sugari* are things of which the representations are embedded with the body sense introduced by the hands. In a simple example, monkeys and chimpanzees often hesitate in front of a branch or a bush they are about to jump onto even if it seems to be in easy reach. Animals probably sense not only whether a tree branch is within their reach, but also whether it is strong enough to support them – that is, assessing it relative to their own body weight – by just looking at the branch.

A branch sticking out of a tree trunk offers the affordance of "*sasae* for climbing" only for primates with hands. The same branch, in comparison, merely offers support for cats with no grasping ability after they have climbed to that level using their claws. The typical *sugari* include small branches and vines. Of course, small claw-footed animals such as squirrels also use flexible branches and vines for locomotion.

Photo 11.1 A bonobo mother swinging infants playing with a sugari. *The female on the left is the mother of the infant in front. She wears a mild play-face as she watches over the playing infants and delights them by shaking the branch from which they are dangling like a swing. In this instance, the branch becomes a socialized thing as play equipment.*

However, squirrels use the same manner of climbing, whether on flexible branches, vines or thick tree trunk, which is by hooking their claws. In contrast, monkeys and apes climb by wrapping their arms around large trunks and, if that's not possible, they use *sugari* to pull themselves up. When they move from one tree to another, they often jump onto a bush underneath to secure the safety of their passage by utilizing the cushioning effect of the bush and the resilience of the flexible branch they are grasping. Although squirrels also jump from one tree to another and cling to bushes using their weak grasping ability, their action is more appropriately called landing on leaves and small branches. In short, many of the various affordances offered by the *sugari*, including "flexibility", are only available to primates.

11.3.4 The specificity of *sugari*

The *sugari* is even more specific than the *sasae*. Small branches, for example, can be drawn closer (elastic deformation) or can be converted to manipulable things when broken off. Their elasticity together with the force and weight of the subject can facilitate movement. Moreover, they might "counter" the subject with their elasticity. For example, bonobos and chimpanzees make bird nest-like beds by snapping and layering small branches. When infants, who are unable to break the branches, mimic the bed-making behavior, the branches spring back as soon as they stop holding them. Some animals fall and occasionally die when the branch they jump to breaks because it is not flexible enough.[11] The branch *sugari* can be regarded as falling outside of the passivity of things; they are things that might defy one's intentions and sometimes cause dangerous accidents.

An examination of the mother-child relationship makes it clear that primates are born into the world of *sugari*. Newborns cling to the breast and belly of their mother using her hair and skin as *sugari* after birth. The child's view from this position is inverted and in almost constant motion, swinging rhythmically as the mother walks. The living body *sugari* is the source of the mother-child relationship unique to primates, that is, a baby sling that keeps the mother and the child close. The baby's fragile hands and feet grasp as the only active action they can perform, turning the mother into a *sugari*. The baby can only grasp a thing that is slender enough for its weak hands and feet to grasp – that thing is by definition a *sugari*. When the mother sits down to rest, the baby uses her body as a *sugari* to crawl upward, grasps a nearby branch as a *sugari* to climb upward although it cannot even walk on its four limbs. It has to grow a little older before it can learn to descend. Juveniles still love the swinging movements of the *sugari* and play by riding on the swinging branches on the tree. When they grow into adults, the *sugari* continues to serve them as a safety rope. When monkeys and apes rest on a tree, they almost always keep one of their limbs grasping either a *sugari* or *sasae* branch, except when sitting in a fork of large branches. They appear to remain almost continuously aware that dangerous falls can happen.

The *sugari* occupies a critically important place in the feeding behavior of primates. Many tree species produce fruit at the thin end of the branch. Young leaves which are important food for many primates also only grow at the end of the branch. Primates use other *sugari* and *sasae* to move closer to the thin end and gather fruits and young leaves by bending or breaking the branch. If they did not have this ability, they could not eat young leaves and they would have to wait until fruits dropped to the ground. Most of these foods would be eaten by birds and land animals and the primates' share would be severely reduced. They probably would not have flourished as they have.[12]

11.3.5 Seeing a thing in another thing
Some interesting cases of primates handling things are found in their play.

Chimpanzee infants often carry around fruit seeds and twigs. Matsuzawa (1991) observed a chimpanzee infant carrying around a piece of wood for several days in the Bossou forest, Guinea, and speculated that it might be doll-play. While this episode alone is not conclusive, other observations have suggested the role of "imagination" in seeing one thing as another thing or, in great apes, seeing a peer in a thing. In Mahale, Tanzania, Hayaki (1990) observed a chimpanzee infant making a play-face (laugh) and play-panting while wrestling with a broken twig. He interpreted this as the infant playing with the tree branch as it would with a peer. In Howletts Wild Animal Park, England, infant gorillas were often found showing a play-face as they played / fought with a rope.[13] Hayes (1951) reported that an infant chimpanzee she had raised in the same way as a human infant developed a play routine which involved pulling an "imaginary" toy.[14]

The ability of chimpanzees and bonobos to imagine things is not commonly accepted, as relevant observations are still scarce. This is perhaps because such an ability is greatly influenced by both species characteristics, up-bringing, and individual capability. I shall discuss the relevance of this to the socialization of things later (11.4.5).

11.4 The co-existence principle of primates and things

While a single thing can produce diversified appearances as affordance to the hand, a thing appearing to more than one individual produces different and diverse meanings. The socialization of things means that a thing arouses a common interest from multiple individuals and triggers interactions towards it, whether as goal or medium. While the primary thing that arouses common interest in primates is food, the inequality principle in which dominance-subordination relationships define fixed relationships of co-existence (Itani 1987) does not allow for multiple individuals to express interests in the same food simultaneously. Simultaneous interests are only accepted in societies where individuals co-exist through interactions under the equality principle (ibid.).

11.4.1 The inequality principle: Non-socialization of food by blocking desire

One species in which society is governed by the inequality principle is the Japanese macaque. There are linear dominance-subordination relationships in which the dominant individual generally obtains food on a priority basis. The subordinate refrains from looking at both the food in the dominant's possession and any other food in its vicinity. Itani (1954) identified dominance-subordination relationships by throwing a mandarin orange between two Japanese macaques and observing which individual would take it (the mandarin orange test). In most cases, one of them would not look at the orange. If the orange came into its field of vision, it would either avert its eyes or leave. The other individual would take the orange, in many cases without rushing, but it might act to threaten the other before taking it. Asymmetry in this behavior is fixed between any two specific individuals and a linear order emerges when all members of a group are ranked with orange-takers as the dominant. The mandarin orange clearly triggers the dominance-subordination relationship between two individuals, reconfirming and entrenching it.

In front of the mandarin orange, the subordinate suppresses its interest in and desire for the food, averting its eyes and avoiding interaction with the dominant. In a way, the food stops the two individuals from getting involved. (By contrast, the opposite dynamic occurs in chimpanzees and bonobos, where meat and tasty fruit draw many individuals, promoting social interaction such as communal feeding, begging and sharing (Kuroda 1999).)

However, there is a strong tendency in primates living in groups for their feeding behavior to become synchronized. One individual starts feeding, another follows and soon the entire troop is in a feeding state. The Japanese macaque is no exception; individuals feeding on nuts and leaves on the same large tree will do so concurrently, keeping a distance of about a meter between them if they are related and more than three meters if they are unrelated. Food only blocks direct social interaction at close range, but the act of eating things prompts other individuals to eat also. This synchronization is not surprising: when one sees another individual reaching for food, mirror neurons simulate the sense that it is one's own action.

Accordingly, the subordinate's act of looking away from food in the possession of the dominant is not merely an expression of fear. It also a way of suppressing desire – or rather, of avoiding desire by avoiding the simulation of the other's act. This behavior can also be witnessed on the part of the dominant, who will also look away to avoid the temptation to try to take food in the subordinate's possession. In fact, the dominant typically would not succeed in taking the subordinate's food even if it tried. Therefore it is in its best interest to leave it be, but this is not the calculation that leads to the blocking of the desire.[15]

In short, the function of mirror neurons means that food becomes an object of desire as soon as an individual sees it, irrespective of who has it and whether it lives under the inequality principle or the equality principle.[16] Food is a universal temptation that invites socialization. Although, on the one hand, food becomes communalized/socialized when the holder abandons its desire in the case of the genus *Pan*, the socialization of food is stopped when the non-holder blocks its desire. Food thus reverts to a mere thing in the possession of an individual in the case of the Japanese macaque. On the other hand, the "sharing of feeding behavior" occurs outside of certain distances as if to compensate for it. The relationships surrounding food are adjusted by distances between individuals.

While the ability to block desire must be genetically based since it is universally found in adults, the act of blocking desire manifests gradually with maturity and does not present clearly in infant monkeys. Newborns in the first several months sometimes get up in the face of a feeding individual to look. In Takasakiyama and Kōjima, infants and juveniles up to the age of two or three often steal food despite threats from adults, whereas adults dare not reach for a pile of favorite sweet potatoes in front of a dominant male.

11.4.2 The inequality principle: Momentary socialization of things

How about things other than food? Stone-play, consisting of the gathering, mixing, striking and stacking of small stones performed by Japanese macaque immatures one to three years of age (Huffman 1984) is a useful example in considering this question. I once observed stone-play between three juveniles two or three years old and a young mother at Arashiyama Monkey Park in Kyoto. When one macaque began to play, another infant approached within one meter, watched, snatched some stones, went away to find its own stones, began to play with them nearby. When the first infant left, the other went and played with its stones.[17] Yet, the two macaques never played with the same pile of stones simultaneously; when an older infant reached for stones, the player ran away carrying the stones.

Shimada (2009) reported branch dragging-play in Japanese macaque juveniles, which appears to be of a similar type. When one infant begins to drag a broken tree branch, which no one else has paid attention to until then, it gets the attention of other individuals, triggers a scramble for possession (but only momentarily before one party grasps it). They repeatedly run and pause and the whole process is over in less than a minute. As one's act spurs others to join in and branch dragging happens intermittently during the process, the action and the thing are shared simultaneously, albeit momentarily. This demonstrates that even juveniles are not very good at sharing acts and things simultaneously. This is why I refer to the interaction as "running away from each other" despite Shimada (2009) description of it as "play-chasing each other". Macaque juveniles manage to produce this hard act of sharing like a streak of lightening by running away with a branch, i.e., "fleeing" from the simultaneous sharing.

On the basis of the above, it is possible to say that the act of manipulating things under the attention of multiple individuals occasionally emerges among Japanese macaque immatures, but it does not develop into simultaneous interaction. It is not found among adults at all. Immatures will eventually develop the ability to block their desire for another individual's food and become full members of their un-equal society. Things try to achieve social status even in this society. However, the anchor to stop direct interactions surrounding things is heavy enough to pull the things down to the bottom as the individual holding again.

11.4.3 The equality principle: Socialized food, non-socialized things

As mentioned, the socialization of things only becomes possible under the equality principle. Food sharing incorporates food into social relationships and transforms individual foraging into concerted action between multiple individuals. This turns food into a social thing and brings it to the fore of society. Interaction between the food holder and the beggar is based in a mutual trust relationship between them, regardless of their status. The food holder can ignore the beggar and instances of food snatching are rare[18] (Kuroda 1984, 1999). The calmness of interactions surrounding food indicates that the parties control their desires and that sharing is voluntary.[19]

In comparison with the socialization of food, there are surprisingly few examples of socialization as far as other things are concerned. Although the equality principle society does not inhibit multiple individuals from showing interest in the same thing in close range, a common interest rarely develops into interaction. Let us look at some of these few cases of social intercourse involving non-food things.

In bonobo research in Wamba, the Democratic Republic of the Congo in September 2008, a young female, newly migrated to E1 group, was frequently seen playing with an infant swinging a twig as if to hit her playing partner. Before long, infants and juveniles two to five years of age also began to play with twigs. They started from the simple swinging of the twig, then running away with a twig and chasing with a twig were added to the repertoire. The following form of play was seen on the final day of my observation.

A three-year-old infant swung a twig at a two-year-old infant and fled upward on the tree. The younger chased the older for a couple of meters, stopped, went out on a limb, broke off a small branch, and resumed chasing. While they were chasing one another up on the tree, both infants accidentally dropped their twigs (once and twice respectively), broke off a replacement twig, and resumed chasing. Three minutes later, the older abandoned the twig, descended the tree, and play was over.

In this instance, the two players acted as if holding a twig was the precondition for the chase. If this was the case, the twig as a thing had become a convention or a rule for the play. The twig can then be regarded as the materialized means or rule of play, or part of the complex goal of "twig-play". However, it appears that the rule of this type of play is "to conform" with the way the other party acts. This two-party twig-play soon went out of fashion and was seldom observed again (private communication from I. B. Izquierdo).

A relatively common example among bonobos is an adult shaking a tree branch and wearing a play-face when infants are sitting on that branch (Kuroda 1999). The infants hold on to the branch and display a play-face as if they are enjoying the shaking. Although this is more of an adult's act to humor infants, it is a kind of social interaction, and the shaken tree branch is a socialized thing.

In another example, collaborative tool use by adult male chimpanzees was observed at Burgers' Zoo in Arnhem, the Netherlands. In order to get to small branches of a tree protected by an electric fence, one male holds a large dead branch propped against the fence as a sort of ladder while another male climbs it to reach the tree safely. He breaks off leafy branches, drops them to the ground, and shares them with his collaborator and females (de Waal 1982). In this case, the dead branch is a medium to realize collaboration between the two individuals; it is a means for production and for achieving a common goal; that is precisely a socialized thing. According to de Waal (1982), when the males became tense and frustrated, they frequently snapped dead branches and eventually started taking this cooperative action.

11.4.4 The equality principle: The structure of food sharing

In many cases, things draw a common interest without becoming socialized. Common tools are typical examples of such things. For example, chimpanzees in Bossou, Guinea, are known to use anvil-and-hammer stones to crack hard nut shells and eat the kernels (Sugiyama 1978). Matsuzawa (1991) reports that a dominant individual would take the stones being used by another individual and a subordinate individual would wait until a dominant individual abandons the stones before taking them. In a video by Matsuzawa and others, one chimpanzee is about to crack a nut placed on an anvil stone and other chimpanzees are staring at it. In other words, a stone as a tool becomes an object of common interest when a nut is placed on it for cracking. Despite this, it does not prompt shared use of the stone, such as handing it over to another individual, taking turns or cracking nuts for another individual.

In captivity, young chimpanzees, bonobos and gorillas use installed ropes and tires, discarded buckets, towels and tree branches for solitary play. Other individuals may take a peek or try to take the thing. Yet, they do not hand it over to others or use it to play with others. For instance, when a gorilla infant is play-wrestling with a rope and laughing on its own, another infant approaches. The second infant either waits for the first infant to leave or pushes the first infant aside to play with the rope on its own; they never play with the rope together.[20] Even Kanzi, who exhibited good language skill (Savage-Rumbaugh 1993), would exchange things such as a ball in play with a researcher but not with another bonobo.[21]

Why does the socialization of food stand out and why is the socialization of non-food things so hard to spread?

The likely answer to the first question is that because interactions surrounding food basically have a simple structure and clear goal of obtaining food. In many cases, when bonobos watch a peer eating food, they make chewing motions with their mouths and their hands lift slightly, as if to touch the food. There is no need to refer to mirror neurons, here: food is highly attractive and pulls the non-holder to the brink of taking action to acquire it. From there, they display their desire directly to the peer by slowly extending their hand, performing a gesture to take food from the peer's mouth or hand, but they have enough self-control to stop short. To maintain a social group, a system to prevent conflicts between individuals over food and mates is necessary. This is the function of the two co-existence principles discussed above. I would like to reiterate that the essence of the inequality principle is the blocking of desires and the essence of the equality principle is the controlling of desires. These appear to be ancient and powerful forces linked to the emergence of groups.

Interactions surrounding food have a common object of desire and consists of each party controlling this desire. Whether it develops into sharing depends on whether the haves respond to the self-control of desire demonstrated by the have-nots by abandoning their own desire in the end. Where there is the means to control desire, the ability to abandon desire seems to appear in most cases. Low-ranked individuals beg the food holder yet rarely share their own food, but as soon as they acquire high-ranked status, they begin to share their food. This coordination of internal self-control by members of the equality principle society is the basis of the socialization of food, which is greatly influenced by the special status of food.

While the use of a dead tree branch as a tool by the chimpanzees at Burgers' Zoo adds complexity at the food acquisition stage, it does not change the linear structure of the set of behaviors, which is to pursue their desire. Wild chimpanzees also routinely engage in this kind of tool-use behavior. For example, they snap off a hard stick, make a hole in a termite nest, take a blade of grass, chew one end into a brush, insert it into the nest, catch termites, and eat them (Suzuki et al. 1995).

11.4.5 The triadic relationship as a difficult obstacle

Why are non-food things not easily socialized? The simplest conceivable answer is that things are generally indivisible. There is no method to cater for one's own and another's desires simultaneously, such as sharing. In fact, giving all of one's food to another individual is very rare; and we suspect that a majority of food sharing acts would not take place if the food in question were indivisible.

A more essential answer appears to be that the species of the genus *Pan* generally do not seem to be good at "continuing" or "exchanging" interactions in a triadic relationship. Food sharing is certainly an interaction in a triadic relationship, but as we have seen, it is simple and the shared food disappears quickly. The play-chase holding a twig is a relatively complex play and the twig is a medium for social intercourse in the sense that it constitutes a rule, but it is not a medium of exchange. In contrast, the mediating role of a thing continues in acts such as playing together with a thing or sharing a tool to accommodate one another. This manner of handling things is possible for chimpanzees and bonobos with humans but not possible with their conspecifics. A lack of aptitude is an anticlimactic explanation, but this is where we find the limit of the ability of the genus *Pan*.

This type of interaction rarely emerges even when the third term is a peer instead of a thing.[22] For instance, they cannot play in a group of three. When three individuals look as if they are playing together, only two of them are actually playing together; the third individual is waiting in the wings. In a type of play in which two infants are striking out at an older individual, closer observation reveals that the older individual is actually interacting with only one of the infants properly and often the two interacting parties will move to another place to continue playing. When a play-faced gorilla or chimpanzee infant is play-wrestling with a rope or a stick, the participation of another individual would form a triadic relationship. Accordingly, another individual cannot participate whether the player considers the thing to be its playing partner (personified) or a thing.

The absence of dyadic interactions mediated by a thing means that there is no exchange of things and that things are not functioned as derived from others. This is equivalent to the absence of reciprocity in food sharing; that is, food is not traded (Kuroda 1999). Food sharing does not extend beyond giving birth to circulatable goods; the world of the genus *Pan* is yet to see the birth of exchange goods, which is a more complete form of socialized things. Despite this limitation, however, we must remember that the structure of their interaction is quite complex. Although it is outside of the scope of this discussion, it is clear that the matrix through which things turn into exchange goods is not reducible to language. Human infants can play by exchanging things before the age of two and engage in more advanced play-exchanging without the medium of language at the age of three or four.

11.4.6 Confusion in the meaning of things

A thing acquires multilayered meanings through the experiences of individuals (i.e., one thing has multiple affordances) but sometimes a markedly different level of complexity is added when it is incorporated into social intercourse. For example, a young female bonobo who migrated from another group would persistently beg a dominant male for food even when the same food is readily available nearby (Kuroda 1982). In this case, it is possible to interpret that the goal of the young female is "to receive a share of food from the dominant male" but the role of the food can also be a medium (or a pretext) for interaction to form an affiliative relationship. This means that the same thing (food) has different "values" when it is acquired for oneself and when it is given by a dominant male (Kuroda 1999).[23] Of course, it is impossible to know whether or not the bonobo in question is aware of these meanings. And it must be recognized that whether a particular thing is a means, a medium, or a goal depends on the way a causal chain is segmented. Therefore, someone could say that any confusion is in the observer's interpretation, especially a confusion of logical types, and not by the socialization of things. Nevertheless, it is clear that the involvement of things in social intercourse complicates their roles structurally irrespective of the party's awareness or language.

An "exchange" of things easily leads to this type of confusion. For example, if human infants are playing by exchanging a twig, the twig "must be that particular twig" and not any other twig for the duration of the exchange. In other words, a thing may be similar to other things but when it is linked to play, it is given special value. However, if a third party carries it away, the players will snap off a new twig and resume playing. It means that the lost twig has always been a replaceable medium even during play but at the same time it "had to be that thing". While this is a question of logical types, the important point is that this type of situation, for example, can only occur in association with continuing interaction in a triadic relationship. With regard to reciprocity by which a thing is given in exchange for a thing, humans perform such acts without being clear about whether the goal is an exchange of utility value or the act of exchange itself, and typically, without unraveling the nexus of the two goals. The limitation of the genus *Pan* discussed in 11.4.5 can perhaps be rephrased as the inability to use things in the presence of this confusion.[24]

11.5 Can the Moon be an object of desire?[25]

One notable difference between things in the primate world and things in the human world is a desire for things on which no one has ever put their hands. Unlike the fox in one of Aesop's fables who says disparagingly that grapes he cannot reach are inedible, chimpanzees persistently try to climb a tree heavily laden with fruit even when it is out of their reach (e.g. Sugiyama 1981). However, the object is a familiar food. In contrast, they rarely show any interest in unfamiliar and inconspicuous things in the vicinity unless another starts toying with them.[26] There has been no report of chimpanzees or bonobos in the wild expressing desire for a thing which they could not reach and had no previous experience with.

Yet, such a case has been reported with Kanzi, a bonobo raised by a researcher. At the age of ten months or so, Kanzi began to reach for things out of his reach together with begging vocalization toward the researcher (Savage-Rumbaugh 1993). As the researcher responded by getting things for him or taking him to things, Kanzi began to use his hand to point at things he wanted. As far as we know, what he pointed at were specific things such as honey, a refrigerator and a dog, as well as a window and a door (when he wanted to go outside). Hand pointing has not been observed in wild bonobos. Even if their infants performed such an action, their mothers would not respond, and therefore the behavior of showing persistent interest in remote things would not be nurtured.

The behaviors and situations are different for human babies. They express their interest in novel and unreachable things by shouting and human adults respond. The babies make the adults get or move unreachable things for them. This situation occurs because here are almost immobile babies who desire and adults who try to understand what the babies want. The social nature of things acquires new dimensions here. While food sharing is sometimes used as a means to form a relationship with another individual in bonobos,[27] human babies use human adults as a means to acquire things. This reversal creates the possibility that unobtainable things fall into their hands through the intermediary of the hands of others and attaches a sense of proximity (availability) to all things. In view of this, the origin of desire is found in the baby's behavior to instrumentalize the adult for the purpose of obtaining things rather than a sense of envy for another's things or circumstances. Moreover, although a remote thing such as the moon is out of reach even for adults, adults tell babies of the moon as if it were an accessible thing and represent it as a thing that will become reachable. Things are not only socialized by the attitude and language of adults but also given a sense of availability for humans, that is, objects of desire.

While language comes to play a larger role at this stage, from a behavioral perspective, the starting point for our desire for unreachable things lies in the behavior of others to satisfy it for us. Our desire must harbor an expectation of the appearance of others who will fulfill it for us; language or information alone cannot prepare for the manifestation of desire. Although things in the contemporary world seem to be characterized as objects of desire more than by their exchangeability, this is based on the behavioral traits of humans as a primate species with mirror neurons which see the action of others and the objects of others as their own.

12 Livestock as Interface: The Case of the Samburu in Kenya

Shinya Konaka

Keywords: interface, body extensions, affordances, livestock-morphism, metaphorical thinking

12.1 Introduction: Toward a holistic theory of material culture

This chapter aims to reconsider the triadic relationship between the body, things and the environment and to explore a holistic theory of material culture based on the proposition that "things are extensions of the body and the environment".

First, we will review preceding studies by distinguishing between two groups of material culture theories: the "material/culture model" premised on mind-body dualism and the "material = culture model" premised on monism. We will then seek to develop the latter, proposing a theoretical direction that defines the body, things and the environment in a more continuous fashion than the former.

In developing this theoretical direction, we will re-examine McLuhan's media theory, which attracted a flurry of attention during the 1960s before being virtually forgotten. According to McLuhan, the media are extensions of the body. Further development of this media theory might provide a perspective from which to understand things and the environment as extensions of the body. We will also discuss Gibson's affordance theory for a different perspective from which to see the body as an extension of the environment and things. By integrating these two perspectives, we will attempt to develop a holistic theory of material culture that sees the body, things and the environment located along a monistic "continuum".

Second, we will present an ethnological study of the cognitive world of the Samburu, a pastoral people in North Central Kenya, and attempt to re-assess the conventional cognitive-anthropological arguments from the perspective of the holistic theory of material culture developed in this chapter. In the cognitive world of the Samburu, man (body), livestock (things) and wild animals (environment) are contiguous through loose metaphorical linkages. It is unlikely that this kind of continuity can be portrayed adequately using the dualistic model of conventional material culture theory. We believe that the holistic theory of material culture can open the way to a new ethnographical understanding of the cognitive world of the Samburu.

12.2 Two models of material culture theory

Theories premised on mind/body dualism clearly divide material and culture. We shall call these the "material/culture theory model" ("slash model"). In many cases, this model postulates that either culture or material is dominant or determinative. Where predominance is given to material while culture is treated as its reflection, the theory suffers from material reductionism (cultural materialism, vulgar materialism), explaining culture as a material condition, as Friedman observes (1966). Where culture is treated as predominant and material as its reflection, the theory suffers from cultural reductionism (semiotics, New Archaeology, etc.), analyzing the materiality of all things in terms of their symbolic meanings. In one case, the world is seen to be constituted by material made of reduced culture, while in the other it is constituted by culture made of reduced material. Needless to say, both are rather too abstracted from the world as it is. In either case, the defense of reductionism has become an end in itself, and the world perceived through these lenses is far removed from the ethnographical mixture of culture and material.

In contrast, theories premised on mind-body monism see material and culture as integrated. We shall call these theories the "material = culture theory model" ("equal theory"). Its theoretical lineage includes consistent and strong critiques against dualism.

The theory of an "embodied mind" proposed by Lakoff and Johnson forms the theoretical foundation of the philosophy of the body. According to Lakoff and Johnson: "The mind is inherently embodied. Thought is mostly unconscious. Abstract concepts are largely metaphorical" (Lakoff and Johnson 1999).

In gender studies, doubts about mind/body dualism arose in the context of questioning gender/sex dualism. As Butler argues, "The sex/gender distinction and the category of sex itself appear to presuppose a generalization of 'the body' that preexists the acquisition of its sexed significance" (Butler 1990). She questions the idea of the passive body inscribed by a culture that is supposedly external to it. In a similar vein, Haraway challenges ideas of body/machine dualism, asking, "Why should our bodies end at the skin, or include at best other beings encapsulated by skin?" (Haraway 1991).

In religious anthropology, nature/culture dualism is being questioned through studies of animism. For example, in a critique of Lévi-Strauss' analysis of totemism, Bird-David notes that "Lévi-Strauss did not question the authority of the Western objectivist view of reality, which accepted a priori the nature/society dualism" (Bird-David 1999: 70). Descola (1996: 98) also criticizes dualist thoughts such as nature/culture, nature/supernature, nature/art, and nature/mind.

In material culture studies, doubts were voiced about the presumed dualism between subjects (who produce things) and objects (things). From such a perspective, Miller introduced agency theory into material culture studies, invoking Latour and Gell, challenging the conventional view that see things as mere artifacts. Miller says

> This introduction will begin with two attempts to theorize materiality: the first, a vulgar theory of mere things as artifacts; the second, a theory that claims to entirely transcend the dualism of subjects and objects. It will then engage with theories associated with Bruno Latour and Alfred Gell that seek to follow a similar path, but with a greater emphasis upon the nature of agency. (Miller 2005: 3)

Although we will not follow up the cross-influences of these theories, it is clear that the critique of dualisms such as mind/body, gender/sex, body/machine, nature/culture, subject/object and so on have spread across all areas of the humanities and social sciences. On this basis, it is time for a fundamental review of the conventional material culture studies model in which human subjects are passive "bodies" governed by active "minds" or determinative "cultures" who use an external and passive "environment" to produce and utilize "things" as artifacts.

In contrast to the "material/culture theory model" which divides and opposes material and culture, the "material = culture theory model" proposed in this chapter aims to rethink the body, things and the environment in the context of a more continuous relationship and to treat the loose dynamic between them as a holistic "material = culture".

12.3 Things as extensions of the body

In that case, we must ask next how the body, things and the environment can be understood in the context of a continuous relationship.

McLuhan's classical media theory is noteworthy in this sense. He looks at the media from a human evolutionary perspective, which is substantially different from the prevailing academic view of the media.

McLuhan redefines a medium as an "extension of ourselves" (McLuhan 1964). He also defines clothing as a medium: "Clothing as an extension of our skin helps to store and to channel energy" (ibid). Bicycles and airplanes are extensions of our feet. The media are extensions of the human body and the "outer/externalized" body. It is therefore as difficult for us to notice the media as it is to notice our own bodies.

In a sense, McLuhan's media theory is a kind of material culture theory originating with the body. From this perspective, it is interesting that he refrains from separating culture and material, treating them both, holistically, as media. He also argues that the human body is constrained by and in the service of the media, rather than taking the Cartesian view that the human mind controls the media at will. McLuhan's understanding here corresponds with Gibson's affordance theory, as we will discuss later.

> Man must serve his electric technology with the same servo-mechanistic fidelity with which he served his coracle, his canoe, his typography, and all other extensions of his physical organs. (ibid)

While *Understanding Media* was published in 1964, McLuhan quotes similar passages from E. T. Hall (1959), implying that he probably drew inspiration from his argument. Although the extent to which McLuhan was influenced by Hall's work is unclear, a host of arguments about bodily extensions appeared in the mid-1960s. For example, Leroi-Gourhan (1965) treats tools in human evolutionary history as "*estérioriser*" (exteriorizations) of the body, while Merleau-Ponty (1968: 255) discusses "extensions of the body". Polanyi describes the process of positioning a sensation far away from the original sensation as "the semantic aspect of tacit knowing," concluding that "all meaning tends to be displaced away from ourselves" (Polanyi 1966).

Thus, McLuhan appears to be part of a new theoretical paradigm which argued that things are extensions of the body, contributing to a material culture theory that treated the body and things as continuous. In Japanese anthropology, Nomura (1997) continues this lineage. In the broader field of anthropology, however, this lineage appears to have been displaced as a new theoretical framework that sees culture as a system of ideas and symbols became mainstream (as Tokoro and Kawai commented in "Introduction"). Regrettably, we must say that the extensions of the body theory became a lost paradigm after the mid-1960s.

12.4 The body as an extension of things

Gibson's affordance theory can be seen as a companion to theories of bodily-extensions. He appears to be arguing from a very similar perspective as McLuhan and Polanyi when he says:

> When in use, a tool is a sort of extension of the hand, almost an attachment to it or part of the user's own body, and thus no longer a part of the environment of the user. But when not in use, the tool is simply a detached object of the environment, graspable and portable, to be sure, but nevertheless external to the observer. This *capacity to attach something to the body* suggests that the boundary between the animal and the environment is not fixed at the surface of the skin but can shift. (Gibson 1979)

Compared with McLuhan's body extension theory, affordance theory places more weight on the side of the environment and things. Gibson's argument revolves around the transmission of the affordances of the environment and things to the body. For instance, Gibson states that "This object in use affords a special kind of cutting, and one can actually feel the cutting action of the blades" (Gibson 1979: 40 Figure 3.1). Despite the strong similarities to McLuhan's body extension theory, we must recognize that it runs in the opposite direction. In other words, Gibson argues not only that the blades of scissors are extensions of the human body from a human perspective but also that their affordance of "cutting" is transmitted to the human body from the perspective of the blades as "things". In this sense, Gibson's affordance theory might be called a theory of the extensions of things to the body. Gibson's view thus provides a strong counterpart to McLuhan's – not contradictory, but complementary.

From this perspective, the human body is never free because it is constrained by the affordances of things. As Sasaki demonstrates using the affordances of a "string" as an example, "We have managed to survive by having our freedom restricted by things and being inconvenienced; being inconvenienced means knowing the diverse properties of things" (Sasaki 2000: 17–18). This argument reinforces McLuhan's claim that humans serve the media.

12.5 Reciprocal extension between the body and environment

Let us now consider the reciprocal relationship between these two theories: the extension of the body to things, and the extension of things to the body. It should be clear by now that my concern is with how to combine them rather than how to choose between them. We aim to combine them in an effort to rethink things, the body and the environment on the same horizon in a holistic fashion. What we call a holistic material culture theory is characterized by this reciprocal extension between the body and things. Merleau-Ponty appears to have had a similar understanding when he stated that "the things are the prolongation of my body and my body is the prolongation of the world, through it the world surrounds me" (Merleau-Ponty 1968: 255).

Let us turn now to how *things* are redefined in this material = culture theory. As Miller (2005: 4) states, materiality is understood by the concept of "artifacts" in our everyday expression. The emphasis on artifacts conforms to the traditional material culture studies in anthropology and archaeology, based on the hypothesis that superior (reasoning) subjects utilize inferior objects rationally and purposefully. For example, Oswalt states "An artifact is the end product resulting from the modification of a physical mass in order to fulfill a useful purpose" (Oswalt 1976: 24).

From the perspective of the reciprocal extension theory, though, *things* can be defined as the "interface" between the body and the environment in a reciprocal relationship between the body, things and the environment. In information and communication technology, the concept "interface" is used to refer to things that serve as connection extension media.[1] What we call *things* in this chapter exist as the interface between the body and the environment. Although livestock in pastoralist society are neither artifacts nor tools, they can be understood as *things* in this sense.[2]

By understanding things as the interface between the body and the environment, we are able to treat the body, things and the environment as a continuum.[3] As Gibson notes, the boundary between the body and the environment shifts constantly after every operation along this continuum; it is not fixed at the skin. The body, things and the environment form a continuum along which a boundary is formed after-the-fact every time a living body operates them. *Autopoiesis* (Maturana and Varela 1980) is a concept which refers to this process of boundary generation.

As in Maturana and Varela's theory of autopoiesis, culture and society in our material = culture theory arise after-the-fact by the operation of the hybrid network comprised of the body, things and the environment. They do not exist a priori, in advance, or independently of the body-things-environment nexus. The idea that distinct communities can be identified by their intrinsic socially and culturally homogeneous structures is premised on the material/culture theory derived from mind/body dualism, which this chapter rejects. By contrast, the material = culture theory proposes that communality and culture are always created after-the-fact in the activities of producing things through the reciprocal extensions between bodies and the environment. Hence, if our discussion of a holistic material culture theory seems to disregard culture and society in their conventional senses, this is only because we take a different view of culture and society.

12.6 The cognitive world of the Samburu, North Central Kenya

12.6.1 An overview of the Samburu and their cognitive world

The preceding formulation of a holistic material culture theory aims to break new ground, especially in the ethnographical study of material culture and body techniques. Unfortunately, I am not yet in a position to provide a detailed ethnographical report corresponding to this theoretical model. Nevertheless, the holistic material culture theory provides a new perspective from which we can review the classical cognitive arguments of conventional ethnographies. In this section, we will look at the pastoralist society of the Samburu in the Republic of Kenya, East Africa, in order to examine their cognitive world ethnographically and rethink the symbolic anthropological approach from the perspective of our holistic material culture theory.[4] This chapter pays particular attention to their understanding of livestock (things), humans (the body), wild animals (the environment), and their inter-relationships.

The subject of our ethnographical study, the Samburu (autonym: *Loikop*), is a pastoral people whose mother tongue is a north Maa dialect of the Eastern Nilotic Maa language. A majority of the population reside in Samburu County and Laikipia County of North Central Kenya. According to the 2009 statistics, the total population in these three districts was 223,947 (including non-Samburu population) (Republic of Kenya 2010: 26). Their society is a gerontocracy characterized by age system and phratry (Spencer 1965).

The Samburu are semi-nomadic pastoralists who subsist on breeding livestock, mainly cattle, goats and sheep. While some people have moved into wage labor and farming in recent years, pastoralism is still the primary livelihood for many Samburu people. The Samburu manage livestock grazing under a division of labor by age and sex and strive to maintain self-sufficiency for food and daily necessities by utilizing animal products. Movement towards a market economy since a periodic livestock market was set up in 1990 has changed their lifestyle dramatically (as detailed in my book, Konaka 2006). Nevertheless, their lives are still deeply connected to livestock today.

One characteristic of the Samburu's cognitive world is a metaphorical understanding of things. They frequently use metaphors and similes in their daily living. Similies such as "X is like Y (X *kotwanana* Y)" and "Y-like X (X *awana* Y)" are used frequently in everyday conversations among the Samburu. Metaphorical thinking is used in various phases of Samburu culture, including naming (Konaka 2000), material culture (Konaka 2007), mythologies, ceremonies, traditions, gossip (Konaka 1997) and so on. Ethnological data used in this chapter were gathered in field studies conducted mainly from 1992 to 2002 in Lorroki Division, Samburu County, and extracted from observations of everyday life and the conversations of the Samburu. These observations were made in various sociocultural contexts but we shall use only those which are related to their understanding of people, livestock and wild animals here.

The Samburu make clear distinction between the categories "people (*oltungana*)", "livestock (*swom*)" and "wild animals (*ngweshi*)". Birds are generally called *nkweni*. Less familiar animals are described using the regional lingua franca of Swahili. For example, the Swahili word *samaki* is used for fish.

12.6.2 Human-livestock recognition

As Tani (1976) points out about pastoralist society in general, the Samburu understand humans and livestock analogically. They draw analogies between the body of their livestock and the human body, and vice versa. For instance, human infants are analogized to baby goats and sheep; a Samburu mother calls her son "My male baby goat (*Lkuo lai*)" and her daughter "My female baby goat (*Nkuo ai*)".

The Samburu people sometimes use these analogies between the human body and livestock body in rites of passage. The practice of extracting infants' teeth (Photo 12.1) is likened to their ear notching practice for goats and sheep. Circumcision in boys is likened to castration of livestock. Unmarried girls are compared to virgin heifers. When a groom makes a marriage proposal, he says "I saw a virgin heifer at your house (*Katodwa utauo tankan lino*)". Circumcised young men are likened to bullocks because castrated male animals cannot reproduce, and young men, although they have been circumcised, are not yet permitted to marry and have children. In a series of age-grade transition rituals called *Ilmugiet*, young men slaughter a bullock that symbolizes them. Elderly men are likened to stud bulls because they are permitted to marry and have children.

Photo 12.1 An old man extracting a tooth from an infant. The Samburu equates the tooth extraction practice for infants to the ear notching practice for goats and sheep.

A stud goat or sheep is slaughtered at the funeral of an elderly man, symbolizing the end of the elderly man's reproduction. The correspondence relationship between the way the human body and the livestock body are recognized by the Samburu is summarized in Table 12.1 for males and Table 12.2 for females. The world of human bodies is neither isolated from nor superior to the livestock bodies in the cognitive world of the Samburu. The human body and the livestock body are understood by the Samburu to be on the same horizon, constituting a cognitive world in which they run parallel to one another according to their growth stage.

12.6.3 The recognition of wild animals

Anthropomorphism of wild animals is sometimes found in the Samburu's cognitive world. In particular, the Samburu use human kinship terms to describe interspecific relationships between wild animals. For example, they use expressions such as "The African elephant is the matrimonial uncle of the cape hare" or "The black-backed jackal and the dog are sisters".

The bodies of wild animals are also analogized to the human body. Some folk tales say that certain wild animals were once human. For instance, "circumcised boys (*laibartag*)" are normally supposed to come home before dark. A circumcised

Table 12.1 Correspondence between human and livestock body recognition (male)

Livestock (cattle)	Human (male)	Transition event
Baby cattle (*lashe nkini*)	Infant (*nkerai nkini*)	
		↓ Tooth extraction, ear notching
Male calf (*lashe sitimaa*)	Juvenile (*laieni*)	
		↓ Circumcision, castration
Bullock (*lmongo*)	Adolescent (*olmurran*)	
		↓ *Ilmugiet* ritual
Stud bull (*laingoni*)	Old man (*olpaiyani*)	

Table 12.2 Correspondence between human and livestock body recognition (female)

Livestock (cattle)	Human (female)	Transition event
Baby cattle (*nkashe nkini*)	Infant (*nkerai nkini*)	
		↓ Tooth extraction, ear notching
Female calf (*nkashe lipong*)	Girl (*ntito*)	
		↓ Circumcision
Heifer (*utauo*)	Circumcised girl (*surmorei*)[a]	
		↓ Marriage, childbirth
Cow (*nketeng*)	Mother (*shiankiki*)	

Note. [a] This stage is skipped if a girl is circumcised at marriage.

boy who once failed to come home before dark is said to have been transformed into the lycaon (*Lycaon pictus*; local name: *suiyan*; a type of dog) (Photo 12.2). A girl who grew her hair too long because she did not like haircuts is said to have been transformed into the black crowned crane (*Balearica pavonina*; local name: *nkaitoole*) with a characteristic crest on its head (Photo 12.3). These examples indicate transformability between the human and wild animal categories in the Samburu's cognitive world.

Wild animals are also analogized to livestock. After the fashion of "anthropomorphism" and "zoomorphism", a certain kind of "livestock-morphism" is found in the Samburu's cognitive world. The following myth is a good example of livestock-morphism.

Livestock as Interface

*Photo 12.2 Boys after circumcision. Circumcised boys (*laibartag*) wear black lobes and the feathers of the birds they have caught until the ceremony to enter an age grade. They are supposed to come home before dark. It is said that those who did not come home before dark were turned into lycaons.*

Photo 12.3 Black crowned cranes (Balearica pavonina; local name: nkaitoole) with a characteristic crest on the head. It is said that a girl who grew her hair too long because she didn't like haircuts was transformed into this bird.

Once upon a time, all animals except hyenas were livestock. Women bred elands like they bred cattle, buffalos like oxen, and Thomson's gazelles, Grant's gazelles and impalas like goats and sheep. Elephants helped collect firewood, and lions served as guard dogs. One day, the women accidentally let all the animals loose. The helpless women went to live with men with cattle, goats and sheep and it was the beginning of marriage in humans. The escaped livestock became today's wild animals. (30 August 1999, collected by author in Lorroki Division, Samburu County)

By contrast to our archaeological knowledge that wild animals were domesticated and became today's livestock, the Samburu's mythology assumes that livestock preceded the appearance of wild animals.

The Samburu classification of wild animals also provides a glimpse of this livestock-morphism (Table 12.3). Although Samburu society does not have a hierarchical taxonomy of animals, it has the following loose classification of wild animals.

1. Eland, buffalo and greater kudu fall in the category of the Samburu cattle (*Bovinae*) equivalent.
2. Thomson's gazelle, Grants gazelle, impala and gerenuk fall in the category of the Samburu goat (*Capra*) equivalent.
3. Common warthog falls in the category of the Samburu sheep (*Ovis*) equivalent.
4. Giraffe falls in the category of the Samburu camel (*Camelidae*) equivalent.
5. Common zebra and Gravy's zebra fall in the category of the Samburu donkey (*Asinus*) equivalent.

This livestock-morphic classification of wild animals by the Samburu is reflected in their daily practices. The Samburu eat the flesh of cattle, goat, sheep and camel among their livestock but they do not eat donkey. Accordingly, they eat the flesh of the wild animals in their equivalent categories and do not eat the animals in the donkey equivalent category (except for the common warthog, which they do not eat although it is in the *Ovis* equivalent category). They often emphasize that the livestock animals and wild animals in equivalent categories share similar characteristics, in statements such as "Buffalo meat tastes the same as cattle meat" or "Thomson's gazelle meat tastes the same as goat meat".

This livestock-morphism is also expressed in their religious views of wild animals. Some wild animal species are considered sacred because they have similar characteristics to livestock. For instance, if a Samburu kills an aardvark (*Orycreropus afer*; local name: *lkerikele*) with a single thrust of the spear, the hunter is believed to get a lucky break. After killing the aardvark, the lucky person

Table 12.3 The classification of wild animals by the Samburu

Classification	Species
(1) Eland, buffalo and greater kudu fall in the category of the Samburu cattle (*Bovinae*) equivalent	Eland (*surwa*), buffalo (*olosowan*), greater kudu (*lmaalo*)
(2) Thomson's gazelle, Grants gazelle, impala and gerenuk fall in the category of the Samburu goat (*Capra*) equivalent	Thomson's gazelle (*nkoipelai*), Grant's gazelle (*ngolii*), impala (*ntarawet*), gerenuk (*irrigo*)
(3) Common warthog falls in the category of the Samburu sheep (*Ovis*) equivalent	Common warthog (*lbiturr*)
(4) Giraffe falls in the category of the Samburu camel (*Camelidae*) equivalent	Giraffe (*lmeot*)
(5) Common zebra and Gravy's zebra fall in the category of the Samburu donkey (*Asinus*) equivalent	Common zebra (*nkoitiko*), Gravy's zebra (*loitiko*)

slaughters a ram and broils ram meat and aardvark meat side by side. It is said that the aardvark is regarded as a sacred animal because its body shape from the back to the buttock is very similar to that of the sheep.

Wild animals with physical features different from those of their livestock are treated as religious taboo. The Samburu recognize the common zebra as having different characteristics than livestock because it has teeth on both the upper and lower jaws and closed hoofs. For this reason, they have a strong aversion to eating zebra meat. If a child eats even a small amount of zebra meat, the child is severely scolded and banned from coming home for a few days.

The Samburu's recognition of wild animals through livestock-morphism extends to birds. Some bird species are considered sacred because their physical or behavioral characteristics are similar to those of livestock. In their society, circumcised boys go out together to catch birds and use their feathers to make head dresses. They aim to catch particular species of birds because they are considered to be sacred and catching them brings good fortune. One of the sacred birds is the Somali fiscal (*Lanius somalicus*; local name: *lkeriketeng*). The local name for this species means "cow pattern" in the Samburu language and its black pattern on a white ground is very similar to the common black-and-white cow pattern (Photo 12.4). In other words, the Somali fiscal is regarded as a sacred bird because it has a physical characteristic similar to that of cattle.

The green winged pytilia (*Pytilia melba soudanensis*; local name: *lkine*) is another sacred bird species. The local name for this bird means "goat" in the

Photo 12.4 Somali fiscal (Lanius somalicus). *This bird is considered sacred because its black pattern on a white ground is similar to the typical cow pattern*

Samburu language. It is characterized by an awkward movement involving walking for a short distance and flying for a short distance. This movement is said to be similar to the awkward gait of the goat. It is considered sacred because of its similarity to the goat.

The yellow wagtail (*Motacilla flava*; local name: *nchokut*) is also considered sacred. The local name for this bird means "herd-boy" in the Samburu language. This bird follows the cattle herd, feeding on mites that infest the cattle. Its behavior is said to resemble that of a herd-boy who grazes the cattle. It is considered sacred because its hovering around the cattle herd makes it closer to the livestock.

12.6.4 Conclusion: Livestock as interface between the body and environment

The Samburu's cognitive system is characterized by their perception of livestock being the origin of various other perceptions. Several species of wild animals are recognized through metaphorical comparison to livestock. The human body is also recognized and perceived using metaphors to the bodies of livestock animals depending on sex and age.

For this reason, Douglas's (1966) classical anomaly theory applies only partially to the Samburu's cognitive system. Although the taboo against eating zebra meat can certainly be explained by the zebra's physical features being anomalous in the livestock categories, the more important point is that livestock creates the value standards of the Samburu's categories. The only question for the Samburu is the subject's similarity to the livestock, not whether it is normative or anomalous to a certain order. Consequently, a metaphor theory appears to be more appropriate than the anomaly theory of symbolic anthropology for understanding the Samburu's cognitive system.

Cognitive scientists studying metaphor have developed a theory of base domain and target domain (Holyoak and Thagard 1995). They hypothesize that humans make an unknown subject comprehensible by projecting the base domain onto the target domain. In this sense, livestock bodies form the base domain in the Samburu's cognitive system and the livestock-based domain is projected onto the target domain of human and wild animal bodies. It is from such a perspective that the meat of wild animals which are considered similar to livestock is used for food and a bird with the coloring of the cow is sacred. Surprisingly, the human body is no exception. The Samburu use the phrase "beautiful as cattle (*Keisupat teembene atwana nketen*)" to describe a beautiful woman or man. This phrase suggests that the human body is re-described as an extension of the livestock body and in terms of the body's sexual appeal. Of course, livestock bodies are also described in terms of human and wild animal bodies metaphorically. In sum, the three entities are in relationships of mutual correspondence through metaphorical thinking.[5]

In any case, the Samburu's cognitive system is characterized largely by livestock-morphism rather than simple anthropomorphism and their metaphorical understanding can be observed everywhere in their pastoralist culture. This is likely because livestock serves as a powerful medium for the Samburu's analogical thinking. In one sense, livestock forms a breeding ground for their metaphor-based pastoralist culture. From the perspective of the relationality between livestock (things), humans (body) and wild animals (environment), the livestock form a powerful cognitive magnetic field towards both the human body and the environment. It is the medium that mediates between the human body and the environment, the "interface" that connects the human body and the environment. From the perspective of affordance theory, the livestock affords the possibilities of metaphorical thinking that connect the human body and the environment for the Samburu people.

Livestock is the object of certain kind of fetishism in pastoralist societies of East Africa. Herskovits (1926) calls this phenomenon "cattle complex". I have discussed the "cattle complex" in Samburu society elsewhere (Konaka 2006) and cannot go into the details here. There are various arguments about why livestock are regarded as sacred and become fetishized objects, but if we accept Tanaka's (2009) argument that a fetish network is "a call and response relationship in which the body and things are connected interactively", then it seems reasonable to assume that the metaphorical field of physical recognition with livestock as interface forms the base for cognitive mediation and livestock fetishism. Livestock of course embodies social values, desires and sacredness which are most likely derived from the cognitive mediation base.

Needless to say, metaphorical thinking is based on the logic of "similarity". Where the logic of "identity" ($X = Y$) is applied, both objects are perceived as the same thing. When the logic of "heterogeneity" ($X \neq Y$) is used, the objects are perceived as having nothing in common. Consequently, "identity" and "heterogeneity" only offer restrictive cognitive frameworks. When the logic of "similarity" ($X \approx Y$) is introduced, though, it opens possibilities for loose and flexible connections between objects. Of course, the Samburu are not confusing these logics. While they recognize differences between livestock, humans and wild animals, they perceive these different objects as parts of a continuum with similarities at the same time. Metaphorical thinking connects heterogeneous objects loosely and flexibly using the logic of "similarity" in the Samburu's cognitive system.

In the Samburu's cognitive system, livestock (things), humans (body) and wild animals (environment) are integrated into a loosely and flexibly connected continuum by the action of metaphor rather than separated as discrete objects. The Samburu's myths and customs speak of the possible transformation of livestock into wild animals or humans into wild animals in their world. Due to the connections by the logic of metaphor, distinctions between livestock, humans and wild animals are ambiguous, inter-penetrable, and sometimes transformable. Thus, a fundamental reconsideration of the pastoralist world view requires a re-examination of dualistic distinctions between "livestock and wild animals" and "humans and animals". Understanding livestock, humans and wild animals as an integrated continuum rather than assuming dualism as given is essential for studies of the cognitive systems of pastoralist societies.

I shall stop at the presentation of this overview of the Samburu's cognitive world due to limitations of space and materials. In order to validate the theoretical model presented in the first half, we need more ethnographical cases exploring material culture and techniques of the body. The proposed theoretical model also has repercussions for the study of human evolution, but I have not yet fully developed it in that context.

However, the ethnographical examples of the Samburu's cognitive system in which the body, things and the environment form a loosely and flexibly connected continuum through metaphors offers various suggestions for a new holistic material culture theory which reinterprets the body, things and the environment in a more continuous relationship and reconsiders things as extensions of the body and the environment.

13 The Cicadas Drizzle of the Chamus

Kaori Kawai

Keywords: The Chamus, pastoral people, grazing as solitary activity, sound environment, solitude, "materiality" of sound

The bell cricket. The cicada. Butterflies. Crickets. Grasshoppers. Water-weed shrimps. Mayflies. Fireflies. The bagworm is a very touching creature. It's a demon's child, and the mother fears it must have the same terrible nature as its parent, so she dresses it in ragged clothes and tells it to wait until she returns for it when the autumn wind blows. The poor little thing doesn't realize that its mother has deserted it, and when it hears the autumn winds begin in the eighth month, it sets up a pitiable little tremulous cry for her.

The Pillow Book by Sei Shonagon
[Translation by Meredith McKinney (2006), Penguin Books]

13.1 *Liiyo* and the sound environment

The Chamus people are pastoralists living near Lake Baringo in the semi-arid area of North Kenya. The population of around 16,000 speaks the Maa language, which is also spoken by the Maasai people, who are well-known as savanna-dwelling pastoralists. Their main livelihood comes from livestock breeding, including cattle, goat and sheep, and small-scale irrigated and non-irrigated farming of crops such as maize and finger millet.

The Chamus call cicadas *liiyo*, which also means "ringing in the ears" as well as "loneliness" or "solitude". Only one species of cicada is known to the Chamus, which is characterized by their chorus in a high-pitched sound. This sound is described as either "tee", "tay" or "yee". This chapter is an attempt to consider what "sound" means for the Chamus in relation to various phenomena represented by the word *liiyo*. In particular, we use the concept of "sound environment" to address the sounds we "hear" when we put ourselves in a certain space, rather than sounds as objects of active "listening", and explore the relationship between people and

Photo 13.1 A herd of cattle moving through an open acacia woodland and a lone Chamus herder following it.

sounds. We shall also consider what "solitude" expressed by the word *liiyo* means to the Chamus in the context of a sound environment. Through this exploration we will contemplate the *mono* nature (materiality) of sound and the physicality of humans who have no choice about receiving sound passively.

13.2 Sounds in a living space

13.2.1 Sounds in a habitat: Human presence and sounds

A majority of sounds in the habitat tend to be artificial sounds such as human voices and sounds produced by human activities. There are some sounds that indicate human presence. The habitat is filled with a wide variety of such sounds. Let us follow the sounds typically heard in a Chamus homestead (*nkang*) in the morning.

As the pre-dawn sky begins to lighten, baby goats begin calling for their mothers. Shortly after that, milking begins and the pen is filled with the loud noise of mother and baby goats calling each other. In the midst, there is a faint but clear "zaa, zaa, zaa" sound of milk gushing into gourd containers. From the cooking hut come the "kacha, kacha, kacha" sound of preparing *chai* (milk tea) and finger millet porridge, which are eventually followed by the clattering of tin plates and utensils. There are voices calling children's names, voices responding to them, and voices saying "kute!" to shoo the dogs away. We can tell how people are beginning their day's activities now that the sun has risen. Soon it is time to put the animals out to pasture. There is a unique glugging sound "gu, gu, gu, gu" that people make when driving the animals out of the pen and the sound of livestock shoving and jostling through the gate. The sound such as "za, za, za, za" of their footsteps gradually moves away. After livestock have been sent away, the homestead temporarily falls silent. Then, there are sounds of sweeping the floor and the ground, of lulling, consoling and calling children, of children running around, and of washing dishes, hands and feet. From the cooking hut come the sounds of lunch preparation – of washing pots and spattering hot oil when vegetables are thrown in. In this way, we can discern what is happening in the habitat by sounds without looking. We get an idea of the activities of a considerable number of people. There are sounds that indicate the presence of others, that is, signs of human life, which fill the habitat.

13.2.2 Sound in a grazing space: An activity with few sounds

In comparison with the habitat of homestead, sounds and voices heard while grazing are simple. When livestock leave the pen to graze, young animals are kept back for a short while so that they graze near the homestead. As they are separated from their mothers heading for a grazing area, mothers and cubs exchange calls loudly. Once the herd of mature animals leaves the homestead and move to the grazing area, they are almost completely silent; only the "za, za, za, za" sound of their footsteps are heard. Goats emit occasional warning sounds such as "bu!", but cattle move to the grazing area silently. Wooden or metal bells tied to the neck of one or two animals in the herd produce dry ringing sounds. Livestock are generally quiet in the grazing area, too. Only the sounds of vigorous grazing are heard – of biting, pulling, gnawing and chewing grass. Again, the bell tied to the neck of an animal occasionally sends an airy sound into the space filled with feeding sounds. The herder[1] rarely uses his or her voice except for the occasional vocalization of "hai!" when s/he throws a stone or a twig to control the livestock's movements. When livestock stop feeding and rest, they make monotonous "kusha, kusha, kusha" sounds of regurgitating grass and chewing the cud. The only other sounds include the winds stirring grass and tree branches, the faint sound of the bell or another herder's call "hai!" in the distance.

In this way, time passes surprisingly quietly in the grazing space. The grazing area is largely silent except for the sounds of livestock feeding and the voices of several bird species. However, there is a space in the grazing area that becomes enveloped in a peculiar sound. The Chamus use two types of pasture land. One is grassland called *lmaine* which becomes a marshland during the rainy season. It extends around Lake Baringo and along the rivers flowing into it. The Chamus mainly graze cattle here as they prefer herbaceous plants, but they also send their goats and sheep. The other type is the acacia bush (woodland), which is called either *iiti* (*Acacia mellifera*) or *ljorai* (*Acacia reficiens*) depending on the dominant tree species (hereinafter called *iiti* for reasons of expediency). It is best suited to goats, which are browsers (feeding on young shoots and leaves). This type of land mainly extends over gentle, rolling hills away from the lake. It is filled with a highly characteristic sound: the sound of cicadas. A chorus of cicadas is called *semi-shigure* (cicada drizzle) in Japanese, but the singing here is rather intense. It is more of a downpour or squall of rain than a drizzle. Cicadas tend to sing even more loudly in the hottest part of the dry season.

The Chamus graze their livestock in the *lmaine* and the *iiti* in slightly different ways. The former is grassland with good visibility. The latter is covered with dense shrubs that reduce visibility. The herder can remain in one place for a relatively long period of time in the *lmaine* thanks to good visibility. In the *iiti*, however, the herder must move frequently in response to the gradual movement of his herd. As the *lmaine* offers plenty of grass and attracts many herds, the herders following different herds often sit together under a tree. This is not possible in the *iiti* because they need to follow their herds constantly. In other words, grazing in the *iiti* requires the herder to follow his livestock alone and when the herd slows down or goes into rumination s/he might spend time sitting under a tree alone. S/he seldom encounters another herd except when they go to a watering hole. In the space dominated by the sound of cicadas, there is no sign of another human life. There are only the sound "hai!" of his/her own voice to warn the herd, the glugging sound "gu, gu, gu, gu" that s/he makes to steer the herd, and the sound of stones or twigs hitting a tree or the ground when thrown to warn the animals. The herder sometimes sings a song to him/herself.

13.3 Two sounds – *buwata* and *ltolilyo*

The Chamus have two words to represent sound[2] – *buwata* and *ltolilyo*. Let us see how they are used based on some examples.

First, voices emitted by wild animals – for example, the hyena's unique whooping "uuuih, uuuih", the ostrich's peculiar grunt "nguh, nguh" that is audible from a distance, and the birds' noisy chirps at dawn are all *buwata*. Loud sounds from distant sources such as cars or tractors driving on a distant road are also *buwata*. The chorus of cicadas is also *buwata*; an extreme *buwata* that is described as *buwata oleng* (*oleng* means "very much"). Human voices, in contrast, are generally *ltolilyo*. A baby's cry is *ltolilyo*. When a single cow or goat vocalizes in a calm state, the voice is *ltolilyo*. Clamoring at the time of milking, however, is *buwata*. These words are not used for natural sounds from sources such as water, wind and rain; they are neither *buwata* nor *ltolilyo*. When they "hear" these sounds or these sounds are "heard", they use the verb *-ning* as in "hear water/water is heard (*-ning nkare*), "hear wind/wind is heard (*-ning suwo*)", and "hear rain/rain is heard (*-ning cham*). The verb *-ning* also means "feel/be felt", "notice (perceive)/ be noticed (be perceived)", "understand" and "accept". Similarly, the word for active or conscious listening is *-inining*, which can be regarded as a derivative of *-ning*.[3]

About the distinction between *buwata* and *ltolilyo*, the Chamus explain ambiguously that "They are almost the same but different". They do not have a clear-cut conceptual distinction. As the voice of one livestock animal is *ltolilyo* while the voices of multiple animals are *buwata*, the distinction appears to be dependent on the context in some cases. Based on various comments, *ltolilyo* seems to be used when the source of a sound or voice can be identified as a single specific thing. By contrast, *buwata* seems to be used when the source of a distant sound or voice can be identified as a category such as hyena or ostrich or motor vehicle but it is not possible to identify which individual specifically. When many voices are mixed together and individual voices are unidentifiable, the sound is *buwata*. This is applicable to the chirps of birds and cicadas. Even for the human voice, the chattering of drunken people at a gathering or the yelping of playing children are also *buwata*.

While the sound of a motor vehicle today is *buwata*, it was *ltolilyo* when I first went to live with the Chamus more than twenty years ago. There were very few passing vehicles in the area surrounding the homestead where I was staying. The only vehicle sound was mine. They told me that children used to yell "It's Kaori! Kaori's here!" every time they heard the sound of a vehicle, even after I had returned to Japan. The sound of a vehicle at the time was the sound of "Kaori's vehicle" and it was *ltolilyo* because the source of the sound was clearly identifiable. But today (in 2010), the sounds of trucks coming to buy charcoal or local and regional shuttle minibuses are heard many times a day. Thus the sound of a vehicle has become *buwata*.

For the time being, it seems reasonable to say that *ltolilyo* is a sound from an identifiable and specific source while *buwata* is a sound from a distant and nonspecific source or a mixture of sounds from multiple sources that cannot be identified individually and has the aspect of "noise".[4]

13.4 "*Liiyo* eats"

I mentioned earlier that the Chamus word *liiyo* means "ringing in the ears" and "loneliness (solitude)" as well as "cicada". Let us now look at *liiyo* when it is used to mean "solitude".

The word *liiyo* here does not refer to "cicada". The Chamus people also state unequivocally, "It is not that *liiyo* that screeches". *Liiyo* in the sense of "solitude" is used in the idiomatic phrase *-tama liiyo*. The verb *-tama* is the past form of *-am*, which means "to eat". So the phrase literally means "*Liiyo* ate (someone)" but the phrase is used to mean that "(someone) is placed in a state of solitude". Other expressions in which *liiyo* means "solitude" include *keti liiyo* (*liiyo* is present), *-ning liiyo* (to hear/feel *liiyo*, *liiyo* is heard/felt),[5] *-oulye liiyo* (to fear *liiyo*). However, one may be physically alone in a space but *meti liiyo* (there is no *liiyo*) if one is engrossed in something. For instance, a woman may be left alone in her homestead after all other members have gone out but "there is no *liiyo*" if she is engaged in cooking, cleaning, other household chores or beadwork. They say that "*liiyo* eats (someone)" when the person is doing nothing or simply sitting around without thinking about anything in particular.

The condition of "solitude" does not happen very often in everyday living but it does happen occasionally. For example, grazing is usually carried out by a single herder and the condition of solitude persists, especially when pasturing in the *iiti* because encountering another person is rare. A woman who is left alone with an infant in the homestead is not alone while the infant is awake but "*liiyo* eats (her)" or "*liiyo* ate", i.e., she is in a state of "solitude", when the infant falls asleep. They say that all people – adults, children, men and women – "have" this condition of "solitude" (and attendant emotions and feelings as mentioned later). Even young children "know *liiyo*". Babies and infants cry when they wake up and find no one around. They say that this is because they "know *liiyo*". During a long-term field study, I once hummed a Japanese song to myself without thinking. I was asked successively, "Did *liiyo* eat Kaori?" and "Were you thinking of (feeling for) Japan?" They also say that "*liiyo* eats" non-human animals in some cases. Livestock always live in a herd and they cry when they are separated from their group. Birds often fly in flocks.

People in the condition described as "*liiyo* ate" are not deemed to be sick or unwell but the condition of their body is said to be not normal. They use expressions such as "*Liiyo* in the heart (*ltau*)", "There is *liiyo* in the belly (*nkochage*)", "There is *liiyo* in the head (*nkwe*)" and "There is *liiyo* in the entire body (*sesen pooki*)". These examples suggest that *liiyo* is something that is felt physically but it is difficult to identify in which part of the body it is present; it seems to vary depending on the individual, the situation, or the context. Some say that *liiyo* interferes with thinking. One person commented that "*Liiyo* is present" in a "thinking place" and hence "It may be the head". Another person stated that "The place must be the heart or the belly because *liiyo* is something that is felt", then immediately added, "No, it may be the entire body".

We can surmise that a person in the condition "*liiyo* ate" has a certain emotion or feeling. This means that some emotion or feeling associated with "solitude" is shared by people, but it does not seem accurate to interpret it as, for example, "loneliness". This is because they describe what is expressed by the phrase "*liiyo* ate" as a condition in which something external is acting on one rather than a condition in which a feeling associated with the condition "wells up from inside". The Chamus have a tendency to explain pain sensations and a sense of unwellness, for example, as material world phenomena that happen to the body as a material entity.[6] Perhaps the same tendency is recognizable in the case of emotions. The metaphorical expression "*liiyo* ate" is highly materialistic in itself and the subject of this sentence is none other than *liiyo*. Before we consider the externality of emotions associated with the condition "*liiyo* ate" or "solitude", we will look at the latent presence of situations in which "*liiyo* eats (people)" in the habitation style of the Chamus.

13.5 The lifestyle of the Chamus

The basic habitation unit of the Chamus is comprised of a husband, wife and their unmarried children. Although their society permits polygamy, co-wives seldom live together in one place. Once their children reach a certain age, each co-wife moves out of the husband's homestead and sets up her own homestead. The youngest co-wife lives with the husband to the end (Kawai 1990). Accordingly, many of the Chamus homesteads are occupied by a married woman and her unmarried children only, but it is not uncommon for married children or unmarried daughters and her children to live at their mother's homestead. The homestead at which these family members reside is called *nkang* in the Chamus language. Each *nkang* consists of one or more thatched huts (*nkaji*), a cattle pen, and a small livestock (goats and sheep) pen (*sum*). The entire site is encircled by a fence called *wata*. The Chamus live in these homesteads scattered across sparsely wooded open lands and acacia woodlands instead of forming residential clusters that could be called "villages" or "settlements". There are several hundred meters between neighboring homesteads, It takes more than a few minutes to walk from one to another and loud voices generally cannot be heard by neighbors.

One of the reasons for the Chamus' tendency to set their homes so far apart and to not live with other co-wives appears to be an aversion to "living with many people" and the noises associated with it. In general, Chamus life consists of quiet and sedate days that are repeated in a calm manner. Those who are prone to shouting or boisterousness and raucous drunken people are often laughed at or criticized. The reprimand of "be quiet / silence (*tegirai*)" is frequently heard in their everyday life.[7] They believe that a gathering of people increases the use of dark magic called *ngopt*. People, especially women, spend much of their time at their own homestead and rarely visit other homesteads. They not only set their homesteads far apart but rarely visit with relatives, in-laws and co-wives. The Chamus engage in activities such as grazing, water fetching and firewood gathering individually in most cases and are seldom seen walking in company with another person except school children on their way home. But it would be mistaken to think that they are unsociable people. They actively participate in ceremonial gatherings and often stand talking for a long time when they cross paths at a watering hole, a grazing area, or in the street. Yet, they believe that they should refrain from going around visiting other homesteads and have less than kind words for those who have such a tendency.

The expression "*liiyo* ate" must be understood on the basis of their lifestyle and behavioral propensity. The potential for falling into the condition of "*liiyo* ate" is embedded in the Chamus way of life. Although they "fear" *liiyo*, it is an inevitable consequence of their choice to lead a quiet life in the form of dwelling with less noise.

13.6 The sound environment and the body

13.6.1 The grazing space of *iiti*

I mentioned in 13.2.2 that the grazing space in the acacia woodland called *iiti* is filled with the sound of cicadas. We discussed in 13.4 that the word for cicada, *liiyo*, is used in the idiomatic expression of "*liiyo* ate" which refers to the condition of "solitude". Why do the Chamus use *liiyo*, the word for cicada, to describe the condition of "solitude"? Their answer to this question is clear-cut: "One strongly feels that one is alone when one hears the sound of cicadas in the *iiti*". One hears (*-ning*) the sound of "*liiyo*" and feels (*-ning*) "*liiyo* (solitude)".

Cicadas buzz most profusely in the hottest period of the dry season, especially at noon when the temperature rises. It is the time of the day when the herder sits in the shade of a tree with nothing to do as his animals stop moving to chew the cud. An animal with a bell sometimes shakes its head and produces dry jingles. Or a yellow billed hornbill (*Tockus flavirostris*) makes a sharp call as it flies by. Tranquility returns in no time. Except for the occasional sound of hot and dry winds shaking grass and trees, the midday woodland is a silent world where only the sound of cicadas is audible. This is the nature of this space. The herder suddenly realizes that s/he is surrounded by the cacophony of cicadas. The herder has no one to talk to and simply gazes blankly at livestock or dozes off.

As mentioned in 13.4, the condition of "*liiyo* eats (someone)" does not happen when a person is active, so the herder does not feel "solitude" when managing the movement of the herd. However, the grazing space of *iiti* forces the herder into the situation of sitting under a tree alone to kill time as soon as the herd stops moving around to rest and ruminate. This is when "*liiyo* eats (the herder)". In other words, the herder has a strong sense of "solitude". The herder may idle away some time while hearing nothing but the sound of cicadas. They say that they attach a bell to their favorite cow or goat because it "tells them that they are not alone". We suppose that the bell provides an awareness of "being with livestock (and not alone)". This is also the reason that the herder often sings when grazing animals alone. Perhaps s/he is trying to resist the condition of "*liiyo* eats" by singing songs or listening to the sound of the bell.

The grazing space called *iiti* is an *iiti*-dominant vegetation environment where cicadas are constantly and intensely buzzing. The space is saturated with the sound of cicadas and the shimmering midday heat that prevent people from "thinking in concentration". It can be described as being overwhelmed by the environment. One is simply dazed and surrenders oneself to the environment.

13.6.2 The characteristics of cicada sound and the passivity of "hearing"

As mentioned at the start, only one cicada species (unidentified) is known to the Chamus. It is a small cicada, about the size of the higurashi cicada (*Tanna japonensis*; approx. 2–4 cm), with a dark brown body and transparent wings. In the *iiti* woodlands, several or many cicadas perch on each tree, producing loud calls. Striking the tree trunk will cause them to fly away, but it is a mere drop in the bucket because the cicadas gathered on other trees continue to buzz. Herders do not make such a vain attempt.

The sound of the cicadas in the *iiti* has the following characteristics. The most prominent is its overwhelming volume. The buzzing of so many cicadas in the middle of the day during the dry season is extremely noisy. The herder sits down and rests under a tree but the trunk of the tree usually has several cicadas calling loudly. The sharp cacophonic sound pierces the herder's ears from just above his head. The overwhelming volume of the sound may drown out other sounds. The second characteristic is the continuity of this never-ending noise. It should be called a "downpour" or "squall" of cicada sound; some cicadas may stop calling but all others continue buzzing. New cicadas fly in, perch on the tree above the resting herder and start calling. The sound of cicadas envelopes the entire woodland and never stops. Finally, the cicada species known to the Chamus makes a uniform and very monotonous sound, which is described by the people as "tee", "tay" or "yee", unlike more unique songs produced by tsukutsukubōshi[8] cicada (*Meimuna opalifera*) or *Tanna japonensis*. The word *liiyo* also means "a ringing in the ears" because the sound of cicadas to the Chamus is a monotonous sound that paralyzes one's head from its core.

These characteristics of the cicada sound – its overwhelming volume, continuity and monotony – offer very little room for people to attribute meaning to it. As in many other societies, the calls of several bird species are recognized as signs of good and bad fortunes by the Chamus. The cicada sound, however, appears to be perceived differently.[9] As mentioned, the Chamus describe the cicada sound as *buwata oleng*, that is, a "very clamorous noise". The *iiti* is an environment characterized by this cicada sound, a sound from which people cannot escape as long as their animals are grazing in it.

People are helplessly passive against the sound environment. This is a characteristic of the body organ called ear. The ear cannot block incoming sounds. Even when people cover their ears with their hands, they cannot completely escape the cicada sound in the *iiti*. The act of covering the ears cannot overcome the passivity of "hearing". I do not recall ever seeing the Chamus people covering their ears. They do not seem to try to prevent sounds from coming into their ears. When they feel some "noise" or "clamor" is unpleasant, the clearest action they take to indicate this is either uttering "Ah, ah, ah, ah" while shaking one hand in front of the face or uttering "Ah" while making fists on the chest and opening the hands as they thrust them forward. But I have never seen them do this against the cicada sound.

The passivity of the ear is clear when compared with, say, the eye, which can be shut so that seeing can be blocked completely. While one can "lend an ear" or "open an ear" to a sound consciously, some sounds are constantly reaching one's ears whether one is conscious of them or not. It is difficult to control this state intentionally. This characteristic, however, is not exclusive to the ear. The nose is similar in that it cannot normally escape environmental scents, although one can actively "smell" something. One can block a scent temporarily by pinching one's nose, but doing so for too long disrupts one's breathing. Consequently, there is no effective way to escape smells other than leaving the place where they occur, just like sounds. Again, I have no recollection of seeing any Chamus pinching their nose shut to unpleasant smells (although I have seen them shaking their hand a little in front of their nose). In short, their attitude toward external stimuli appears to be passive.

13.6.3 The sound environment and "solitude"

The cicadas in the *iiti* are a material presence that gives people an intense feeling of "solitude" in the sound environment they create. There is a sound that is an extension of a creature called cicada which becomes an auditory stimulus that permeates the human body and triggers an experience of *liiyo* ("solitude"). The Chamus associate the physical condition of "solitude", or the social condition of singularity, with the environment of the *iiti* woodland filled with the endless, monotonous and overwhelmingly loud calls of cicadas. What is expressed here is the physicality of "solitude" in the Chamus. In other words, their experience of "solitude" seems to intensify in the midst of their relationship (interaction) with the environment mediated by their own bodies.

People feel "solitude" strongly in the *iiti* woodland when they go into a temporary state of inactivity. The condition "*liiyo* eats" does not occur while they move around with the herd and actively engage in controlling the animals by throwing stones or vocalizing. We can assume that the sound of cicadas recedes in the background during periods of activity. As soon as they stop voluntary movements, however, the sound of cicadas begins to assert itself, overwhelms them, and prevents them from "thinking about things". It continually sends a single message: "solitude". It demonstrates that the environment is not always a mere background or a simple stage for human activity.

The Chamus speak of *liiyo* in the condition "*liiyo* eats" as being "in the head" and hence paralyzing their thinking. They say that *liiyo* "in the heart" or "in the belly" stops them from feeling anything. As we have seen, people "have a strong sense of *liiyo* (solitude)" when they are encased in a sound environment created by the cicada sound characterized by an overwhelming sound volume, continuity and monotony while grazing their livestock in the *iiti* woodland. In other words, it creates a state of mind and body in which the head is thinking nothing and the heart (or the belly) is feeling nothing other than the sense of "being alone". The loud chorus of cicadas seems to infiltrate the body through the ears, saturate the body and make the person unable to think. It can be called a type of paralysis. Sounds directly infiltrate very deeply into human physiology (Kawada 1992a: 129) and excessive acoustic stimuli numb our auditory senses or confuse our thinking (Kawada 1992a: 249). While it is possible that some emotion associated with the condition "*liiyo* eats" is shared among people, it appears to permeate the body from outside, unlike an emotion arising from within. It is difficult to identify where in the body *liiyo* (solitude) is felt, or "where (in the body) it is present" in their terms, but it seems to be something that threatens the locus of intellect or feeling in any case.

In this way, we can perhaps treat *liiyo* used in the sense of "solitude" as something permeating the body, regardless of whether one chooses it or not, just as the sound of cicadas. It is considered that "hearing" – or we should say "being heard" in this case – means linking the environment and the body through the ear, which involves a fluctuating boundary between the environment and the body. In other words, the sound (of cicadas), the environment (the grazing area) and the body (our auditory sense) melt or fuse in the condition of *liiyo* or "solitude". It represents one condition in which people are faced with sounds and made to interact with sounds. Yet, the sound of cicadas becomes meaningful and begins to assert itself specifically under the social condition of "solitude". In this sense, the expression "*liiyo* ate" not only calls us to examine the relationship between the sound environment and the individual body, but also reminds us that the condition of being alone and doing nothing and thinking nothing looms large in their social consciousness, whether good or bad. We must remember here that the expression "*liiyo* ate" is also deeply linked to the social condition, i.e., the way the Chamus people live and conduct themselves socially.[10]

13.7 In closing: The *mono* (thing) nature or materiality of sound

In closing this chapter, I would like to touch on the question of the *mono* (*thing*) nature of sound. This is an attempt to raise the question "Is sound a thing?" which invokes the more fundamental question "What is the materiality of a thing?". Let us consider step by step.

Generally speaking, sound is intangible. Hence it may be physical but not material, in which case it can hardly be called a *thing*. For instance, in his discussion of the condition of physical things in non-human primates in Chapter 11, Kuroda defines things as "objects of movable size" (even of imagined movability) and states that "we seem to intuitively perceive objects of movable size as things ("thing-like things")". But does this mean we should reject the possibility that sound is a *thing*, i.e., the materiality of sound, simply because it is immaterial and intangible (i.e., it is not a "matter or material object").

Sound has a source, which is a *thing*, and the materiality of sound can be maintained as long as there is an awareness of the source. The Chamus use the word *ltolilyo* for sounds from identifiable and specific sources and the other word *buwata* for sounds whose sources are not identifiable or specific. This demonstrates that when the Chamus perceive sounds, they also trace them back to their sources. In other words, the Chamus recognize each sound in a form associated with a *thing* that is its source. This is where we can see glimpses of the materiality of sound. Nevertheless, the main subject of this chapter is the sound of cicadas, which is *buwata* (noise) whose source is unidentifiable and which they call "the worst *buwata*". As it is impossible to differentiate individual cicadas that produce the sound, the chorus of cicadas was perceived by the human ear as the noise that creates the sound environment saturating the *iiti* woodland. Thus, the Chamus do not always perceive sounds reaching their ears on the basis of how it relates to identified sources. Let us confine ourselves to stating that the Chamus make a distinction between sounds with identifiable sources and sounds with unidentifiable sources. This should sufficiently explain that they are aware of the sources of sounds.

At the same, it is possible to recognize materiality in sound in the sense that it is undoubtedly perceived physically through the ear or that it directly acts on the body through the sensory organ ear (agency) even though it is intangible. Moreover, while we have been discussing sound in relation to the auditory sense, sound is also perceived as tactile stimulation by physical pressure in the form of vibrations sensed by one's entire body. From this perspective, we need not hesitate to say that sound is a *thing*. Indeed, we may be over-emphasizing the visual as well as (and perhaps more importantly) the mass-centric perspective in considering "the materiality of things".[11] My opening statement in this section conforms to those biases, nominating tangibility as a requirement for the materiality of things without qualification. Although it is beyond the scope of this chapter, non-solid *things* such as wind, air and smell that "cannot be touched directly" in the ordinary sense should be examined in future research, along with sound. Perceiving intangible sounds through auditory senses or the tactile senses in the form of physical pressure is analogous to perceiving wind, air and smell through tactile or olfactory senses as a gaseous flow, a temperature or humidity, or sometimes pressure or irritants (chemicals) floating in the atmosphere. In this sense, wind, air and smell can be regarded as things with materiality. In other words, "the materiality of things" being discussed here may be one aspect of *things* that can be recognized only in the context of their relationship with the human body, equipped with five senses that are always open to the environment. It does not feel too far off the mark to say that this is one way for *things* to manifest. Sound, wind, air and smell are all constituent elements of the environment in which people place themselves and act. I would like to think that they can be regarded as entities with materiality – i.e., *things* – in that they manifest their presence by infiltrating human space through the medium of various physical sense organs.

How can we treat the intangible conceptual representation of sound? What perspective do we need to adopt to discuss the domain of emotional life evoked by sound? What language can we use to describe the way a sound, which is "heard" and not "listened to", permeates one's heart? While we have examined the very human behavior among the Chamus of attaching the meaning "solitude" to the cacophony of cicadas that they perceive, we still have many unexplored questions. There is a substantial body of excellent research on sound and sound environments in the field of anthropology but many of them center on either "music" created by humans (ethnomusicology), including songs – for ceremonial or entertainment purposes – or "human voice (speech sound)", be it conversation, monologue or oration.[12] But we will still need to study how the world of sound, especially various sounds in the natural world – the voices of wild animals, the sounds of rain and winds, the sound of trees swaying in the wind, the rustling of grass blades in the wind sweeping across the meadow, the murmuring of the river, and so on – influences human emotions and social life.[13] This chapter might serve as a research note for the purpose of opening the possibility of approaching the thing-like medium of sound from the perspective of the study of *things*.

Epilogue
Stonehood: Agency as Inagency

Motomitsu Uchibori

1 The meaning of being meaningless

A stone sometimes manifests in a way that resonates with the heart precisely because it presents in this world in a way that is opposite to the condition of human existence. As an immovable and unchanging object with no intention, a stone is as far as possible from what we commonly call agency.

There are a few research areas in the humanities that examine natural objects not processed by human hands. They include the history of religion and the study of symbolism in anthropology. In these domains, a *thing* is not always exchanged between people. Such a thing is spoken of as simply existing, and as meaningful in itself, regardless of whether it has humanly exchangeable commodity value or not. In this sense, the thing appears to be brimming with *exogenous* forces or meanings that overwhelm people. However, these *natural* forces or symbols can be regarded as constituent elements of a purely human semantic field ironically because of their exogenous nature. Hence, paradoxically, they seem to diverge from the thing itself, using these forces and meanings as a springboard. Can we find a path to circumvent this divergence? How should we follow it?

I am following a stone because its "stonehood" appears to offer a possibility of circumventing this divergence. To what extent does a stone remain a thing independent of human meaning? A stone on the side of the path, for example, is certainly the most typical of the "meaningless things" pervading the world; yet this "meaninglessness" is entirely human. In other words, meaninglessness only exists where there is meaning; hence it is impossible in anthropology, by definition, for anything to exist outside of the semantic domain or free from meaning. Nevertheless, I have an inkling that a stone can offer a concrete sort of proxy for meaninglessness. That is because I see in the relationship between people and a stone the very essence of the convention which regards humans as subjects and locus of agency in the strongest sense.

2 *Thing*-telling being story-telling

Let a thing tell its story, they say. A thing in this context can be an "object", but can we successfully let a *thing* (object) tell its own story? Answering this question is difficult even when the thing is presented to us in the form of a museum exhibit, for example – more difficult than figuring out how to present the thing. But what form of telling would approximate the right answer if we attempt it in human language in the absence of the thing itself? This is what I am exploring here.

Humans are eager to tell stories about things. Things never tell stories themselves. Letting a thing tell a story is in fact one way of telling a story about the thing, and we need to erect a levee somewhere to stop us from talking about this in endless cycles. I shall therefore assign the role of the levee to my denial of the privileged nature of story-telling itself. This will make the argument of this essay appear self-contradictory, but I believe that it is only when we take that risk that the attempt to invert the generally-accepted relationship between things and humans will become possible in a more or less significant way. Let us begin with a discussion of what sort of significance it might be.

In short, the degree of significance here will be the distance that can be achieved in moving away from the human-centric view of human story-telling. The narratives about things have been biased towards human-made things (artefacts) and their production. Even when this was not the case, the ontological meaning of the things tended to be presented in terms of their utilitarian or symbolic value for humans. By contrast, this exercise to lay the groundwork for the aforementioned possibility is oriented towards thing-telling without the anthropocentric perspectives of utilitarianism and symbolism. A story generally owes its meaning to its storyline or narrative structure, but we are attempting to circumvent or at least suspend temporarily the need for utilitarianism or symbolism to construct a "storyline" about things.

I will give the principal role to a stone in the hope that the broadness of the relationship offered by this thing will allow us to try to tell a story in the way that highlights the condition of being a stone, that is the stonehood, within the world which consists of variegated things that exist around and are related to it. Note that, when we try this, these things could include humans, even though they may not be in the equal capacity as other things.

3 Linkage

On the entrance floor of our home, there is a stone that looks like an old-fashioned weight stone for pickling, although slightly larger. It surely weighs more than seven kilograms. This stone was sitting by the side of an upper stream of a river until mid-2005. There is nothing special about its composition, nor does it have an attractive color or shape. An attribute that proved decisive in its relocation to the present position was that its size and weight would be just within the carry-on baggage allowance for our airplane. This attribute led my wife to decide to assign the role of its transporter to her husband. Its association with that particular river bank constitutes in her awareness the precondition for her selective intention and action, for it must have appealed to her sentiment in her reminiscence of living in the village nearby three decades ago. From another perspective, however, to say that the contingent or ontic fact of the stone's being just there *caused* her exogenously and non-intentionally to exercise her intention in that way is not inconsistent with seeing the present state of the stone as a consequence of a chronological chain of events. But where will we end up if we pursue this way of speaking or narrating?

If we dare to approach this question as a caricature, we will find ourselves ending up in a contradiction similar to what relates the so-called "stumbling block" in the logic of the causal link. In other words, it is the question of which term – the state of affairs of a human bodily movement of "stumbling" on the one hand or the contingent existence of the "stone" as an ontic thing on the other – we should treat as the origin of the event as we follow and narrate the relationship thread that links them. We can rephrase this and speak of a comparative assessment of the agency of the people and the thing involved in a particular event. Perhaps any apparent self-contradiction means that this assessment is constantly fluctuating and has no stabilization point. More specifically, it concerns the inconclusiveness of the absurd argument of "becausality", so to speak, rather than causality as such, about whether the person stumbled over the stone *because* of their own gait or the stone has made that person stumble *because* of its form or mode of existence.

Although the introduction of this "becausality" is likely to contribute somehow to the well-received broadening of the concept of agency to include things beyond the privilege conferred on language and meaning, it is still an unusual and limited approach. To make it a bit more conventional, we can introduce something like "linkage" or "connectedness", but if we turn that into something akin to a causal or chronological chain – or a Saussurian syntagmatic chain – we do more harm than good. Such a chain implies a form of relationship that is relatively more restrictive within the range of "becausality" as applied above. It may, indeed, include even a causal necessity. What we want to introduce with the term "linkage" or "connectedness" is a relationality that is more fundamentally contingent than the indeterminable "becausality". Akin to a paradigmatic relationality, that might be a relationality among the things with the attribute of "co-location" or even a primarily fictitious relationality as in the relationship between elements in a parallel set of things that do not see the presence of the other things at each particular moment.

4 The context of self-contradiction

The people who engage in swidden agriculture in the hills of Borneo speak about the topography of the land along their local rivers on the basis of whether the river banks are pebbled or not. They are distinguishing between upstream and downstream, or valley and plain, but their terminology focuses on stones. They do not seem to be thinking of large rocks, but rather of round stones of various sizes. Of course, the one sitting in my house is one of them. For these people, the closest pebbled river bank to human dwellings functions as a daily bathing area as well as a children's playground. Not long ago, it was the source of water, including drinking water, for a considerable number of people. A pebbled river bank is spoken of in the same breath as the "clarity (cleanliness)" of the domestic water source. It is one of the major advantages of living in the upper reaches of a river. To my wife, who visited me in my field-site with our two-year-old son and stayed in the village for several months in the mid-1970s, the stone from the pebbled river bank is a reminder of our son bathing in the river.

Once we have figured out that a particular stone has meaning for a particular person based on the context of their encounter, we are unlikely to discover anything new there, because context is basically a one-dimensional extension, so to speak, of a chronological or syntagmatic chain. In contrast, looking at the expansion of the relationship between elements of a parallel set has the potential to allow us to move within the inner space of an operating network between things while reducing or nullifying the agency of the people involved by destroying contextuality, and perhaps logic as well.

The parallel set is not limited in size. It can be expanded or reduced in any way. Starting with stones on a river bank, this set can be expanded to include crystals used by shamans to read the condition of a human life, or the rocks that appear in the river current as the petrified marks of punishment for sins such as incest, or megalithic monuments found somewhere in Borneo as vestiges of human activity, and, beyond the boundaries of the Bornean world, even to stone money as man-made objects with profound signification. Needless to say, roadside stones, meteoric stones from space, and various attributes of stones that evoke a wide range of metaphors of "stonehood" encountered outside conventional ethnography can all be told within the confines of this place. Conversely, we can jump over to the place of a set of various growing and changing plants – including the aptly defined rhizomes – and, as if at the opposite end of stone metaphors, line up, for example, metaphors generated by bananas in this place.

Unfortunately, the extension, reduction and jump are all performed by humans, who should be described as subjects rather than agents, and therefore my first attempt for *thing*-telling must end in self-contradiction.

Essay I
The Appearance of "*Mono*"

I-1 Where a Name Acquires a Form: Motifs of Javanese Batik

Junko Sato

This essay describes the way that the environment, including things and the experiences of people, forms traditional motifs on cloth focusing on the production of Javanese batik. I introduce the case of the work of female waged workers who take jobs on a piece rate basis from Bunga Istana, a batik workshop in Yogyakarta in Central Java where I conducted research over a period of twenty one months from 2005, to illustrate that the apparently simple task of motif drawing is only possible due to the accumulation of interactions between the workers, the environment and the objects..

⦿ What is Javanese batik? ⦿

Batik is a generic term for textile fabrics with motifs which are made using a wax resist dyeing technique. There are many examples throughout the world that were originally produced by people for their own use and later came to be goods traded in the market, such as the Uzbek *kashta* embroidery described by Imahori in Essay I-2. Javanese batik, however, does not originate from the local production techniques or organizations of the workers themselves. Javanese batik was being produced as goods for the Javanese court at least by the 18th century, but it was not worn by those who produced it (Brenner 1998: 34). Since then, despite competition from batik made using a stamp technique and print batik, hand-drawn batik is still traded in the market, favored by collectors and devotees, not only in Indonesia, but all over the world. Many people who had accumulated wealth in batik production founded the Islamic Union (formerly Islamic Commercial Union) in 1912 which supported the independence movement of Indonesia. Javanese hand-drawn batik (*batik tulis*, hereinafter referred to as "batik") is far from the products of simple manual labor by common people for self-sufficiency and has been elevated to a symbol of national pride.

The batik from Central Java in this case study is made with abstract traditional motifs in white, blue and brown dyes. According to motif classifications in specialized textile books, numerous motifs on the batik produced at Bunga Istana correspond to Yogyakarta court- and merchant-style (*Saudagar*) motifs. Yet, the workshop owner and workers simply state that they are local Yogyakarta motifs. They do not use this kind of classification. The workshop owner gives work instructions by the name of the motif or a rough pencil-drawn sketch to the workers, who draw patterns using hot wax. Some of the motif names are derived from the Indian epics Mahabharata and Ramayana, which are popular in Java as shadow puppetry stories. Because of its production history and its former status as prestige goods, many researchers have said that the meaning and value of motifs are rooted in court culture and philosophy. These symbolic meanings are elucidated in many books. Working in batik production is sometimes described as an ascetic practice based on Javanese mysticism (Darmosugito 1990: 100–101). However, workers reject these interpretations, insisting that they draw these motifs for no reason other than wages.

Of course, engaging in this work does not necessarily mean subordination to court culture or political affiliation. Work is exchanged with wages in the end. Nevertheless, when we focus on the process of work itself, it becomes clear that the seemingly simple act of "drawing" has depths that go beyond voluntarism and the mechanical manipulation of materials.

⦿ Things in the workspace of batik motif drawing ⦿

The workers normally call the batik production site "factory" (*pabrik*), the term used for a modern production factory. They do not use the term *workshop*. Many workshops have a workspace for motif-drawing (hereinafter referred to as "workspace") in addition to the dyeing space. The Bunga Istana workshop that I researched is situated in the urban area of Yogyakarta, a regional capital city, and a very different environment from the rural hamlets in which the workers live. However, the work procedures in the workspace at this "factory" and those done in the worker's or her neighbor's home have very similar compositions of physical objects.

The materials and tools needed to draw batik motifs include wax and a wok, heating oil, a tool called *canting*, and a stand called *gawangan* at the workers' homes – all of which are purchased by the workers – and the batik cloth, which is provided by the workshop owner. Those who use the *canting* (see Photo I-1.1)

Photo I-1.1 Wax resist filling using the canting (nembok). A worker uses a tool called canting to apply the resist wax to the parts of the outlined motif that are not to be dyed. She needs to continually ensure that the temperature of the wax running out of the canting is appropriate and that the wax permeates the cloth without blurring. In this design, each square is divided into five parts. An area is customarily divided into five or seven parts in this way.

in their work buy and use several different types of this tool. Materials and tools other than wax and *cantings* are common household items.

The workers who draw motifs on batik by hand are usually women who live in or are from rural hamlets. Some not only work in the workshop but also take cloth home to work on. As they do not need workshop equipment such as stamp tables, dye baths and large gas burners, they can work anywhere as long as they have the aforementioned tools and materials.

The portability of the relatively light-weight cloth is an important factor that makes drawing at home possible. In batik production in Japan, Indonesia and other Asian countries, the cloth is often fixed to the table because hardened wax on the cloth tends to crack or fall off when moved. The wax used in Javanese batik production contains additives such as vegetable oil which gives it elasticity so it does not suffer this problem when the worker folds it to take it home.

Besides the basic tools and materials, miscellaneous and trivial items found in the everyday environment are utilized as auxiliary tools in motif drawing work both at the workshop and home. For example, the *canting* is a pen-like instrument with a small cup (Photo I-1.1) into which hot wax melted in a wok is scooped. Motifs are drawn with wax flowing out of a small tube at the tip of this cup. This tube is cleaned with worn-out bristles pulled from an old broom and the tip of the tube is sanded with a stone or a piece of concrete so that it glides more smoothly on the cloth. The *canting* attachment to the handle is reinforced with some threads pulled out of a rag. Cooked rice grains are used as glue when a small piece of cloth is wrapped around the *canting* tube so that thicker lines can be drawn. A brush to paint out a large space is made of a bundle of cotton fibers from a frayed garment and a piece of scrap wood from broken furniture. These things are not universally needed or owned by all the workers. They appear as a result of individual responses to the requirements of the cloth, wax, *canting* and motif. The same function can be performed by different things that are available in the particular environment such as a rag instead of a woolen garment or a wooden chopstick instead of a piece of broken furniture. Interactions with these things in the process of motif drawing are the same whether they take place at a defined production site such as a workspace in a workshop or someone's home in a rural hamlet.

⦿ The appearance of motifs on a cloth ⦿

The environment surrounding work at these two work sites influences not only things but also the manner of realizing motifs on a cloth. Although the workshop owner has books of color photos with the names of traditional motifs, the workers rarely look at a photo or the real sample when they draw traditional motifs. Instead of following a sample, they rely on the name of the motif told by the owner or their own memory evoked by a sketch or outlines (Table I-1.1 Stage 2). However, there are times when the workers falter after they have started drawing with wax because they are unsure of its details.

At other traditional batik workshops operating over three generations, the motif drawing work is divided into stages performed by different workers (Table I-1.1). The worker who has experience of drawing a certain motif at a particular stage is not necessarily able to draw another stage of the same motif. One day at Bunga Istana, Suminah was alone with me in the workspace and began to draw a traditional motif saying "I can draw the outline, too". She eventually became confused and returned the cloth to the manager to go back to her background filling work.

Because of its guiding function for subsequent stages, the outline stage (*klowong*) is usually performed by the most experienced workers. Nevertheless, even they become unsure when they face a motif or a combination of motifs for the first time about matters such as the space between lines, whether lines should be connected or not, whether a decorative motif will be inserted later, whether wax should

Table I-1.1 The process of making batik in white, blue and brown

1	Sketch (*sket*)	Drawing ruled lines or a sketch on a cloth with a pencil.
2	*Klowong*	Drawing the outlines and dots with wax.
3	*Nembok*	Filling or covering the resist areas with wax.
4	Dyeing (blue)	Dipping in blue dye.
5	Wax removal	Wax is removed in boiling water, leaving white patterns in the blue ground
6	*Mbironi*	Covering the parts that are not to be dyed brown with wax.
7	Dyeing (brown)	Dipping in brown dye.
8	Wax removal	Wax is removed in boiling water.
9	Finish	

cover the dyed ground, and so on. Because some rules are presumed to apply to traditional motifs, they work through these problems in consultation with one another, sometimes asking a co-workers to draw some part of it, or discussing ways to produce something that is consistent with the sketch. In other words, motifs are formed by the experience and general feel of the people at the scene. There are no clear verbal instructions that can be formalized into a manual; supplementary explanations and views are provided verbally based on the unfinished motif currently on the cloth.

The same problem is encountered when dots are added to the outline as well as during other tasks at the *nembok* and *mbironi* stages. The traditional motif will finally appear on the cloth only after the workers utilize things at hand and consult the experience of the co-workers on the scene to deal with the partially visible motif. The use of things and the use of workers' experience together shape the act of drawing a motif and cannot always be treated as separate elements.

This essay has illustrated that in the process of drawing traditional batik motifs, miscellaneous things of similar functions are utilized to aid the work process of the workers who confront the tools and materials whether they are in the workspace at the workshop or working at home. Although the process of producing a traditional motif on the cloth tends to be assumed as reproduction of a predetermined sample, the traditional motif appears as a form actually through mobilization of the environment, including things, and the experience of people rather than by an act of realizing planned designs.

The process in which a traditional motif manifests based on a given motif name and a sketch without using the kind of standardized and institutionalized sample in other places has much in common with the "appearance of a form" pointed out by Niwa in Chapter 1. It may offer a glimpse into the limitations of the concept of "the human as master designer" who performs an act of "making" as the subject, and redirect us to a new analytical perspective.

I-2 Kashta Drives People: The "Mono" Power of Uzbek Embroidery

Emi Imahori

Tampering with natural objects and adorning them with seemingly useless decorations is common across humanity. Embroidery, the art of decorating woven fabrics with colored threads, is the most popular decoration technique in many societies. It has been produced in a wide variety of distinctive ornamentations. One possible reason for its widespread popularity is simplicity with which one can produce an infinite number of decorative design patterns by combining three essential "*mono*" (things) (needle, colored thread and textile/leather) with human hands and techniques. Although it is made with three simple "things", the agency exerted by the embroidered "things" on humans is far from trivial (see Introduction). This essay will consider how embroidered "things" become subjects with the power to mobilize humans through embroidery production in Uzbekistan.

Uzbekistan, situated almost at the center of the Eurasian Continent, has a style of embroidery called "*kashta*". The resultant embroidery characteristically covers the entire surface of a garment or large cloth. In Central Asia from the late 19th to the early 20th century, *kashta* developed as an art of decorating dowry items – large wall hangings (*suzani*), prayer rugs, sheets, blindfolds etc. Young girls learned from their mothers or other female relatives and prepared these items for themselves before they married (Cheperebestkaya 1961; Jumaev 2003). In those days, it was said that "A bride with a dowry is a valuable bride" and "Evaluate a new bride by checking her dowry". The dowry provided by the bride was supposed to be presented in grand style to the female relatives of the groom. Among the dowry items, those which had been decorated with *kashta* in particular were considered to represent the bride's character and capability. The quality of *kashta* influenced the status of the bride in her matrimonial family (Bo'riev & Xojamurodov 2006). In this case, the *mono* called *kashta* acted as an agent speaking for the bride's character and personality and formed her relationships within the matrimonial household.

By the time I began my research in the Central Uzbek village of Bukhara in 2002, however, a dowry including *kashta* handmade by the bride was no longer

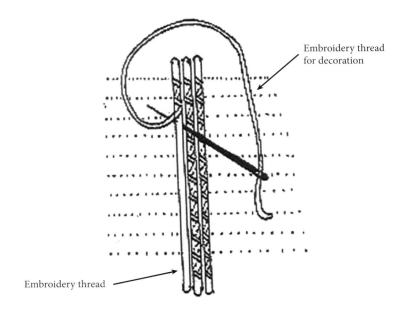

Figure I-2.1 Qars do'z *(Stitch A)*

the dominant norm. Nevertheless, rural women continued to produce *kashta*, but commercially, to cater for demand from a rapidly increasing number of foreign tourists under government tourism policy after the country gained independence from the Soviet Union in 1991 (Imahori 2006). *Kashta* production became a means to earn a living, which was different from when rural women produced *kashta* as a medium for self-representation. This does not mean that *kashta* has lost its agency to influence people. In fact, it became a significant factor that influenced business policy and its success or failure at the new sites of commercial production. Let us look at the difference between two *kashta* stitch techniques used by two embroidery producers to compare the way *kashta* as the agent creates difference in their business policies and production methods.

Embroidery producer and entrepreneur Zulayho (pseudonym; female, born in 1953) is a pioneer who began producing *kashta* commercially in S District of the Bukhara Region in 1992. The embroidery stitch predominantly used in her *kashta* production is a type of satin stitch (making stitches spanning from one end to the other of a motif) called *qars do'z* (hereinafter referred to as "Stitch A") (see Figure I-2.1, Photo I-2.1, Table I-2.1). Stitch A involves stitching the embroidery

Table I-2.1 Comparison of kashta *producers*

Kashta producer (pseudonym)	Zulayho	Nargiza
Main stitch used (abbrev.)	*Qars do'z* (Stitch A)	*Qarso do'z* (Stitch B)
Decorative feature	Straight line	Curved line
Number of pieceworkers (permanent – seasonal maximum)	116–200 or more	12
Business policy	Mass production	Small team of highly skilled workers
Customers	Zulayho's own outlets, art shops at prestigious hotels, craft association outlets, Europe, USA, Turkey, Middle East, Japan etc.	Made to order except through the Golden Heritage Crafts Association.

Note. Numbers as at 2006.

thread along the shape of each motif and then stitching across the first stitches for a decorative effect. This technique emphasizes beautiful straight lines when decorative stitches are made along the weave pattern of the fabric.

Another embroidery producer, Nargiza (pseudonym; female, born in 1963), came up with a new technique by modifying Stitch A. While the basics are the same as those of Stitch A, this technique called *qarso do'z* (hereinafter referred to as "Stitch B") involves spanning the decorative stitches across the first stitches so as to create curved lines rather than straight lines (Table I-2.1, Photo I-2.2). Let us compare Photos I-2.1 and I-2.2. In the first photo showing Stitch A, we can see straight lines inside each motif whereas we see curved lines forming circular shapes in line with the round flower motif in the second photo. Stitch B devised by Nargiza can be considered an ideal stitch that can adjust the curved lines to match any motif shapes so that, together with the luster of the silk thread, it can clearly emphasize the design.

The difference between Stitch A and Stitch B is merely a difference in the way decorative stitches are made over embroidery threads. However, there is a considerable difference in the degree of difficulty experienced in learning these two techniques. According to women who are subcontracted to embroider (embroidery pieceworkers) using Stitch A, "Anyone with moderate dexterity wouldn't take long to learn; anyone can produce a beautiful work as long as she counts grain lines patiently". The guideline for Stitch A certainly says that making decorative stitches along the weave pattern of a plain-woven fabric will produce

Photo I-2.1 Qars do'z *(Stitch A)*

Photo I-2.2 Qarso do'z *(Stitch B)*

beautiful straight lines. Even unskilled embroiderers can produce beautiful *kashta* if they follow this guideline faithfully. Consequently, difference in the skill levels of individual pieceworkers is minimized and it is possible to produce *kashta* products of relatively homogeneous quality in large quantities.

In contrast, Nargiza's Stitch B provides no guidelines for the sizes of the decorative stitches and the angles of the curved lines. Learners must learn them through their own experience of making stitches repeatedly. The quality of work with Stitch B depends on so-called "tacit knowledge" acquired by producers and clearly reflects differences between the skilled and the unskilled. It takes time and effort to learn this technique, and thus mass production is difficult.

The *kashta* produced with Stitch A and Stitch B respectively exerts unignorable power as the agent who influences the producer's business policies and management.

At the time of my follow-up research (2006), Zulayho was selling her predominantly Stitch A *kashta* products to a wide range of customers, including art shops in the country's prestigious hotels, the craft makers' association outlets, souvenir shops, and foreign buyers visiting her home from Europe, the USA., Turkey, Arab countries, Japan etc. This broad-based business operation is supported by the division of labor of pieceworkers in charge of embroidering (*tikish*). To produce a highly priced product such as a large wall hanging or bedspread, for example, multiple narrow fabrics that form part of one large item are allocated to multiple pieceworkers, who embroider them separately and sew them together to complete the item. While this system enables production of large quantities of products in short periods, the pieceworkers who are collaborating on the job are required to make stitches in a uniform manner. This requirement is satisfied by Stitch A. Stitch A is a vehicle for minimizing skill differentials between embroidery pieceworkers, thus enabling mass production of products of almost homogeneous quality in a short time. As a result, Zulayho was able to develop a large scale operation employing over 200 pieceworkers.

Nargiza's business, however, sells *kashta* made with Stitch B exclusively and runs a small operation dealing with regular customers only. It employs only ten or so pieceworkers, who may collaborate on one large *kashta*, but they are unable to produce in large quantities. The reason for this is the difficulty of teaching Stitch B to pieceworkers. Nargiza has opened one room in her home for training where she personally teaches the stitch to a new recruit for one month or even longer depending on her skill level. One of her pieceworkers told me, "I was told to undo the stitches and do them again many times until I could make beautiful curves. Not everyone can do that stitch. Many women have given up halfway". Certainly, Stitch B is avoided by would-be pieceworkers who generally hope to start earning money immediately because it is difficult to learn and has produced a succession of dropouts. For this very reason, however, *kashta* with beautiful Stitch B embroidery is made to order in limited quantities. Because of the limited production, Nargiza's *kashta*, which cannot be easily imitated, sells for a premium price and secures repeat customers.

The relationship between *kashta* and humans is not limited to the direction in which human subjects produce *kashta*. Rather, *kashta* itself seems to possess the power to pull producers and pieceworkers into its production and to push them away from it. If we consider the *mono* called *kashta* as the subject, *kashta* always pursues beauty because it is an ornament. In this example, we have looked at the way *kashta* drives two individual producers to formulate completely different business operations, management policies and employment relations with pieceworkers in order to realize the "beauty" of the two similar but different stitch techniques. However, its influence is not just applicable to the producers alone. We will see an increasing number of occasions on which *kashta* appears in front of us as the agent to bring more buyers and tourists from all over the world in the future.

I-3 "Play" Between Mono and Humans: Interdependence with bananas?

Kaori Komatsu

◉ *"Mono"* called crops ◉

Plants and animals which exist in the natural environment independently of humans become crops and livestock through processes called domestication. They come to find it easier to survive when favored by humans, who help them to acclimate to the environment disturbed by humans, and who manage their reproduction. The term domestication derives from the Latin word *domus*, literally meaning home or family, but also "bringing into the home/family" (Harlan 1992). Rather than an event that happened once-and-for-all, or only a few times in history, domestication involves numerous ongoing processes that take place in various forms all over the world (Yamamoto 2009).

While the term domestication emphasizes human actions and intentions, domesticated plants and animals have never been completely under human control. Nor have they changed characteristics only in the ways humans intended. They sometimes manifest unexpected changes due to the effect of human control, the natural environment, hybridization or mutation. Indeed, the term implies both human action (cultivation or breeding) and the plants' and animals' reactions (genetic change). Domestication is a reciprocal relationship between two groups of life forms – humans and plants/animals. This relationship, whether viewed from the perspective of all humanity and a particular animal or plant species, or only the humans in a particular locale and a particular animal or plant species, is subject to continuous change. It is never fixed. In this complex process, plants and animals can fall anywhere along a broad spectrum from natural beings that keep their distance from humans to artificial products, made and controlled by humans. Considering that these crops and livestock are destined to be ingested by humans, there is also a very real sense in which they become part of "humans" as well, but we shall leave that aside for the moment.

Thus, the reciprocal changes in each other's behavior and character makes "crops" and "livestock" a unique field for discussing the relationship between humans and *mono*.

⦿ Diversity of human-plant relationship ⦿

When we look at the relationship between humans and plants from a domestication point of view, we see many intermediate stages between the use of wild plants and the cultivation of crops. Various examples of these intermediate stages are mentioned in Harlan's *Crops and Man*, a comprehensive account of the relationship between crops and humans (Harlan 1992).

For instance, African oil palm (*Elaeis guineensis* Jacq.) originally grew wild in West African forests. It later spread to large areas of woodland in West and Central Africa, accompanying slash-and-burn agriculturalists. The plant favored burned fields with more sun light over its original habitat of deep forests. Humans utilize the plant in various ways, including extracting oil from its fruit, making an alcoholic beverage from the sap and building houses with the bark. While humans and African oil palms exploit one another in these ways, the plant remains genetically unchanged from the wild species (although some high-yielding cultivars, whose yield increases proportionally to increases in fertilizer use, have recently been developed through genetic engineering and used for plantation).

Human intentions are absent in some cases. Ethiopian oats (*Avena barbata* Pott ex Link) arrived in Ethiopia as a wild companion plant for barley (*Hordeum vulgare* L.) and emmer wheat (*Triticum dicoccum* Schrank). Although it was not sowed purposely on its own, its growth among sowed barley and emmer wheat was tolerated. Ethiopian oats gradually changed genetically, acquiring a non-shattering habit. As wild plants must drop their seed to reproduce, this non-shedding habit means that the plant is reliant on deliberate sowing by humans. Ethiopian oats is an example of a plant becoming domesticated without being selected by humans.

Foxtail (*Sateria* sp.) in Mexico reverted to its wild state when it was abandoned as a crop. Although this plant is excavated frequently from ancient ruins, it has gone out of cropping and back to wild since the domestication of corn.

Harlan demonstrates the ambiguity of boundaries between wild plants, crops and weeds by reporting on the cases of a plant that shuttles between wild and cultivation and one that is treated as both a crop and a weed in the field.

Photo I-3.1 Intensive banana cultivation in western Tanzania, the Great Lakes region of East Africa (source: S. Maruo)

◉ Bananas grow without humans ◉

Banana is a crop that is controlled to varying degrees depending on where it is growing. Bananas belong to the genus *Musa* of the Musaceae Family and produce edible fruit. They were cultivated in a region from Southeast Asia to New Guinea before spreading to other tropical regions in the world, including Africa, Pacific Islands and South America. Now they are grown by small farmers both commercially and for their own consumption in most tropical and subtropical humid areas. As well as bananas that are eaten raw, many bananas are eaten cooked in tropical areas. Bananas for cooking are sometimes called plantain in the West (Komatsu et al. 2006).

Except for the large corporate-run plantations, the world's most intensive banana farming is practiced by people on the highlands of the Great Lakes Region in East Africa. They plant bananas throughout the home garden, thin out suckers to guide them to the next growing position, protect the soil by covering it with banana leaves, control the timing of fruit setting by cutting male buds (which are called flowers) at the appropriate time, and achieve successfully high yields (Photo E1-3.1) (Maruo 2002; Satō 2004). In contrast, people living in the Central African rainforests provide little husbandry after they transplant suckers from their old fields to newly burnt fields. They will weed a couple of times before harvesting the fruit a little over a year later. Yet, they can keep harvesting bananas

Photo I-3.2 Extensive banana cultivation in southeastern Cameroon, Central Africa

of reasonable size for several years from the suckers left behind after harvesting (Photo EI-3.2) (Shikata 2004). In the first case, bananas are carefully cultivated through intensive human management whereas the level of human intervention is very low in the second case, as the growing environment, the burnt field, is left to natural vegetation succession. We sometimes find bananas that continue to regenerate autonomously in secondary forests several decades after the burnt fields have been abandoned.

The Baka Pygmy people, who subsisted on hunting and gathering for a long time in southern Cameroon, have come to farming open fields by slash-and-burn over the last few decades. Their main crops are bananas for cooking. They have long known how to create fields, as they have always helped slash-and-burn farmers in their neighborhood. But the Baka never had their own fields. This is perhaps because they were so used to receiving an immediate reward for their labor (an immediate-return system) that they were slow to adopt the idea of accumulating daily labor under a delayed-return system. Bananas are not selective about the timing of planting. People can expect reasonable harvests

Photo I-3.3 Standardized banana planting at a plantation in Ghana

planting suckers whenever they feel like it and leaving them unattended. One need not pass up the opportunity to gather tree nuts growing wild in the forest in the peak season in order to work in the banana field. As bananas are not stored like grains, they do not need to plan their consumption. Bananas that grow independently of humans have enabled the Baka people to have their own fields (Kitanishi 2002).

It is likely that the wide range of banana cultivation methods stems from the low level of human intervention in crop breeding for domestication. While wild bananas are packed with seeds, cultivated bananas have very few of them. Humans have had almost no part in this process of seed loss. It is thought that humans accidentally found wild plants of diploid bananas that had lost seeds by spontaneous mutation and propagated them by suckers. It is highly likely that the only interest humans took in growing seedy bananas was in using the leaves as wrappers and dishes, rather than in eating the fruit.

The characteristics of domesticated bananas are almost the same as those of wild bananas. Although they cannot be propagated by seed, each plant will continue to generate new suckers for several decades without the need for intervention. The banana plant is not totally reliant on humans, as it is able to regenerate on its own without human assistance as long as it has suitable environmental conditions.

PhotoI-3.4 Different cultivars of bananas found in one day at a market in Tinambung, West Sulawesi, Indonesia

⦿ "Play" in the relationship ⦿

The bananas grown in plantations for our everyday consumption belong to a cultivar group called Cavendish. Another cultivar named Gros Michel was the main variety grown all over the world until the mid-20th century. When Gros Michel bananas were wiped out by Panama disease in the 1960s, the more resistant and fertilizer-responsive Cavendish bananas were introduced into plantations around the world. A great majority of bananas currently produced by multinationals and marketed under various brand names throughout the world are Cavendish (Photo EI-3.3). There are similarities between production on banana plantations and the pearl production described by Tokoro in Chapter 3. Like banana plantations, pearl oysters farms are thoroughly managed and produce completely standardized pearls. However, pearl oyster management requires higher skill levels in order to meet specifications while making fine technical adjustments in response to changing ecological conditions, whereas operational procedures on banana plantations are highly formalized (see Chapter 3 by Tokoro).

In contrast to the standardization of the corporate plantations, diversity is preferred by local banana growing cultures around the world. In many areas where bananas are marketed locally and the producers are also consumers, more than ten cultivars of bananas are cultivated in a single area (Photo EI-3.4) (Komatsu et al. 2006). In the Great Lakes Region of East Africa, a single village may grow over seventy different cultivars. The cultivations of multiple varieties in one location can be explained at least in part by functional reasons such as catering for different purposes, being able to harvest all year round, and being able to avoid a complete wipeout when attacked by pest or disease. However, these suggestions cannot fully explain why one village would grow seventy varieties of bananas. Some of them are purposely grown despite their low productivity and unpalatability. Most domesticated bananas are seedless. The chance to find a new cultivar hinges on the human ability to identify and name spontaneous mutation of very low probability. In inland Africa, subtle variations from limited rootstock varieties have been discerned, preserved and cultivated to form unique cultivars over the last 2,000 years or so.

While domestication means the enclosure of plants and animals by humans, there is considerable variation in the intensity of management and the degree of standardization. The range of characteristics and behaviors humans expect from domesticated plants and animals, the level of management provided by humans, and the level of management that plants and animals require of humans are all variables dependent upon the species and the locality. The relationship between bananas and humans varies greatly depending on locality and situation. Compared with other crops, their relationship has much more room for "play" that produces variation. In this sense, bananas appear to be at the opposite end of the scale from "stones" addressed by Uchibori in the Epilogue.

Essay II
Mysterious "*Mono*"

II-1 Fetishism on Pagodas and Buddha Images

Keiko Tosa

⦿ Pagodas and Buddha images as *mono* ⦿

In Buddhism, pagodas are essentially "towers" in which the hair and bones of the Buddha and / or saints are enshrined. "Images" of the Buddha and saints are *mono* (*things*), representations of their figures. Pagodas and Buddha images are regarded as holy objects of faith in a localized context, but sometimes questions arise about their condition as *mono* or their *materiality*. I would like to consider the materiality of pagodas and Buddhist images, which has rarely been examined in earlier studies, from the perspective of fetishistic interest.

According to Pietz, *fetico*, the root of the word "fetishism", was initially used only for things, people and practices associated with magic. It later came to refer to African religious practices in the discourse of European intellectuals in the 17th to mid-18th centuries. Their religious practices, including iconolatry, were associated with materiality and primitiveness by the dualistic theory of Protestant Christianity as a spiritual religion (Pietz 1987; Murakami 2009). However, iconolatry has rarely been addressed in the studies of Theravada Buddhist society. The only study on fetishism in Theravada Buddhist society is by Tambiah, who expatiates on Mauss' theory of gifts and Marx' commodity fetishism with a focus on the amulet cult in Thailand (Tambiah 1984). Tambiah interpreted amulets as the objectified manna of charismatic saints, discussing the processes of differentiation and commercialization, of provenance and potency. In my research fieldwork in Myanmar, however, Buddhists attach importance to amulets but they are rather indifferent about exchange and commercialization. Instead, their fetishistic interests are directed at Buddha images and pagodas.

In Myanmar, "sightseeing" is almost synonymous with a visit to a pagoda (*hpaya hpu*). The itinerary of any domestic travel by tour bus (*hpaya hpu ka*) always includes visits to famous local pagodas. And pagoda construction brings a Buddhist the highest merit; "pagoda donor" is the greatest honor used as an official title. Pagoda construction is seen as a difficult project. Five rituals presided by religious experts are considered to be imperative to its success – pile-driving (*panet yaik mingala pwe*), cornerstone-laying (*okmyit kya pwe*), treasure-placement (*htapana peik pwe*), umbrella-placement (*hti tin pwe*) and consecration (*anaygaza tin pwe*) (Tosa 2000, 2014). The last two rituals are particularly important, as a pagoda becomes an object of worship only through their performance. Conversely, religious forces are indispensable even during the construction process when the *mono* is turned into a religious object through rituals.

Images of the Buddha and saints are treated as beings who abide by the same precepts as the Buddha and saints. Food offerings are withdrawn by noon according to a precept forbidding afternoon meals and people are careful to avoid contact between the Buddha images and women's clothing according to a precept forbidding monastics from touching women. For instance, famous Buddha images from overseas are much-prized souvenirs but it is basically inappropriate to transport them in a suitcase packed with miscellaneous items and clothes. If, after being treated temporarily as *mono* they are placed on the altar and offered the chants for consecration and protection (*paritta*), they become religious objects again. Even if they have been placed in a suitcase with miscellaneous items, the question of defilement does not arise. In other words, pagodas and Buddha images retain their materiality but their holiness can be detached or attached by rituals.

⦿ From a heritage protection perspective ⦿

A different kind of value is added to pagodas and Buddha images in another context. It is the value of history and heritage. Pagan (Bagan), which prospered as the capital of a Burmese kingdom from the 10th century to the 14th century, is one of the world's three greatest Buddhist heritage sites with the remains of over 2,500 ancient pagodas and temples. After a major earthquake of 1975 damaged many of them, UNESCO and the government undertook joint restoration work. The oppression of the democracy movement and the military coup and takeover in 1988 attracted strong criticisms from the West and slowed foreign aid for cultural projects. However, the government led by Secretary-1 Khin Nyunt showed interest in the preservation of cultural heritage and the restoration of pagodas and established committees such as the Committee for All-Round Perpetual Renovation of Shwedagon Pagoda to undertake restoration works at various locations. UNESCO Japanese Funds-in-Trust for the Preservation of the World Cultural Heritage Projects agreed to provide $283,400 in 1994 and the Department of Archaeology, Ministry of Culture conducted a survey in Pagan to make a list of buildings in need of repair. At the same time, Khin Nyunt sought cooperation from businesses and individuals and set up a fund-raising system by which donors were able to choose their preferred pagodas for donation.

Pagan was included in the 1996 interim list of World Heritage nominations but it was left out of the final selection in the following year. It is believed that UNESCO found some problems with the way restorations were carried out. Hudson mentions three organizations as the main players in restoration efforts: UNESCO, Department of Archaeology, and the local trusties (Hudson 2008). While the local trusties are identified as a local NGO on the World Heritage listing application form, it includes groups that responded to the aforementioned government appeals. Hudson, based on the Bagan Working Database, divided the repaired buildings into two groups; major construction and complete rebuild. Although most repaired buildings might maintain structural authenticity, some additions or modifications such as interior whitewashing or the addition of the *hti* (metal umbrella), a standard feature of modern pagodas which is not seen in the wall art of surviving interior stucco pagoda shapes from the Bagan period, are observed (Hudson 2008:563). Examples of rebuilding include laying new colored bricks to replace historic weathered bricks in some collapsed walls and placing a new white plastered Buddha statue on what appears to be a Buddha statue pedestal in a monastery. These examples in Hudson's photos give an impression of incoherence.

Here we find a tug of war between two extreme types of obsession with *mono*. On one end is the "universal" concept of world heritage preservation and management. From the adoption of the Convention concerning the Protection of the World Cultural and Natural Heritage at the UNESCO general conference in 1972 through the 1980s, a majority of registered properties were in Europe. The concept of "authenticity" at that time had "materials" at its core, based on European properties built with hard materials such as stone. This concept subsequently became shaky, though, as more non-European properties were listed. For example, it was pointed out at the 1994 UNESCO World Heritage Expert Meeting in Nara that the Japanese practice of *sengū* (the moving of shrines to new sites) deviated from the standard notion of heritage. Thus the word heritage underwent a gradual change from the "standardized heritage concept" to the "diverse heritage concept" (Nishimura 2006).

However, the diverse heritage concept was not a shared understanding in Myanmar's reconstruction. Manhart, the head of UNESCO's world heritage programs, told a reporter, "They use the wrong materials to build wrongly shaped structures on top of magnificent ancient stupas" (Crampton 2005). This critique to "rebuilding" in Myanmar invokes the Western material-centered authenticity concept.

On the other end of the rope is the local concept of pagoda restoration. A collapsed ruin is just a pile of bricks and dirt, that is, merely a *mono*. It becomes an object of worship only when it is restored to a pagoda form and an umbrella is placed on top of it. Restoration for the purpose of merit-making means the transformation of a *mono* into an object of faith. Original building materials and methods of the pagoda are not so important for many Buddhists. In other words, the Western concept of heritage preservation that stresses consistency with the heritage building is not of importance here. Interestingly, archaeological evidence shows that the original bricks were plastered with decorative patterns (Hudson 2008: 567). Hudson, an archaeologist, argues from a cultural relativist perspective that local repair is not necessarily the wrong way of restoration in a historical context on the basis of the archaeological evidence.

⦿ Kitsch modernology and novelty temples ⦿

In contrast, there is a form of iconography that, unlike cultural relativism, is completely indifferent to the cultural values of others. Modernology is a movement that began in the 1980s, whose origins can be traced to Wajirō Kon in Japan. It involves searching and gathering kitsch places, advertisements and so on. *Kenbutsuki* (The Buddha watching journal) by Jun Miura and a magazine named *Wonder Japan* specialized in Buddha images and Buddhist temples. Today, of course, information is gathered by individuals and disseminated on the Internet. Popular websites are sometimes turned into books. Examples include *Chindera daidōjō* (A collection of novelty temples) (http://www41.tok2.com/home/kanihei5/chindera-kaigaihen.html) and *Nippon chin supotto hyakkei* (One hundred bizarre spots in Japan) (http://b-spot.seesaa.net/) (Kojima 2004 and Igarashi 2008 respectively). The overseas edition of the former provides information about Myanmar, Thailand, Malaysia, Hong Kong and others.

Kojima calls Myanmar a "superpower in the world of novelty temples" and provides full descriptions of its unique temples and designs. The information is quoted in the blogs of other individuals. For example, "Ryokōki" (http://www.

rz-zel.com/trip/myan/hajieni.htm) states that "I decided to travel to Myanmar after reading *Chindera daidōjō*". It is also quoted in the blog of a Japanese tour operator in Myanmar who has incorporated visits to novelty temples in sightseeing itineraries for Japanese tourists. A similar tendency is found in the blog of the operator of Lotus*sari News & Message who states that "Pagodas are the Myanmar version of Disneyland" under the title "Talking nonsense in Burma" (http://blog.lotus-sari.com/?eid=441818).

What they have in common is an approach that suspends the religious significance, cultural value and historical interpretation of Buddha images and Buddhist buildings, so as to concentrate on filming, gathering and introducing forms and designs that they consider unusual and interesting at a superficial level. This, of course, reflects the tendency among contemporary Japanese people to perceive Buddha images and temples as *mono* – as historic relics and works of art and craft – rather than as objects of worship.

We have had a quick look at three modes of fetishistic interest in pagodas and Buddha images as *mono* in this essay. To a majority of local Buddhists, the completion of the pagoda and Buddha forms as objects of worship is important. Merit-making deeds leading up to sanctification are highly valued. For the West-initiated projects for restoration and heritage site preservation, the historicity of *mono*, including materials and production methods, is important and its conservation is paramount. While Japanese kitsch novelty temple collectors are similar to local Buddhists in the sense that they are fixated on their forms, they are interested in their unusual shapes and designs exclusively outside of the local cultural contexts such as their holiness. A closer examination of the actual construction or production of pagodas and Buddha images would further reveal ways that the relationship between people and *mono* is not unilateral. For example, the agency of *mono* becomes apparent even before the actual *mono* come into being in some cases. A Buddha image may be discovered through a dream or vision, or the final form of a pagoda is indicated in advance and restoration and production are carried out in order to realize it. In any case, this exercise to see pagodas and Buddha images as *mono* and to re-examine their relationship with people seems to offer abundant potential.

II-2 "Mono" Sucked Out of the Body: Shamanic Rituals of Ladakh

Kiyoshi Miyasaka

⦿ The *"Mono"* extracted in psychic surgery ⦿

The primary interest of anthropologists with regard to psychic surgery and similar practices has been with questions about veracity and fakery, how to address the ethics of healers if it is fakery, and its effectiveness. The *mono* (*things*) that are taken out of the body by hand or sucked out the body by mouth have attracted little interest, perhaps because they are regarded as obvious devices of deceit. In one well-known example reported by Lévi-Strauss, Quesalid in Kwakwaka'wakw, North America, sucked a "worm" from out of his patient's body, but the worm was in fact a tuft of down soaked in his own blood and hidden in his mouth in advance (Lévi-Strauss 1958). The issues surrounding the trick draw people's attention while the extracted thing is no longer mentioned.

How could the thing extracted from the body be a "worm" and a "pathogenic agent" at the same time? In this essay, I would like to discuss the perception of *mono* using the ones extracted from the body in the shamanic rituals of Ladakh.

⦿ Sucking treatment of Ladakh ⦿

Ladakh is situated in the eastern region of the northernmost Indian state of Jammu and Kashmir adjacent to Pakistan and China. It has a population of 236,639 living in an area of 59,146 square kilometers with a population density of only 4 people per square kilometer (Census of India 2001). It extends from the Karakoram Range to the Himalayas and has an alpine climate with low rainfall and harsh winter conditions. Most settlements scatter across the upper Indus River valley at 3,000–4,000 meters above sea level where the villagers grow barley and wheat. The population in the eastern part is predominantly Tibetan Buddhist as the area was ruled by the kingdom of Ladakh from the 9th to the 19th centuries, while the western part, closer to Kashmir, is predominantly Muslim. My research field is the city of Leh and its surrounds in the eastern part.

Shamanic beliefs similar to those found throughout the Tibetan cultural sphere are common in Ladakh. There are many professionals, called *lha-mo* (female) and *lha-pa* (male), who perform rituals, mainly to cure illnesses through possession by the *lha* (deity). A majority of *lha-mos* and *lha-pas* are lay Tibetan Buddhists, The *lha* seems to be an indigenous deity who has been added to the guardian deities of Tibetan Buddhist temples in many cases. The position of *lha-mo/lha-pa* is sanctioned and overseen by Rinpoches (high Lamas, or Buddhist monks). The association is apparent from their ritual implements. The *lha-mo/lha-pa* wears a coronet depicting Mahavairocana and the rest of Five Dhyani Buddhas and holds the *dorje* (*vajra*), *drilbu* (*ghanta*) and *damaru* (pellet drum) in the hands. These ritual objects are normally worn or used by Buddhist monks in certain rituals and clearly indicate that the *lha-mo/lha-pa* is conducting the rituals under the authority of Buddhism. In Leh and its surrounds, a number of *lha-mos* and *lha-pas* are operating from their homes and receive ten to fifty clients almost daily.

Their primary treatment method is *jip*, which literally means "sucking out". They suck either directly by mouth, through a metal pipe, or by placing one end of the *damaru* on the diseased site of the client's body. What is sucked out is a black slimy fluid or semisolid substance in many cases. Everyone frowns at the sight of this substance, which arouses an instinctive repulsion. A rolled up paper is sucked out on rare occasions while pins and metal objects are routinely sucked out of livestock. The most common part of the body for this treatment is *ninga* (chest), followed by the area around an eye. The sucked substance is placed in a container, covered with ash, and thrown out of the house after the ritual.

The sucked out "thing" is generally called *grib*. The word means "shadow", "dark" and "pollution". For example, a space such as a village or a house as well as the body are comprised of three tiers of which the upper tier is inhabited by the *lha*, the middle tier is inhabited by humans, and the lower tier is inhabited by the *klu* (spirits), G*ribs* are said to be found at lower tiers. However, the phrase "There is *grib*" is generally understood to refer to the state of being polluted, not the presence of an actual pollutant, a thing. The rituals performed by the *lha-mos/lha-pas* draw curious stares as they suck out the polluted thing. The *grib* as an idea is given materiality and presented in front of our eyes. It is natural that this is sometimes regarded as a dubious act. The vital question for their profession is how to make the act look authentic, how to maintain credibility. However, it appears that the *grib*'s presence is already sensed by the clients, even though it is ostensibly detected by the *lha-mos/lha-pas*. Almost all of the clients who visit the *lha-mos* and *lha-pas* receive the sucking treatment, and many simply present the diseased body part without saying anything.

The sucking operation is practiced similarly throughout the Tibetan cultural sphere but its origin is unclear. It may be a syncretism of modern surgery with beliefs in bloodletting in Tibetan medicine, indigenous spirits or sorcery, or influenced by exorcism practiced at temples and villages, but none of the theories have conclusive evidence.

⦿ Entrance of the spirit into the body ⦿

What is the state of the body of a *lha-mo* or *lha-pa* who performs the sucking operation? Their body is possessed by the *lha*. The *lha* is normally invisible but it becomes "visible" by possessing the body of the *lha-mo/lha-pa*. The *lha-mo/lha-pa* is sometimes called "*luyar*" (container), reflecting how the state of possession is perceived. It is generally believed that when a person's soul (*la*) weakens, other spirits (*gongmo*, *dre* etc.) invade the body, causing illnesses (*gongmo zhugshes*, *dre zhugshes* etc.). This is a representation of the relationship between the body and the soul or spirit by analogy to the relationship between a container and its contents.

This is clear from the procedures for spirit possession. First, the *lha-mo/lha-pa* sets up an altar, makes offerings, purifies the venue and prostrates (*wutitoudi*) while chanting a mantra. The shaman goes outside, washes her/his face and gargles with water poured by an attendant, and instantly starts shaking and shouting in a high-pitched voice to reach the state of spirit possession. As soon as the face and the mouth are purified, the *lha* enters the body through the mouth. The *lha* is said to waft in the atmosphere "like a wind", enter by the mouth and stay in the area around the back, shoulders or chest. One *lha-mo* describes the feeling as follows. "When I wash my hands while chanting, soon the *lha* approaches me. I gradually feel sleepy and heavy in my back. It feels as if something heavy is pressing down on my shoulders. It gets darker and I feel something is on my back and pushing me". Evil spirits (*dre*) are also believed to wander around in the atmosphere. The *lha-mos/lha-pas* cover their mouths with cloth during spirit possession so that they do not inhale the *grib*. This suggests that the *grib* and the *lha-mo/lha-pa* are interrelated like the content and the container.

◉ The container for the spirit ◉

Let us take a step further and see how the generation of the *grib* is explained. The *grib* is attributed to a variety of sources: food or drink improperly consumed and degenerated in the body, or a wounded spirit (*klu* or *sadakh*) that has entered the body via food, drink or inhalation, or the ill will of others (*gongmo*, *mikha* or *jadu*) that has entered also via food, drink or inhalation. It is believed that when a *grib* enters through the mouth via either inhalation or ingestion, they remain in the body and cause illnesses.

Klu is a spirit that is often mentioned in relation to the *grib*. It is sometimes referred to as the creator or the ancestor of the material world. Fish and lizards which live underground or underwater are likened to the *klu*. Sometimes spring water and field crops are referred to as *klu*. It is said that polluting a water source or wantonly cultivating a field hurts the *klu* residing in that place and the wounded *klu* enters the body via water or crops (food and drink) to become a *grib*, which brings illness to the person who has committed such an impropriety. Water and crops are containers for the *klu*, spirits that govern the earth, while the *grib* as a *mono* is a container for the wounded *klu* (Miyasaka 2006).

In that case, the *grib* as a *mono* can be regarded as a new container acquired by the content (wounded spirits) that has been in limbo in the body after losing its old container (food). Although a wounded spirit or another's ill will cannot be seen or touched, the *lha-mo/lha-pa* places it in a container and sucks it out. In this way, people get to see the wounded spirit or ill will in the form of a dark, slimy *grib*. This image is lucid, albeit precarious.

◉ A system of explanations made by "*mono*" ◉

A *mono* that has been assigned a certain identity is easily spoken of as an altogether different *mono* in some cases. Narratives surrounding possession are a clear example. When a *lha* enters a person's body, the person is suddenly called *lha*. In this case, the container is still the same but the content has changed. Nevertheless, when the person puts on a costume such as a coronet, i.e., overlaying another container on the container (the body), the container matches the content. The *grib* emerges almost out of the blue. It is a strange *mono*. While it is difficult to assign an identity to this dark, slimy *thing*, it appears to be a container matching its content. In other words, the *grib* as a *mono* conjures up negative images such as pain, illness, and memories of actions that may have damaged the spirit or aroused ill will in others. The *mono* constructs a system of explanations. And it is not difficult to imagine that witnessing the removal of a *mono* that invokes negative responses can lead to healing.

Essay III
Fluctuating "Mono"

III-1 Globalization of Aboriginal Paintings, Localization of "Art"

Sachiko Kubota

⦿ A *mono* perspective ⦿

The recognition given to the *mono* (*things*) made by the Aboriginal people of Australia, the subject of my research, has changed greatly in the post-19th century social context. They were initially defined by Western society as practical articles used in ceremonies and daily living rather than works of so-called "fine art". In other words, they were treated as craft products and ethnographic materials which had been fostered by the local climate, customs and religious beliefs, and not as "art for art's sake". By the end of the 20th century, however, they came to capture people's attention as "art". This change symbolizes the global expansion of *things* made by Aboriginal people and at the same time means that the recognition of their value as "art" has spread to the local scenes.

The focus of this essay is this dynamic state of *things* made by Aboriginal Australians. Craftwork moves beyond its local context and takes on new meanings. At the same time, the global art market influences local scenes. How do the two vectors interact and what is the substance of the change produced by the interaction? Focusing on the *things* of craft/art, I would position this essay as a sketch that provides a perspective from which concrete aspects of the change are elucidated and the interlocking of the local and global as well as the interpenetration of craft and art are considered anthropologically in order to contribute to the future discussion of the agency of *things*.

⦿ Changes in Australia and Aboriginal craft/art ⦿

Since the start of colonization by the British in 1788, the lives of Aboriginal people in Australia have changed dramatically. Aboriginal people, especially in the southern part of Australia, were deprived of their land and livelihood. Their culture and population were eroded significantly by diseases brought in by, and their struggles against, the settlers. Their basic human rights were largely ignored. The situation began to improve after the Second World War and there have been repeated efforts to recognize their human rights and give them equal rights. Against this backdrop, the *things* they made began to draw attention. The Aboriginal Arts Board was set up in 1971 and supported the establishment of Aboriginal Art Centres. The Centres bought the *things* made in remote communities and sold them in cities, employing and dispatching white advisors to do so. The aim was to set up a commercial distribution system for the *things* Aboriginal people made in order to establish an industry that would assist with their self-sufficiency (Kubota 2008).

In Aboriginal society, ceremonies representing their creation mythology have socially important meanings. The mythology is expressed in ceremonies in the form of paintings and designs. They symbolize close connections between Aboriginal people and their land. In Arnhem Land, designs are painted on the human body and the ground as well as wooden caskets, bark and carved objects. These paintings are used to pass cultural knowledge on to younger generations (Morphy 2007). Bark paintings using strips of flattened Eucalyptus tree bark and pigments were produced in this area at least by the beginning of the 20th century. While bark painting in Arnhem Land had been deeply embedded in their social context for centuries, it provided a feature product for commercialization.

The motifs in bark paintings, however, basically come from the knowledge only available to adult clansmen. Selling these paintings could mean disclosing clan secrets. Commercializing these paintings became a major issue. Some clans chose to paint mostly animal figures and exclude secret designs, while others decided to sell only specific mythological paintings. We can see that they actively manipulated their paintings from an early stage in order to facilitate their entry into the market. This was part of an attempt to communicate their unique connection with the land and mythological world view to the outside world (Morphy 2007).

In contrast to the bark paintings of Northern Australia, Australia's Central Desert Region did not have instantly marketable *things*. Ceremonial designs were painted or drawn on the ground or the body and vanished once an event was over. Some communities introduced wax resist textile featuring the patterns the women painted on their bodies. Other communities applied technology to make boomerangs, coolamons (wooden vessels) and carvings of small animal figures. Dot paintings with acrylic paint emerged in a community called Papunya. An art teacher spotted this style of painting practiced by local men and discovered its commercial potential. Their designs were painted on canvas with acrylic paint and brought to the market. The paintings were based on mythological stories drawn on the sand for ceremonial purposes. As they created a sensation, the dot painting style was gradually adopted by more Aboriginal communities in the Central and Western Desert Region. Although dot paintings were popular, they were initially regarded as inauthentic. It was thought that they were not "traditional" or "authentic" in a true sense because they were *things* made with newly introduced Western materials, not materials native to these communities.

These *things* made by Aboriginal people were, however, gradually incorporated into Australia's national identity from the 1980s. The year 1988 marked 200 years since the arrival of the First Fleet in Australia and 2001 was the centenary year of Australia's federation. When Australia was searching for a new identity in the lead up to these historic occasions, treatment of Aboriginal people became an important issue. There was much debate about the repositioning of Aboriginal people in the nation's history (Kubota 2008b). Various initiatives were actively pursued in order to include Aboriginal people, who had been excluded until then, as part of the nation's history. These efforts point to an increasing awareness that the Aboriginal people are an important element of Australia's national identity.

This change manifested symbolically in treatment of *things* made by Aboriginal people. They came to be actively adopted as Australia's national symbols. Aboriginal works and designs were frequently used to adorn the Parliament House and other public places (Kubota 2008a). The National Gallery of Australia, opened in Canberra in 1984, and other public and major art galleries began to actively collect Aboriginal works, which had rarely been purchased by art galleries before then. Aboriginal exhibits at museums also changed dramatically from the exclusively historic representation of their past existence to the presentation of contemporary Aboriginal issues (Kubota 2011).

⦿ Globalization of Aboriginal paintings ⦿

Despite the aforementioned shift, *things* made by Aboriginal people, including dot paintings, were still not valued highly during the 1980s. That situation changed in the 1990s. In particular, an exhibition titled *Dreamings: The Art of Aboriginal Australia*, held at the Asia Society Galleries, New York, in 1989, exerted a major impact. The exhibition subsequently toured other cities in the USA to international acclaim. A series of Aboriginal Art exhibitions were also staged in Europe during the 1990s. Aboriginal works received increased recognition mainly overseas. Galleries specializing in Aboriginal Art appeared in the USA and Europe. The changing appreciation of Aboriginal works abroad led to increased recognition within Australia (Myers 2002). Many exhibitions were held domestically. The recognition of *things* made by Aboriginal people as "fine art" became established.

The auction market for Aboriginal Art emerged by the mid-1990s, transforming the market structure. Sotheby's, an international auction house, founded its Aboriginal Art Department in 1996. Other auctioneers such as Deutscher Menzies and Christies also entered this field in quick succession. Bidding prices for Aboriginal works at auctions escalated, attracting a great deal of attention. Particularly in the 2000s, paintings by Rover Thomas and Emily Kame Kngwarreye were sold for record-breaking prices. Their works were painted in an abstract, avant-garde style; completely different from the dot paintings that dominated the auction market in the 1990s. Their reputations soared at home and abroad. Some of their paintings have sold for more than a million dollars (Kubota 2011).

Today Aboriginal Art has grown into a major industry worth 100 million Australian dollars (approx. 75 million USD). All state and territorial governments are making serious efforts to promote it. For example, the Queensland state government set up the Queensland Indigenous Arts Marketing and Export Agency (QIAMEA) in 2003 to promote Aboriginal artists of the state at home and abroad. Aboriginal Art has also attracted the attention of investors. The opening of the National Aboriginal and Torres Strait Islander Art Awards and exhibitions held annually in August in Darwin has become a national event which brings in large numbers of tourists, art collectors and investors.

The opening of Musée du Quai Branly in Paris in June 2006 has also contributed to the recognition of *things* made by Aboriginal people. The interior and exterior of one of the buildings at this museum were decorated with the works of eight Aboriginal artists. This event created a strong impression that *things* made by Aboriginal people had moved outside of their local contexts and achieved global recognition. Four of the chosen artists hailed from remote regions and their paintings presented their individually unique abstract styles. Gulumbu Yunupingu from Arnhem Land was one of the artists who drew attention for interpreting bark painting designs into abstract representation in the late 1990s. Another bark painter among the selected artists, John Mawurundjul, also introduced abstract representation to his bark painting at around the same time.

It is conceivable that this shift to abstract representation was prompted by multiple factors, including the aforementioned success of Emily and Rover, the subsequent emergence of a wide variety of Aboriginal artists, and the soaring prices of Aboriginal artworks. The tastes of the art world and consumers were communicated via art advisors and guidance was provided. And artists themselves had opportunities to experience the tastes of buyers directly as they attended exhibitions and award presentations, visited museums and art galleries, and travelled abroad. In this multi-layered environment, Aboriginal people changed their styles of representation in paintings.

⦿ Localization of arts ⦿

The shift toward a more abstract style seen in Aboriginal art from around the year 2000 is a major departure from the past relationship between craft and art. Aboriginal people themselves changed their techniques and turned their works into art, unlike, say, the case of primitive art, in which the Western art world borrowed local craft and "deemed" it to be "art". The Aboriginal case can be regarded as voluntary negotiations carried out entirely by themselves. In other words, the change was effected as a result of negotiations between Aboriginal people and the mainstream society, not the result of a unilateral takeover by the art world.

If we look at representations in paintings, it seems as if Mawurundjul and Gulumbu merely changed their style to suit the tastes of the outside world. However, their connection with the land and with the world of spirits and myths at the core of their paintings has never been lost. Their paintings have continued to represent their respective mythical worlds, which have continued to be shared by the locals. This continues to be both an essential element of, and the source of power for, their paintings at the same time. Their paintings represent a strong connection between them and a mythology which is embedded in their living and of utmost importance in their lives. It was not an appropriation by a third party; it was a new style they devised for the purpose of communicating with the outside world. They created the new artistic representation on their own volition.

As mentioned earlier, Aboriginal Australians have continued to produce paintings in view of selling them as they interact with the outside world since the 1970s. Cash income was of course one aim but their greater aim was to explain, through their paintings, local concepts such as their mysterious connection with spirits and their relationship with the land to mainstream society; seeking understanding. They have continually changed the style of their work so that the outside world can understand their concepts. The aforementioned shift towards an abstract style that happened around the turn of the 21st century was also an attempt to foster understanding. In effect, Aboriginal artists chose to use styles of representation favored by the globalized audience that would best communicate their world view.

Their paintings as *things* have never moved away from local values such as their connection with their land, spirit mythology, and ceremonies. These values continue to be central in their paintings. Despite large incomes, they continue to live the way they have always lived, in the environment that allows them to carry on hunting and gathering and continuing to perform ceremonies based on their ancestral mythology, confirming their connections with it and the land. They continue to move to and from the local and the global while maintaining their local culture. This is the very source of the power of Aboriginal paintings. The historical change in the *things* made by Aboriginal people represents the interaction between the *things* and people. The *things* made by Aboriginal people continue to change by encompassing their social history and thereby Aboriginal people also continue to change.

III-2 The Bodies and Art Forms of Pacific Islander Artists

Matori Yamamoto

Something once hailed as "Pacific Art" originated from local customs. Although there was certainly something aesthetic in it, there was no specific intention on the part of its creators to create "works of original art". In the first place, "art" as a creative activity was not part of the culture of the people indigenous in the region.

The art activities of the Pacific Islanders in their homelands and in the circum-Pacific developed countries, especially in New Zealand, are new endeavors for the Pacific Islanders. While inheriting various heritages of "Pacific Art" these activities conform to the general understandings of art in global society, including that they are creative activities undertaken by individuals and that they have unique characteristics. Their activities are generally known as "contemporary Pacific art" (D'Alleva 1998; Stevenson 2008; Tautai at www.tautai.org). The term "contemporary" is used to mean that it is art practiced by artists today and that the category includes a wide variety of artistic activities not limited to so-called contemporary art.

There are 266,000 Pacific Islanders living in New Zealand, comprising 6.9% of the country's total population (Census 2006, excluding the Maori) (NZ statistics 2007). About one half of them are Samoan. They form the most established community among all Pacific Islanders in the circum-Pacific developed countries. The community has spawned many artists engaged in a wide range of activities, including painting, sculpture, installation, film, photography, jewelry, theatre, music, dancing, and various performances.

From the reservoir of diverse contemporary Pacific artists, this essay will focus on three who use their bodies: performance artist Yuki Kihara, and dance company directors Lemi Ponifasio and Neil Ieremia. In an art form that put the body on show, the body is intentionally objectified. It is turned into a *mono* (*thing*). What is the relationship between the body as a *thing* and the human being who is the owner of this body?

⦿ Yuki Kihara ⦿

Kihara was born to a Samoan mother and a Japanese father who was a Japan Overseas Cooperation Volunteer. She spent her childhood in Japan, returned to Samoa, received secondary education in New Zealand, and studied fashion and design at university. Kihara is what Samoans call "*fa'afafine*" (male transgender) who prefers the feminine way although she is physically male. As she told me, she was like this from the beginning, as far as she remembers. I shall refer to Kihara using feminine pronouns.

After designing T-shirts and being involved in fashion shows, she became a self-portrait artist. She is also known as a performance artist. She says that she pursues this activity to show the world the discrimination experienced by *fa'afafine* and to achieve social acceptance. When she was living in Samoa, she was severely beaten by her parents whenever she exhibited her preference for feminine manners and clothes. She was deeply hurt as a child by this denial of her identity. Samoan society is generally more tolerant of people such as Kihara compared with countries such as Japan, yet she says that her family life was filled with conflict (Kihara's interview, September 2008).

Kihara has a somewhat small stature for a man and looks natural in women's clothes. In high-heel shoes and a miniskirt or a pair of shorts, she passes as a flamboyantly dressed woman. Her early works are photographs in which she dresses as the heroines of oral tradition. Unsuspecting viewers would think she is a woman. Although Kihara openly stated that she was *fa'afafine* at the time, the fact might have escaped the attention of those who were unfamiliar with Samoan or Polynesian culture.

Her next series of works presented in 2004 was titled *Fa'afafine: In a Manner of a Woman*, revealing her body to present herself as a *fa'afafine*. It amounts to a coming out about her way of life. The most revealing of all is a triptych of photographs in which she reclines on a couch with her long hair hanging down over her bare breasts – enlarged by hormone treatment. She is wearing a grass skirt in the first print entitled *Fa'afafine: In a Manner of a Woman*. The second photograph presents her fully naked womanly body and the third photograph also has her lying naked but her penis is showing between her thighs.

Another work conceals a surprising element, which I did not notice when I first saw it. It is a photograph called *Ulugali'i Samoa* (Samoan Couple) in the *Tama Samoa ma Teine Samoa: A Man and A Woman of Samoa* series in which Kihara with a fan in her hand is sitting next to a mustached man wearing a pandanus

Photo EIII-2.1   Samoan Couple by Yuki Kihara (2005) In the Fa'afafine: In the Manner of a Woman *series, this photographic print is staged to look like a 19th century postcard depicting a Samoan couple in a colonist's gaze but the faces of both the husband and the wife are actually composites based on Kihara's own face. This work was produced as a challenge to the dichotomized thinking about gender and the view of* fa'afafine *as "primitive peculiarity" and "the exotic". By courtesy of Sean Coyle and Yuki Kihara.*

seed necklace and holding a fly whisk (accessories of the Samoan chief) as if they are a married couple. When I asked her who the man was, she told me that she used photomontage to add a moustache to her own face and attach her head to a muscular male body. It was a sly attempt to demonstrate that there was only a fine line between man and woman. Kihara laughed with delight when I showed my surprise.

Kihara has succeeded in demonstrating the richness of her being by using her body as a photographic object. I was initially surprised by the "violent act" of exposing her naked body. When I study closely the sepia-toned photographs in which the photographic object is a Polynesian woman in a sex symbol-like pose evoking the colonial era, however, I find a representation of Kihara's androgynous being: both man and woman as well as being open to multiple interpretations.

Kihara's work stands in sharp contrast to Yasumasa Morimura, for example. Morimura, is a famous self-portrait artist in Japan and abroad, whose work consists of photographs of himself masquerading as someone else. Hence his works always have an element of fiction. Kihara, as we have seen, is presenting herself as herself; quite the opposite to Morimura's approach. Kihara turns her own body into an "object" in an unadorned state. What is interesting is the richness of being that is expressed through letting the objectified body speak freely.

The photograph of her in a grass skirt was purchased by the Metropolitan Museum of Art in New York together with another print and exhibited in the fall of 2008.

⦿ Lemi Ponifasio and Mau ⦿

Lemi Ponifasio was born in Samoa and moved to Auckland, New Zealand, to go to university. He worked in Japan after graduation. He was reluctant to talk about his life in Japan in detail but he reportedly earned good money during Japan's economic boom and travelled widely, including to Europe, to broaden his experience. He returned to New Zealand after ten years and started a dance company. According to Wikipedia, he formed Mau in 1995 (http://en.wikipedia.org/wiki/Lemi_Ponifasio). Mau is a multi-ethnic group comprised of mostly Samoans as well as Maori, other Pacific Islanders and Kiwis. Mau – literally "protest" – was the name of the Western Samoan anticolonial movement, of which Samoans are very proud. At the time, Ponifasio was known as a Samoan Butoh practitioner living in New Zealand due to his background as a former member of a Japanese Butoh group. He has somewhat distanced himself from Butoh in recent years and asked me to focus on his originality when I interviewed him in 2008.

There is nevertheless still a discernible Butoh influence in his choreography. He once told me about his experience in his early days in Auckland (his talk show in March 2009). He had tried break dancing and ballet but he felt that conventional Western dance styles did not suit him because everyday lifestyle is highly relevant in mastering dance moves. This is similar to the Butoh practitioners' attempts to express the texture of the body while emphasizing stillness because they thought that Western dance moves were unsuitable for Japanese bodies. Butoh is generally known as an obscure, alternative dance style featuring "white body paint, bow-legs, shaven head, and askance gaze" but it is an attempt to present the body through extreme objectification. Tatsumi Hijikata famously described Butoh as "a corpse standing straight up in a desperate bid for life" (Harada 2004: 18).

Ponifasio's choreography and stage direction are rather recondite, featuring movements such as stomping the floor and spinning the arms while standing still, rather than airy jumps and turns. Acoustic accompaniment often involves large sounds or sound effects rather than music. When music is used, it tends to be contemporary music with no mechanical rhythm. He often combines some performances of Pacific heritage. His latest work *Tempest* (http://www.youtube.com/watch?v=WfLqv85uCww) incorporates an oration delivered by indigenous activist Tame Iti in the Maori language. Aside from the argument about the suitability of Polynesian bodies to European-style dances, Tame Iti's face is tattooed with traditional Maori markings which, together with the rhythm of his oratory, adds striking character to the performance. What is important here is Tame Iti's unique presence, his objectified body itself.

Lately Mau have been spending much more time touring abroad than at home, performing in many parts of the world, including London, Paris and New York.

⦿ Neil Ieremia and Black Grace ⦿

Black Grace, founded by Neil Ieremia, provides a marked contrast to Mau in terms of the way they use their bodies.

Neil grew up in a small country town called Cannons Creek outside of Wellington. The dance company he formed with his friends there developed a reputation and eventually shifted its base to the city of Auckland. His group is made up of predominantly male dancers of Samoan and Maori heritage, many of whom are of mixed ethnicity, and some are white. Neil himself was probably born in New Zealand and the dance company appears less exotic than Mau. While many of the members have tattoos of Samoan or Maori designs, their application to non-traditional parts of the body speaks of their distances to traditional cultures as multi-ethnics or second-generation immigrants. Black Grace must have been founded at around the same time as Mau (http://www.blackgrace.co.nz/).

On video, all of the dancers show brilliantly muscular flexibility and dynamism. They exhibit the refinement to be able to dance to Bach's piano pieces as well as the skill to perform traditional Samoan dances with a more contemporary taste. *Fa'ataupati* (slap dance) – also known as the mosquito dance because it looks like a person slapping mosquitos all over his body – and the *sāsā* – a seated dance with synchronized hand movements – are rhythmic dances performed to the sound of percussive instruments in Samoa, but I have never seen Samoan dance moves as refined as those performed by Black Grace. Their performance of Manu Samoa's

Siva Tau – the Samoan version of the famous haka of the All Blacks, performed by the Samoan national rugby team – is spectacular. The dance company embodies the brilliant fusion of dynamic dances with Western music and beautifully executed Samoan dances.

Gathering Clouds was produced in 2008 to protest against the discourse that Pacific Islander immigrants were a burden on the New Zealand economy. It depicts the way Pacific Islanders made an honest living in the country despite various forms of persecution as it traces the history of their migration with a diverse blend of various dance styles of Pacific Island peoples. It is clear that the show adopts the authentic dance approach of embodied expression in contrast to Ponifasio's attempt to make a statement through objectified bodies. What is objectified here is body movements that disappear in a blink of an eye rather than the body itself.

⦿ Thoughts on the materiality of the body ⦿

We have so far discussed the body and its materiality in the art of three Pacific Islander artists based in New Zealand.

In the works of Yuki Kihara, her attempt to objectify her own body would not have been feasible without the body. While it contrasts to the works of Yasumasa Morimura, however, what is interesting more than the blunt exhibition of the object itself is the intense presence of the *fa'afafine* who uses her body to assert herself. Her works have been adapted and staged in an ingenious fashion rather than as straightforward portraits.

Lemi Ponifasio's Mau Company is all about presenting the body. The body is objectified and presented drawing on the influence of Butoh.

By contrast, in Neil Ieremia's Black Grace, it is the movements of the body not the body itself that is to be objectified.

This essay has considered the relationship between *things* (bodies) and human beings (artists) in art forms that objectify bodies. As I have insufficient space to discuss the relationship between *things* and human beings (audience), I shall address that topic in a future study, but I believe talking about "the body" in association with the consideration of *things* is a highly effective approach.

III-3 Staying Authentic: Between *bingata* and Ryukyu Bingata

Akiko Muramatsu

⦿ The birth of *bingata* and Ryukyu Bingata ⦿

Okinawa Prefecture is made up of approximately 160 islands on the southernmost part of the Japanese Archipelago. The famous subtropical resort region is known for many woven and dyed textiles. Okinawa is credited with eleven types of woven and dyed textiles among Japan's Traditional Crafts (designated by the Ministry of Economy, Trade and Industry), a number unmatched by any other prefecture. However, most of these are textile products. The only dyed product is Ryukyu Bingata, which was designated a Traditional Craft in 1984 (Photos EIII-3.1 and EIII-3.2). The name Ryukyu Bingata was adopted at the time of this designation.

The term *bingata* refers to both the textile dyeing technology (craft) used to produce clothes for the royals and nobles of the Ryukyu Kingdom and its products (*mono/things*). One of the accepted theories claims that the technology was influenced by textile dyeing technologies from abroad through the Kingdom's trade with China and Southeast Asia from around the 15th century and established its style by around the 18th century (Tonaki 1980; Hoshi 1987). A common theory holds that the Chinese character for *bin* is a collective name for the colors used and the Chinese character for *gata* (*kata*) means a pattern or design. Therefore the term means textile dyeing using patterns and multiple colors. Another theory suggests that the term is a corrupted form of Bengal, indicating the influence of Indian chintz (Iha 1974: 128). We can fairly safely assume that *bingata* is a dyeing technology/product which developed by blending heterogeneous elements in both its name and craft.

Okinawa was once a sovereign nation called the Ryukyu Kingdom. The kingdom was abolished when it became part of Japan. It was designated a prefecture in 1879, following a reorganization of Japan's feudal domain system. The *bingata* dye houses lost their largest customer base, the royalty and aristocrats who bought their dyed clothing. Dye houses either switched trades or closed down as their businesses

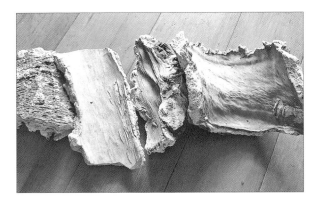

Photo III-3.1   The bark of fukugi (Garcinia subelliptica) *is the source of a yellow dye, one of the base colors of* bingata. *(Shiroma Bingata Kōbō)*

Photo III-3.2   Fabric for a Ryukyu dance costume. The yellow ground color was dyed with fukugi. *See Photo EIII-3.1. (Shiroma Bingata Kōbō)*

became unviable, and only a handful were still operating in the the late 1920s. The survival of *bingata* was under threat. However, a turning point came when a party led by Sōetsu Yanagi, the founder of the *mingei* (folk art) movement who appreciated "*yō no bi*" (functional beauty) in handicraft, visited Okinawa in 1938. Yanagi lauded *bingata* out of nostalgia for the art of hand-dyeing on a beautiful southern island and reignited interest in *bingata*. However the battle in Okinawa during the Second World War completely devastated the townships of Shuri and Naha, the home of many *bingata* producers, destroying their age-old stencils and equipment, and disrupting production. After the war, *bingata* was revived and began to expand its sales by targeting the souvenir market for foreign tourists. It became widely known following the reversion of Okinawa to Japan (from the USA) in 1972 and a tourism boom triggered by the Okinawa Ocean Expo in 1975. It has solidified its reputation as a Japanese traditional craft since its inclusion in the list of Traditional Crafts under the designation of Ryukyu Bingata in 1984.

⦿ Names and descriptions ⦿

Those who are interested in *bingata* may be aware that it has multiple names, including *hon-bingata* (meaning *bingata* dyed in Okinawa), Ryukyu Bingata, *bingata* (stencil-dyed fabric), and *wazome-bingata* (meaning *bingata* dyed in mainland Japan). This is intertwined with questions of authenticity; about what is the "true" *bingata*.

The type of textile dyeing that had been referred to as *katachiki, binsashi* and others among its producers came to be called *bingata* at around the time Yoshitarō Kamakura[1] used the term in a lecture at Tokyo Fine Arts School in 1925 (Hoshi 1987: 12). Kamakura had a teaching position at Okinawa Teacher Training College in the early 1920s, where he became fascinated by the textile dyeing method that was locally called *katachiki* or *binsashi*. He took lessons from veteran dyers (Kamakura 1976: 171—172). Other visitors from mainland Japan trickled in, became similarly captivated by the beauty of *bingata*, and learned the craft before returning to Japan. Since then, textile dyeing producers in regions such as Tokyo, Kyoto and Shizuoka have incorporated the patterns and technology of *bingata*.

Before long, key figures in the kimono fabric industry decided that kimono made from Okinawan *bingata* (or *hon-bingata*) and kimono made from *wazome-bingata* dyed in mainland Japan should be distinguished and they came to be called by different names. The designation of Ryukyu Bingata as a national Traditional Craft in 1984 entailed the detailed specification of a number of elements, ranging from the technology and raw materials used to the production areas, of Okinawan-dyed *bingata*. According to the Act on the Promotion of Traditional Craft Industries, Ryukyu Bingata basically uses *bingata* patterns for which the stencil is made of paper sheets bonded by persimmon juice, underlain by *rukujyū*[2] and carved using

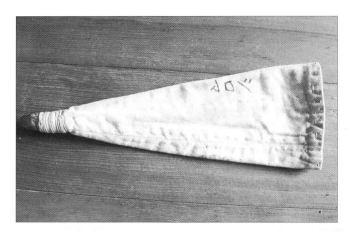

Photo III-3.3 A paste bag used in a technique called tsutsubiki *involving dyeing hand-drawn patterns used in making products such as* furoshiki *(wrapping cloth). The tale of postwar producers who made nozzles out of shell casings is still talked about among the craftsmen. (Shiroma Bingata Kōbō)*

the *tsukibori* (dotted outline) technique. The resist paste is a mixture of glutinous rice flour, rice bran, salt etc. There are six other requirements. A dyeing craft must satisfy all these requirements to receive designation as a Traditional Craft from the Minister of Trade and Industry (at the time) (Ryukyu Bingata Jigyō Kyōdō Kumiai 1987: 63). Such a move towards the specification of materials, equipment and the segmentation of the craft differentiated Ryuky Bingata from the *bingata* that had been practiced in Okinawa until then (*hon-bingata*).

⦿ The practices of producers during the *bingata* revival period ⦿

In considering the authenticity of *bingata*, it is interesting to note the practices of producers during the postwar *bingata* revival period. *Bingata* production, which had been disrupted for a while in war-torn Okinawa, was revived by the efforts of producers and the momentum provided by their supporters. Let us look at the situation at the time.

Upon completion of his apprenticeship in Yaeyama, Eiki Shiroma became a *bingata* craftsman after learning the traditional skills from his father over a period of several months from the spring 1928 until his father's death in December. The dyeing equipment and stencils that he inherited from his father, which had been handed down for generations, were destroyed during the war. His eldest son, Eijun

Staying Authentic 331

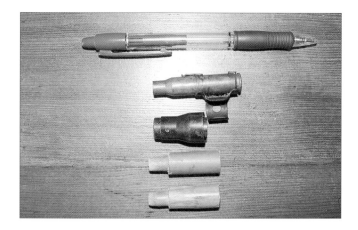

Photo III-3.4   Nozzles from the postwar era. Some were made of bamboo. (Shiroma Bingata Kōbō)

Shiroma, who was a young child at the time, told me about the *bingata* revival as follows.

> Our family returned to Okinawa after the war, began to live in tents at Shuriyamagawa, and attempted to revive *bingata* using whatever materials and tools we could find. We couldn't get pigments due to a supply shortage, so we used any colored things, including artists' paint from Pentel. We substituted ground red roof tiles and even red lipsticks we got from the U. S. Military personnel for red pigments, and ground the shells of *yakōgai* (*Turbo marmoratus*) to use as a white pigment. There was no heavy paper to make stencils, so we collected maps discarded by the Japanese Army and carved patterns out. We unraveled flour bags and dyed them because we did not have fabrics to dye. (…) In the early stage of the revival period, we made Christmas cards, neckties, and tapestries mainly as souvenirs for the U. S. Military personnel.

Sekihiro Chinen, Sekigen Chinen's eldest son, was one of the producers who led the *bingata* revival. He told me:

> During the revival period, we had to begin with tool making for *bingata* dyeing. For example, we didn't have small knives, so we took springs out of clocks and sharpened them to make knife blades; we made a round gimlet by burning and fabricating an umbrella rib and shaved off the rubber shoe sole to use it as an underlay for carving the

stencil... My father seems to have begun with *tsutsugaki*[3] during the revival period. He dyed quilt covers and flour bags and looked for anything that might be usable because there were no fabrics. Although indigo was relatively available, most pigments were unavailable at the time; he substituted all sorts of things and used charcoal too, for shading.

There were some people who said, "This is no time to dye fabrics", to criticize people such as Shiroma and Chinen who were scrambling for equipment and materials for *bingata* dyeing when they were living from hand to mouth. Nevertheless, postwar *bingata* was revived and passed down through what Levi-Strauss calls bricolage, entailing the use of whatever tools and materials come to hand. In a sense, craftsmanship was put into effect through the practices of *bingata* in order to reclaim the way people had been living in Okinawa before the war. However, *bingata* practices during the revival period can be regarded as deviations from the traditional craft of Ryukyu Bingata under the detailed specifications for raw materials and equipment. Some producers consider the dyeing of souvenirs such as Christmas cards, ties and tapestries to be a lower grade work, so to speak, that deviates from *bingata* for both Okinawan kimono and Japanese kimono. This is despite the fact that applying *bingata* to anything other than Okinawan kimono, be it a tie for Western clothes or Japanese kimono, is a deviation from the original craft of *bingata* in view of its history as a textile dyeing technology that had been developed and refined for Okinawan kimono making during the Ryukyu Kingdom period.

The discourse about authenticity is further complicated by the existence of the *wazome-bingata* dyeing technology, which was undisturbed by the war because mainland Japan was spared ground war damage. On the one hand, in view of the history of *wazome-bingata* in which technology and equipment were passed on to Kamakura in the 1920s, when *bingata* was still called *katachiki* by the locals, it is possible to consider *wazome-bingata* to be an authentic continuation of the *bingata* tradition of the Ryukyu Kingdom.

On the other hand, Ryukyu Bingata is designated as a Traditional Craft by the government with detailed specifications to assure its authenticity. Yet, its producers do not always comply with these specifications. Some workshops use the *rukujyū* underlay for stencil carving as stipulated, but they also use a rubber underlay when it is more convenient. Some workshops occasionally resort to chemical dyes despite the stipulation to use Ryukyu Ai (indigo blue dye made in Okinawa) for Aigata (*bingata* dyed in shades of indigo blue) because the availability of this natural dye is limited. In other words, the *bingata* producers in Okinawa do not always conform to the national designation to guarantee the authenticity of *bingata*.

⦿ What is authentic *bingata*? ⦿

So what is their perception of the authenticity of *bingata*? One producer spoke about the tools devised by Shiroma and others in the years of postwar shortages and said: "For me to use handmade knives and *rukujyū* means that my work is connected with my life in Okinawa. Even when I buy a knife, I don't use it as it is; I modify it to fit my own requirements before I start carving stencils" (Photo EIII-3.5). Another producer, who uses a chemical dye when Ryukyu Ai is unavailable, said: "Our workshop always uses red in some parts of our *bingata* designs. We were instructed by our predecessor to use a red dye, no matter how little, even for kimono fabrics for older people for which it is uncommon to use red, so we adhere to it".

In short, they place importance on the way they inherited their *bingata* craft from their predecessors, and the fact that their craft is practiced in their everyday living in Okinawa. It is not a question of which raw materials and tools they use. It is obvious that this condition of transmission of the craft, including some elements not covered by the government's specifications, does not exclude the bricolage-like impromptu practices of their predecessors during the revival period (Photo EIII-3.6).

Genroku Yagi, who had been trained by Eiki Shiroma and who, with his teacher, supported the *bingata* revival, spoke about his students from mainland Japan who came to Okinawa to experience *bingata* dyeing.

> While they are in Okinawa, they quickly assimilate and learn to express our colors. What mystifies me is that they revert to their own colors as soon as they return to the mainland. This means that "Okinawan *bingata* can develop only in the climate of Okinawa"… those vivid colors come to life only in the climate of Okinawa and one can express those colors only because one lives in Okinawa. (Yagi 1988: 112)

On the surface, this discourse of heavy reliance on the local climate sounds like an essentialist assertion which excludes non-Okinawans, or like a counter to the *wazome-bingata* of the mainland which is technically authentic. However, as evidenced by Yagi's saying that even the students from the mainland can express "Okinawan colors" albeit temporarily, Okinawan *bingata* is open to everyone as

Photo III-3.5 The underlay called rukujyū *is made by drying Okinawan* shima-dōfu *in winter. It is firm to touch but has just enough softness for the knife blade to carve patterns in the stencil. Fat from soy beans prevent the knives from rusting (top right). Carving knives were reportedly made from umbrella ribs during the postwar shortages. Today's producers buy their knives and modify them to suit their requirements (bottom).*

Photo III-3.6 Final checking of pattern carving. (Futenma Bingata Kōbō)

long as "one lives in Okinawa". In other words, the "climate" referred to above has something in common with the following description by Takashi Uchiyama, a philosopher: "I believe that a climate is something that is created by sustained relationships. A climate comes into existence when there is a sustained relationship between nature and human beings and between human beings" (Uchiyama 2006: 220). The *bingata* craftsmen in Okinawa place importance on their connection with their predecessors, their technology and the equipment born thereof, as well as the place called "Okinawa" where they have sustained relationships with people living there. The fixed authenticity of Ryukyu Bingata can be shaken by changes in raw materials and dyeing technology in changing times and circumstances. By contrast, the word "climate" in the discourse of the *bingata* craftsmen in Okinawa to describe relationships rooted in the fabric of life and their connection with their forefathers guarantees that the bricolage is built by the hands of "true craftsmen". The story surrounding *bingata* suggests that authenticity lies in this condition of a living tradition.

Notes

Introduction

1. Our description of the outline and historical background of material culture studies relies on various works, including Yoshida (1999), Uchibori (1997), Boivin (2008), Henare, Holbradd and Wastell (2007), Knapett (2005), Knapett and Malafouris (2008), Miller (1998) and Tilley (2007).
2. This account is of course a rather loose generalization. Closer examination of the work of individual anthropologists would reveal a continuous thread of interest in *mono* even though it was not mainstream. Space does not permit much elaboration here but even with Malinowski, the so-called "father of modern anthropology", for example, the study of the Kula exchange is, in a broad sense, themed on the exchanging of *mono*. Similarly, Levi-Strauss, regarded as the leading proponent of structuralism, focused on structures abstracted from the relationships between individual objects (including myths) rather than objects in the field themselves. At the same time, though, he consistently maintained his interest in *mono* as specific individual and sensuous objects. His structuralism did not lose the characteristic of being a "science of the concrete" and "bricolage" (French for DIY) after all. Levi-Strauss also positively appraised Boas' material culture studies in *The Way of the Masks* (Levi-Strauss 1972).
3. In the context of this epistemological reflection on ethnography, however, Clifford's art-culture system theory and other critical re-evaluations of material culture studies in anthropology raised questions and exerted influence on the study of arts and material culture in a broad sense in anthropology.
4. See the works of Appadurai (1986), Candlin and Raiford (2009), Gell (1998), Henare, Holbradd and Wastell (2007), Knapett and Malafouris (2008), Kopitoff (1986), Miller (1987, 1998, 2005) and Latour (1993) among others. The launch of *Journal of Material Culture* led by University College of London in 1996 is indicative of the revitalization of material culture studies in anthropology in the Anglo-sphere. Although there is insufficient space

for details, we would like to note that there have been sustained efforts also in Japanese anthropology, including Kawada's discussions of "technological culture", *mono* and body techniques, and Yoshida's material culture studies in relation to museum exhibits (see Kawada 1992c and Yoshida 1999 among others). In related fields, studies of folk implements and Matsui's study of the folk arts movement are worth noting (Innami et al. 2002; Matsui 2005). In recent years, studies on material culture in a broad sense have been undertaken as part of the "Anthropology of Resources" project (Grants-in-Aid for Scientific Research on Priority Areas; "Distribution and Sharing of Resources in Symbolic and Ecological Systems: Integrative Model-building in Anthropology") led by the small products unit (distribution and consumption of small products (commodities)) and the recognition & processing unit (recognition and processing of natural resources). Our joint study project at Research Institute for Languages and Cultures of Asia and Africa (ILCAA), which forms the basis of this book, inherited many questions and members from the Anthropology of Resources project (Uchibori 2007).
5. See Lakoff and Johnson (1999) and Lave and Wenger (1991) among others.
6. See Braudel (1985–1999) among others for social history emphasized by him and the Annales School. Also in Japan, there is a lineage of quality historical studies themed on mono independent of Braudel. See Tsunoyama (2001) and Hasegawa (1997) for example.
7. On this point, see Niwa (Chapter 1 in this volume) and Sugawara (Chapter 2), both of which focus on the linguistic practices surrounding *mono*. Konaka (Chapter 12) examines the use of metaphor in the study of *mono*. Tilley (1999) is also informative.
8. See Miller (1998: 18–22) and Edwards, Gosden and Phillips (2006) for anthropology and senses or qualia.

Chapter 1

1. The house is decorated for the Spring Festival with these items on which auspicious phrases or wishes for the coming year are written in a couplet form. Various couplets are pasted on either side of and above the outside gate and the entrance door to the house. In Shanbei, red couplets are replaced with white ones for one year after the death of a family member, and with green or yellow ones for several years after that. The same green and yellow sheets of paper are used for paper-cutting as well.

2 In Shanbei from the late 1970s, an administrative agency called "local culture center" (*wenhuaguan*), which was responsible for the cultural education of the masses, oversaw various training programs for the promotion of "folk art" such as paper-cutting patchwork pictures and peasant painting under expert artists' instruction. These days there are many farming women who are also paper-cutting artists who sell or exhibit their work within and outside of China. See Wu (2015) and Niwa (2015) for more information about the political or gender history of Shanbei paper-cuts having been changed into "folk art".

3 The term "representation" consists of two components: "re" meaning "again" or "acting for or on behalf of", and "presentation" meaning "being presented". Accordingly, it can be said that a "representation" appears "again, in place of something else". For instance, a painting or verbal narrative depicting or describing an apple is generally regarded as a representation which is in lieu of a real apple. However, they are also a painted surface or sound which present themselves as *things* now and here, each having its own physical entity and inherent material characteristics.

4 The illiteracy rate among women (aged 6 and older) in my research field of Yanchuan County was 44.31% in the 1990 statistics (National Bureau of Statistics of China population and employment statistics 2000). The proportion of rural women in their mid-50s and older with school education is extremely small. It is not uncommon for a person to carry various ID cards showing her name in different homophonic characters because she does not care how her name is written.

5 In Shanbei, scissors are considered to be the most familiar tools for women. Similarly, Satō (in Essay I-1, this volume) reports that the wax drawing in Indonesian batik-making uses tools that are also used in the everyday home environment. Sekimoto (2007) argues that women like this work and are motivated to pass on these skills to their children because it is "work embedded in everyday living," which can be carried out in the home, between household chores. The pair of scissors used for paper-cutting is a common tool used in various household tasks, including sewing, cooking and harvesting from the vegetable garden. The scissors are always lying about on the edge of the kang bed-stove, which is effectively the living area of the cave-house. Children are often seen casually playing with them. By contrast, writing instruments and craftsman's knives are relatively unfamiliar tools for women. Although space does not permit a full exploration of this point, how the paper-cutting scissors relate to women in their everyday lives is an important point of consideration.

6 In addition to these items, human-shaped cut-outs to ward off diseases and evil spirits and other paper offerings and decorations for funeral rites were classified as a type of paper-cutting in earlier studies of paper-cutting (e.g., Chen 1988). However, since the local people basically consider paper-cuts as "celebratory" and the makers of religious and ritual paper-cuts tend to be professional shamans and healers, these are excluded from our discussion.

7 The entry for the word "*hua*" in dictionaries of Chinese characters includes not only "botanical flowers" but also "things having a form similar to a flower", "things with a pattern or design", "small things" and even "cotton", "fireworks", "female prostitutes", and "smallpox" (verbs excluded) (*Hanyu da zidian* (Sichuan cishu shubanshe 1995) among others).

8 Our discussion of the appearance of "tangible and intangible images" refers to the concept of "image" presented by Yanai (2008). While drawing on the idea of "image" discussed by the aesthetics scholars Iwaki (to be discussed in the closing section of this chapter), Yanai focuses on the dimension of "formless" images in the anthropologist's physical experience of fieldwork before theorization or verbalization. As Yanai points out, the practice of trying to capture the "whole" of the subject matter while interacting with such "images" parallels "art" as sensory experience (Yanai 2008). The present study is an attempt to capture Shanbei paper-cutting as a similar sensory experience.

9 I held experimental exhibitions on the theme of the ephemerality and intensity of Shanbei paper-cuts as "flowers" in collaboration with the local people and Japanese artists. Aiming to invite visitors to feel the art and life of Shanbei in which these "flowers" are grown with their five senses, just as we experienced it in the field, we did fieldwork specifically for the exhibition and to film scenes from Shanbei everyday life, bringing real objects – including a façade of the cave-houses – from there, creating installations in the exhibition rooms. See Niwa & Yanai (2017) for more information about this art-anthropology exhibition, 'Window Flowers: Chinese Paper Cuts in Huangtu Plateau', in Fukuoka Asian Art Museum and in Seikatsu-Kobo gallery between October 2013 and March 2014.

10 In this chapter, the term "motif" is used to mean "the subject matter expressed through cut-out forms". It covers both the theme of the work as a whole (the content of a wish, a story in mythology or song, or a worksite scene) and the individual subject matters (a cat, peony etc.).

11 Paper-cutting artists in Yanchuan County, Shanbei, such as Gao Fenglian

have been trained at the local culture center mentioned in Note 2 above. They produce "paper-cut works" nowadays with new motifs and compositions of their own which are distinct from traditional window-flowers. However, Feng Shanyun, a former center officer, said, "We do encourage '*maojiao*' when we teach but we choose not to teach techniques for it". While individual artists adopt various approaches, I believe that the paper-cut makers discussed in this chapter more or less follow the process of traditional "flower-cut" making for practical purposes.

12 The "yin/yang" concept is applied to paper-cutting in the form of motifs such as man/woman, sun/moon and heaven/earth, as well as through compositions such as coarse/fine and concave/convex.

13 Examples of homophony-based design include "年年有余" (*niannian-you-yu*: a picture of a fish to wish for "a prosperous life year by year" because "余" (*yu*: surplus) and "魚" (*yu*: fish) are homophonic), and "馬上封侯" (*mashang-fenghou*: a picture of a monkey on horseback, signifying advancement in life because "馬上" (*mashang*) is a play on words for "horseback" and "at once" and "侯" (*hou*: high official) and "猴" (*hou*: monkey) are homophonic).

14 Story-telling in rural villages of northern China alternates between narratives and songs. According to Iguchi (1999), the mode of expression for "traveling", "fighting" and "expressing emotions" is always a song. The "sound symbolism" (a function that conveys more than linguistic meanings) found in songs is one reason for this preference. And because rhyming generates concatenation of sounds, more emphasis is placed on spoken sounds than textual meaning. More detailed studies will be needed to elucidate the different emotions and images evoked in paper-cut makers by various words and songs.

15 For instance, the Hegelian notion of "objectification" proposed by Miller's material culture study (1987) is founded on a dialectic understanding of materiality which posits that the object manifests through the subject's cognition and the subject is sublated by inconsistency between them. Kearns (2003) argues that Miller's thesis and other studies influenced by it lapse into an essentialist dichotomy between the objective and the subjective by treating objects as the essentially, universally and externally given "matter".

16 Iwaki's argument is based on Bergson's (1978) view of *things* as an aggregate of "images", defined as "an existence placed halfway between the 'thing' and the 'representation'". In *Matter and Memory*, Bergson broke through the dichotomy of mind/matter on the basis of this view of matter as "images".

Chapter 2

1 The G|ui is one of the language groups of the San hunter-gatherers inhabiting the Kalahari Desert. They had been living in the Xade area under the Botswana government's settlement policy since 1979. They were relocated to Qx'oensakene (New Xade) under a new government re-settlement policy in 1997 and since then have been living in a community of more than 1,000 residents.

2 The gender of the university students is indicated by small letters following hyphens; -f and -m. The symbols in the transcripts denote the following. =: Separate utterances in quick succession. →: A succession of utterances made by the same speaker. {xxx}: Simultaneous utterances. (xxx): Ambiguous transcription. (......): Inaudible. xxx: Utterance with laughter. ((xxxxx)): Description of gestures/motions. [xxxxx]: Author's note or an addition in Japanese translation of G|ui. (0.9): Length of silence by seconds. The following abbreviations are also used. x·x: Pause shorter than 0.5 seconds. (-): Pause approximately 0.5 seconds long. (+): Gap approximately 1 second long. Xxx---xx: Restart. ↓: Momentary insertion of a notable gesture or action, or the beginning of such a gesture or action. ↑: The moment a notable gesture or action ends. [[Go: Eheh]]: Agreement response not regarded as an independent turn.

3 The "anthropology of corporeality" that I called for in my recent book can be seen in this light (Sugawara 2010).

4 "Double contingency" refers to the fundamental impossibility of starting a theoretically constructed communication (Luhmann 1995). My action is contingent upon your action. Your action is also contingent upon my action. According to Luhmann, in ordinary life, we are rarely frozen by this theoretical impossibility because some communication system actually operating reduces the double contingency that is always latent behind every interaction. From the reversed perspective, double contingency is the most fundamental condition that every communication is made possible. "Double contingency"-like situations can clearly happen between animals and humans. For instance, during my fieldwork as a primatologist, I encountered a big hound in a forest. As he was wagging his tail, I began to stroke his throat. Soon I noticed that I was afraid of him and he was aware that I was afraid, and I was aware that he was aware that I was afraid, and..... However, I could not keep stroking him all day long. Just when I took my hand off

him, his jaws snapped near my hand. Such a kind of interaction can never occur between the vending machine and myself.

5 In a semiotic analysis of nonverbal behavior, body movements were broken into the following categories: illustrator, emblem, adaptor, regulator, and facial expression (Ekman and Friesen 1969). Gesture is a concept combining illustrator and emblem. Similarly, Kendon describes three types of gestures: gesticulation, quotable gesture, and signs (Kendon 1990). The first two terms largely correspond to the first two categories devised by Ekman and Friesen above. The third term refers to sign languages.

6 The gender of the G|ui participants is distinguished by abbreviated names, e.g., KK (two large letters) : male; Go (a large letter+a small letter): female. Qg and Go are co-wives, the first and second wives of KK, who appears in Case 5.

7 Go, who appears in Case 2 in Section 2.2, is the mother of Ga. After her husband (Ga's father) died, she remarried KK's elder brother. When he died of illness, KK married Go in the form of levirate marriage.

8 I have been laughed at by my local assistants for explicitly demanding a share of meat, in violation of local customs. This episode is described in another paper (Sugawara 2009).

9 Kendon pointed out the importance of paying attention to "instrumental behavior". He observed that "friends" aligned on the same side in an argument were amazingly synchronized in their drinking actions (Kendon 1970).

10 Goodwin has focused on the involvement between *mono* and humans. For example, Professor Ann is instructing her post graduate student Sue by pointing at the markings on the ground at an archaeological dig site.

What Sue must see if she is to understand Ann's action in a relevant fashion is not only a gesture, but the patterning in the earth she is being instructed to follow. (…) The finger indicates relevant graphic structure in the soil (…), while simultaneously that structure provides organization for the precise location, shape and trajectory of the gesture. Each mutually elaborates the other (and both are further elaborated by the talk that accompanies the gesture) (Goodwin 2003, p. 20).

Goodwin calls action complexes of this type Symbiotic Gestures, which contain not only the body movements of the speaker but also something other than the body, that is, the surrounding structure.

Chapter 3

1. See Tokoro (2007) for ethnographic details about pearl culture referred in this chapter. See Kunz and Stevenson (1908) for the relationship between pearls and humans before the modern pearl culture industry.
2. See Matsuzuki (2002) and Akamatsu (2003) among others for definitions of the pearl and an overview of pearl oyster species.
3. See Akamatsu (ibid.) for the history of pearl cultivation in Japan.
4. However, this does not (necessarily) mean that verbalized and propositional knowledge is not important in pearl cultivation. For "tacit knowledge", see Polanyi (1966) and Fukushima (2001a). Incidentally, Yasutomi proposes to use "tacit knowing" in place of "tacit knowledge" as the latter expression is open to the misunderstanding that it is a static and fixed system of knowledge (2006: 32). While we agree with Yasutomi's view in principle, we opt for the commonly-used expression of "tacit knowledge" for expediency and simplicity. For the importance of "embodiment" in human cognition and practice, refer to various arguments surrounding "embodied mind" proposed by G. Lakoff et al. (Lakoff and Johnson 1999).
5. See *Shinju nenkan* (Pearl yearbook 2005) for a special feature about the Akoya pearl oyster mass-mortality problem.
6. See Fukushima (2001b) for the limitations of "skills learning", including the "communities of practice" model in a changing environment or situation. In particular, "the paradox of skill" discussion in this chapter has been inspired by Fukushima's argument about "the purgatory of skill" (Fukushima 2001a: 156–158). However, we use "the paradox of skill" in this chapter to highlight the dysfunction of skill in a fluctuating environment.
7. See Bestor (2003) among others for memorial services and memorial towers for *mono*, including living and non-living things, in various parts of Japan. Borrowing Wittgenstein's expression, we can find "an attitude toward a soul" of *mono* here.
8. Some readers may question whether the argument in this chapter applies only to lifeforms such as pearl oysters, and not to manmade things. Space does not permit a detailed discussion, but we would draw your attention to the fact that the boundary between living and non-living things is much fuzzier than is commonly assumed. For example, as mentioned in the Introduction, the boundary between *humans* and *mono* can be expanded, contracted or changed as in the examples of a walking stick for the visually impaired or a

vehicle and its driver. In the case of so-called "car animism" and fetishism, humans engage with lifeless manmade things as if they were entities with agency. Thus, the boundary between "lifeform" and "manmade things" is also a potentially negotiable (changeable) boundary. See also Yasutomi's suggestion about the applicability of the dialogic model as mentioned in this chapter to *mono*, including manmade things (Yasutomi 2008: 136–137).
9 A departure from the anthropocentric world view that sees non-human things as manipulatable object is proposed in various actor-network-theory type arguments (e.g., Latour 1993; Knapett and Malafouris 2008).
10 Latour presents a detailed analysis of this common-sense dichotomy between human and non-human as a "constitution" of modern society (Latour 1993).

Chapter 4

1 In this chapter, "pottery" refers to unglazed earthenware fired at low temperatures.
2 Although the style of pottery, including decoration, is an important focus of pottery studies because it sometimes reflects social rules and ideologies, it is excluded from this discussion due to space limitations.
3 The temperature varies depending on the kind of minerals contained in the clay (Rye 1981; Tite 1972).
4 The analysis will be made using archaeological materials, the final stage of pottery production. It is difficult, however, to reconstruct things such as the way fingers are used during the manufacturing process.
5 Increasing the ratio of temper sand can reduce the plasticity and shrinkage rate but it also reduces the strength of the fired pottery (Rye 1981). Hence its use is generally avoided.
6 Yap beach sands contain calcium carbonate ranging from 14% to as high as 98% in some places (Intoh 1990: 43). The problem with using calcium carbonate sand for tempering is explained in Section 4.4.
7 Yap is divided into ten districts, with ten to twenty villages in each. Its social class structure was village-based. Hence a person's class was determined by the village the person was born into (Lingenfelter 1975; Ushijima 1987). The lowest-ranked villagers called *milingay* had no land ownership until recently. They were allowed to live on highest-ranked villager's land in exchange for labor and subjected to various kinds of discrimination. The labor they provided to the landholders included farming, construction and repairs of community halls, as well as grave digging and pottery making.

on their lifestyle (Sue 1965: 45–50), she found that the Hare children were not fully utilizing the school "teachers" and that White teachers were having difficulty teaching them (Hara 1979: 199).
11 Differences in clay characteristics may be a background reason for the different order of learning between S village and G village. Although I have not tested the composition of clay, I observed the following two points. First, clay found in S Village has higher water content (water is scooped out before clay is excavated). Second, potters in G village add a large amount of sand of a type that is not found in S village when they prepare clay bodies (20% more than the amount of finely ground fired clay that is added to clay bodies in S village).
12 I have conducted a survey of two such products – *inkilt* (charcoal stove) and *durizen* (roof ornament) (Table 5.3). The former is frequently used by day-laborer households for cooking and the latter came into use as a rooftop ornament from the 1970s with the spread of Protestant Christianity.
13 When I tried to videotape, male relatives expressed disapproval but the potter was unconcerned and agreed to the filming.

Chapter 6

1 Sex without the need for erection, i.e., a sexual act not involving penetration of the vagina or anus of a woman by a man, is outside the scope of discussion in this chapter. Our discussion is confined to heterosexual intercourse involving genital penetration.
2 Formulas for sexual rejuvenation and erection enhancement are also used. The difference between male sex stimulants and aphrodisiacs will be explained later.
3 The Cartesian view of the body has been thoroughly criticized in various fields since Merleau-Ponty. See Ichikawa (1975) for example.
4 The sex industry is thus also a giant masturbation industry.
5 The penis can still be seen as an instrument if the pleasure center is understood to be located in the brain, but we refrain from any further exploration of this perspective here.
6 It would be reasonable for us to suspect that the purposive rationalist world view behind the instrument might be incompatible with one's own sexual pleasure or even any physical pleasure in a more general sense. Furthermore, the goal of sexual intercourse of giving a woman pleasure by using the penis (or a substitute) does not always give the male body genuine pleasure even when penetration is possible. This is because purposive rationality is paramount

here and the mind always tries to control the body (penis) with reference to this rationality. The mind is always the active agent, turning its own body into a means here, but genuine pleasures come about when one casts aside such rationality, that is, being passive, in my view (Tanaka 2010).

7 Of course, the question of why they are effective has been given various scientific explanations (Koizumi 2010). Vitalism is not inherently incompatible with scientific analysis as far as male sex stimulants are concerned.

8 "Natural" in this chapter does not mean a biological body or a universal human body. From the viewpoint of what kind of external nature (the environment, lifeforms etc.) influences the body, the naturalness of the body means the body that is subject to such influences. By contrast, the cultural aspect of the body does not relate to the difference in the view of the body between different cultures. It concerns cultural means, or more specifically, the body as an instrument and the body that uses instruments.

9 Yohimbine is extracted from the *Pausinystalia yohimbe* tree native to West Africa.

10 Steam-baked in an earthenware oven.

11 *Hachimigan* contains eight ingredients – *Rehmanniea radix* (root), *Cornus fructus* (fruit), *Batatis rhizoma* (root), *Poria* (fungus sclerotium), *Alisma plantago aquatica* (root), moutan cortex, cinnamon, and *Aconitum* (root).

12 For more details, see Koizumi (2010), Takenaga (1997), Tachiki (1993) and Watanabe (2004).

13 Broader categorization would have to include mineral and chemosynthetic/biosynthetic types, the latter of which would include Viagra (Koizumi 2010: 19). Mineral-type includes actinolite.

14 Accounts of the history of the Pharmaceutical Affairs Act are based on Ogino (1994).

15 Although it is outside of the scope of this chapter, we must note that increasing numbers of women are entering the market for sex-related goods and drugs. See Tanaka (1996) on this point.

16 See Uchihara (1994, 2001) for example.

17 See Saitō (2006) for details.

18 Levitra was released by Bayer in the U.S. in 2003 and approved by the Health, Labour and Welfare Ministry of Japan in 2004. Cialis was released by Eli Lilly in the U.S. in 2003 and approved by the Health, Labor and Welfare Ministry of Japan in 2007.

19 It has been claimed (Simons 2004) that the launch of Viagra curtailed the poaching of endangered species.
20 Packaging is also important in terms of images but I was not able to obtain sufficient data from the advertisements.
21 Perhaps we should also consider rarity, which is closely associated with marginality.
22 It has been pointed out that bizarre things are also effective (Katō 1996).
23 See Tanaka (2010) for details. See Holler (2002) for the contrast between Logos and Eros.

Chapter 7

1 The term *topeng* means both a masked performance and a mask itself. To avoid confusion, a *topeng* mask is referred to as a mask in this chapter while a masked performance is referred to as *topeng*. Local terms are italicized and Indonesian terms are marked [I] for the purpose of distinguishing them from Balinese terms. A majority of interviews were conducted in the Indonesian language.
2 What we have in mind here is the argument of A. Gell, who used the term "agency" for the capacity of a person or thing "who/which are seen as initiating causal sequences of a particular type, that is, events caused by acts of mind or will or intention, rather than the mere concatenation of physical events" (Gell 1998: 16).
3 *Topeng wali* is also called *topeng Sidakarya*. When it is performed by one actor, it is called *topeng pajegan*.
4 Slattum et al. is a book for a general readership rather than academic (Slattum & Schraub 2003). It offers a systematic overview of Balinese mask culture, including *topeng*. It covers the characteristics and functions of performances in each genre as well as the process of producing masks and associated rituals. However, it devotes a lot of space to a systematic arrangement of photographs of masks against a black background. It seems to follow, in some respects, the tendency of Young and Dunn to extract and schematize the characters represented by the masks, focusing on comparative presentations of the characters represented by particular masks.
5 The account of *topeng wali* performances presented here will be brief due to space limitations. For a more detailed description of *topeng wali* performances, see Emigh (1996: 118–170).

6 Among various stories about the origin of Sidakarya, the most well-known legend claims that it was Brahmana Keling, a priest with supernatural power who came from Java to Bali at the time of King Waturenggong, around the 16th Century (Dunn 1983: 74–75; Coldiron 2004: 70–71).
7 These two photos were taken by Warren Fong. All other photos are by the author.
8 Fushiki refers to *taksu* in the context of bamboo flute (*suling*) performances in Chapter 8. *Taksu* is a concept widely used in all forms of performing arts and other general activities as well as *topeng*.
9 Conversely, it is possible to influence *niskala* from the *sekala* realm. *Topeng* is regarded as an activity to entertain the *niskala* dwellers who gather at the scene of a ritual and ask them for assistance.
10 At least in the village where I stayed, the higher caste people never ate the food offerings made by lower castes to their ancestral spirits. This further supports the idea that *lungsuran* carries the power of a specific deity to which the offering is made.
11 I have never conducted the *pewintenan* purification ritual because I do not play the part of Sidakarya. Nevertheless, I did receive a smaller purification ritual called *melukad*. It was recommended by my host family and friends who were concerned about my safety as I was frequently participating in ritual *topeng* performances.
12 The Japanese word for mask is "kamen", which literally means "temporal face".
13 In his study of *noh* and other Japanese masks, T. Watsuji stated, "Although it is actually the actor wearing a mask who moves, the mask has acquired a body from the standpoint of the effect" (Watsuji 1988: 15–16).
14 Dewa Agung was conversant in religious and literary knowledge and remained very influential inside and outside Klungkung even after the establishment of the Republic of Indonesia (Vickers 1989: 136–137, 166–167).
15 As mentioned earlier, many *topeng* masks are owned by actors today. It appears that in previous times masks were usually owned by temples in some regions.
16 It is interesting to compare this point with the "ephemerality/transience" of paper-cutting discussed by Niwa in Chapter 1. The "transience" of paper cutouts leads to their yearly replacement, encouraging new production activities periodically. The solidity of wooden masks and the fragility of paper cutouts are quite different material characteristics, but both influence people into the future.

Chapter 8

1. It is believed to have been established in the medieval period (around the 16th century) according to the historical classification system for Balinese gamelan. It is performed at temple ceremonies and court rituals as part of the ritual proceedings. There is a tendency to choose a program that is suitable for the particular occasion but the performance itself does not contain ritual acts. The story, music and dance can be completely different depending on the traditions of individual villages.
2. Ethnomusicological studies include Sugiyama (2005, 2008), acoustic engineering studies include Shiokawa (2005 etc.), Carterette and Kendall (1994), and Sven-Amin (2009), and psychoacoustical studies include Carterette, Kendall and DeVale (1993), and Rapoport, Shatz and Blass (2008) among others.
3. One example of this force is orchestration, a systematized application of the limitations and characteristics of musical instruments to music, especially orchestral music.
4. *Gambuh* in this village emphasizes dances with fewer traditional songs (and very few instrumental numbers) compared to other places. The dances of this village reportedly feature consciously polished movements and more lively expressions than those of other villages. Only fragments of the melodies and rhythms have been passed on and some songs had not been played in an ensemble for a long time. Consequently, the melodies and rhythms were playing two different beats in some compositions. Under these circumstance, the village frequently initiated revitalization activities, willingly accepting assistance from foreign scholars and the willing participation of young people.
5. Unlike fipple end-blown flutes, a ring flute has no block (fipple) inside the duct. The windway (duct) is cut at the node of the bamboo, a ring is wrapped around it, and air is blown through the labium (edge) for sound production.
6. Circular breathing is a playing techniques for wind instruments in which the player blows air into the duct while simultaneously inhaling in order to play the melody with no interruption. There are a number of ways to achieve this.
7. The word *saih* needs to be used carefully as it is sometimes used to mean a scale.
8. *Pathetan* was originally a Javanese gamelan term which scholars borrowed to discuss Balinese gamelan. It is not in common use in Bali. In the context of *gambuh*, *tekap* is a more common term.

9 *Selisir* is the most basic, *baro* has more borrowed notes, *lebang* is more variable, and *senaren* consists of the lowest notes.
10 According to *suling* players from B village, the fingerings reported in earlier studies were provided by an informant who mainly played in the traditional style of another village but who had some ties with a player from B village in the past. The authors appear to have failed to reconfirm the B village fingerings, confusing the two styles when they wrote their studies.
11 The measurement was carried out through an analysis of recordings (wav format, 16 bit, sampling frequency of 44,100 Hz) using a spectrum analyzer called WaveSpectra (4,096 point FFT (minimum frequency resolution 10.77 Hz), Hanning). The spectrum and the cent were used for comparison. The formula $n = 1200 \cdot \log_2$ (frequency ratio) was used for conversion into cents.
12 I have numbered the fingerings in the figure for convenience. Where there are variations of a particular fingering, they are indicated by an alphabetic character next to the number for that particular fingering.
13 Based on C's interview (August 2009). All of C's comments hereafter come from the same interview.
14 It appears, however, that K was originally a dancer and not necessarily an excellent *suling* maker himself. I asked his son W but he was unclear how good K's knowledge and skills were concerning *suling* (interviewed in August 2009).
15 I attended these classes while studying in this department from 1995 to 1998.
16 The interviewee was the only surviving *suling* maker-player of B village as at August 2009. Information gained from the interview is reliable.
17 Because of this, the manufacturing technology from P village, D city, is now widely known and its terminology and technique are spoken of as if they are commonly used throughout Bali.
18 *Suling* players who do not manufacture *suling* often try to make one by measuring the finger width (*nyali*) instead of the diameter and the circumference, copying the *suling* they already have.
19 The ratio called *sikut kutus* or *asta pada* in P village, D city, means eight times the circumference, and *sikut sanga*, an old ratio that is no longer used today, means nine times.
20 An earlier researcher reported that the bamboo variety was *Tiying tamblang*, but that is the same variety as *Tiying gendanpal*. *Tiying gendanpal* produces clear and beautiful sounds. Another variety, *Tiying jajan* (reportedly a *Bambusa* sp. but that is unconfirmed), is often mentioned. It has thicker walls

and is commonly used to make *semat* (whittled bamboo sticks to secure or shape offerings or vessels made of palm leaves; sometimes replaced by staplers these days) for making palm leaf offerings.
21 Many people use a file to make an opening, but C says that he never uses a file. Tools used in *suling* making, especially in the hole making stage, include *mutik*, *taji* (a steel blade tied to the rooster's leg in cock fighting), thin bamboo stick and sandpaper.
22 In P village, D city, the fingerhole size is derived on the basis that the (inner) diameter of the bamboo equals the fingerhole circumference.
23 The verb form of *tekap* is *nekap*, which is synonymous with *nutup* (to close).
24 Obviously, this much difference in size produces completely different sounds, giving the impression that it is a completely different gamelan. The size of this smaller *suling gambuh* is the same as that used in university classes. This may be attributed to the influence of the ISI-Denpasar teacher S of P village, D city (pseudonyms).
25 Gamelan is commonly played with paired instruments, which are tuned to produce subtly different pitches in order to generate interference beats (*ombak*). The instruments are made so that an acoustic characteristic described as "sounding well" is achieved when the beats are organized well in an ensemble as a whole. Adjustment of interference beats is often given priority in tuning. Instruments that are pitched the same do not produce the beat effect and the sounds are drowned out; this condition is described as "cowering". This is also the case with *suling gambuh*. It is likely to be the matching of frequency ratios perceived by human ears that is required, and not the complete matching of pitches. I must defer discussion on this point to a future study.
26 Applying oil to the inside of the flute can resolve this *getap* state. Further fine-adjustments can be made using sandpaper so that the forces (of air) applied to *pemanis* and finger-holes are equal (*magang*).
27 The concept of *rasa* is generally translated as emotion or feeling but it is not a human emotion or feeling. In Balinese gamelan performance, direct expression of human emotions in music or dance is avoided. Students are taught that emotion (*emosi*) and expression (*ekspresi*) are different.
28 In Chapter 13, Kawai points out "one aspect of *things* [*mono*] that can be recognized only in the context of their relationship with the human body, equipped with five senses that are always open to the environment.". The memory mentioned here is *mono* in this sense and should be understood as

mono because it directly connects to the embodied playing techniques and the senses that perform them as well as the compositions learned through human hearing, memory, and bodily kinesthetic learning that is repeated until the body can move naturally. These are not passed on in the form of musical scores or recordings.

29 Taboos concerning bronze musical instruments are generally described from the perspective of the symbolist world view. It is said that "gods reside" in the sounds of bronze musical instruments but I have not studied how this belief relates to the sense of the *suling*'s "aliveness" as discussed in this chapter and whether the sense of "aliveness" exists for bronze musical instruments as well. Nevertheless, the relationship between bronze musical instruments and humans is probably different from that between *suling* and humans because modifications to the former are actively carried out even after they have been used in performances. I would like to research this topic in the future.

30 The instrumentalist and symbolist world views are concepts drawn from Tanaka (2009), used to examine the dynamics operating on humans and *mono* (*things*). The term *things* is used in place of *mono* here as per Tanaka. According to him, "the typical relationship governing humans and *things* is the 'instrumentalist relationship' in which the former use the latter". The term *things* in this case is used to include instruments and resources and the relationship entails the dynamic in which "the former (humans) control and use the latter (*things*)". Tanaka calls this type of perspective where "the subject-object relationship is always unilateral" the "instrumentalist world view". He also says that the study of *things* has a viewpoint to see (*things*) as symbols" from which it is regarded that "*things* are signs carrying meanings" or "the object to be deciphered as texts" and "the unilateral subject-object directionality of decipher remains the same even if *things* as texts carry multiple meanings". In other words, it is no different from the aforementioned instrumentalist world view in terms of dynamics. Tanaka calls this "standpoint that positions *things* as texts" the "symbolist world view." I follow this usage when I use the term in this chapter.

31 If people listened to the sound as *mono* with utmost care, the sound would not change and people could endeavor to stop it from changing as soon as they noticed a sign of change. The sound continues to change because people deliberately "do not listen". I have not mentioned it in this chapter, but we come across many occasions in Balinese gamelan in which some significantly out of tune keyboard instruments are played with other instruments in an

ensemble. In these situations, people deliberately "do not listen"; they "ignore" the out of tune sound no matter how loud it may be.

32 In Chapter 13, Kawai states,
> It does not feel too far off the mark to say that this is one way for *things* to manifest. Sound, wind, air and smell are all constituent elements of the environment in which people place themselves and act. I would like to think that they can be regarded as entities with materiality – i.e., *things* – in that they manifest their presence by infiltrating human space through the medium of various physical sense organs.

33 Although I could not discuss it in detail in this chapter, it is worth noting that changes in people's lifestyle, the living environment and the natural environment in Bali in recent years have dramatically reduced the availability of bamboo and timber materials, significantly affecting the manufacture of musical instruments.

Chapter 9

1 See Imamura (1992) for arguments surrounding fetishism after Marx. The power of *mono* (*things*) is expressed in Japanese words such as *misemono* (freak show) and *mononoke* (specter) (Yamaguchi, Kinoshita and Sakairi 1999; Kamata 2009).

2 Among studies that are critical of a functionalist understanding of divination, Zeitlyn (1993) is informative. Zeitlyn focuses on the place where divination is performed and its format (how things are used, how questions are asked). (See Hamamoto 1993 for a similar perspective.)

3 Ishii (2005) argues that, in a ritual paired with divination, *things* alter the client's destiny by taking the client's place. Kondō (2009) discusses African society, where magical reality construction and non-magical reality comprehension coexist based on Kuki (2000)'s argument on contingency. If I borrow Kuki's expressions, what *things* show in divination is a hypothetical contingency by "encounter of two" independent variables. A contingency such as this takes on the aspect of destiny.

4 Similarly, Kawai (2006) finds the generation of meanings in divination at the intersection of the act of perceiving *things* and the act of interpretation.

5 Astrology arrived in India from Greece and Babylonia in around the 1st century BCE and the foundations of astrology (*jōsyam*) were laid by the 6th century CE (Varahamihira 1995; De Fouw & Svoboda 1996).

6 Since the 1960s, astrology has spread to various levels of Indian society

across geographical and caste boundaries thanks to the development of information and transportation networks. There are many magazines and books concerning astrology in book stores and many divination websites on the Internet. While drawing horoscope charts used to require specialist knowledge, anyone can prepare them using computer applications these days.
7 This chapter is based on interviews and participant observation studies I conducted in Tamil Nadu for about two months in August 2005 and September 2008.
8 A small drum made of teak (*tēkku*; *Tectona grandis*) and its sound. The Nāyakaṉs play it in front of the door in order to draw householders' attention. The Nāyakaṉs are commonly known as Kuṭukuṭupai kāraṉ (people who play drums).
9 See Coleman (1996) for reified words in evangelical religious practices.
10 Cuvaṭi also plays the role of "ancient wisdom" in the practice of nadi astrology (*nāṭi jōsyam*), using the so-called Agastya Leaves. This style of divination was started by a caste called Valluvar during the 1960s and experienced a global boom.
11 Both gods are worshipped in Tamil Nadu. Mahamāi ("great mother", Māriyammaṉ) is a goddess who brings and cures smallpox. Murukaṉ was originally the god of mountain tribes but syncretized with Skanda (Ganesha's younger brother) in the 4th or 5th century.
12 Similarly, the sets of cards used in Cameroon's spider divination are not standardized in terms of their number, size, shape, drawn symbols, material and pairing, either (Gufler 1995: 54)

Chapter 10
1 Chimpanzees in Bossou eat at least 200 kinds of food (Sugiyama 1992).
2 S.J. Gould (1977) suspected that Engels "stole" the idea from Ernst Haeckel.

Chapter 11
1 The bonobo is a great ape, also known as the pygmy chimpanzee. The bonobo and the chimpanzee are the two species of the genus *Pan* which are closest to humans phylogenetically and genetically. It is thought that humans diverged from their common ancestors about six to seven million years ago and that the chimpanzee and the bonobo diverged about 2.4 million years ago. Because food sharing is found in these two species, it is reasonable to conclude that this behavior pre-existed the divergence of humans and the genus *Pan*.

2 We are referring to food sharing between adult individuals. This behavior is also found in capuchin monkeys. However, they are excluded from discussion here because their sharing interaction seems different from that of the genus *Pan* in that they do not exhibit stinting (see Note 3 below) as far as I can deduce from videos by F. de Waal and therefore a comparative analysis is not possible.
3 Many primatologists do not recognize this behavior as significant because they consider food sharing in the genus *Pan* to be a passive act of letting another have part of food only in response to begging. However, it is clear that the food-holder exhibits internal conflict about its desire for exclusive possession in the course of deciding to share. The passivity can thus be interpreted as "stinting", a reluctance to give. Recognizing this aspect of the behavior is tantamount to crossing the Rubicon, changing primates from the subject of behaviorist research to the subject of sociological research. This allows us to take up the socio-psychological aspect of food sharing such as value sharing and the renunciation of desire for analysis, and hence to explore the horizons of the genus *Pan* society as we are doing in this chapter. The socio-psychological traits of chimpanzees inferred from the interpretation of "stinting" are consistent with findings in animal psychology, artificial language learning and observations in captivity (Kuroda 1999).
4 This "ownership" is incomplete in the human sense, however, in that as soon as an individual moves away from the food, it no longer belongs to anyone. Furthermore, as this "ownership" only applies to food that is instantly consumed, "someone's thing" is a temporary condition and therefore it is never attributed with the meaning "a thing from someone," nor does it infer a history of relations.
5 Although some extant primates such as colobus and spider monkeys have vestigial thumbs and they use the remaining four fingers to grasp, it is thought that five fingers with an opposed thumb were of the utmost importance for primates to get a firm grasping ability in their evolution.
6 For example, the human is the only primate species that can move the individual fingers almost independently of one another (a requirement for playing the piano and the flute, for example) and the human ability to use the thumb and the index finger to pinch small things is outstanding.
7 Objects in very close range are sensed tactually without actually touching. This is different from the perception of touch, and is called anticipatory touch (Rizzolatti & Sinigaglia 2009).

8 A symptom involving the inability to perceive both space and objects on one side of the field of vision. In cases of hemispatial neglect of distal space, patients can see and draw things in the unrecognizable side of distal space by using a stick to touch them.
9 It is easy to confirm that a similar situation occurs in humans, too. For instance, imagine there is an open notebook on top of a stack of closed notebooks before you. When you begin to extend your hand with the intention to shift the open notebook to the side, you might notice that your fingers are spread or your wrist is turned over from the start and the sensation of strength in the fingers as you are about to shift it is already different than when you extend your hand towards the stack of closed notebooks. This may be clearer when you extend your hand to a heavy book because you sense its weight in advance and prepare an appropriate grasp force for it. This condition of the fingers demonstrates that hand that is "about to grasp it" has its own perception of the forms of things. It suggests that a simulation has been generated on the assumption that the object is something to be touched or grasped in that way based on previous experience.
10 Needless to say, these things, *sugari*, *sasae* and substrates form a continuum; their boundaries vary depending on the weight and strength of the individual.
11 For example, there was an incident in E1 group in Wamba in which a young male bonobo engaging in furious displays on a tall tree fell to the ground when a branch snapped. The broken branch pierced his belly and killed him (private communication from T. Sakamaki).
12 I think that *sugari* is the thing that is most profoundly linked with the existence of primates. It lurks in the depths of human life, too. Every form of play that makes human infants feel dizzy and excited can be traced to the world of primate *sugari*. We are almost continuously grasping in one way or another, and can feel profound emptiness when we have no-thing to cling to.
13 I was able to observe this in the gorilla enclosure at Howletts Wild Animal Park by courtesy of J. Aspinal in 1994.
14 Viki, a female chimpanzee raised by the Hayeses, one day began to mimic the act of dragging something by her hand behind her and started pretending that the imaginary string was sometimes caught by something, looking back and pulling the string with a jerk. One time, she acted as if the invisible string was caught by a handle, landed on her bottom with both arms extended as if she was holding on to a taut string, and called "Mama!". When Mrs. Hayes pretended to remove the string from the handle and give it back to Viki, Viki gave her a pleased expression and resumed her pretend dragging. Next, Mrs.

Hayes began pretending to drag something and get stuck with another thing. Viki stared at the point where the imaginary thing was supposed to be tied to the imaginary string and said "Boo". This imaginary thing-play eventually stopped when Mrs. Hayes began to play again which behavior somehow frightened Viki.

15 Some might conclude that there is an ownership-like relationship between a thing and the subject in Japanese macaques because the dominant does not take food from the subordinate, but "ownership" does not arise in a society without sharing according to this interpretation. See Kuroda (1999) for more details.
16 They are thought to be two different systems acquired in the respective phyletic lines (Kuroda 2010).
17 The phenomenon in which one individual starts playing with stones and another individual, who has not shown any interest until then, begins to take an interest in the stones was called "popularity" by M. Huffman (1984).
18 Theft is in fact a characteristic of the sociality of food. The rare occasions of stealing actually demonstrate that food sharing and ownership in the genus *Pan* operate on the basis of mutual self-control. In the un-equality principle society, the highly restrictive self-control towards food in another individual's possession prevents both sharing and stealing. In other words, it blocks the sociality of things. See Kuroda (1999) for more details.
19 See Note 3 above.
20 My observations of great apes in captivity include gorillas at Howletts Wild Animal Park, England, and the Brazzaville Gorilla Orphanage, Congo, chimpanzees at Burgers' Zoo in Arnhem, the Netherlands, and bonobos at the Planckendael Zoo, Belgium.
21 According to my direct observations as well as video recordings.
22 As evidence against this argument, some people may be aware of an episode in which a third party reaped benefits by alternately supporting two individuals fighting for dominance (de Waal 1982; Nishida 1981). However, it is rare even for a cunning individual to change sides on the same day and supportive behavior is so simple that it is unlikely to provide a lasting medium.
23 This type of interaction is confined to young females who are in a sexual rut and highly promiscuous. In general food sharing of the genus *Pan*, the process is structured to be controlled for food as the immediate goal and there is no confusion (promiscuity) as to its meaning (11.4.4).
24 Behaviorally, primates use multiple logics. For example, grooming provides lice

as food for the groomer but it also serves to form an affiliative relationship (Mori et al. 1977).
25 The topic of this discussion is derived from the Edo-period haiku of Issa Kobayashi: "'Gimme that harvest moon!', cries the crying child" [Translation by D. G. Lanoue]. While this haiku can be interpreted in many ways, because of Issa's longing for a deceased child and love of children, I use it literally as the description of an infant asking an adult to get an unreachable thing in order to satisfy his/her desire.
26 Wild bonobos and chimpanzees seldom pick up the writing utensils and towels left behind by observers. Even in an experiment in which towels and other objects were thrown in the enclosure at Burgers' Zoo, it was generally more than several tens of seconds before chimpanzees picked them up.
27 See the case of a young female referred to in 11.4.6.

Chapter 12

1 The early computer scientists who invented this technology, including Alan Kay, were strongly influenced by McLuhan.
2 In fact, treating objects such as animals which are normally not considered to be "things" as "things" has heuristic significance, as Tokoro and Kawai state in the "Introduction". McLuhan's theory of body extensions may appear to be instrumentalist on the surface, and it includes animals. "An artifact pushed far enough tends to reincorporate the user. The Hun lived on their horse day and night" (McLuhan and Powers 1989).
3 In a holistic material culture theory, neither the body, things, nor the environment are privileged in advance. Of course, there is always a value hierarchy surrounding the body, things and the environment in everyday social life. However, this hierarchy is generated by a society's value system and must not be assumed a priori by researchers.
4 The ethnological examples discussed in this chapter have also been addressed in a report for general readership (Konaka 2002) and a comparative study of pastoralists (Konaka 2010).
5 Some may think it is contradictory that livestock, as a 'mere' interface between the body and the environment, forms the important base domain. From our perspective, however, the concept of "interface" does not carry any connotations of being secondary. The base domain and the target domain are mutually interchangeable, in this case.

Chapter 13

1. The Chamus customarily allocate one herder to each herd. The herder can be male or female. An increasing number of married middle-aged and older people (but rarely older women) are assuming the grazing duties because schooling has made unmarried boys and girls unavailable for this task.
2. The Chamus language does not make a distinction between "sound" and "voice".
3. Other verbs of perception associated with the five senses include "see/watch/look at: *-dol/-rip/-ingurr*", "be seen: *-duaa*", "smell: *-inguaya*", "taste: *-ichamicham*", and "touch (something): *-ibung*" which are independent words with different etymologies. Unlike "hear/be heard: *-ning*", these verbs do not contain other meanings such as "feel", "notice", "understand" and "accept". While these are only a few examples of perception verbs, this suggests that the verb *-ning* is the prototype perception verb in the Chamus language and that the auditory sense plays the central or primary role in their experiences of perception, sensation and cognition.
4. According to Kawada (1992b: 18), the Mossi people in Burkina Faso make a distinction between a meaningful sound (a sound with message: *koega*) and a meaningless noise (*buure*). The word *koega* also refers to the vocalizing organ of throat and includes emotive songs and dance drum sounds as well as all comprehensible words. Incomprehensible songs sung in the languages of other tribes, songs that are unpleasant to the ear, and drum sounds unsuitable for dancing are called *buure*. The source of sound is irrelevant to the sound classification system of the Mossi. Animal voices such as the voice of a dog telling the owner about an approaching visitor, the voice of a mother goat calling to her baby goat, and the voice of a rooster declaring the approach of dawn are all regarded as *koega*. Although *buwata* in the Chamus language is similar to *buure* in some aspects, the Chamus sound classification system is different from that of the Mossi in that the voices of wild animals and the sounds of vehicles coming from afar are considered to be *buwata*, that a voice carrying no particular message is considered to be *ltolilyo* if it comes from a single identifiable animal, and the clamoring of livestock during milking is classified as *buwata* even though it probably carries stronger messages.
5. The verb "listen to *(-inining)*" is never used in conjunction with *liiyo* (solitude). This suggests that *liiyo* is not something to which one actively and "consciously listens" or "lends one's ear" but it is something that is passively "heard" or "felt".

6   For instance, where the Japanese would describe a headache as "having a throbbing headache", the Chamus would explain the condition as "too much blood is coming into the blood vessels in my temple and jumping around violently" (Kawai 1998: 210–211).
7   The Chamus repeat the expression "Be quiet / Silent (*tegirai*)" earnestly when children are too excited or complaining loudly, when people are vociferously protesting, slandering or moaning about others, and especially when someone is crying.
8   Tsukutsukubōshi is a Japanese onomatopoetic name, referring to its song (sound).
9   Bird songs are turned into onomatopoeic phrases or treated as harbingers in many parts of the world. For insect sounds, Uchibori (1996: 10–11) reports that the Iban people of Borneo consider the voice of a cricket called lon (lo:n), which is heard only on clear nights, to be announcing that "All is well", for example.
10 While I have interpreted *liiyo* as "loneliness (solitude)" for this chapter, I have no space to discuss in detail the relationship between the condition of "solitude" or "*liiyo* ate" in the Chamus and the extent of the meaning of the word "loneliness" here. I must stress that we cannot consider it synonymous with "loneliness" in modern society, as in Sartre's philosophy, where it is defined as isolation from a social network or exclusion from the sociality that makes life meaningful (Sartre 2012) or as containing the implication that we choose our own existence (Sartre 1948: 57). Nonetheless, according to Uchibori (2013: 45) for example,

> The common image of solitude seems to refer to the concrete and self-conscious existence of human individuals, who came to be referred to as egosyntonic in modern society. Undeniably, there is an affiliative relationship between solitariness and modernity. However, the central point of the current discussion is the proposition that the basis of the development of such affinity is something inherent in human assemblage, and in fact characterizes the existence of human groups in crucial aspects within an evolutionary framework, and there is no reason to think that the concept of "loneliness" is specifically modern. In contrast, Luhmann argues that one of the important aspects of the relationship between society and interaction is time, which can be understood using the concept of episode.

Interactions are episodes of societal processes. They are possible only on the basis of the certainty that social communication has been going on before the episode begins, so that one can presuppose sediments of earlier communication; and they are possible only because one knows that social communication will still be possible after the episode concludes. The beginning and end of an interaction are merely caesuras in society's autopoiesis (Luhmann 1995: 406–407).

This suggestion that people become "individuals" in the gaps in the autopoiesis of society for the period between the end of one interaction and the beginning of the next seems to describe the condition "*liiyo* ate (solitude)" in the Chamus well. Similarly, Sugawara (2007: 117–118) has analyzed the social lives of a hunter in a San hunting-and-gathering community in Botswana about his experience of bow-and-arrow hunting alone and found that the hunter returns to his camp community loaded with the events he has lived through on his own in the middle of an isolated wilderness, desperate to surrender his isolated experience to communal understanding. In other words, we can assume the universality of the desire that "one's singular experience has significance to the communal interest".

11 Kuroda states in Chapter 11 that "non-solid objects such as water, air and fire should perhaps be placed in a different category of things" and suggests that the materiality of things is attributed to their solidity in our common perception.

12 For example, Niwa in Chapter 1 of this volume, Kawada (1988, 1992a, 1992b), Kimura (2003), Sawada (1996), Takemitsu and Kawada (1992), Yamada (ed.) (2000), Roseman (1993), and Helliwell (1988) among others.

13 Schafer's concept of the soundscape (landscapes composed of sounds) is informative for understanding the phenomena addressed in this chapter in that it covers a wide range of sounds that fill our everyday world. The relationship between natural sounds in the environment and human perception is one of its central questions. However, the proponents of this school focus their discussions on actively "listening" to sounds, in contrast to this chapter's focus on "(passive) hearing" or "being heard", be they natural or artificial, and its emphasis on the importance of the normally unnoticed sound worlds and the act of "listening" (and associated emotional senses) that has been relegated since the emergence of vision-dominant literal culture and its reinstatement as well as their application and development in conjunction with education (music education) and practices such as sound design (the creation of new sound environments) (Schafer 1992, 1977; Yamagishi and Yamagishi 1999; Nakagawa 2004; Torigoe 2008 among others).

I have therefore been unable to directly address soundscape theory in this chapter. Meanwhile, in a collection of papers written by ethnomusicologists and cultural anthropologists (Yamada (ed.) 2000), the editor points out issues with the soundscape framework, including that "soundscape is treated as if it exists independently of human activity" and that "being biased towards listening, that is, listening activity is over-emphasized (an environment is regarded too much as an object of listening activity whereas it is supposed to be perceived through all of the five senses or the whole body sense combining all of them in the first place)" (Yamada 2000: 8–9). The latter has also been rephrased in the book: "the visual sense and the auditory sense should not be treated in an oppositional manner" and that "various senses are interactive and such interactions between the senses are produced in varying ratios and proportions depending on culture" (ibid: 272). Further, Yamada notices that humans acoustically act on their soundscape and cause its acoustic features to change constantly, pointing to the importance of the interrelationship between humans and their sound environment, i.e., that humans hear sounds from the environment and at the same time they act on the environment acoustically or utilize the environment acoustically (Ibid: 9–10). Schafer also represents the interrelationship between humans and their sound environment using the concept of "acoustic ecology" and proposes to deal with sounds in relation to life and society as well as to study how a soundscape influences the physical response and behavioral characteristics of lifeforms living in a certain environment (Schafer 1977). In contrast, the leading ethnomusicologist Feld (1988, 2000) proposes the concept of "acoustemology", stating that "Soundscapes are invested with significance by those whose bodies and lives resonate with them in social time and space… By acoustemology I wish to suggest a union of acoustics and epistemology, and to investigate the primacy of sound as a modality of knowing and being in the world". He also states that "Sound both emanates from and penetrates bodies" and that "Following the lead established by Maurice Merleau-Ponty's *Phenomenology of Perception*, then echoed in Don Ihde's *Listening and Voice: A Phenomenology of Sound*, my notion of acoustemology means to explore the reflexive and historical relationships between hearing and speaking, listening and sounding" (Feld 2000: 40). Yamada, also an ethnomusicologist, proposes the theory of "acoustic body" and focuses his argument on "the dynamic interaction between the voice and the body" in the Waxei people in the tropical forests of Papua New Guinea. In explaining that "The voice and the body that resonates with the voice have the power to mediate the relationship between humans and the environment", Yamada states that "Songs combine with the stream of water through the body and depict the way the voice flows in the stream as songs; I would like to call this body that oscillates and flows as it resonates with the voice the acoustic body" (Yamada 2000: 109). As these arguments are developed with the "human voice or song" as an essential element, again I have been unable to address them directly in this chapter. It will be a major challenge for the future to connect these arguments to our understanding of "the Chamus sound environment" in general or an even broader "Chamus sensory environment" of the five senses not confined to sound that is reliant on the auditory and tactile senses.

* This chapter is based on the research project supported by Grant-in-Aid for Scientific Research provided by the Japan Society for the Promotion of Science (Project numbers: #15520513, #20242026, #15K03034), and the ILCAA (of Tokyo University of Foreign Studies) Joint Research Project, "Human Society in Evolutionary Perspective (4)".

III-3

1. Yoshitarō Kamakura was designated a living national treasure in 1973 as a practitioner of *kataezome*.
2. *Rukujyū* is made by sun-drying the Okinawa-style hard tofu made from thick soy milk (*shima-dōfu*) until it is completely free of moisture in winter. It is used as an underlay for pattern carving.
3. *Tsutsugaki* is a *bingata* dyeing technique which does not use stencils. It involves drawing the pattern freehand with paste based on a sketch before dyeing. The process requires fewer tools as the stencil is not used.

Bibliography

Adorno, T. W. (1963), *Dissonanzen, Musik in der verwalteten Welt*. Göttubgen: Vandenhoek & Ruprecht.

Aiello, L. C. and P. Wheeler (1995) "The expensive-tissue hypothesis: The brain and the digestive system in human and primate evolution". *Current Anthropology*, 36: 199–221.

Akamatsu, S. (2003) *Karuchādo pāru – Shinju no miryoku* (Cultured pearl: The attraction of the pearl). Shinju Shimbunsha.

Appadurai, A. (1986) "Introduction: Commodities and the politics of value". In A. Appadurai (ed.), *The Social Life of Things: Commodities in Cultural Perspective*. New York: Cambridge University Press, 3–63.

Ari Astika, I N., I Gst. N. Hari Mahardika et al. (2005) *Laporan Penelitian Pasang Surut Gambuh Pedungan di Tengah Laju Budaya Global* (How to install the declining Gambuh Pedungan in rapidly changing global culture). Denpasar: ISI-Denpasar.

Arnold, D. E. (1985) *Ceramic Theory and Cultural Process*. Cambridge: Cambridge University Press.

Arnold, D. E. (1993) *Ecology and Ceramic Production in an Andean Community*. Cambridge: Cambridge University Press.

Artana, I Md. (1986) *Mengenal Gending-gending Gambuh di Desa Pedungan* (Get to know Gambuh pieces in Pedungan Village). Denpasar: Akademi Seni Tari Indonesia.

Arya Sugiartha, I Gd. (2008) *Gamelan Pegambuhan 'Tambang Emas' Karawitan Bali* (Traditional Balinese music Gamelan Pegambuhan 'Tambang Emas'). Denpasar: Institut Seni Indonesia-Denpasar and Sari Kahyangan.

Bateson, G. (2000), *Steps to an Ecology of Mind: Collected Essays in Anthropology, Psychiatry, Evolution and Epistemology*. Chicago: University of Chicago Press.

Beck, B. B. (1980) *Animal Tool Behaviour: The Use and Manufacture of Tools by Animals*. New York: Garland STPM Press.

Beeman, W. O. (1993) "The anthropology of theater and spectacle". *Annual Review of Anthropology*, 22: 369–393.

Bergson, H. (1978) *Matter and memory*. N. M. Paul & W. S. Palmer (trs.). New York: Humanities Press.
Best, S. B. (1989) *Lakeba: The Prehistory of a Fijian Island*. Michigan: University Microfilms.
Bestor, T. (2004), *Tsukiji: The Fish Market at the Center of the World*. Berkeley: University of California Press.
Bharathi, S. B. (1998) "Ritual healing: Metamedical discourse and discursive practice of a South Indian nomadic sub-caste". *Man in India*, 78 (3 & 4): 239–253.
Bird-David, N. (1999) "'Animism' revisited: Personhood, environment, and relational epistemology". *Current Anthropology*, 40 Supplement: 67–91.
Black Grace. http://www.blackgrace.co.nz/ (accessed 17/07/2010).
Boʻriev, O. and I. Xojamurodov (2006) *Oʻzbek xalgining boqiy qadriyatlari*. Toshkent: Qarsh Nasaf.
Boinski, S., R. P. Quatrone, and H. Swartz (2000) "Substrate and tool use by Brown capuchins in Suriname: Ecological contexts and cognitive base". *American Anthropologist*, 102: 741–761.
Boivin, N. (2008) *Material Cultures, Material Minds: The Impact of Things on Human Thought, Society, and Evolution*. New York: Cambridge University Press.
Boswall, J. (1977) "Tool using by birds and related behavior". *Aviculture Magazine*, 84: 162–166.
Braudel, F. (1955–1979) *Civilisation matérielle, économie et capitalisme, XVe-XVIIIe siècle*. Paris: Armand Collins.
Braun, D. P. (1983) "Pots as tools". In J. A. Moore & A. S. Keene (eds.), *Archaeological Hammers and Theories*. New York: Academic Press, 107–134.
Brenner, S. A. (1998) *The Domestication of Desire: Women, Wealth, and Modernity in Java*. New Jersey: Princeton University Press.
Brunet, M., F. Guy, D. Pilbeam, H. T. Mackaye, A. Likius, D. Ahounta, A. Beauvilain, C. Blondel, H. Bocherens, J.-R. Boisserie, L. De Bonis, Y. Coppens, J. Dejax, C. Denys, P. Duringer, V. Eisenmann, G. Fanone, P. Fronty, D. Geraads, T. Lehmann, F. Lihoreau, A. Louchart, A. Mahamat, G. Merceron. G. Mouchelin, O. Otero, P. Pelaez Campomanes, M. Ponce De Leon, J.-C. Rage, M. Sapanet, M. Schuster, J. Sudre, P. Tassy, X. Valentin, P. Vignaud, L. Viriot, A. Zazzo and C. Zollikofer (2002) "A new hominid from the upper Miocene of Chad, Central Africa". *Nature*, 418: 145–151.

Buchli, V. (ed.) (2002) *Material Culture Reader*. New York: Berg.
Butler, J. (1990) *Gender Trouble: Feminism and Subversion of Identity*. New York: Routledge.
Canale, G. R., C. E. Guidorizzi, M. C. M. Kierulff, and C. A. F. R. Gatto (2009) "First record of tool use by wild populations of the yellow-breasted capuchin monkey (*Cebus xanthosternos*) and new records for the bearded capuchin (*Cebus libidinosus*)". *American Journal of Primatology*, 71: 366–372.
Candlin F. and G. Raiford (2009) *The Object Reader*. New York: Routledge.
Carpenter, A. (1887) "Monkeys opening oysters". *Nature*, 36: 53.
Carterette, E. C. and A. K. Roger (1994) "On the tuning and stretched octave of Javanese gamelans". *Leonardo Music Journal*, 4: 59–68.
Carterette, E. C., A. K. Roger & S. C. DeVale (1993) "Comparative acoustical and psychoacoustical analyses of gamelan instrument tones". *Journal of the Acoustical Society of Japan* (E) 14(6): 383–396.
Chen, Shanqiao (1988) "Ansai ren yu jianzhi yishu" (Ansai People and Paper-Cuts Art). In Ansai wenshi ziliao bianji weiyuanhui (ed.) *Ansai jianzhi yishu* (The art of Ansai paper-cuts). (Publisher unknown).
Cheperebestkaya, G. A. (1961) *O'zbekiston So'zanasi*. Toshkent: O'zSSR Davlat Badiiy Adabiyoti Nashriyoti.
Chiang, M. (1967) "Use of tools by wild macaque monkeys in Singapore". *Nature*, 214: 1258–1259.
Claridge, G. G. C. (1984) "Pottery and the Pacific: The clay factor". *New Zealand Journal of Archaeology*, 6: 37–46.
Clark, J. T. & M. G. Michlovic, (1996) "An early settlement in the Polynesian homeland: Excavations at 'Aoa valley, Tutuila island, American Samoa". *Journal of Field Archaeology*, 23: 151–167.
Coldiron, M. (2004) *Trance and Transformation of the Actor in Japanese Noh and Balinese Masked Dance-Drama*. New York: The Edwin Meller Press.
Clifford, J. and G. Marcus (1986) *Writing Culture: The Poetics and Politics of Ethnography*, Berkeley: University of California Press.
Coleman, S. (1996) "Words as things: Language, aesthetics and the objectification of Protestant evangelicalism". *Journal of Material Culture*, 1 (1): 107–128.
Crampton, T. (2005) "Concrete overlay for an ancient Burmese landscape". *New York Times*, 25 April. (http://www.nytimes.com/2005/04/21/world/asia/21iht-burma.html)
D'Alleva, A. (1998) *Arts of the Pacific Islands*. New York: Harry Abrams Ltd.
Darmosugito, Astuti Hendrato (1990) "The Philosophy of Batik". In Himpunan

Wastraprema (ed.), *Sekaring Jagad Ngayogyakarta Hadiningrat*. Jakarta: Himpunan Wastraprema, 98–104.

De Fouw, H. and R. Svoboda (1996) *Light on Life: An Introduction to the Astrology of India*. New Delhi: Penguin Books.

de Waal, F. B. M. (1982) *Chimpanzee Politics: Power and sex among apes*. New York: Harper and Row.

de Waal, F. B. M. (1999) "Cultural primatology comes of age". *Nature* 399: 635–636.

Denoon, D. (1997) "Human settlement". In D. Denoon, S. Firth, J. Linnekin, M. Meleisea & K. Nero (eds.), *The Cambridge History of the Pacific Islander*. Cambridge: Cambridge University Press, 37–41.

Descola, P. (1996) "Constructing natures: Symbolic ecology and social practice". In P. Descola and G. Pálsson (eds.), *Nature and Society: Anthropological Perspectives*. London: Routledge, 82–102.

Douglas, M. (1966) *Purity and Danger: An Analysis of Concepts of Pollution and Taboo*. London: Routledge and K. Paul and New York: Praeger

Dunn, D. G. (1983) *Topeng Pajegan: The Mask Dance of Bali*. Ph. D. dissertation, University of Union, Graduate School.

Edwards, E., C. Gosden and R. B. Phillips. (2006) *Sensible Objects: Colonialism, Museums and Material Culture*. Berg.

Ekman, P. and W. V. Friesen (1969) "The repertoire of nonverbal behavior: Categories, origins, usage and coding". *Semiotica*, 1 (1): 49–98.

Emigh, J. (1996) *Masked Performance: The Play of Self and Other in Ritual and Theater*. Philadelphia: University of Pennsylvania Press.

Engels, F. (1968) Dialectics of Nature. *Marx-Engels Collected Works*. London: Lawrence & Wishart.

Enthoven, R. E. (1990) *The Tribes and Castes of Bombay, Vol.III*. New Delhi: Asian Educational Services.

Feld, S. (1982) *Sound and sentiment: Birds, weeping, poetics, and song in Kaluli expression*. Durham: Duke University Press.

Feld, S. (2000) "Onkyō ninshikiron to oto sekai no jinruigaku: Papuanyūginia Bosabi no mori kara" (Anthropology of acoustemology and soundscape: From the Bosavi rainforest of Papua New Guinea). In Y. Yamada (ed.) *Shizen no oto, bunka no oto – Kankyō tono hibikiai* (Sounds of nature, sounds of culture: Reverberating with the environment) (Kōza ningen to kankyō Vol. 11). Shōwadō.

Fellers, J., and G. Fellers (1976) "Tool use in a social insect and its implications for competitive interactions". *Science*, 192: 70–72.

Fernandes, M. E. B. (1991) "Tool use and predation of oysters (*Crassostrea rhizophorae*) by the tufted capuchin, *Cebus apella apella*, in brackish water mangrove swamp". *Primates*, 32: 529–531.

Focillon, H. (1992) *The Life of Forms in Art*. C. B. Hogan & G. Kubler (trs.). New York: Zone Books.

Formaggia, M. C. (2000) *Gambuh Drama Tari Bali: Tinjauan Seni, Makna Emosional dan Musik, kata-kata dan Teks, Musik Gambuh Desa Batuan dan Desa Pedungan* (Balinese dance drama Gambuh: Artistic views, the meaning of emotion, music, lines and text, Gambuh music of Batuan Village and Pedungan Village). Jakarta: Yayasan Lontar.

Foucault, M. (1966) *Les mots et les choses: Une archéologie des sciences humaines*. Paris: Éditions Gallimard.

Fragaszy, D., P. Izar, E. Visalberghi, E. B. Ottoni, and M. G. de Oliveira (2004) "Wild capuchin monkeys (*Cebus libidinosus*) use anvils and stone pounding tools". *American Journal of Primatology*, 64: 359–366.

Friedman, J. (1974) Marxism, Structuralism, and Vulgar Materialism. *Man* (n.s.), 9–3: 444–469.

Fukushima, M. (2001a) *Anmokuchi no kaibō: Ninchi to shakai no intāfēsu* (The anatomy of tacit knowledge: Interface between cognition and society). Kaneko Shobō.

Fukushima, M. (2001b) "Jōkyō, kōi, naisei" (Situation, action, introspection). In Y. Moro (ed.) *Jissen no esunografī* (Ethnography of practice). Kaneko Shobō.

Gell, A. (1986) "Newcomers to the world of goods: Consumption among the Muria Gonds". In A. Appadurai (ed.), *The Social Life of Things: Commodities in Cultural Perspective*. Cambridge: Cambridge University Press.

Gell, A. (1998) *Art and Agency: An Anthropological Theory*. Oxford: Clarendon Press.

Gibson, J. J. (1979) *The Ecological Approach to Visual Perception*. New York: Psychology Press.

Gifford, E. (1919) "Field notes on the land birds of the Galapagos Islands and Cocos Islands, Costa Rica". *Proceedings of California Academy of Science*, 2: 189–258.

Gifford, E. W. & D. S. Gifford, (1959) *Archaeological Excavations in Yap*. Anthropological Records 18(2). Berkeley: University of California.

Goffman, E. (1963) *Behavior in Public Places: Notes on the Social Organization of Gatherings*. New York: The Free Press.

Goodwin, C. (2003) "The body in action". In J. Coupland & R. Gwyn (eds.), *Discourse, the Body, and Identity*. New York: Palgrave Macmillan, 19–42.

Gosselain, O. P. (1998) "Social and technical identity in a clay crystal ball". In

M. T. Stark (ed.), *The Archaeology of Social Boundaries*. Washington D. C.: Smithsonian Institution Press, 78–106.

Gosselain, O.P. (2008) "Mother Bella was not a Bella: Inherited and transformed traditions in southwestern Niger". In M. T. Stark, B. J. Bowser & L. Horne (eds.) *Cultural Transmission and Material Culture*. Tucson: University Arizona Press, 150–177.

Gould, S. J. (1977) *Ever Since Darwin*. New York: W. W. Norton.

Green, R. C. (1974) "A review of portable artefacts from Western Samoa". In R. C. Green & J. M. Davidson (eds.), *Archaeology in Western Samoa*. Bulletin of the Auckland Institute and Museum 7(2). Auckland: Auckland Institute and Museum, 245–276.

Gufler, H. (1995) "Yamba spider divination". *Journal of the Anthropological Society of Oxford*, 26 (1): 43–67.

Gumert, M. D., M. Kluck, and S. Malaivijitnond (2009) "The physical characteristics and usage patterns of stone axe and pounding hammers used by Long-tailed macaques in the Andaman Sea Region of Thailand". *American Journal of Primatology*, 72: 594–608.

Gunther, M. M. and C. Boesch (1993) "Energetic cost of nut-cracking behaviour in wild chimpanzees". In H. Preuschoft and D. J. Chivers (eds.) *Hands of Primates*. Wien: Springer-Verlag, 109–129.

Hall, E. T. (1959) *The Silent Language*. Doubleday: Garden City.

Halliwel, C. (1988) "Good walls make bad neighbors: Public and private space in a Dayak long-house". *Canberra Anthropology*, 11 (1).

Hamamoto, M. (1983) "Bokusen (divination) to kaishaku" (Divination and interpretation). In K. Ebuchi and A. Itō (eds.) *Girei to shōchō: Bunka jinruigaku teki kōsatsu* (Ritual and symbolism: A cultural anthropological study). Kyushu Daigaku Shuppankai: 21–46.

Hamamoto, M. (1993) "Duruma no uranai ni okeru setsumei no mōdo" (Modes of explanation in Duruma divination). *Minzokugaku kenkyū* (The Japanese journal of ethnology) 58 (1): 1–28.

Hamamoto, M. (2006) "Tasha no shinnen wo kijutsusuru koto: Jinruigaku ni okeru hitotsu no giji mondai to sono kaishō shian" (Describing the beliefs of others: A simulated question and tentative solutions in anthropology). *Kyushu Daigaku Daigakuin kyōikugaku kenkyū kiyō* (Education research bulletin of Kyushu University Graduate School) 9: 53–70.

Hanks, W. (2005) "Explorations in the deictic field". *Current Anthropology*, 46 (2): 191–220.

Hara, H. (1979) *Kodomo no bunka jinruigaku* (Cultural anthropology on children). Tokyo: Shobunsha.

Harada, H. (2004) *Butoh taizen: Ankoku to hikari no ōkoku* (Butoh corpus: The kingdom of darkness and light). Gendaishokan.

Haraway, D. (1991) *Simians, Cyborgs, and Women: The Reinvention of Nature*. Free Association: London.

Harlan, J. (1992) *Crops & Man*, 2nd ed. Madison: American Society of Agronomy Inc. & Crop Science Society of America Inc.

Hasegawa, H. (1997) "Kagu/dōgu to karada: 'Osan isu' no rekishi kara kangaeru" (Furniture/tool and body: Thinking about the history of parturition chair). In M. Uchibori (ed.) *Iwanami bunka jinruigaku kōza – Mono no ningen sekai* (Iwanami cultural anthropology series: The human world of things). Iwanami Shoten, 73–108.

Hata, N. and T. Moriya (1981) "Kamen no jinruigaku" (Anthropology of masks). In T. Umesao (ed.) *Kamen* (Masks). Kodansha, 145–167.

Hauser, M. D. (1988) "Invention and social transmission: New data from wild vervet monkeys". In R. Byrne and A. Whiten (eds.) *Machiavellian Intelligence: Social Expertise and the Evolution of Intellect in Monkeys, Apes and Humans*. Oxford: Oxford University Press, 327–343.

Hayaki, H. (1990) *Chinpanjī no naka no hito* (The human inside the chimpanzee). Tokyo: Shōkabō.

Hayes C. (1951) *The Ape in Our House*. Oxford: Harper.

Heidegger, M. (1962) *Being and Time*. J. Macquarrie & E. Robinson (trs.). New York: Harper & Row.

Helliwell, C. (1988) "Good walls make bad neighbours: Public and private space in a Dayak long-house", *Canberra Anthropology*, 11(1).

Henare, A., M. Holbradd, and S. Wastell (eds.) (2007) *Thinking through Things: Theorizing Artifacts Ethnographically*. London: Routledge.

Herbich, I. and M. Dietler (2008) "The long arm of the mother-in-law: Learning, postmarital resocialization of women, and material culture style". In M. T. Stark, B. J. Bowser & L. Horne (eds.) *Cultural Transmission and Material Culture*. Tucson: University of Arizona Press, 223–244.

Herskovits, M. (1926) "The cattle complex in East Africa". *American Anthropologist*, 28: 230–272, 361–388, 494–528, 633–664.

Hidaka, K. (1996) "Seiryokuzai gyōkai, sono kanōsei no chūshin wo motomete: Tōsei 'yotsumeya' moyō" (The invigorant industry and its potential: Modern-day 'sex shops'). In Bessatsu Takarajima Henshūbu (ed.) *Genki ga deru kusuri:*

Kaishunzai, kyōsōzai, biyaku, gōhō doraggu – tanoshii ecchi no tameno kusuri no subete (All about drugs for better sex: Sexual rejuvenation formulations, sex stimulants, aphrodisiacs and legal drugs). Takarajimasha, 162–169.

Higaki, T. (2008) "Berukuson" (Bergson). In S. Washida (ed.) *Tetsugaku no rekishi 20-seiki 3 Jitsuzon, kōzō, tasha* (History of 20th century philosophy 3: Existence, structure, other). Chūōkōronsha.

Hobbes, T. (1992) *Leviathan*. Oxford: Basil Blackwell.

Hobbes, T. (1992) *Rivaiasan* (Leviathan). H. Mizuta (trs.). Tokyo: Iwanami Shoten.

Hodder, I. (1982) *Symbols in Action: Ethnoarchaeological Studies of Material Culture*. Cambridge: Cambridge University Press.

Hohmann, G. (1988) "A case of simple tool use in wild liontailed macaques (*Macaca silenus*). *Primates*, 29: 565–567.

Holler, L. (2002) *Erotic Morality: The Role of Touch in Moral Agency*. New Brunswick: Rutgers University Press.

Holyoak, K. J. and P. Thagard (1995) *Mental Leaps: Analogy in Creative Thought*. MIT Press, Cambridge.

Hopkins, J. (2006) *Asian Aphrodisiacs: From Bangkok to Beijing: The Search for the Ultimate Turn-On*. Singapore: Peripuls.

Hoshi, M. (1987) "Ryukyu bingata no rekishi" (The history of Ryukyu bingata). In Ryukyu Bingata Jigyō Kyōdō Kumiai (ed.) *Ryukyu bingata no rekishi to gihō* (The history and techniques of Ryukyu bingata). Ryukyu Bingata Jigyō Kyōdō Kumiai, 1–33.

Hudson, B. (2008) "Restoration and reconstruction of monuments at Bagan (Pagan), Myanmar (Burma), 1995–2008". *World Archaeology*, 40(4): 551–571.

Huffman, M. A. (1984) "Stone-play of Macaca fuscata in Arashiyama B troop: transmission of a non-adaptive behavior". *J. Human Evolution*, 13(8): 725–735.

Iacoboni, M. (2009) *Mirroring People: The new science of empathy and how we connected with others*. New York: Farrar, Straus and Giroux.

Ichikawa, H. (1975) *Seishin toshite no shintai* (The body is the mind). Keisō Shobō.

Igarashi, M. (2008) *Nippon chin supotto hyakkei* (One hundred bizarre spots in Japan). Pia.

Iguchi, J. (1999) *Chūgoku hoppō nōson no kōshō bunka – Katarimono no sho, tekisuto, pafōmansu* (Oral culture in rural villages of northern China: Script, text and performance of story-telling). Fūkyōsha.

Iha, F. (1974) "Ryukyu sarasa no hassei" (The origins of Ryukyu chintz). *Iha Fuyū zenshū* (Collective works of Fuyū Iha), Vol. 5. Heibonsha, 121–139.

Imahori, E. (2006) "Shijō keizai ni okeru kashutachi (shishūya) jigyō no tanjō

– Uzubekisutan Shōfirukōn chiku no jirei kara" (The birth of kashtachi (embroidery business) in the market economy: A case of the Shofirkon district of Uzbekistan), *Shakai jinruigaku nenpō* (The annual of social anthropology), 32: 57–84.

Imamura, H. (1992) "Kakureta fetishizumu" (Hidden fetishism). In H. Kawai et al. (eds.) *Shūkyō to shakai kagaku* (Religion and social science). Iwanami Shoten, 145–172.

Imamura, K. (2001) "Kannōsuru sekai: Gui/Gana Busshuman no shochō girei" (Sympathetic world: Menarche rituals of the Gui/Gana Bushman). M. Sawada (ed.) *Afurika shuryō saishū shakai no sekai kan* (The world views of the African hunter-gatherer societies). Kyoto Seika Daigaku Sōzō Kenkyūjo, 95–128.

Ingold, T. (1992) "Comment on 'Beyond the original affluent society' by N. Bird-David". *Current Anthropology*, 33: 34–47.

Ingold, T. (2007) "Introduction" (to Part 1 Modes of Creativity in Life and Art). In T. Ingold & E. Hallam (eds.), *Creativity and Cultural Improvisation*. Oxford: Berg, 45–54.

Innami, T., Y. Kamino, K. Sano, and H. Nakamura (eds.) (2002) *Mono, mono, mono no sekai* (The world of things of all sorts). Yūhikaku.

Intoh, M. (1990a) *Changing Prehistoric Yapese Pottery Technology: A Case Study of Adaptive Transformation*. Michigan: UMI Press.

Intoh, M. (1990b) "Ceramic environment and technology: A case study in the Yap Islands in Micronesia". *Man and Culture in Oceania*, 6: 35–52.

Intoh, M. (1995) "Oseania no doki bunka no shosō" (Aspects of pottery culture in Oceania). In S. Yoshida (ed.) *Seikatsu gijutsu no jinruigaku* (Archaeology of life technology). Heibonsha, 185–206.

Intoh, M. (2000) "Oseania no tōshokan kōryū" (Island interactions in Oceania). In H. Ogawa (ed.) *Kōryū no kōkogaku* (The archaeology of interaction), (Shirīzu gendai no kōkogaku 5) (Contemporary archaeology series 5). Asakura Shoten, 50–72.

Intoh, M. (2002) *Oseania: kurashi no kōkogaku* (Archaeology of island life in Oceania). Asahi Shimbunsha.

Intoh, M. (2003) *Oseania no dentō doki bunka: Tayōsei wo unda mekanizumu no kenkyū* (Traditional pottery culture of Oceania: A study of the mechanism for diversity). Grant-in-Aid Research Report 2001–2002.

Intoh, M. (2006) "Tōsho sekai no doki tsukuri: Shigen no katayori to gijutsu henka" (Pottery making in an island world: Resource bias and technological change). M. Intoh (ed.) *Kankyō to shigen riyō no jinruigaku* (Anthropology of the environment and resource use). Akashi Shoten, 129–150.

Intoh, M. & B. F. Leach (1985) *Archaeological Investigations in the Yap Islands, Micronesia: First Millennium B. C. to the Present Day* (BAR International Series 277). Oxford: BAR.

Iriki, A. (2004) *Dōgu wo tsukau saru* (Tool use in monkeys). Tokyo: Igaku Shoin.

Irwin, G. (1981) "How Lapita lost its pots: The question of continuity in the colonisation of Polynesia". *Journal of the Polynesian Society*, 90: 481–494.

Ishii, M. (2005) "Mono/ katari toshite no unmei: Gāna no bokusen Afa ni okeru jujutsuteki sekai no kōsei" (Destiny as story, destiny as object: Storytelling and ritual in Afa divination in southern Ghana). *Bunka jinruigaku* (Japanese journal of cultural anthropology), 70(1): 21–46.

Itani, J. (1953) *Takasakiyama no saru* (Japanese monkeys in Takasakiyama). Tokyo: Kodansha.

Itani, J. (1987) *Reichōrui shakai no shinka* (The evolution of primate social structures). Tokyo: Heibonsha.

Iwaki, K. (2001) *Kansei ron – Esutetikkusu: Hirakareta keiken no riron no tameni* (Aestetics = Theory of Aisthesis: A philosophical study on the flexibility of human experience). Kyoto: Shōwadō.

Izawa, K. and A. Mizuno (1977) "Palm-fruit cracking behaviour of wild black-capped capuchin (*Cebus apella*)". *Primates*, 18: 773–792.

Jin, Zhilin (1994) *Shengming zhi shu* (Tree of Life). Beijing: Zhongguo shehui kexue chubanshe.

Jumaev, Q. J. (2003) *19asr ohari 20asr boshlarida Buxoroning An'anavity Kashtado 'zlik San 'atida*. Nashriyotlanmagan Ilmiy Nomozodlik Desserbastiya. Toshkent: O'zbekiston Badiy Akademiyasi San 'atshunoslik Ilmiy Tadqiqot Institut.

Kamakura, Y. (1976) "Kataezome ni kansuru geijutsu ronkō" (An artistic study of kataezome). *Kamakura Yoshitarō kagaezome sakuhinshū* (Collection of stencil dyeing works by Yoshitarō Kamakura). Kodansha, 171–188.

Kamata, T. (2009) *Mono gaku no bōken* (An adventure of the study of things). Sōgensha.

Kaneko, M. (2005) *Bunmyakuka sareru doki zukuri no katei: Echiopia seinanbu Omo kei nōkōmin Ari no josei shokunin ni yoru chien gijutsu no shūtoku, jissen, sōzō* (Anthropological study of pottery makers: The Aari people in southwestern Ethiopia). Ph. D. thesis, Graduate School of Asian and African Area Studies, Kyoto University.

Kaneko, M. (2006) "Seigyo toshite no doki zukuri" (Pottery making as livelihood). *Asian and African Area Studies*, 6(2): 522–539.

Kaneko, M. (2007) "Variations in pottery making by Aari potters in southwestern Ethiopia: Analysis of the finger movement patterns used in forming pots". *Nilo-Ethiopian Studies*, 11: 1–15.

Kaneko, M. (2007a) "Echiopia seinanbu ni okeru doki shokunin no tekuno raifu hisutorī: Jinsei no kiseki ni gijutsu no henka wo atozukeru kokoromi" (The techno life history of the pottery maker in southwestern Ethiopia: An attempt to trace technological changes in the life history). In A. Gotō (ed.) *Doki no minzoku kōkogaku* (Ethnoarchaeology of pottery). Dōseisha, 15–25.

Kaneko, M. (2007b) "Teyubi wo tsukatte doki wo tsukuru: Echiopia seinanbu Ari josei shokunin no shintai gihō" (Making pottery with fingers: The body techniques of Aari female potters in southwestern Ethiopia). In K. Sugawara (ed.) *Shintai shigen no kōchiku to kyōyū* (Building and sharing of body resources) (*Shigen jinruigaku* series Vol. 9). Kōbundō, 113–140.

Kaneko, M. (2010) "Variations in pottery making in southwestern Ethiopia". In S. Ege, H. Aspen, B. Teferra and S. Bekele (eds.) *Research in Ethiopian Studies: Selected Papers of the 16th International Conference of Ethiopian Studies, Trondheim July 2007*. Aethiopistische Forschungen, 72. Wiesbaden: Harrassowitz Verlag, pp, 187–199.

Kaneko, M. (2013) "The creation and sale of pottery in Southwestern Ethiopia" *Busshitsu Bunka*, 93: 17-30.

Kani, M. (2005) *Jōmon doki no gihō* (Jōmon pottery techniques). Dōseisha.

Katō, M. (1996) "Kusuri karuto ō Katō Michihiro no gedoku koramu 4: Getemono ryōri tte hontō ni seiryokuzai ni naru no?" (Drug cult king Michihiro Katō's detox column 4: Do bizarre foods really invigorate?). In Bessatsu Takarajima Henshūbu (ed.) *Genki ga deru kusuri: Kaishunzai, kyōsōzai, biyaku, gōhō doraggu – tanoshii ecchi no tameno kusuri no subete* (All about drugs for better sex: Sexual rejuvenation formulations, sex stimulants, aphrodisiacs and legal drugs). Takarajimasha, 189.

Kawada, J. (1988) *Koe* (Voice). Chikuma Shobō.

Kawada, J. (1992a) *Nishi no kaze, minami no kaze: Bunmeiron no kumikae no tameni* (West wind, south wind: To recompose civilization theory). Kawade Shobō Shinsha.

Kawada, J. (1992b) *Kōtō denshōron* (A study of oral traditions). Kawade Shobō Shinsha.

Kawada, J. (1992c) "Shintai gihō no gijutsuteki sokumen: Yobiteki kōsatsu" (Technological aspect of the body techniques: Preliminary discussion).

Nishi no kaze, minami no kaze (West wind, south wind). Kawade Shobō Shinsha, 64–122.

Kawai, K. (1990) What does marriage mean to each gender of the Il Chamus? Husband-wife relationship of an East African agro-pastoral people. *African Study Monographs, Supplementary Issue*, No. 12: 35–49.

Kawai, K. (1998) *No no iryō: Bokuchikumin Chamusu no shintai sekai* (Pastoralists' View of Body and Therapeutic Practice). Tokyo Daigaku Shuppankai.

Kawai, K. (2006) "Kyanpu idō to chō uranai: Dodosu ni okeru rinsetsu shūdan tono kankei wo meguru shakai kūkan no seisei kijo" (Camp relocation and divinatory reading of animal intestines: The mechanism for social space generation of the Dodoth surrounding their relations with neighboring communities). In R. Nishii and S. Tanabe (eds.) *Shakai kūkan no jinruigaku: Materiariti, shutai, modaniti* (Anthropology of social space: Materiality, agency and modernity). Sekaishisōsha, 175–202.

Kearns, M. (2003) "Geographies that matter: The rhetorical deployment of physicality?". *Social and Cultural Geography*, 4(2): 139–152.

Kendon, A. (1970) "Movement coordination in social interaction: Some examples described". *Acta Psychologica*, 32: 100–125.

Kendon, A. (1990) "Gesticulation, quotable gestures, and signs". In M. Moerman & M. Nomura (eds.) *Culture Embodied* (Senri Ethnological Studies 27), National Museum of Ethnology, 53–77.

Kimura, D. (2003) *Kyōzai kankaku: Afurika no futatsu no shakai ni okeru gengoteki sōgo kōi kara* (Sense of coexistence: Verbal interaction in two African societies). Kyoto Daigaku Gakujutsu Shuppankai.

Kirch, P. V. (1997) "The Lapita peoples". *The Peoples of South-East Asia and the Pacific*. Cambridge: Blackwell Publishers.

Kishimoto, Y. (2004) "Shimotabarushiki doki no bunrui to hennen shian" (Tentative classification and chronology of Shimotabaru pottery). *Okinawa maibun kenkyū* (Okinawa archaeological heritage studies), 2: 1–12.

Kitanishi, K. (2002) "Chūō Afurika nettai urin no shuryō saishūmin Baka ni okeru banana Saibai no juyō" (The acceptance of banana cultivation among the Baka hunter-gatherers in tropical rainforest of Central Africa). *Yamaguchi Daigaku kyōiku gakubu kenkyū ronsō* (Bulletin of the faculty of education, Yamaguchi University), 52 (1): 51–68.

Knapett, C. (2005) *Thinking through Material Culture: An interdisciplinary perspective*. Philadelphia: University of Pennsylvania Press.

Knapett, C. and L. Malafouris (eds.) (2008) *Material Agency: Towards a Non-anthropocentric Approach*. Berlin: Springer.

Köhler, W. (1917) *Intelligenzprüfungen an Menschenaffen*. Berlin: Springer.

Koizumi, T. (2010) *Zetsurin shoku* (Diet for virility). Shinchōsha.

Kojima, D. (2004) *Chindera daidōjō* (A collection of novelty temples). East Press.

Kolb, C. C. (ed.) (1988) *Ceramic Ecology Revisited: The Technology and Socio-economics of Pottery* (BAR International Series 436). Oxford: BAR.

Komatsu, K. et al. (2006) "Banana Saibai bunka no Ajia Afurika chiiki kan hikaku: Hinshu tayōsei wo megutte" (Comparative study of banana farming cultures in Asia and Africa: with special reference to the diversity of local cultivars). *Ajia Afurika chiiki kenkyū* (Asian and African area studies) 6-1: 77–119.

Konaka, S. (1997) "Keiken sekai no rakusa ha ikani katarareruka: Kenia chūhokubu Sanburu no sekenbanashi no jirei" (How gaps in the empirical world are narrated: The case of small talk in the Samburu, North Central Kenya). Shizuoka Kenritsu Daigaku Kokusai Kankei Gakubu (ed.) *Seiki tenkan ki no sekai to Nihon* (The world and Japan at the turn of the century), Kokusai kankeigaku sōsho 14. Shizuoka Kenritsu Daigaku Kokusai Kankei Gakubu, 251–282.

Konaka, S. (2000) "Bokuchikumin no meimei gihō to keiken sekai no gurōbaruka: Kenia chūhokubu Sanburu no jirei" (Pastoralists' naming techniques and the globalization of the empirical world: The case of the Samburu, North Central Kenya). *Shakai jinruigaku nenpō* (TMU social anthropology), 26: 157–168.

Konaka, S. (2002) "Kachiku wo miru manazashi de shizen to ningen wo miru" (Seeing Nature and man as one sees livestock). *Kikan riratio* (Relatio quarterly), 13: 90–95.

Konaka, S. (2006) *Bokuchiku nijū keizai no jinruigaku: Kenia Sanburu no minzokushiteki kenkyū* (The pastoralist dual economy: An ethnographic study of the Samburu in Kenya). Sekai Shisōsha.

Konaka, S. (2007) "Shō seisanbutsu (shōhin) no bisai na gurōbaraizēshon: Kenia chūhokubu Sanburu no haibutsu shigen riyō" (Microscopic globalization of small products (commodities): Waste resource utilization by the Samburu, North Central Kenya). In R. Ogawa (ed.) *Yakudōsuru shō seisanbutsu* (*Shigen jinruigaku* dai yonkan) (Vibrancy of small products (Anthropology of resources series volume 4)). Kōbundō.

Konaka, S. (2010) "Metaphorical projection and integrated cognitive systems: The Samburu in North Central Kenya". In F. Stammler and H. Takakura (eds.)

Social Significance of Animals in Nomadic Pastoral Societies of the Arctic, Africa and Central Asia (Northeast Asian Studies Series 11). Sendai: Tohoku University, 63–73.

Kondō, H. (2009) "Gūzenka to jujutsu: Aru kigyōka no kake to kukyō wo megutte" (Randomization and magic: Gambles and predicaments of a certain entrepreneur). In T. Ochiai (ed.) *Supirichuaru Afurika: Tayōnaru shūkyōteki jissen no sekai* (Spiritual Africa: A world of diverse religious practices). Kōyōshobō, 131–173.

Kopitoff, I. (1986) "The Cultural Biography of Things". In Appadurai, A. (ed.) *The Social Life of Things: Commodities in Cultural Perspective*, New York: Cambridge University Press, 64–91.

Kubota, S. (2008) "Planning the local museum: Anthropology and art in the postmodern era". *People and Culture in Oceania*, 23: 53–72.

Kubota, S. (2008a) "Aborijini bijutsu no henbō" (Transformation of Aboriginal Art). In S. Yamashita (ed.) *Shigenkasuru bunka* (Culture as a resource) (M. Uchibori (ed.) *Shigen jinruigaku* (Anthropology of resources), Vol. 2). Kōbundō, 181–208.

Kubota, S. (2008b) "'Ōsutoraria no nagai chinmoku' no nochi: Rekishi to Aborijini no ējenshī" (After 'Australia's long silence': History and Aborigine's agency). *Bunka jinruigaku* (Japanese journal of cultural anthropology), 73 (3): 400–418.

Kubota, S. (2011) "Aborijini ātisuto no tanjō: Gurōbaru to rōkaru no hazama de" (The birth of Aboriginal artists: Between the global and the local). In T. Matsui, K. Nawa, and A. Nobayashi (eds.) *Gurōbarizēshon to 'ikiru sekai'* (Globalization and the 'living world'). Shōwadō, 339–387.

Kuki, S. (2000) *Gūzensei no mondai/ Bungeiron* (The Matter of Contingency / Theory of Literature). Tōeisha.

Kunz, G. F. and C. H. Stevenson (1908) *The Book of the Pearl*. New York: The Century Co.

Kuroda, S. (1982) *Pigumī chinpanjī: Michi no ruijinen* (Pygmy chimpanzee: The unknown ape). Tokyo: Chikuma Shobō.

Kuroda, S. (1984) "Interaction over food among pygmy chimpanzees." In R. L. Susman (ed.) *The Pygmy Chimpanzee: Evolutionary biology and behavior*. New York: Springer US, 301-324.

Kuroda, S. (1999) *Jinrui shinka saikō: Shakai seisei no kōkogaku* (Reconsideration of human evolution: Archeology of the emergence of hominid society). Tokyo: Ibunsha.

Kuroda, S. (2002) *Shizen gaku no mirai: Shizen tono kyōkan* (Future of nature study: Empathy with nature). Tokyo: Kobundo.

Kuroda, S. (2010) "'Ningen byōdō kigen ron' ni okeru byōdō gensoku no keifu" (The genealogy of the equality principle in 'the origin of human equality'). *Ningen bunka* (Humanities and sciences, Kobe Gakuin University), 27: 3–6.

Kuroda, S. (2013) "Collective excitement and primitive war: What is the equality principle?". In K. Kawai (ed.), *Groups: The Evolution of Human Sociality*. Kyoto and Melbourne: Kyoto University Press and Trans Pacific Press, 273-292.

Lakoff, G. and M. Johnson (1999) *Philosophy in the Flesh: The Embodied Mind and its Challenge to Western Thought*. Basic Books: New York.

Latour, B. (2005) *Reassembling the Social: An Introduction to Actor-Network-Theory*. Clarendon Lectures in Management Studies. Oxford: Oxford University Press.

Latour, B. (1993) *We have never been modern*. C. Porter (tr.). Cambridge: Harvard University Press.

Lave, J. and E. Wenger (1991) *Situated Learning: Legitimate Peripheral Participation*. Cambridge: Cambridge University Press.

Le Moine, G. (1987) "The loss of pottery in Polynesia". *New Zealand Journal of Archaeology*, 9: 25–32.

Leach, H. M. (1982) "Cooking without pots: Aspects of prehistoric and traditional Polynesian cooking". *New Zealand Journal of Archaeology*, 4: 149–156.

Leonard, G. (1983) *The End of sex: Erotic love after the sexual revolution*. New York: Tarcher Perigee.

Leroi-Gourhan, A. (1965) *Le Geste et la Parole: La Mémoire et les Rythmes*. Albin Michel: Paris.

Lévi-Strauss, C. (1958) *Anthropologie structurale*. Paris: Plon.

Lévi-Strauss, C. (1969) *The Elementary Structures of Kinship*. J. H. Bell and J. R. von Sturmer (trs.). Oxford: Alden Press

Levi-Strauss, C. (1972). *La Voie des masques*. Paris: Editions Albert Skira.

Lingenfelter, S. (1975) *Yap: Political Leadership and Cultural Change in an Island Society*. Honolulu: The University Press of Hawaii.

Lovejoy, O. W. (1981) "The origin of man". *Science* 211: 341–350.

Luhmann, N. (1995) *Social Systems*. J. Bednarz, Jr. and D. Baecker (trs.). Stanford: Stanford University Press.

Lyotard, J.-F. (1984) *The Postmodern Condition: A Report on Knowledge*. Minneapolis: University of Minnesota Press.

Malaivijitnond, S., et al. (2007) "Stone-tool usage by Thai long-tailed macaques (*Macaca silenus*)". *American Journal of Primatology*, 69: 227–233.

Marshall, Y. (1985) "Who made the Lapita pots? A case study in gender archaeology". *The Journal of the Polynesian Society*, 94: 205–233.

Maruo, S. (2002) "Afurika daiko chihō ni okeru banana nōkō to sono shūyakusei: Tanzania hokuseibu Haya no jirei" (Banana farming and its intensiveness in the Great Lakes region of Africa: A case of the Haya in northwestern Tanzania). *Nōkō no gijutsu to bunka* (Farming technology and culture), 25: 108–134.

Matson, F. R. (1965) "Ceramic ecology: An approach to the study of the early cultures". In F. R. Matson (ed.), *Ceramics and Man* (Viking Fund Publications in Anthropology 41). London: Methuen, 202–217.

Matson, F. R. (1989) "Shell-tempered pottery and the fort ancient potter". In G. Bronitsky (ed.), *Westview Special Studies in Archaeological Research*. Colorado: Westview Press, 15–31.

Matsui, K. (2005) *Yanagi Sōetsu to mingei no genzai* (Yanagi Sōetsu and folk arts now). Yoshikawa Kōbunkan.

Matsuzawa, T. (1991) *Chinpanjī maindo* (Chimpanzee mind). Tokyo: Iwanami Shoten.

Matsuzuki, K. (2002) *Shinju no hakubutsu shi* (Natural history of the pearl). Kenseisha.

Maturana, H. R. and F. J. Varela (1980) *Autopoiesis and Cognition*. D Reidel Publishing Company: Dordrecht.

MAU. *Tempest: Without a Body*. http://www.youtube.com/watch?v=WfLqv85uCww (accessed 17/07/2010)

Mauss, M. (1950) *Sociologie et anthropologie*. Paris: Les universitaires de France.

McGrew, W. C. (1992) *Chimpanzee Material Culture: Implications for Human Evolution*. Cambridge: Cambridge University Press.

McGrew, W. C. (1996) *Bunka no kigen wo saguru: Chinpanjī no busshitsu bunka* (Chimpanzee material culture: Implications for human evolution). T. Nishida, K. Adachi and S. Suzuki (trs.). Nakayama Shoten.

McLuhan, M. (1964) *Understanding Media: The Extensions of Man*. McGraw-Hill: New York.

McLuhan, M. and B. R. Powers (1989) *The Global Village: Transformations in World Life and Media in the 21st Century*. Oxford University Press: New York.

McNeill, D. (1992) *Hand and Mind: What Gestures Reveal about Thought*. Chicago: University of Chicago Press.

Mcphee, C. (1966) *Music in Bali: A Study in Form and Instrumental Organization in Balinese Orchestral Music*. New Haven: Yale University Press.

Merleau-Ponty, M. (1945) *La phénoménology de la perception*. Paris: Editions Gallimard.

Merleau-Ponty, M. (1968) *The Visible and the Invisible*. A. Lingis (trs.) Evanston: Northwestern University Press.

Miller, D. (1987) *Material Culture and Mass Consumption*. Oxford: Basil Blackwell.

Miller, D. (ed.) (1998) *Material Cultures: Why Some Things Matter*. Chicago: University of Chicago Press.

Miller, D. (ed) (2005) *Materiality*. Durham & London: Duke University Press.

Minato, O. (2009) "Kōru & resuponsu aruiha yūai no kioku" (Call & response or memories of friendship). In K. Kasahara & M. Terada (eds.), *Kioku hyōgen ron* (Memory expression). Shōwadō, 85–110.

Misra, P. K. (1992) "Oral strategies among the nomadic peoples". *The Eastern Anthropologist*, 45 (3): 215–226.

Mithen, S. (1996) *The Prehistory of the Mind: The Cognitive Origins of Art, Religion and Science*. London: Thames & Hudson.

Miyasaka, K. (2006) "Seirei no hairu kuchi: Radakku no fusha ni miru hyourei to suidashi" (Spirit entry by mouth: Possession and sucking in spiritual mediums of Ladakh). *Ajia yūgaku* (Intriguing Asia), Tokyo: Bensei Shuppan, 84: 123–133.

Mori, A., U. Mori, and T. Iwamoto (1977) "Kōjima no yasei nihonzaru no mure ni okeru mesu kan no jun'i hendō" (Fluctuations in the rank order among females in wild Japanese macaque troops on Kōjima Island). In T. Katō and S. Nakao (eds.) *Keishitsu, shinka, reichōrui* (Morphology, evolution, primates). Tokyo: Chuo Koron Shinsha, 311–338.

Morphy, H. (2007) *Becoming Art: Exploring Cross-Cultural Categories*. Oxford & New York: Berg.

Moura, A. C. and P. C. Lee (2004) "Capuchin stone tool use in Caatinga dry forest". *Science*, 306: 1909.

Müller, W. (1917) *Yap. Efgebnisse der Südsee-expedition, 1908–1910*. II, B, 2, Hamburg: Friederichsen.

Munn, N. D. (1983) "Gawan kula: Spatiotemporal control and the symbolism of influence". In J. W. Leach and E. Leach (eds.) *The Kula: New Perspectives on Massim Exchange*. Cambridge: Cambridge University Press, 277–308.

Murakami, T. (2009) "Shūkyō toshite no fetishizumu: Kindai "shūkyō" gainen rikai heno hitotsu no apurōchi" (Fetishism as religion: An approach to an understanding of the modern concept of 'religion'). In M. Tanaka (ed.)

Fetishizumu ron no keifu to tenbō (Genealogy and prospect of fetishism theories). Kyoto Daigaku Gakujutsu Shuppankai, 41–63.

Muroi, H. (1987) *Take wo shiru hon: Take ha ki ka kusa ka* (The book of bamboo: Is bamboo a tree or a grass?). Chijinshokan.

Muroi, H. (1993) *Take no sekai* (The world of bamboo) Part 1. Chijinshokan.

Myers, F. R. (2002) *Painting Culture: The Making of an Aboriginal High Art.* Durham & London: Duke University Press.

Myers, F. R. (2001) "Introduction: The Empire of things". In F. R. Myers (ed.), *The Empire of Things: Regimes of Value and Material Culture.* Santa Fe: School of American Research Press.

Nakagawa, S. (1994) "Shinsō ga iki wo fukikaesu: Indoneshia Bari tō" (Reviving the deep layer: Bali, Indonesia). In K. Yoshida (ed.) *Kamen ha ikiteiru* (Living masks). Iwanami Shoten, 53–88.

Nakagawa, S. (2004) *Heiankyo oto no uchū: (Zōho) Saundo sukēpu heno tabi* (The ancient Kyoto universe of sound: A journey to a soundscape (enlarged edition)). Heibonsha (Heibonsha Library).

Nakata, J. (1996) "Seiryokuzai no okashina okashina kōkoku sekai! Dentsu, Hakuhodo niha zettai tsukurenai" (The weird world of male sex stimulant advertising! Ads Dentsu and Hakuhodo can never make). In Bessatsu Takarajima Henshūbu (ed.) *Genki ga deru kusuri: Kaishunzai, kyōsōzai, biyaku, gōhō doraggu – tanoshii ecchi no tameno kusuri no subete* (All about drugs for better sex: Sexual rejuvenation formulations, sex stimulants, aphrodisiacs and legal drugs). Takarajimasha, 170–178.

Nakata, T. (2002) "Sonraku shakai ni okeru shōchō tōsō: Minami Raosu Nge no mura no 'kī kapo' uranai kara" (Symbolic conflicts in village society: From 'kigapo' divination of Nge village in southern Laos). *Minzokugaku kenkyū* (The Japanese journal of ethnology), 67 (1): 21–42.

National Bureau of Statistics of China (ed.) (2000) *Zhongguo renkou tongji nianjian 2000* (China Statistical Yearbook 2000). Beijing: Zhongguo tongji chubanshe.

Natsuhara, T. (1996) "Sennyū! 'Kokusai hogo dōbutsu' mitsuyu rūto wo ou: Kyōsō to hōshoku no hate ni" (Infiltration! Tracking the 'internationally protected animals' poaching route: At the end of lust and gluttony). In Bessatsu Takarajima Henshūbu (ed.) *Genki ga deru kusuri: Kaishunzai, kyōsōzai, biyaku, gōhō doraggu – tanoshii ecchi no tameno kusuri no subete* (All about drugs for better sex: Sexual rejuvenation formulations, sex stimulants, aphrodisiacs and legal drugs). Takarajimasha, 210–218.

New Zealand Statistics (2007) *Quick Stats National Highlights 2006 Census.* Wellington, NZ Statistics.

Nishida, T. (1973) "The ant-gathering behaviour by the use of tools among wild chimpanzees of the Mahali Mountains". *Journal of Human Evolution*, 2: 357–370.

Nishida, T. and K. Hosaka (2001) "Reichōrui ni okeru shokumotsu bunpai" (Food distribution in primates). In T. Nishida (ed.) *Hominizēshon* (Hominization) (kōza seitai jinruigaku 8). Kyoto: Kyoto Univ. Press, 255–304.

Nishimura, M. (2006) "'Isan' gainen no saikentō" (Reappraisal of 'heritage'). *Bunka jinruigaku kenkyū* (Japanese journal of cultural anthropology), 7: 1–22.

Niwa, T. (2009) "Chūgoku kōdo Kōgen ni saku senshi no hana: Negai wo takusu katachi, hasami de tsutaeru kokoro" (Paper-cut flowers of the Huangtu Plateau, China: Wishes in forms and feelings shown by scissors). *Kikan ginka* (Ginga quarterly), 160: 75–102.

Niwa, T. (2015) "'Madohana' kara 'Senshi' he: Chūgoku Kōdo Kogen ni okeru josei no shutai -ka no keifugaku ni mukete (From "Window Flowers" to "Paper-Cutting Works": A Genealogical Approach to the Subjectification of the Rural Women in Shanbei, China). *Journal of Asia and Africa Studies*, 90: 5–27.

Niwa, T. & T. Yanai (2017) "Flowers' Life: Notes and Reflections on an Art-Anthropology Exhibition", A. Schneider (ed.) *Alternative Art and Anthropology: Global Encounters.* London: Bloomsbury, 75–87.

Nomura, M. (1997) "'Shintai gihō ron' heno nōto" (A note to 'Techniques of the body'). In M. Uchibori (ed.) *'Mono' no ningen sekai* (A human world of 'things'). Iwanami Shoten, 25–42.

Nomura, M. (1999) "Gijutsu to shite no shintai: 20 seiki no kenkyū shi kara" (Body as a technology: From the history of studies in the 20th century). In M. Nomura & M. Ichikawa (eds.) *Gijutsu to shite no shintai* (Body as a technology). Taishūkan Shoten, 8–20.

Nuckolls, C. W. (1993) "The structure of emotions in Jalari divination". *The Eastern Anthropologist*, 46 (2): 111–144.

Ogino, S. (1994) "Sei no kusuri to yakuji hō: Biyaku ga 'kokumin eiyōzai' ni naru hi" (Sex drugs and the Pharmaceutical Affairs Act: The day aphrodisiacs become 'national nutrition drugs'). *Otoko to onna no sei no kusuri: Biyaku toiu na no adaruto doraggu no uraomote 1, adaruto doraggu no sekai, Hanashi no channeru bessatsu* (Male and female sex drugs: The two sides of sex drugs called aphrodisiacs 1, the world of sex drugs, Hanashi no channeru supplementary issue), Vol. 2, 10–25.

Ōkubo, S. (1989) *Otoko wo pawā appu saseru hiyaku, hijutsu: Chūgoku yonsennen no rekishi ga oshieru sokkō no kenkō, kyōsei hō* (Secret elixirs and alchemy to enhance male power: Fast-acting health and energy improvement taught by the 4000-year history of China). KK Ronguserāzu.

Ong, W. J. (1982) *Orality and Literacy: The Technologizing of the Word*. London & New York: Methuen.

Orenstein, R. (1972) "Tool use by the New Caledonian crow (*Corvus moneduloides*)". *Auk*, 89: 674–676.

Oswalt, W. H. (1976) *An Anthropological Analysis of Food-getting Technology*. John Wiley & Sons: New York.

Parthasarathy, J. (2001) *Report on Community Status*. Chennai: Tribal Research Centre, Department of Adi Dravidar and Tribal Welfare. (unpublished report)

Peirce, C. S. (2001) *Renzokusei no tetsugaku* (Philosophy of continuity). K. Itō (tr.). Iwanami Bunko.

Phillips, K. A. (1998) "Tool use in wild capuchin monkeys (*Cebus albifrons trinitatis*)". *American Journal of Primatology*, 46: 259–261.

Pietz, W. (1987) "The Problem of the Fetish II", *RES*, 13: 23–45.

Polanyi, M. (1966) *The Tacit Dimension*. London: Routledge.

Poulsen, J. (1988) *Early Tongan Prehistory* (Terra Australis 12). Canberra: The Australian National University Press.

Qiao, Xiaoguang (ed.) (2004) *Zhongguo minjian jianzhi tiancai chuanchengzhe de shenghuo he yishu* (Life and Arts of Folk Paper-cutting Genius Inheritors in China). Taiyuan: Shanxi renmin chubanshe.

Rapoport, E., S. Shatz and N. Blass (2008) "Overtone spectra of gongs used in music therapy". *Journal of New Music Research*, 37: 37–60.

Reed, E. S. (1996) *Encountering the World: Toward an Ecological Psychology*. Oxford: Oxford University Press.

Rembang, I Ny. (1973) *Gambelan Gambuh dan gambelan2 lainya di Bali* (Gamelan Gambuh and other gamelans of Bali), Workshop Gambuh (Denpasar).

Republic of Kenya (2010) *The 2009 Kenya Population and Housing Census "Counting Our People for the Implementation of Vision 2030" Vol. 1A Population Distribution by Administrative Units*. Nairobi: Kenya National Bureau of Statistics.

Rice, P. M. (1984a) "Technological analysis of pottery". In P. M. Rice (ed.), *Pots and Potters: Current Approaches in Ceramic Archaeology*. Los Angeles: University of California Press, 165–170.

Rice, P. M. (1987) *Pottery Analysis: A Sourcebook*. Chicago: The University of Chicago Press.

Rice, P. M. (ed.) (1984b) *Pots and Potters: Current Approaches in Ceramic Archaeology*. Los Angeles: University of California Press.

Rizzolatti, G. and C. Sinigaglia (2009) *Mirā nyūron* (Mirror neurons). H. Shibata and K. Mogi (trs.). Tokyo: Kinokuniya Shoten.

Rodman, P. S. and H. M. McHenry (1980) "Bioenergetics and the origin of hominid bipedalism". *American Journal of Physical Anthropology*, 52: 103–106.

Roseman, M. (1993) *Healing sounds from the Malaysian rainforest*. Berkley: University of California Press.

Rye, O. S. (1981) *Pottery Technology: Principles and Reconstruction* (Manuals on Archaeology 4). Washington D. C.: Taraxacum.

Ryukyu Bingata Jigyō Kyōdō Kumiai (ed.) (1987) "Shiryō hen" (Archival material). *Ryukyu bingata no rekishi to gihō* (The history and techniques of Ryukyu bingata). Ryukyu Bingata Jigyō Kyōdō Kumiai, 59–72.

Saitō, Y. (2006) *Madogiwa OL tohoho na asa, ufufu no yoru* (A shunted office girl, morning blues, evening happiness). Shinchō Bunko.

Sartre, J.-P. (1956) *Being and Nothingness*. H. E. Barnes (trs.). New York: Washington Square Press.

Sartre, J.-P. (1964) *Nausea*, L. Alexander (trs.). New York: New Directions Publishing.

Sartre, J.-P. (2012) *Saint Genet: Actor and martyr*. B. Frechtman (trs.) Minneapolis: University of Minnesota Press

Sartre, J.-P. (1948) *Existentialism and Humanism*. New Haven: Yale University Press.

Sasaki, M. (2000) *Chikaku ha owaranai: Afōdansu heno shōtai* (Perception never ends: An invitation to affordances). Seidosha.

Satō, Y. (2004) "Hito to banana no orinasu seikatsu sekai: Uganda chūbu Buganda chiiki ni okeru banana no saibai to riyō" (Life-world Woven by People and Bananas: Cultivation and Use of Bananas in Buganda, Central Uganda). *Biostōrī* (Biostory) Vol. 2: 106–121.

Savage, T. S. and J. Wyman (1943–44) "Observation on the external characters and habits of the *Troglodytes niger* Geoff". *Boston Journal of Natural History*, 4: 362–386.

Savage-Rumbaugh, S. (1993) *Kotoba wo motta tensai zaru Kanzi* (Kanzi, a genius ape with language). E. Kaji (trs.). Tokyo: NHK Shuppan.

Sawada, M. (1996) "Onsei komyunikēshon ga tsukuru futatsu no sekai" (Two worlds created by speech communication). In K. Sugawara and M. Nomura (eds.) *Komyunikēshon toshite no karada* (Body as a means of communication). Karada to bunka series Vol. 2. Taishūkan Shoten.

Schafer, R. M. (1977) *The Tuning of the World*. New York: Random House.

Schafer, R. M. (1992) *A Sound Education*. Indian River: Arcana Editions.

Sekimoto, T. (2007) "Mono wo tsukuru waza no kōsatsu: Indonesia no batik gyō kara" (Rethinking the skill of making objects: Indonesian batik industry). In T. Matsui (ed.) *Shizen no shigenka* (Nature to Natural Resource). Tokyo: Kōbundō, 287–315.

Semaw S, P. Renne, J. W. K. Harris, C. S. Feibel, R. L. Bernor, N. Fesseha, and K. Mowbray (1997) "2.5-million-year-old stone tools from Gona, Ethiopia". *Nature,* 385: 333–336.

Sept, J. M. and G. E. Books (1994) "Reports of chimpanzee natural history, including tool use, in 16th- and 17th-century Sierra Leone". *International Journal of Primatology*, 15: 867–878.

Setia, P. (1994), *Putu Setia no Bali annai* (Putu Setia's guide to Bali). H. Kagami & K. Nakamura (trs.). Mokuseisha.

Shepard, A. O. (1956) *Ceramics for the Archaeologist* (Publication 609). Washington, D. C.: Carnegie Institution of Washington.

Shigeta, M. (1988) "Hito shokubutsu kankei no jissō" (Person-plant interactions). *Kikan jinruigaku* (Anthropological quarterly), 19(1): 191–281.

Shikata, K. (2004) "Niji rin ni okeru purantein no jizokuteki seisan: Kamerūn tōnanbu no nettai urin tai ni okeru yakihata nōkō shisutemu" (Sustainable plantain production in secondary forest: A shifting cultivation system in the tropical rain forest of southeastern Cameroon). *Ajia Afurika chiiki kenkyū* (Asian and African area studies) 4 (1): 4–35.

Shimada, M. (2009) "Nihonzaru no asobi no minzokushi: Kinkazan, Arashiyama, Kōjima, Shiga Kōgen no kodomotachi" (An ethnography of play in Japanese macaques: Children in Mount Kinka, Arashiyama, Kōjima and Shiga Highlands). In N. Kamei (ed.) *Asobi no jinruigaku kotohajime: Fīrudo de deatta 'kodomo' tachi* (Anthropology of play: 'Children' in the field). Kyoto: Showado, 81–133.

Shinju Shimbunsha (2005) *Shinju nenkan* (Pearl yearbook). Shinju Shimbunsha.

Shiokawa, H. (2005) "Indoneshia Bari tō no gamuran no onkyō tokusei ni tsuite: Sono 3 gongu kubyāru no pomade no unari" (Acoustics of Balinese gamelan: No. 3 Interference beats of pemadé in gong kebyar). Research presentation. Nippon Onkyō Gakkai.

Simons, C. (2004) "Vaiagura ga hogo ni kiku?" (Is Viagra good for conservation?). *Newsweek Japan*, 19 May, 64–65.

Slattum, J. and P. Schraub (2003) *Balinese Masks: Spirit of an Ancient Drama*. Hong Kong: Periplus Editions.

Sotomori, K. (1989) *Otoko to onna jiten: Sex no subete ga wakaru* (Encyclopedia of man and woman: All about sex). Seitōsha.

Souto, A., C. B. C. Bione, M. Bastos, B. M. Bezerra, D. Fragaszy, N. Schiel (2011) "Critically endangered blonde capuchins fish for termites and use new techniques to accomplish the task". *Biology Letters*, 7: 532–535.

Spencer, P. (1965) *The Samburu: A Study of Gerontocracy in a Nomadic Tribe*. London: Routledge & Kegan Paul.

St Amant, R. and T. E. Horton (2008) "Revisiting the definition of animal tool use". *Animal Behaviour*, 75: 1199–1209.

Stark, M. T. & W. A. Longacre (1993) "Kalinga ceramics and new technologies: Social and cultural contexts of ceramic change". In W. D. Kingery (ed.), *The Social and Cultural Contexts of New Ceramic Technologies* (Ceramics and Civilization 6). Ohio: American Ceramic Society, 1–32.

Stevenson, K. (2008) *The Frangipani is Dead: Contemporary Pacific Art in New Zealand, 1985–2000*. Wellington: Huia Publishers.

Sue, H. (1965) *Pre-school Children of the Hare Indians*. NCRC, 65-1. Otawa: Northern Co-ordination and Research Center.

Sugawara, K. (2000) "Busshuman no minzoku dōbutsugaku" (Ethnozoology of the Bushman). In K. Matsui (ed.) *Shizen kan no jinruigaku* (Anthropology of perspective on nature). Yōju Shorin, 159–210.

Sugawara, K. (2007) "Kari=karareru keiken to shintai hairetsu: |Gui no otoko no danwa kara" (Hunt=hunted experience and body configuration: From the statements of /Gui men). *Shintai shigen no kyōyū* (Sharing of body resources). (Shigen jinruigaku Vol. 9). Kōbundō, 89–121.

Sugawara, K. (2009) "Speech acts, moves and meta-communication in negotiation: Three cases of everyday conversation observed among the |Gui former-foragers". *Journal of Pragmatics*, 41 (1): 93–135.

Sugawara, K. (2010) *Kotoba to shintai: "Gengo no temae" no jinruigaku* (Words and the body: Pre-language anthropology). Kōdansha.

Sugishita, K. (1996) "Bokusen kenkyū no kanōsei: Inpeisareta kaishaku kōi toshiteno bokusen" (Perspectives in the study of divination: Divination as concealed interpretative act). *Minzokugaku kenkyū* (The Japanese journal of ethnology), 60 (4): 354–365.

Sugiyama, M. (2005) "Bari no gamuran hensei sumaru puguringan no onritsu taikei to senhō" (Tuning systems and scales in Balinese gamelan ensemble semar pegulingan). *Mūsa* (Mousa), 6: 83–95.

Sugiyama, M. (2008) "Bari tō no gamuran hensei sumaru puguringan ni okeru onritu taikei no kinshitsuka" (Homogenization of tuning systems in Balinese gamelan ensemble semar pegulingan). Research presentation at Tōyō Ongaku Gakkai 59-kai taikai (The 59th Congress of the Musicological Society of Japan).

Sugiyama, Y. (1978) *Bossou mura no hito to chinpanjī* (People and chimpanzees in Bossou village). Tokyo: Kinokuniya Shotan.

Sugiyama, Y. (1981) *Yasei chinpanjī no shakai* (Wild chimpanzee society). Tokyo: Kōdansha.

Sugiyama, Y. and J. Koman (1992) "The flora of Bossou: Its utilization by list of chimpanzees and humans". *African Study Monographs*, 13: 127–169.

Suharta, I Wy. (1994) *Mengenai Suling dalam Karawitan Bali: Studi Mengenai Identitas dan Fungsi* (About Suling in Balinese traditional music: A study of its identity and function). Denpasar: STSI Denpasar.

Suzuki, S. (1995) "Joshō" (Introduction). *Taishō seimeishugi to gendai* (Taishō-era vitalism and modernity). Kawade Shobō Shinsha, 2–15.

Suzuki, S., S. Kuroda, and T. Nishihara (1995) "Tool-set for termite fishing by chimpanzees in the Ndoki forest, Congo". *Behaviour*, 132: 219–235.

Sven-Amin L. (2009) *Investigation of Balinese Gamelan Gongs: Acoustical Analyses, Perceptually Relevant Attributes and Evaluation of Computationally Modelled Sounds*. (Final Term Project of Graduate Seminar MUMT 618: Computational Models in Musical Acoustics) McGill University, Schulich School of Music, Music Technology Area. (Web site: http://mt.music.mcgill.ca/~lembkes/)

Tachiki, T. (1993) *Biyaku no hakubutsu shi* (The natural history of aphrodisiacs). Seikyūsha.

Takemitsu, T. and J. Kawada (1992) *Oto, kotoba, ningen* (Sound, speech, humanity). Iwanami Shoten (Dōjidai Library).

Takenaga, M. (1997) *Labu doraggu: Seiryōkuzai jittaiken repōto* (Love drugs: Based on a real experience). Tokuma Kōkai.

Tambiah, S. J. (1984) *The Buddhist Saints of the Forest and the Cult of Amulets*. Cambridge: Cambridge University Press.

Tamura, T. (1996) "Jibun ni atta seiryokuzai ha kōshite erabe: Taipu betsu kōka no mekanizumu" (Which invigorants suit you: Types and efficacy mechanisms). In Bessatsu Takarajima Henshūbu (ed.) *Genki ga deru kusuri: Kaishunzai, kyōsōzai, biyaku, gōhō doraggu – tanoshii ecchi no tameno kusuri no subete*

(All about drugs for better sex: Sexual rejuvenation formulations, sex stimulants, aphrodisiacs and legal drugs). Takarajimasha, 82–89.

Tanabe, S. (2002) "Saikiteki jinruigaku ni okeru jissen no gainen: Bourdieu no habitus gainen wo meguri, sono kanata he" (The concept of praxis in anthropology: On Bourdieu's concept of habitus). *Kokuritsu Minzokugaku Hakubutukan kenkyu hōkoku* (Bulletin of the National Museum of Ethnology), 26(4): 533–573.

Tanaka, H. (1996) "Kusuri wo meguru Nihonjin no mittsu no chōryū: Kakuseizai ryūkō patān wo bunsekisuru" (Three trends of drug use among the Japanese: Analysis of the spread pattern of stimulant drugs). In Bessatsu Takarajima Henshūbu (ed.) *Genki ga deru kusuri: Kaishunzai, kyōsōzai, biyaku, gōhō doraggu – tanoshii ecchi no tameno kusuri no subete* (All about drugs for better sex: Sexual rejuvenation formulations, sex stimulants, aphrodisiacs and legal drugs). Takarajimasha, 222–231.

Tanaka, I. (1999) *'Chie' wa dō tsutawaruka: Nihonzaru no oya kara ko he watarumono* (How the 'knowledge' is transmitted: What is transferred from mother to offspring in Japanese monkeys). Kyoto: Kyoto Univ. Press.

Tanaka, J. (1971) *Busshuman: Seitai jinruigakuteki kenkyū* (The Bushmen: An ecological anthropological study). Shisakusha.

Tanaka, M. (1999) "Shaseisuru sei: Dansei no sekushuariti gensetsu wo megutte" (Ejaculating sex: Discourse on men's sexuality). In Y. Nishikawa & M. Ogino (eds.), *Kyōdō kenkyū dansei ron* (A joint study on men). Jinbun Shoin, 183–200.

Tanaka, M. (2009) "Fetishizumu kenkyū no kadai to tenbō" (Challenges and prospect of fetishism studies). In M. Tanaka (ed.) *Fetishizumu ron no keifu to tenbō* (Genealogy and prospect of fetishism theories) (Fetishizumu kenkyū 1). Kyoto Daigaku Gakujutsu Shuppankai.

Tanaka, M. (2010) *Iyashi to iyarashi: Erosu no jinruigaku* (Healing and horniness: The cultural anthropology of Eros). Chikuma Shobō.

Tanaka, M. (ed.) (2009) *Fetishizumu ron no keifu to tenbō* (Genealogy and prospect of fetishism theories) (Fetishizumu kenkyū 1). Kyoto Daigaku Gakujutsu Shuppankai.

Tani, Y. (1976) "Bokuchiku bunka kō: Bokufu – Bokuchiku kachiku kankei kōdō to sono metafā" (An essay on pastoral culture: Herdsman, pastoralism and livestock-related behaviors and their metaphors). *Jimbungakuhō* (The journal of social sciences and humanity), 42: 1–58.

Tantra, I Ny. (1992) *Bentuk Saih Tetekep dan Patutan dalam Gamelan Tujuh Nada di Bali* (The form of Saih Tetekap and Patutan in seven tone Gamelans in Bali). Denpasar: Sekolah Tinggi Seni Indonesia.

Tautai Contemporary Pacific Art Trust. http://www.tautaipacific.com/ (accessed 03/09/2010).

Tempest: Without a Body. http://www.youtube.com/watch?v=Wflqv85uCww (17/07/2010)

Tenzer, M. (1991) *Balinese Music*. Berkeley: Periplus Editions.

Terborgh, J. (1983) *Five New World Primates: A Study in Comparative Ecology*. Princeton: Princeton University Press.

Tilley, C. (1999) *Metaphor and Material Culture*. London: Blackwell.

Tilley, C. (2007) "Metaphor, materiality and interpretation". In: A. Henare, M. Holbradd, and A. Wastell (eds.) *Thinking Through Things: Theorizing Artifacts Ethnographically*. New York: Routledge, 23–56.

Tite, M. S. (1972) *Methods of Physical Examination in Archaeology*. London: Seminar Press.

Tokoro, I. (2007) "Shinju no shigen jinruigaku: Akoya shinju to shirochō shinju no yōshoku wo chūshin ni" (Anthropology of pearl as a resource: Centering on aquaculture of Akoya pearls and South Sea pearls). In R. Ogawa (ed.) *Yakudōsuru shō seisanbutsu* (*Shigen jinruigaku* dai yonkan) (Vibrancy of small products (Anthropology of resources series volume 4)). Kōbundō.

Tomikura, M. (1973) "Uranai" (Divination). In I. Oguchi and I. Hori (eds.) *Shūkyōgaku jiten* (The dictionary of religion). Tokyo Daigaku Shuppankai, 40–43.

Tonaki, A. (1980) "Gaisetsu bingata" (An overview of bingata). *Senshoku no bi* (Textile art), No. 6. Kyoto Shoin, 53–60.

Toren, C. (1993) "Making history: The significance of childhood cognition for a comparative anthropology of mind". *Man* (N.S.), 28(3): 461–478.

Toren, C. (1999) *Making Sense of Hierarchy: Cognition as Social Process in Fiji*. London School of Economics Monographs on Social Anthropology, 61. London: Athlone Press.

Torigoe, K. (2008) *Saundo sukēpu no shigaku: Fīrudo hen* (Poetics of soundscapes: In the field). Shunjūsha.

Tosa, K. (2000) *Biruma no weizā shinkō* (Weikza cults in Burma). Keisō Shobō.

Tosa, K. (2014) "From bricks to pagodas: Weikza specialists and the rituals of pagoda-building". In B. Brac de la Perrière, G. Rozenberg and A. Turner (eds.) *Champions of Buddhism: Weikza Cults in Contemporary Burma*. Singapore: National University of Singapore Press, 114–140.

Tsunoyama, S. (2001) *'Seikatsu shi' no hakken: Fīrudowāku de miru sekai* (Discovery of 'life history': The world seen through fieldwork). Chūōkōronsha.

Uchibori, M. (1996) *Mori no tabekata* (Between longhouse and forest: Everyday life among the Iban of Sarawak). Tokyo Daigaku Shuppankai.

Uchibori, M. (1997) *'Mono' no ningen sekai* (A human world of 'things'). Iwanami Shoten.

Uchibori, M. (1997) "Mono to hito kara naru sekai" (The world made of things and people). In T. Aoki et al. (eds.) *'Mono' no ningen sekai* (A human world of 'things') (Iwanami kōza bunka jinruigaku 3). (Iwanami Course of Cultural Anthropology 3) Iwanami Shoten, 1–22.

Uchibori, M. (2013) "Assembly of solitary beings – Between solitude and 'invisible' groups". In K. Kawai (ed.), *Groups: The evolution of human sociality*. Kyoto and Melbourne: Kyoto University Press and Trans Pacific Press, 43–57.

Uchibori, M. (ed.) (1997) *Iwanami bunka jinruigaku kōza – Mono no ningen sekai* (Iwanami cultural anthropology series: The human world of things). Iwanami Shoten.

Uchibori, M. (ed.) (2007) *Shigen jinruigaku* (Anthropology of resources), 9 volumes. Kōbundō.

Uchihara, S. (1994) *Kiku! Seiryōkuzai, biyaku* (Effective! Invigorants and aphrodisiacs). Gendai Shorin.

Uchihara, S. (2001) *Darenimo kikenakatta seiryokuzai kanzen gaido* (Complete guide for invigorants). Gendai Shorin.

Uchiyama, T. (2006) *Nō no itonami kara* (From agricultural activities). Nōsangyoson Bunka Kyōkai.

Uchiyamada, Y. (2008) "Geijutsu sakuhin no shigoto: Gell no hanbigakuteki abudakushon to Dushan no bunpaisareta pāson" (The work of artworks: Gell's anti-aesthetic abduction and Duchamp's distributed person). *Bunka jinruigaku* (Japanese journal of cultural anthropology), 73 (2): 158–179.

Ushijima, I. (1987) *Yappu tō no shakai to kōkan* (Society and exchange in the Yap islands). Kōbundō.

Van Schaik, C. P., E. A. Fox, and A. F. Sitompul (1996) "Manufacture and use of tools in wild Sumatran orangutans". *Naturwissenschaften*, 83: 186–188.

Van Schaik, C. P., R. O. Deaner and M. Y. Merrill (2006) "The conditions for tool use in primates: Implications for the evolution of material culture". *Journal of Human Evolution*, 36: 719–741.

Varahamihira (1995) *Uranaijutsu daishūsei 1 – Kodai Indo no zenchō uranai* (Brihat-

Samhita 1 – Omen reading in ancient India). M. Yano and M. Sugita (trs.). Heibonsha.

Vickers, A. (1989) *Bali: A paradise created*. Melbourne: Penguin.

Waga, I. C., A. K. Dacier, P. S. Pinha, and M. C. Tavares (2006) "Spontaneous tool use by wild capuchin monkeys (*Cebus libidinosus*) in the Cerrado". *Folia Primatologica* 77: 337–344.

Wallaert, H. (2008) "The way of the potter's mother: Apprenticeship strategies among Dii potters from Cameroon, West Africa". In M. T. Stark, B. J. Bowser & L. Horne (eds.) *Cultural Transmission and Material Culture*. Tuscon: University of Arizona Press, 178–198.

Watanabe, O. (2004) *Genki shu, pawā ga minagiru yakuyō shu zukuri* (How to make medicinal liquors for power and wellbeing). Ienohikari Kyōkai.

Watsuji, T. (1988) "Men to perusona" (Mask and persona). In H. Gotō (ed.) *Kamen* (Masks). Iwasaki Bijutsusha, 11–31.

Watts, C. M. (2008) "On meditation and material agency in the Peircean semeiotic". In C. Knappett and L. Malafouris, *Material Agency: Towards a Non-Anthropocentric Approach*. New York: Springer, 187–207.

Weber, M. (1956) *Wirtschaft und Gesellschaft, Grundriss der verstehenden Soziologie. Mit einem Anhang: Die rationalen und soziologischen Grundlagen der Musik*. 4., neu hrsg. Aufl. Besorgt von Johannes Winckelmann, Tübingen: Mohr.

Weber, M. (1967) *Ongaku shakaigaku keizai to shakai furon* (Rational and social foundations of music), with additional comments. E. Andō, H. Ikemiya and I. Sumikura (trs.). Sōbunsha.

Wenger, E., R. McDermott and W. M. Snyder (2002) *Cultivating Communities of Practice: A Guide to Managing Knowledge*. Cambridge: Harvard Business Review Press.

Wheeler, P. E. (1991) "The influence of bipedalism on the energy and water budget of early hominids". *Journal of Human Evolution*, 21: 117–136.

Whiten, A, J. Goodall, W. C. McGrew, T. Nishida, V. Reynolds, Y. Sugiyama, C. E. G. Tutin, R. W. Wrangham, C. Boesch (1999) "Cultures in chimpanzees". *Nature*, 399: 682–685.

Whiten, A., V. Horner and S. Marshall-Pescini (2003) "Cultural panthropology". *Evol. Anthropology* 12: 92–105.

Wikipedia (Ponifasio, Lemi). http://en.wikipedia.org/wiki/Lemi_Ponifasio (accessed 17/07/2010).

Wrangham R. W., F. B. M. de Waal and W. C. McGrew (1994) "The challenge of behavioral diversity". In R. W. Wrangham, W. C. McGrew, F. B. M. de Waal and P. G. Helme (eds.) *Chimpanzee Cultures*. Harvard University Press, 1–18.

Wrangham, R. (2010) *Catching fire: How cooking made us human*. London: Profile Books

Wu, K. (2015) *Reinventing Chinese Tradition: The Cultural Politics of Late Socialism*. Urbana, Chicago, and Springfield: University of Illinois Press.

Yagi, G. (1988) "Bingata no dentō to atarashii nichijōsei" (The bingata tradition and a new everydayness). *Bingata*. Tairyūsha, 108–133.

Yamada, Y. (ed.) (2000) *Shizen no oto, bunka no oto – Kankyō tono hibikiai* (Sounds of nature, sounds of culture: Reverberating with the environment) (Kōza ningen to kankyō Vol. 11). Shōwadō.

Yamagishi, M. and K. Yamagishi (1999) *Oto no fūkei toha nanika: Saundosukēpu no shakaishi* (A landscape of sounds: A sociography of soundscapes). Nihon Hōsō Shuppan Kyōkai (NHK Books).

Yamaguchi, M., N. Kinoshita, and N. Sakairi (1999) "Misemono no kasetsusei" (Temporality of freak show). *Shizen to bunka tokushū: Misemono* (Nature and culture featuring: Freak show), 59: 46–57.

Yamakoshi, G. (1998) "Dietary responses to fruit scarcity of wild chimpanzees at Bossou, Guinea: Possible implications for ecological importance of tool use". *American Journal of Physical Anthropology*, 106: 283–295.

Yamakoshi, G. (2001) "Ecology of tool use in wild chimpanzees: Toward reconstruction of early hominid evolution". In T. Matsuzawa (ed.) *Primate Origin of Human Cognition and Behavior*. Tokyo: Springer-Verlag Tokyo, 537–556.

Yamakoshi, G. (2004) "Evolution of complex feeding techniques in primates: Is this the origin of great-ape intelligence?". In A. E. Russon and D. R. Begun (eds.) *The Evolution of Thought: Evolutionary Origins of Great Ape Intelligence*. Cambridge: Cambridge University Press, 140–171.

Yamakoshi, G. and Y. Sugiyama (1995) "Pestle-pounding behaviour of wild chimpanzees at Bossou, Guinea: A newly observed tool-using behaviour". *Primates*, 36: 489–500.

Yamamoto, N. (ed.) (2009) *Domesutikēshon: Sono minzoku seibutsugakuteki kenkyū* (Domestication: Ethnobiological studies). Kokuritsu Minzokugaku Hakubutsukan.

Yanai, T. (2008) "Imēji no jinruigaku no tame no rironteki sobyō: Minzokushi eizō wo tsūjite no 'kagaku' to 'geijutsu'" (Outline of a theory of anthropology of images: 'Science' and 'art' through ethnographic audio-visual media). *Bunka jinruigaku* (Japanese journal of cultural anthropology), 73 (2): 180–199.

Yano, M. (1992) *Senseijutsushi tachi no Indo* (Astrologers' India). Chūkōshinsho.

Yasutomi, A. (2006) *Fukuzatsusa wo ikiru* (Living in complexity). Iwanami Shoten.

Yasutomi, A. (2008) *Ikiru tame no keizaigaku: 'Sentaku no jiyū' kara no dakkyaku* (Biophilic economics: A departure from 'freedom of choice'). NHK Books.

Yoshida, K. (1999) *Bunka no 'hakken': Kyōi no heya kara vācharu myujiamu made* ('Discovery' of culture: From amazing rooms to virtual museums). Iwanami Shoten.

Yoshida, Y. (2008) "Bari tō kamen buyō geki topen to jendā: Ru Rwi no jirei wo chūshin ni" (The Balinese masked dance topeng and gender: A case study of the Luh Luwih female dance troop). *Bunkakōryū Kenkyū* (Cultural exchange studies) 3: 69–90.

Yoshida, Y. (2009) "Bari tō kamen buyō geki topen wari to 'kankyaku': Shiatā to girei no hazama de" (Balinese mask dance drama topeng wali and its 'audience': Between theatre and ritual). *Tōhōgaku* (Eastern studies) 117: 156–139.

Yoshimoto, T. (1984) *Masu imēji ron* (The theory of the mass image). Fukutake Shoten.

Young, E. F. (1980) *Topeng in Bali: Change and Continuity in a Traditional Drama Genre*. Ph. D. dissertation, University of California, San Diego.

Zeitlyn, D. (1993) "'Spiders in and out of court, or 'the long legs of the law': Styles of spider divination in their sociological contexts". *Africa* 63 (2): 219–240.

Zhang, Tongdao (2009) *Jin Zhilin de Yan'an*. Beijing: Wenhua meishu chubanshe.

Name Index

Beck, B. B., 214
Bergson, H., 340
Bird-David, N., 243
Brenner, S. A., 281
Butler, J., 242

de Waal, F. B. M., 235
Deleuze, G., 26
Descola, P., 243
Douglas, M., 254

Ekman, P., 342
Engels, F., 210–213

Focillon, H., 48
Foucault, M., 59
Friesen, W. V., 342

Gell, A., 190–191, 349
Gibson, J. J., 241, 244–245
Goffman, E., 69
Goodwin, C., 342

Hall, E. T., 244
Hamamoto, M., 191–192
Hanks, W., 77
Haraway, D., 242
Hayaki, H., 231
Hayes, C., 231
Heidegger, M., 60–61, 76
Herskovits, M., 255

Hosaka, K., 223
Huffman, M. A., 233

Iacoboni, M., 224–225
Ingold, T., 57
Iriki, A., 226
Itani, J., 222–223, 231
Iwaki, K., 42, 55–56, 339–340

Johnson, M., 242

Kanzi (the name of a bonobo), 236, 239
Kendon, A., 342
Kuki, S., 355
Kuroda, S., 210, 363

Lakoff, G., 242
Leroi-Gourhan, A., 244
Lévi-Strauss, C., 59, 243, 308
Luhmann, N., 341, 363

Mauss, M., 116
Matsuzawa, T., 230, 235
Maturana, H. R., 246
McLuhan, M., 241, 244–245
McNeill, D., 63, 71
Merleau-Ponty, M., 225, 227, 246
Miller, D., 243

Nishida, T., 223

Name Index

Peirce, C. S., 191
Pietz, W., 303
Polanyi, M., 244–245

Reed, E. S., 62
Rizzolatti, G., 224–227
Roseman, M., 363

Sartre, J.-P., 58, 60–61, 64–65, 221, 362
Savage-Rumbaugh, S., 236, 239
Schafer, R. M., 363
Shimada, M., 233
Sinigaglia, C., 224–227
Sugawara, K., 363
Sugishita, K., 191

Sugiyama, M., 235, 239
Suzuki, S., 236

Tambiah, S. J., 303
Tanaka, M., 227

Uchibori, M., 362

Varahamihira, 193, 355, 392
Varela, F. J., 246

Watsuji, T., 350

Yanai, T., 339
Yoshimoto, T., 191–192, 395

Subject Index

abandoning desires (ability to abandon desire), 232, 236, see "desire"
abduction, 191
Aboriginal Australians, 315
acacia bush (woodland), 261
acoustic ecology, 364, see "ecology"
action, 1, 157, 160, 168–170
Actor Network Theory, 31
adaptation, 110–111, see "technology"
affordance, 62–63, 76, 224–229, 231, 245
Agastya Leaves, 356
agency, 1, 23–24, 26–27, 30–31, 33, 155, 190–192, 273, 288, 349
 inagency, 273
almanac, 192
Andra Pradesh, 193
animal, 1, 155
anthropomorphism, 249–250, 255, see "de- anthropocentrism"
anticipation, 227
anvil stone, 235
appearance of a form, 286
appearance of things, 37, 40, 55–57
appropriation, 64
arasan, 177
Arashiyama Monkey Park, 233
art, 315
 art object, 167
 fine art, 315
artefacts, 274
astrologer, 192–194, 200

astrology (*jōsyam*), 192–195, 201, 355–356
astronomy, 192–193
auction market, 318
auditory sense, 271, 364, see "sense"
augury, 191
Australia, 315
authenticity, 327, 329–330, 332, 335
 questions of authenticity, 329
Autopoiesis, 26, 246

Backward Class House Scheme, 193
Baka people (Pygmy), 296
Bali, 155–158, 160–162, 164, 166, 350
banana, 293–299
bark painting, 316
basic habitation unit, 264
basis of the socialization of food, 236
batik, 281–283
becausality, 275
be quiet / silent (*tegirai*), 362
being alone, 266, see "isolation", "loneliness", "solitude"
being heard, 269
being-in-itself (*l'être-en-soi*), 65
being transience, 350
bestowal, 164
Bhadrakāli, 200
Bingata (Okinawa's traditional textile dyeing technology / craft), 327, see "Ryukyu Bingata"

bipedalism, 210–213
blocking of desire, 233–234, 236, *see* "desire"
body, 21, 23–24, 26–27, 29, 33, 60, 134, 157, 160, 165, 170, 265, 269–270, 308–311
  bodily technique, 96–97, 101
  body–*mono* relationship, 136, *see* "*mono*"
  extension of the body, 241, 243–246, 255, 257
  human body, 16, 271
  instrumentalist view of the body, 5, 152
  modernist view of the body, 137
bonobo, 223, 229, 234–239, *see* "Pan"
Bossou forest, 208–209, 212, 218, 220, 230, 235
Brahman, 192–193
branch dragging-play, 233
Burgers' Zoo, 235–236
buwata (noise), 261–262, 270

capuchin, 216–220
Cavendish, 298
Central Asia, 287
Chamus people, 16, 258, 361
Chennai, 200, 202
chimpanzee, 207–213, 215, 218, 223, 227–231, 235–237, 239, *see* "Pan"
cicadas, 263, 265–267, 269
  cicada drizzles (chorus of cicada sounds), 16, 258, *see* "auditory sense", "*semi shi gre*", "sound"
circulatability, 224
  circulatable goods, 237
clamor, 267

clay, 99
cloth, 281–287
co-existence principle, 231, 236
collaboration, 235
communication, 60, 77–78, 341
communities of practice, 117
confusion, 238
contingency, 6, 189–191, 201, 204, 355, *see* "double contingency"
controlling of desire, 234, 236, *see* "desire"
conversation, 58, 77
cooperative action, 235
craft, 315
cuvaṭi, (a sheaf of divining cards), 6, 189, 197–201, 203, 356

de-anthropocentrism, 30, *see* "anthropocentrism"
decorative pattern, 97
deity, 156, 158, 160–163, 168–170, 350
deixis, 67, 70, 76–77
demonstrative, 77
dengaku (*noh* troupe), 58, 70
design, 286
desire, 65–67, 76
  abandoning desire (ability to abandon desire), 232, 236
  blocking desire, 233–234, 236
  controlling desire, 234, 236
  origin of desire, 239
  self-control of desire, 236
  suppressing desire, 232
destiny, 190–192, 197, 204, 355
dialogue, 81, 95
  dialogical model, 81, 94
distance, 77

divination, 189–198, 200–201, 203–204, 355–356
diviner, 190–192, 197, 200–201, 203–204
doll-play, 230
domestication, 293–294, 297, 299
dominance-subordination relationship, 231–232
double contingency, 60, 341, *see* "contingency"
drawing, 282–286
dry season, 267

ear, 268, 270
ecological participant observations, 224
ecology
  acoustic ecology, 364
  feeding ecology, 208
emblem, 342
embodiment, 21, 23, 26–27, 90
  embodied knowledge, 96, 101, *see* "knowledge"
  embodied mind, 23, 25
  embodied technique, 101
embroidery, 287–288
emotion, 269, 271
encephalization, 211–213
environment, 16, 26–29, 61, 87–90, 110, 293, 296–297, 338, 343, 348, 353, 355, 360, 363–365
  everyday environment, 283
  environment–technology relationship, 98, *see* "technology"
  local environment, 101
  sound environment, 258–259, 265, *see* "sound"

equality principle, 222–223, 231, 234–236, *see* "inequality principle"
equality principle society, 236
objectification of the equality principle, 223
erection, 136, 140–41
Ethiopia, 119
event, 156–157, 160, 349
evil spirit, 156, 160–161
exchange, 237–238
  generalized exchange, 59
exchangeability, 223
  semi-exchangeability, 224
exorcism, 310
extension of the body, 241, 243–246, 255, 257

fa'afafine (male transgender), 322–323
feeding ecology, 208 , *see* "ecology"
feeling, 269
female, 281
fine art, 315, *see* "art"
fingering, 173
five senses, 16, 271, 361, *see* "sense"
food sharing, 222–224, 234–235, 237
food snatching, 234
fortune-teller, 6, 189, 192–194, 200
frame reference, 74
freedom, 223–224
functionalist, 190, 355
function-specific, 62, 76
future, 162, 168–169, 350

|Gui people (Bushman), 58, 67, 341, *see* "San people"
gambuh (Balinese classical dance-drama), 168, 171

Subject Index

generalized exchange, 59, *see* "exchange"
gesture, 60, 62–63, 76–77, 342
  iconic gesture, 71
getap (scared), 180
gift, 162, 166–167
gorilla, 231, 235–236, *see* "Pan"
grand narrative, 210–211
grasping, 225–226, 230
  precision grasping, 225
grassland, 261
grib (pollution), 309–311
Guinea, 208

hammer stone, 235, *see* "stone"
hand, 124, 126, 129–131, 225–227, 236
heard, *see* "being heard"
hearing, 267, 269
Hindu, 169
holding a twig, 237
horoscope, 192–193, 200, 356
household item, 283
Howletts Wild Animal Park, 231
human body, 16, 271, *see* "body"
human–thing relationship, 40–41, 136, 326

iconic gesture, 71, *see* "gesture"
identity, 157
idup (alive), 180
iiti (*Acacia mellifera*), 261, 265–270
illness, 309–312
illustrator, 342
imagination, 231
inagency, 273, *see* "agency"
index, 189, 192, 197
  indexicality, 6, 201

India, 308
individual, 363
Indonesia, 1, 155, 281
inequality principle, 231, 233, 236, *see* "equality principle"
inheritance, 164–166, 168, 170
in-itself, *see* "being-in-itself (*l'être-en-soi*)"
insertion, 220–221
  insertion feeding, 220
instrumentalist view of the body, 5, 152
instrumentality, 61
intangible, 16, 155, 160, 164, 169, 271, *see* "tangible"
  intangible image, 42
intention, 169–170, 349
interaction, 58
interface, 246, 254–256
interpretationist, 190
intervention, 60
  intervention of *mono*, 59
involvement, 69
isolation, 362, *see* "being alone", "loneliness", "solitude"

Jakkamma (a female deity of the Nāyaka<u>n</u> people), 194
Japanese macaque, 227, 231–233
Java, 281–282
jip (sucking out), 309
Jogis (a religious mendicant), 193

key, 173
knowledge
  embodied knowledge, 96, 101
  tacit knowledge, 290

Kōjima, 233
kuṭukuṭupai, 194, 196–197, 203, 356

labor, 210–212
Ladakh, 308–309
layers of complexity to the meaning of things, 222
lebang (one of the keys in *gamelan*), 173
legitimate peripheral participation (LPP), 116
lha (deity), 309–311
  lha-mo (female shaman), 309–311
  lha-pa (male shaman), 309–311
liiyo (solitude, cicada), 16, 258, 263, 265, 268–269
  liiyo ate, 265–266, 269, 362–363
linear dominance-subordination relationship, 231
linguistic turn, 24–26
livestock-morphism, 250, 252–253, 255
ljorai (*Acacia reficiens*), 261
lmaine (swamp, swampy grassland, grassland), 261
locality, 293, 298–299
  local environment, 101, *see* "environment"
loneliness, 258, 263–264, 362, *see* "being alone", "isolation", "solitude"
ltolilyo (voice), 261–262
luyar (container), 310

Maasai people, 258
macaque, 215, 217–218
Mahābhārata, 201
Mahale, 231
making, 286

mandarin orange test, 231
manipulation, 222, 282
mask, 1, 155–161, 163–170, 349–350
material, 283, 286, 350
  material culture, 20–24
  material or technological determinant, 111
  material thing, 1, 155
materiality, 1, 37, 42–43, 55–56, 155, 157, 168–170, 259, 271
  materiality of sound, 269–270, *see* "sound"
meaning, 273
  multilayered meanings, 238
medium, 160
metaphorical thinking, 248, 255–256
metonymy, 203
microscopic analysis, 58, 77
mirror neuron system, 224, 232, 236, 240
modernist view of the body, 137, *see* "body"
mono (things), 18–19, 118, 132, 134, 189, 259, 269, 287
  mono no ke (spirits), 31
  mono–body relationship, 136, *see* "body"
  social function as *mono*, 99, *see* "socialization of things"
multilayered meanings, 238, *see* "meaning"
multiple affordances, 238
music, 167

narrative , *see* "grand narrative"
national identity, 317
Nāyakaṉ, 6, 189–190, 192–201, 203, 356

needle, 287
nglubit (manner of opening hands/fingers), 179
noise, 267, 361
nomad, 193
non-intentionality, 6, 201
nonverbal behavior, 342
now-and-here, 77

objectification, 223
oil palm, 209, 294
Okinawa, 329
ontic thing, 275
opposable thumb, 225
oral culture, 42, 53
origin of desire, 239, see "desire"
ownership, 158, 166, 223–224
owning, 161, 163

Pacific Art, 321
Paleolithic period, 96
palmyra palm, 198–199
Pan, 223, 232, 237–238, see "bonobo", "chimpanzee", "gorilla"
paradigm, 276
paradox of skill, 81, 90, 94, see "skill"
past, 166, 169–170
past performance, 168
pastoralist, 258
pearl, 81–87
people indigenous, 321
performance, 1, 155–160, 162–166, 169–170, 349–350
phenomenology, 59
physicality
  physical pressure, 16, 270–271
  physical response, 364

physical sense organ, 271, see "sense"
physicality of humans, 259
pieceworker, 291
pitung ilah (seven circumferences), 176
plantain, 295
play, 121, 229–231, 237–238, 293, 298–299
  play equipment, 229
  play in a group of three, 237
  play with twigs, 234
  play-chasing, 233, 237
  play-exchanging, 238
  play-face, 229, 231, 235, 237
  playing by exchanging a twig, 238
  play-wrestling, 236–237
  twig-play, 235
pointing, 73, 77
possession, 193–194, 309–311
posture, 67
pottery, 96–99, 103
  pottery culture, 101
  pottery on the Yap Islands, 108
practical satisfaction with the completed mono, 110
pragmatics, 77
precision grasping, 225, see "grasping"
Present Being (*Dasein*), 61
product names of sex stimulant, 144
production, 210, 282
project, 65
psychic surgery, 308

questions of authenticity, 329, see "authenticity"

quiet / silent (*tegirai*), *see* "be quiet / silent"

rainforest, 295
Ramayana, 201
rasa, 181
ratio principle (*sikut ibane*), 176
reciprocity, 237–238
  reciprocity involving exchanges of food, 223
relevance, 64, 76
religion, 273
representation, 224, 227–228
  representation of sex stimulant, 145
resistance rate, 60
resource, 66, 77
rhizome, 277
ritual, 156, 158, 160–164, 166–167, 169–170, 349–350
  shamanic ritual, 308
Ryukyu Bingata, 327, 329, *see* "*bingata*"

sacredness, 159, 161–163, 166, 169
saih (key), 173
Samoa, 109
San people (Bushman), 212, *see* "|Gui people"
sasae (cling), 228–230, *see* also "*sugari*"
self-control of desire, 236, *see* "desire"
selisir (one of the keys in *gamelan*), 173
semi-exchangeability, 224, *see* "exchangeability"

semi-shigure (cicada drizzle), 261, *see* "auditory sense", "cicada drizzle"
sense
  auditory sense, 271, 364
  five senses, 16, 271, 361
  physical sense organs, 271
  tactile sense, 226, 271
  visual sense, 364
sex enhancement technique, 5
sex stimulant, 136, 140–141, 144
  advertisement of male sex stimulant, 136, 144
  product names of sex stimulant, 144
  representation of sex stimulant, 145
sexual intercourse, 137, 139
shaman, 276, 309
  shamanic ritual, 308, *see* "ritual"
shape, 99
share of the food, 223
sign, 76, 189, 199–201
  sign language, 342
silent, *see* "being quiet / silent (*tegirai*)"
sikut ibane (sizing or ascertaining of ratios), 176
skill, 26–27
  paradox of skill, 81, 90, 94
smell, 268
social and cultural satisfaction with production time and energy consumption, 110
social and cultural satisfaction with the completed mono, 110
social communication, 363
social function as *mono*, 99, *see* "*mono*"
socialization

socialization of food, 234
socialization of things, 222–223, 227, 229, 231, 233–234, 237
solitary play, 235
solitude, 16, 258–259, 263–266, 268, 271, 362
sorcery, 310
soul (*la*), 310
sound, 16, 258–259, 270–271, 361
  sound classification system, 361
  sound environment, 258–259, 265, *see* "environment"
  sound in a grazing space, 260
  materiality of sound, 269–270
  sounds in a living space, 259
Soviet Union, 288
spirit, 309–312
  spirit possession, 310
  spiritual image, 97
stable technique, 111, *see* "technique"
stimulant, *see* "sex stimulant"
stone, 155, 299
  stone tool, 96
  stone-play, 233
  "stonehood", 273
  hammer stones, 235
substrate, 210, 216–220, 220, 228
sucking, 309
  sucking treatment, 308, 310
sugari (support), 228–230, *see* also "*sasae*"
  world of *sugari*, 230
suling gambuh (main instrument of the *gambuh* gamelan ensemble), 171
suppressing desire, 232, *see* "desire"
symbolism, 156, 273

symbiotic gestures, 342
symbolic meaning, 1, 155
syntagm, 275

tacit knowledge, 290, *see* "knowledge"
tactile perception, 226
tactile sense, 226, 271, *see* "sense"
Takasakiyama, 233
taksu (spiritual power / agency of the things), 157–158, 160, 163, 169, 350
Tamil Nadu, 6, 190, 193, 356
tangible, 155, 168–169, *see* "intangible"
  tangible image, 42, 51, 56, 339
  tangible phenomenon, 55–56
technique, 97, 111
  stable technique, 111
  technique of the body, 116
techno life history, 117
technology
  technologies in pre-industrial society, 110
  technological adaptation, 96, 101, 105
  technological change, 96
  technology–environment relationship, 98, *see* "environment"
tegirai, 265, *see* "being quiet / silent (*tegirai*)"
tekap (fingering/key of *suling gambuh*), 173
  tekap lebang, 173
textile, 281, 287
Thanjavur, 200, 202
thematization, 76
thing, 41, 270, *see* "mono"
  thing-like things, 227
  appearance of things, 41

Tibet, 309–310
Tibetan Buddhist, 308–309
tonality, 173
Tonga, 109
tool, 282–283, 286
  tool-using behavior, 96, 207, 209, 211–220
traditional Chinese medicine, 136, *see* "sex stimulant"
traditional motifs, 282, 284–285
traditional pottery, 104, *see* "pottery"
transience, *see* "being transience"
triadic relationship, 237–238
trick, 308
tsukibori (dotted outline) technique, 330
twig-play, 235, *see* "play"
two sounds, 261

unconsciousness, 59
uncontrolled nature, 81, 90, *see* "environment"
ungkur (grows older), 181

utilitarianism, 274
utterance, 77
Uzbekistan, 287
  Uzbek embroidery, 287

Vaghri, 193, 198–200
Valluvar, 356
value, 223–224, 238
verisimilitude, 191, 203–204
Viagra, 140, 151, *see* "sex stimulant"
Vīramma Kali, 200, 202
visual sense, 364
voice, 271, 361, *see* "auditory sense"

waged worker, 281
Wamba, 234
wazome-bingata technology, 332
wood, 155, 157, 167, 350
workshop, 282
world of *sugari*, 230, *see* "*sugari*"

Yap, 103
Yogyakarta, 281–282